TOUCHSTONE

BY WILL DURANT

The Story of Philosophy
Transition
The Pleasures of Philosophy
Adventures in Genius

BY WILL AND ARIEL DURANT
THE STORY OF CIVILIZATION:

The Lessons of History
Interpretations of Life

INTERPRETATIONS OF LIFE

A Survey of Contemporary Literature

The Lives and Opinions
of Some Major Authors of Our Time:
Faulkner, Hemingway, Steinbeck, Sinclair, O'Neill,
Jeffers, Pound, Joyce, Eliot, Maugham, Proust, Gide,
Wittgenstein, Kierkegaard, Husserl, Heidegger, Sartre,
de Beauvoir, Camus, Mann, Kafka, Kazantzakis,
Sholokhov, Pasternak, Solzhenitsyn, and Yevtushenko

by

Will and Ariel Durant

A TOUCHSTONE BOOK PUBLISHED BY
SIMON AND SCHUSTER

Table of Contents

Why This Book?

WHY should a novice of eighty-four, after immersing himself for the last half century in philosophy and history, break out with a book on literature? What competence has he in this field? What can he say that has not been said long ago by specialists who have devoted their adult lives to the study of literature?

And yet literature was my first intellectual love. I have told elsewhere[1] how, aged twelve, I saw my equally aged inamorata reading *Pickwick Papers*, how I borrowed the book from her, and then ungratefully divided my affection between her and Dickens. I saved fourteen cents, bought *David Copperfield*, read every word of its eight hundred pages, and ranked it, for a time, next to the Bible and *The Imitation of Christ*. Literature became an almost divine revelation, a miraculous multiplication of the world and life.

Ariel has preserved, through sixty-six years, a tattered notebook of 248 pages, dated November 30, 1904, containing in my then legible handwriting (1) a "Chronological List of the World's Literature," with a thousand entries, (2) a "List of English Writers," with 729 entries, and (3) a "List of American Authors," with 180; apparently I proposed to read all of these predecessors, and then, in due time, join them among the immortals of the pen. Page 139 of the notebook proclaimed a wild resolve: "I must someday, when I have made a closer study of the subject, and shall have learnt the arts of style and criticism, write a series of 'Literary Lives' . . . Volume I might treat of Asiatic literature; Vol. II of Greek; Vol. III of Roman," and so on through twenty-five volumes. Long after I had half-forgotten this resolution, I unwittingly accomplished it, on a tiny scale, and with Ariel's help, in the ten (in the French and German translations thirty) volumes of *The Story of Civilization*, which includes, among other matters, a history of the world's literature from 500 B.C. to A.D. 1789.

Having reached the age of nineteen, I wrote a "History of English Literature." I sent the typescript to Benziger Brothers, a Catholic pub-

7

lishing firm in New York; it was rejected as slightly immature. A year later (1905), I pored through Darwin's *Origin of Species* and *Descent of Man*, Haeckel's *History of Creation*, and Spencer's *First Principles of a Synthetic System of Philosophy*. I lost my faith and found philosophy.

This new love affair lasted some twenty years, and begot *The Story of Philosophy* (1926). Soon thereafter I became discontent with contemporary philosophy as a mist and mirage of logic and epistemology, and turned to history in the belief that there, rather than in the philosophers, I would find the nature of man and states. This third devotion proved lasting, as it fitted well with another devotion: my wife too was mad about history. But we paid a price for our forty years' immersion in the past: we lost touch with the thought and art of our own times. We realized, to our shame, that we knew almost nothing about Faulkner, Joyce, Proust, Gide, Thomas Mann . . . We resolved to become pupils again, and sit at the feet of contemporary novelists, poets, and philosophers.

I say "philosophers" not in the professional sense of that word, but as embracing all who have persistently inquired into the meaning and possibilities of life, or who have tried to live in the perspective of a humane intelligence. I was not surprised to find that most great writers were philosophers in all but academic terminology and technique. I discovered that in studying such men (as in studying history) I had not really abandoned philosophy; that what interested me in them—behind their varieties and skills of literary art and form—was their views of what significance our life retained now that the gods had departed, and what way of life seemed most worthy of mature men.

So the title of this book is honest; it tells just what I have proposed to do: to seek and clearly express the diverse but thought-stirring interpretations of life offered to us in the literature of the last fifty years. You must not expect here any professional literary criticism, any learned discussion of styles, meters, movements, or schools. These pages will rather be the confessions of an amateur who has been philandering among a variety of loves these last eighty years, and has forfeited the authority that might have been earned by a lifelong specialized devotion. Worse yet, you will see in me many prejudices and mental blocks. I have a Gallic distaste for obscurity, especially when it is cutely and laboriously intentional, as in some twentieth-century verse. After forty years of wandering among older centuries I find it difficult to appreciate new forms of expression (or concealment), as in *The Waste Land* or *Finnegans Wake;* and with an uncertain few years left me I move with some impatience among authors who deliberately make a puzzle of their thoughts—as if life were not puzzle enough.

I need another indulgence. In almost all these studies I have found the author himself more interesting than any character in his books, and his career more instructive than the imaginary world by which he revealed or cloaked himself. I varied an old motto, and told myself, *Cherchez l'homme*—search for the man. So let me spread myself out, according to an old habit, about the personalities of these writers as well as about the stories they tell. I would rather have known Somerset Maugham—grouch though he was—than his gay and tempting Sadie Thompson; and I regret that I could not know Thomas Mann as leisurely as he made me know his Hans Castorp, his Jacob, and his Joseph. Literature, like history, has been lived, has been enacted or written upon human nerves and flesh.

Originally this book was begun as my personal reaction to contemporary literature, while Ariel worked on her chapters for our dual autobiography. But when she saw the earlier essays she felt that they were insubstantial and inadequate, and proposed a more thorough study of each author. In this amended enterprise she joined me; and though she asked me to keep the intimate first-person approach, she entered so actively into the project that we found ourselves, happily, co-authors again.

WILL DURANT

Los Angeles
May, 1970

CHAPTER I

William Faulkner

I. PRELIMINARY

THESE belated studies began with contemporary American literature, and were soon sharpened to attention by its vitality, originality, and force. Faulkner, O'Neill, and Hemingway were authors of
depth and power, who raised the American novel and drama to full competition with their like in England, Germany, and France. The lions of
European letters were startled when in 1949 the Nobel Prize was
awarded to an obscure author seemingly lost in Mississippi swamps, and
in 1954 to an aging bewhiskered safarian whom Paris had known thirty
years before as an impoverished journalist pecking at an old typewriter
under a crumbling roof. I live in a glass house, for till 1966 I had read
only one novel by Hemingway, one by Steinbeck, none by Faulkner;
and to this day I am ignorant of the literatures of Canada, Mexico, and
South America. Any alert reader might have guessed this from my
careless use of "American" as a lazy, convenient, shortsighted, insulting
substitute for "United Statesian." Who will give us a national adjective?

I was a bit shocked by the blatant "candor" of many minor American
authors about the private functions of our bodies. I am no sinless Puritan,
and I have enough French-Canadian blood in me to relish a subtly
pointed bawdy joke, or a revealing film; but I had supposed that anyone
clever enough to write a book would know that some plain curt words
carry the odor of their surroundings, or dishonor the poetry that can
rise from the flesh; and that, in works meant for our eyes and hands,
they would use a deodorized vocabulary, an educated indirectness, in
referring to the secrecies of the privy or the bed. Wit sharpens itself,
and conflict is blunted, by recognizing such restraints. Now that our
courts have almost given up the attempt to define obscenity we shall
be swamped for a time with pornography crude or adorned. Probably
the situation will be eased by the excesses of liberty; books like *Candy*
will become commonplace, and will no longer agitate readers beyond
the college years—just as women's legs have ceased to agitate men's
bones. Meanwhile I should admit that such novels as *Last Exit to*

Brooklyn, however emetic, are not pornography; it is desirable that literature, as "a criticism of life," should be free to reveal to us the depth of degradation lying under our blind and hectic affluence. (I should also admit that I have read these books.)

I have read some other books, about which I should like to say a word before sitting down leisurely to Faulkner's feast. There are many vigorous and inventive writers working in the United States, and some have resisted the temptation to pornography. I respect Saul Bellow as an honest craftsman who never lets his manuscript go to print until he has put into it his sensitive sympathy and his finished art. Our pullulating cities generate yearly a thousand men like Bellow's Herzog: a cuckolded husband wearing his horns patiently, a fond but negligent father, a man of good intentions and flaccid will floundering in the flotsam of a wrecked theology.

John Updike's *Rabbit, Run* builds up a somber but impressive picture of a man suffering from a deadening environment, a swollen ego, and an atrophied sense of right and wrong; every town in America has a hundred Rabbit Angstroms, and we feel ourselves *participes criminis* as we see him collapsing from the loosening of his moral vertebrae. The literature of our time reeks with the ruins of men who presumed that the Ten Commandments had been abrogated by the reputed death of their reputed author. In *Couples* Updike spent his full force, for good and evil: a masterpiece of penetrating perception, angry satire, and social surgery, marred by a reckless resolve to bring all the sweet secrets of love and flesh, all the corrosive speech of sullied men and women into the light and language of literature. I was shocked by every second page, but amid the moral mire I found many a flashing percept, and an understanding summary: "The fate of them all suspended in this one of those dark ages that visit mankind between millennia, between the deaths and rebirths of gods, when there is nothing to steer by but sex and stoicism and the stars."[1]

Francis Scott Fitzgerald (1896–1940) was born into a pious Catholic family. He lost his faith, and suffered proscription of his books by the Church. Perhaps for these reasons I responded more warmly to *Tender Is the Night* than to *The Great Gatsby,* which was generally rated his best. Essentially it was a mystery story—who killed whom?—with a suspense plot and a dramatic denouement; there are thousands such. The other book was the brave attempt of a romantic Irishman to describe, almost clinically, the degeneration of an idealist, under temptation and misfortune, into a mediocrity ruled by adultery and drink; I was surprised to find no rosy tints sprayed upon the hurried end. Here was a hardly disguised account of the author's own alcoholic and moral collapse after a long devotion to a distempered wife, and long resistance to economic strains and proffered charms. It was Fitzgerald's lovable character and sensational career that gave his books a passing fame.

II. FAULKNER'S COUNTY

Faulkner stemmed from James Joyce's *Ulysses* via Erskine Caldwell's *Tobacco Road*. He pursued the stream of consciousness through an entire class of Mississippians, and chronicled their decay by baring their flesh and souls. Having read much Balzac, he set out to write the *comédie humaine* of a single county in one of the United States. It was really Lafayette County, with its capital at Oxford, proud seat of "Ole Miss"—the University of Mississippi; but Faulkner rechristened the city Jefferson, and called the county Yoknapatawpha. This, he tells us, is a Chickasaw Indian word meaning "water runs slow through flat land"—an excellent description of his books. He ascribed to his imaginary county a population of 9,313 Negroes and 6,298 whites. At least a hundred of these whites and a score of these Negroes move in and out of the novels, just as the same evolving characters appear in different parts of Balzac's works. Through Faulkner's microscopic exposure the people on his chosen foot of earth were more intimately and candidly revealed than any other sector of America's population.

He was born on September 25, 1897, at New Albany, Mississippi. His father moved the family to Oxford in 1902, and became business manager of the university. William received no formal education beyond high school. He tried to enlist in the Army for World War I, but was rejected by the examiners. He went to Canada and joined the Royal Flying Corps, but the war ended before he finished his training. He returned to Oxford and attended the university for a year. In 1924 a volume of his poems was published in Boston; the title page wrongly put a *u* in his name; he let the error stand, and so signed all his later books. A good prose writer almost always begins with poetry, as feeling precedes thought.

While working as a newspaperman in New Orleans Faulkner met Sherwood Anderson, who encouraged him to continue writing despite a succession of rejection slips. In June, 1925, he shipped on a freighter to Europe; he walked through Italy and France, and served for a time on a Paris journal. Back in Oxford, he supported himself with whatever employment he could find, however menial. After some minor publications that dropped with hardly a sound or an eddy into the ocean of print, he persuaded a New York firm to issue (1929) the book which began his fame.

Sartoris opened the annals of Yoknapatawpha County by describing an old Southern family gradually yielding its supremacy and property to members of an enterprising, unscrupulous, expanding mercantile class. The founder of the family's prominence was Colonel John Sartoris, who led a cavalry regiment in the Civil War with a dashing bravery that supplied his descendants with repeatedly recounted and embroidered tales. He died in 1876, leaving Bayard Sartoris I as heir to his patriarchal power. The novel begins with this aging Bayard as bank president in Jefferson, courtly and comfortable with his whiskey and cigar, universally respected but showing signs of decline in his inability to discipline his offspring and his servants. The devil of the book is his grandson Bayard Sartoris II, who returns from World War I addicted to violence, irresponsibility, and speed. His new car, dreaded by his grandfather, becomes the symbol of the changing world, and the instrument of catastrophe.

The Sartorises retain pride of blood, old standards of manner and tastes, some sense of duty to family, class, and community. They use and hector their Negro servitors, treat them as accepted and nourished members of the household, but never think of them as other than a permanently servile caste. They look with futile contempt upon the rootless, cunning, innovating newcomers from the North, who recognize no social bonds, no aesthetic restraints, and no other driving force than the urges to money, sex, and power. The chief representatives of this new breed, in the Faulkner novels, are the Snopeses, "a seemingly inexhaustible family which for the last ten years has been moving to town [Jefferson] in driblets from a small settlement known as Frenchman's Bend." Flem Snopes, destined to mount to wealth and authority, "had appeared unheralded one day behind the counter of a small restaurant on a side street. . . . . With this foothold, and like Abraham of old, he brought his blood and legal kin, household by household, individual by individual, into town, and established them where they could gain money." They "spread to small third-rate businesses of various kinds—grocery stores, barber shops, . . . where they multiplied and flourished. The older residents, from their Jeffersonian houses and genteel stores and offices, looked on" this influx "with amusement at first," then with "consternation."[2] As the novels proceed, the new class spreads until the Sartorises disappear before the Snopeses; the plantation, the village, the mansion, and the carriage give way to the store, the town, the bank, and the automobile, and the face of the South is changed into a degraded image of the North.

The only Snopes in this volume is a bookkeeper in Bayard Sartoris' bank. He embezzles on a tentative scale, saves his gleanings, lives in squalid surroundings, and sends unsigned love letters to Narcissa Benbow, who is beyond his reach because she is related to the Sartoris family. Her brother, Horace Benbow, is a lawyer marked by "his air of fine and delicate futility."[3] He saddens her—who is all virtue and tenderness—by going off with the flirtatious wife of his best friend. Narcissa herself falls silently and fearfully in love with Bayard Sartoris II, who ignores her, having lost his soul to his car. When he breaks several ribs in an accident she nurses him in mute devotion till he marries her. When ribs and fenders are repaired he takes his reluctant grandfather for a ride, and runs into a ditch; Bayard I dies of the shock. Bayard II soon thereafter comes to his end by flying a damaged plane. He was then twenty-seven, and the year was 1920.

So much for the story; it would be nothing without the art. There is structure here, an unhurried filling in of the picture: of the town and its shops and tradesmen and idlers; of the old residential districts with the quiet, lawned, and shaded homes of the dying gentility; of these defeated families, with their sad proud recollections of a gracious past; of the former slaves and their descendants—propertyless, shiftless, cunning, remodeling the English language to their tongues and needs and songs. Best of all is Faulkner's fond recording of the Southern atmosphere: the color and composition of the soil, the characteristic plants and flowers making a "mazed and scented jungle" of "crape myrtle and syringa and lilac, . . . and massed honeysuckle";[4] "the scent of jasmine drifting steadily into the house";[5] the native birds "demurely mellifluous in the late afternoon";[6] the Southern sky drenching the earth and the Spanish moss, or turning the soil red with a burning sun. We perceive that much labor and love have gone into the book; Faulkner would not exchange his South, despite its "old miasmic swamps of spiritual sloth,"[7] for all the wealth and rush of the trampling North. He spends himself in seeking unhackneyed words to describe the sharply observed scene. He writes sensitively of a mule's burdened day[8] as if it were his brother; he notes how a young dog "soon must dash away with his tongue flapping and the tense delicate feathering of his tail in pursuit of the maddening elusive smells with which the world surrounded him and tempted him from every thicket and copse and ravine."[9] Sometimes the venturing author overreaches himself for novelty, as when he describes sumptuous ladies rising from the dinner table "with sibilant gathering motions [of their skirts] above the petulant modulation of the hostess";[10] but also he has passages of quiet flowing beauty unspoiled by bizarre adjectives or perfumed prose.[11]

Sartoris gradually found an audience; royalties dribbled in, and Faulkner could eat with confidence. In 1929 he married Mrs. Estelle Franklin, a widow who brought him two children by a previous marriage. William accepted them as her dowry.

Even before the publication of *Sartoris* he had finished the novel which he later rated his best. The theme of *The Sound and the Fury* (1929) is again the decay of an upper-class family—here the Compsons. As if to bear out Macbeth's view of life as "a tale told by an idiot, full of sound and fury, signifying nothing," the tale is first told by an idiot, Benjy, who is described as "been three years old thirty years." He is too loose in his bearings to tell the story connectedly; it is dimly conveyed to us by images that float through Benjy's mind; the result resembles some contemporary paintings in its transformation of order into chaos, of clarity into obscurity. In the pivotal scene Benjy, not quite comprehending, sees a neighbor seduce his sister Caddy Compson; she resists, yields, repents, and kneels before Benjy. " 'I won't,' she said, 'I won't anymore, Benjy, Benjy.' Then she was crying and I cried, and we held each other."[12] Soon a child announces itself; Caddy hurries off into marriage. In the final chapter the son and heir of the Compson family, hearing of Caddy's slip, kills himself. It is a powerful story if you can make head or tail of it, but Faulkner has left no device unused to make it obscure.

"In the summer of 1929," Faulkner tells us,

> I got a job in the power plant [at Oxford], on the night shift from 6 P.M. to 6 A.M. as a coal passer. I shoveled coal from a bunker into a wheelbarrow and wheeled it in and dumped it where the fireman could put it into the boiler. About 11 o'clock the people would be going to bed, and it did not take much steam. Then we could rest, the fireman and I. He would sit in a chair and doze. I had invented a table out of a wheelbarrow. . . . On those nights, between 12 and 4, I wrote *As I Lay Dying* in six weeks.[13]

In that ambling novel the epic of degeneration turns to a family of poor whites working their stingy acres near Frenchman's Bend. Faulkner was a city man, but he knew the lore and language of the farms, the peasants, even of their animals; he describes in confident detail the breaking of a horse by a man. The story runs around the death and funeral of Addie Bundren after bearing five children to a shiftless husband thick in skin and head. Dewey Dell, the only daughter, fans her dying mother tirelessly; son Cash builds Addie's coffin under her window and subject to her approval. The other sons rival their father in profanity; they talk at the rate of thirty goddamns an hour. The mother has found little happiness with her surly husband; she anticipates no pleasure in lying near his forebears in the earth; she begs her sons to take her corpse to Jefferson and bury her with her own people; the husband consents because he hopes to find new dentures in the city. Soon after her death they squeeze the body, still warm, into the skimpy coffin, load the box on a rickety truck, hitch up their two mules, and begin the long procession to the county seat.

A hundred calamities delay them. A storm drenches them, and the swollen river destroys the bridge they had expected to cross. They detour several miles to another bridge and find it too demolished. They try to ford the stream, and their mules drown. They buy a team from Flem Snopes, and finally reach Jefferson. The burial accomplished, Dewey Dell arranges to abort the fetus she has been secretly carrying, and husband Anse gets new teeth, a gramophone, and a new wife. — *As I Lay Dying* is widely highly praised, but I found it dismal and tedious. Faulkner confessed: "I thought of all the natural calamities that could happen to a family, and I let them all happen."[14] I admit that a wheelbarrow is no spur to ecstasy, but I trust I shall never again have to follow a forty-mile funeral.

Honest William made another confession: he had deliberately crowded *Sanctuary* (1931) with sex and violence as lures to customers[15] —and perhaps as invitations to an invitation to Hollywood. The film makers responded, the picture prospered, and a critic called the book "one of the finest novels in modern literature."[16] It is terrible. Into a mess of "poor white trash" walks Temple Drake, a high-school girl with a fancy for fornication; around and after her runs a rabble of men eager to soothe her itch; a murder is committed; a Negro is lynched; Temple, irretrievably pregnant, is reclaimed by her father and a husband, and waits for her sequel in *Requiem for a Nun* (1950). In that dramatic postlude she gratefully allows her nurse to suffocate the unwanted infant; she runs off with a lover, returns to her husband, takes fifty pages to confess her adultery, but lets her nurse be hanged for the infanticide. Here were flesh and blood enough for a dozen films, but quite unworthy of the man who was about to write his masterpiece.

I am still in the dark as to the meaning of the title, *Light in August* (1932)—unless it refers to the changing shades of dawn and noon and night during the month that encloses the tale. Lena Groves, barefoot and pregnant (no woman stays long unburdened in Faulkner's books), walks through thirty days from Alabama to "Jefferson," seeking the vagrant father of her child. It is a touching story, which Faulkner tells with leisurely sympathy, lingering over every aspect of the road and sky, every act or word of help or kindness that greets the girl and her trustful quest. She reaches Jefferson at last, only to find that the faithless seducer is a drunken bootlegger, who, at her approach, takes again to his heels, in terror of stability. Two tense episodes adjoin the central narrative: how the gossipers of the town consciously and resolutely wreck the life of an innocent preacher whose wife goes astray; and how a fanatic puritan, by harsh and pious discipline, turns a hapless boy into a criminal. But there is a hero here: Byron Bunch, who befriends Lena in all her troubles, falls in love with her, and finally gets bride and child in a happy ending rare in Faulkner's memories. But the plot must not be further exposed, for this is the one single volume of Faulkner that the reader must travel with in person through every page and to its close.

In November, 1932, Faulkner went to Hollywood as a script writer. Dissatisfied with his earnings there, he returned to Oxford and the novel, and won critical praise for *Absalom, Absalom!* (1936) and *The Unvanquished* (1938). But no public acclaim followed; until the Nobel Prize (1949) aroused an audience for him his readers numbered only four or five thousand, and by that time "he was virtually out of print."[17]

Obstinately he dipped his pen ever more deeply into the darkest layers of his county's life. In a trilogy that constitutes his greatest achievement he traced the history of the Snopes family through the complex legend of their tenacious rapacity. In *The Hamlet* (1940) Flem Snopes is a poor but competent helper in a café in Frenchman's Bend; he rises to a position of trust in the village store; when its owner finds his daughter Eula pregnant by a stranger never seen in those parts again, Flem agrees to marry the girl for the store and some acres; before the volume ends he has promoted himself to the county bank in Jefferson.

In *The Town* (1957), amid acid etchings of dour whites and cheerful fearful blacks, amid pages of trivial superfluities and dialectic gab, Faulkner intertwines stories of the near-lynching of an innocent Negro, the polite adultery of Major de Spain, president of the bank, with Eula Snopes, and the self-denying love of Gavin Stevens for Eula's exciting daughter Linda. Gavin is the most interesting, decent, and ineffective character in Faulkner: a Harvard graduate, the most trusted lawyer in Jefferson, too busy helping people to tidy his clothes or his hair. Eula falls silently in love with him, Linda falls recklessly in love with an irresponsible mechanic; Eula commits suicide, de Spain decamps, Flem becomes president of the bank, and Stevens rescues Linda from Flem's tyranny by sending her to Greenwich Village to wear out her dreams. In *The Mansion* (1959) a lesser Snopes, imprisoned for a passionate murder, and asking in vain for Flem's intercession, escapes from jail, and kills him to make the saga's end.

III. FAULKNER'S NEGROES

Bit by bit, as he filled his canvas, the leisurely artist softened the colors in which he presented the black people of his realm. In *Sartoris* he still called them "niggers"; in later volumes he described them as mentally retarded by poverty, poor schooling, and "the old-fashioned religion." In *The Sound and the Fury* they are clever in their elusive way, especially in avoiding work; one of them explains, "Ain't nobody works much in dis country sep de boll-weevil, noways."[18] In that same book, however, Faulkner gave a sympathetic portrait of old "Mammy" Dilsey, who seems to have the best heart in the whole Compson ménage. At the grave of his own "Mammy," Caroline Barr, who "has known me all my life," he spoke of her with warm affection and respect. In *Go Down, Moses* (1942) he drew favorable pictures of Southern Negroes. Finally, in *Intruder in the Dust* (1948), he took up their cause.

That story is presented as told by Charles Mallison, the seventeen-year-old nephew of Gavin Stevens. Charles remembers a kindness received in childhood from a Negro, Lucas Beauchamp, who now is falsely accused of murdering a white man. All the Negroes in Jefferson hide in their cottages that night, fearing a lynching, even a massacre. Charles enlists the aid of his uncle and other whites to exhume the corpse of the victim, proving that the bullets that killed him were quite different from those in Beauchamp's revolver. After an exciting confrontation with the lynching mob Stevens and the boy triumph, Beauchamp is freed, and Stevens discourses to his nephew on the race problem.

"The injustice is ours, the South's," he says, "we must expiate and abolish it ourselves, alone, and without help nor even (with thanks) advice."[19] North and South are so deeply different in origins, memories, and ways that neither can understand the other. "The North shows an almost helpless capacity and eagerness to believe anything about the South, not even provided it be derogatory but merely bizarre enough," and the South, proud of its Anglo-Saxon blood, scorns "the rootless ephemeral cities [of the North] with . . . the coastal spew of Europe." "We are defending not actually our politics or beliefs or even our way of life," continues Stevens-Faulkner, "but simply our homogeneity, from a federal government to which the rest of the country has to surrender more and more of its personal and private liberty. . . . And of course we will continue to defend it."[20] "Only from homogeneity comes anything of a people or for a people of durable . . . value—the literature, the art, the science, that minimum of government and police which is the meaning of freedom, . . . and, perhaps most valuable of all, a national character worth anything in a crisis." And the author in his own person adds, about young Mallison: "The dirt, the earth, which had bred his bones and those of his fathers for six generations, . . . was still shaping him into not just a man but a specific man, . . . with specific hopes and convictions and ways of thinking and acting of a specific kind and race."[21]

Stevens wants to see the Negro freed, but "what we [Southerners] are really defending" is "the privilege of setting him free ourselves."[22] Nevertheless, freedom for the Negro "won't be next Tuesday. The people in the North believe it can be compelled even into next Monday by the simple ratification, by votes, of printed paragraph"; but they "have forgotten that although a long generation ago Lucas Beauchamp's freedom was made an article in our constitution, and Lucas Beauchamp's master [the Southern white] was not merely beaten to his knees but trampled for ten years on his face in the dust to make him swallow it, yet only three short generations later they are faced once more with the necessity of passing legislation to set Lucas Beauchamp free."[23] The problem remains as a living curse on the white race for having so long enslaved black men; "the curse of every white child that . . . ever will be born; none can escape it."[24] In Jefferson there is a white woman, Joanna Burden, who, by organizing schools for Negro children, hopes to dull the curse; but when a mulatto, Joe Christmas, asks her, "Just when do men that have different blood stop hating one another?" she answers sadly, "I don't know."[25]

In 1956, in a letter to *Life* magazine, Faulkner braved the wrath of his white neighbors by declaring for integration. They called him "weeping Willie Faulkner," sent him abusive letters, and chided him over the telephone. He fought back: demanded equality of educational opportunity for all, lauded the accomplishments of Negroes, and condemned the churches of the South for not responding to the Negroes' cry for justice.[26] At the same time he lost friends in the North by repeating Stevens' view that the problem could not be solved by Northern compulsion of the South.

Possibly Faulkner's appeal for the liberation of both whites and blacks through education shared with the mounting scope and power of his novels to win him the Nobel Prize for Literature in 1949. He went to Stockholm (1950) to receive the award in person; there he made a brief but impressive speech, declaring that "man will not merely endure, he will prevail." Twice already he had used the phrase; "the capacity to survive and absorb and endure and still be steadfast"[27] became the banner under which he moved to his end, as if recalling Edgar's lines in *Lear*:

> *Men must endure*
> *Their going hence, even as their coming hither:*
> *Ripeness is all.*[28]

IV. THE WRITER'S ART

Faulkner is nothing if not original. I know of nothing like him in narrative method, plot structure, vocabulary, and style. He borrows from Balzac the device of recalling, in a novel, characters introduced in a previous work; so Joanna Burden, in *Light in August*, is a granddaughter of the reformer whom Colonel Sartoris, in *Sartoris*, had killed for trying to get Negroes to vote; and Flem Snopes binds several volumes into one by his sly metamorphoses and sinuous rise. By this plan, by centering most of the stories in or near Jefferson or Frenchman's Bend, and by revealing ever new aspects of the same souls and scenes, Faulkner makes us feel that we have met these people, seen these places, before, and that they are not fiction but history. He never lets his creatures rest; he probes them again and again, on every side, until they are exposed in all the powers and blemishes of their bodies and souls.

Other authors had used their *personae* as masks through which to see and report events, but no other had employed this method of indirect narrative so persistently. Almost all of Faulkner's stories are told by one or more of the participants. We are reminded of Browning's *The Ring and the Book*, but there the same action is described by each main actor in turn; or we may recall an O'Neill play in which the diverse but related occurrences of a moment are simultaneously presented to the eye. In Faulkner one character narrates all, or each tells a different part or aspect of the tale; so *The Town* is divided not into chapters but into narrators. Faulkner felt that no event has a simple objective reality; it is an amalgam of human sensations, perceptions, memories, interpretations, illusions, and beliefs; every participant sees it in part and with blinders; "truth" is a precarious kaleidoscope of these partial views. The plan helps to create the feeling of intimacy, of being there; but Faulkner often weakens that effect by putting subtle perceptions, profound meditations, or recondite phrases into the mouths of adolescents or illiterates, and by making the narrator remember page after page of conversation.[29] So Darl, the simplest of the Bundren sons, says of his budding sister: her "wet dress shapes . . . those mammalian ludicrosities which are the horizons and valleys of the earth."[30] (They are treasures or tragedies, but ludicrosities—what blasphemy!)

Faulkner's plots are always complex, and as confused as he can make them. He seems determined to keep the reader guessing, on every page, what has happened, or to whom. So in *Sartoris* we are informed that Narcissa is pregnant, and are left to conclude, unwarrantably, that she has at last married Bayard II;[31] and in *Light in August*, two hundred pages after learning that Lena is swelling with child, we are told who was the *male*factor in that collision. Repeated flashbacks ignore chronology, even in their own sequence: the present is illuminated by a scene from the past, which in turn is explained by a scene from an earlier past. Past and present mingle as contemporary forces in compounding a thought or an event; the present is a penalty paid for the past. Nearly all the plots are mysteries, and, as in a good detective story, we have to digest a hundred or more pages of unintelligible incidents before we are taken into the secret of their significance. Some readers enjoy such treasure hunts, but I bequeath them to Presidents tired by a day of finding plums for senators or youths for Mars. Usually the plot is well constructed, and the major threads are untangled in the end. Sometimes, however, as in *The Town* and *Intruder in the Dust*, the master forgets his art and tags onto his completed tale several pages of incidents or ideas quite unrelated to the preceding narrative. We must not look in Faulkner for an orderly sequence of events, or the patient development of a character.

His style is as strange as his people and as mystifying as his plots. Much of it is Negro or peasant dialects; Faulkner is an expert mimic of these, and multiplies them to tedium. When he speaks in his own person, or through educated mouths, it is a unique style—complicated, involved, rambling, cumulative, forceful, and often picturesque. So he conveys the mood of a "long still hot weary dead September afternoon," and he describes the sexual urge as "the immortal unsentient [unthinking?] demanding ancient meat." It is a hurried style, piling clause upon clause, chary of commas, and as delayed in periods as Faulkner's deflowered heroines. Faulkner could hold his breath indefinitely, and thought nothing of spreading a sentence over a page.[32] He makes a direct-action woman like Eula Snopes say to her impatient daughter, "You—a girl anyway—don't really hate your father no matter how much you think you do or should or should want to because people expect you to or that it would look well to because it would be romantic to";[33] even Juliet's nurse was clearer. Sometimes I wore myself out hunting the person referred to by a pronoun, or finding the forgotten subject of a tardy verb.

The vocabulary is baroque, with unexpected twists of phrase, shunning worn-out words, fondling fresh ones shamelessly; so, within two pages, a plow turns up "viscid shards" of earth, and a mulatto woman "came sibilantly [with rustling dress?] into the house"; a little later we see a Negro "richly static" [erect and adorned?] behind a tethered horse; and farther on we are told of Horace Benbow's "fine spatulate hands."[34] In *Light in August* some wayfarers "came in sight vaguely against the defunctive dust"[35]—which is too much for me. Balancing such bizarre conjunctions are picturesque phrases on almost every page: the Confederate lady's "voice was proud and still as banners in the dust";[36] and Lena tells her story again "with that patient and transparent recapitulation of a lying child."[37] Sometimes the imagery touches poetry, as when, on a much traveled country road, the "identical and anonymous and deliberate wagons" of farmers move to market "through a succession of creak wheeled and limpeared [donkey-led] avatars moving forever and without progress across an urn."[38] Faulkner has imagination, and knows Keats.

But I am losing proportion: while picking flaws in Faulkner's art I have forgotten to say that it is, all in all, a splendor of illumination and originality. It is an art conceived in proud withdrawal from models and traditions, and molded by feeling, fancy, and experiment to a continuing sense of human character and struggle in communities, classes, and souls. If you have the fortitude to read a dozen of these novels in due sequence you will see emerging a vast composite picture of Mississippi—or Yoknapatawpha—man. It does not claim to be complete, or to reveal all the South; there is no color here of "Southern hospitality" (which I found comfortingly real on my weary lecture tours); no paragraph of a Southern mother rearing a family to courtesy and grace, to generosity and strength. It is "a slice of life," but mostly cut from the middle layers. John Faulkner thought that "my brother Bill" deliberately stressed the "seamier side and most outlandish doings" of his countrymen as more calculated to sell the books.[39] This seems to be a harsh judgment; much in these volumes—their slow movement, their complicated style, their dark mood, their rarely lovable characters—might rather have made them hard to sell. William admitted that he had described only a segment, but "I like to think of the world I created as being a kind of keystone in the universe; that, small as that keystone is, if it were taken away the universe itself would collapse."[40] Without these somber, dreary, patient, cunning people tilling the soil, herding the cattle, and taking their pennies to the store, the bank, the church, and the government, how could there be an America?

V. A VIEW OF LIFE

Faulkner loved America, if only because it was his, if only because of the unforgettable dream it had been. Like so many of us, in this long and painful transition, he had transferred his sustaining dream from heaven to utopia. He pictured his utopia as one of individual freedom rather than social security—of liberation from religious dogma, economic exploitation, governmental domination, and mass pressure to conformity; his visioned America was to be "a sanctuary on the earth for individual man." But "we dozed and slept, and the dream abandoned us."[41] He mourned that liberty had become license, that the press violated the individual's right to privacy, that catch phrases like "subversion" and "anti-Communism" could be used to destroy a man's good name or confuse the public mind. He shrank from crowds, cities, industrialism, speed, and greedy fortunes dissipated in luxury or display.

He reluctantly realized that man is not made for utopia, that evil is written somewhere in almost every heart. He saw no heroes on his landscape; apparently they had all died in the Civil War. He despised the lower-middle-class culture that was engulfing the North and overflowing into the South: "the cheap shoddy dishonest music, the cheap flashy baseless overvalued money, . . . the noisy muddle of political activity, . . . the spurious uproar produced by men deliberately fostering —then getting rich on—our national passion for the mediocre; who will ever accept the best provided it is based and defiled before being fed to us; who are the only people on earth who brag publicly of being second-rate, i.e., lowbrows."[42] Faulkner seems to have agreed with Flem Snopes that "the normal condition of a bank was a steady decorous embezzlement" of its patrons' funds by its controllers and employees.[43]

He was easier on women than on men. He had good words for Narcissa and Miss Jenny in *Sartoris*, for Addie Bundren and Dewey Dell in *As I Lay Dying*, for Lena Groves and Joanna Burden in *Light in August*, even for Eula and Linda Snopes in *Intruder in the Dust*. But he doubted if any man had ever understood women. Farmer Samson says, "A man can't tell nothing about them. I lived with the same one fifteen years and I be durn if I can."[44] Another farmer reckons that "women folks are likely to be good without being kind. . . . It is only a bad woman herself that is likely to be very kind to another man that needs a kindness."[45] And Samson adds, "They [women] make life hard on them[selves], not taking it as it comes up, like a man does."[46] (A man forgets, a woman cannot.) One kind of woman particularly displeased Faulkner—the proud and aging virgin. Rosa Coldfield's room exuded "the rank smell of female old flesh long embattled in virginity."[47] Correspondingly he allowed wide freedom to his males: Joe Christmas' "life, for all its anonymous promiscuity, had been conventional enough, as a life of healthy and normal sin usually is."[48]

So he interpreted Puritan morality as unnatural and hypercritical, and came down heavily upon the old Protestant ethic of hard work, thrift, pride, and prayer. He satirized the "old-fashioned religion" in McEachern, who deformed Joe Christmas with harsh discipline, and Calvin Burden, who informed his children, "I'll beat the loving God into the four of you as long as I can raise my arm."[49] Faulkner made fun of his county's preachers, "all looking like . . . bankers or doctors or store-keepers . . . , all very grave and long in the face, like horses."[50] And, resenting God's permission of evil, he made one of his farmers ask, "If there is a God what the hell is he for?"[51] In Faulkner God is chiefly an expletive.

But neither had he any faith in science or philosophy. He was among the first to feel the impotence of science to keep its inventions from enlarging and implementing crime. He found no answer to the riddles of the universe in the philosophers. He kept his praise for poetry. "The poets are almost always wrong about facts. That's because they are not really interested in facts, only in truth; which is why the truth they speak is so true that even those who hate poets . . . are exalted and terrified by it."[52] We gather from elusive echoes that he found the deepest truths in Whitman and Keats.

Faulkner resigned himself, in his books, to pessimism, determinism, even fatalism. He spoke of "an infallibility in events."[53] He found no purpose or meaning in history. He spoke of life as something to be borne rather than enjoyed. He saw "old men . . . drawn thin by the slow attenuation of days";[54] every tick of the merciless clock announcing and advancing the agonizing end. A man is the sum of his misfortunes, and "victory is an illusion of philosophers and fools."[55] He relented a bit in accepting the Nobel Prize, and thought that man "will prevail"; but in his books it is evil that prevails, or some neutral, undiscriminating, meaningless irony of fate or web of circumstance. In *Requiem for a Nun* (1951) even hope disappears; "hoping is the hardest thing of all to break, to get rid of, to let go of, the last thing of all poor sinning man will turn loose."[56] In *A Fable* (1954) we are again assured that man will "endure" and "prevail," but the story tells how a soldier mutinies, is betrayed by his companion, and is finished by a firing squad. In *The Town* (1957) the word "prevail" drops out, and only "endure" remains. "It is for us to cope, to resist, to endure, and, if we can, survive."[57] Here at the outset of our literary tour, we find—as, near its end, in Kazantzakis—the stoic message: all hope abandon, but fight on; the fight must be its own reward.

Between his dirges Faulkner sipped his fame. In 1952 he was lionized by the international literati in Paris. In 1955 he undertook with flattering success a lecture tour of Japan. In 1957–58, as "Writer in Residence" at the University of Virginia, he explained to his students the art of fiction and the secrets of style. In 1960 he had the comfort of reading, in England's magisterial *New Statesman*, "Mr. Faulkner . . . is the greatest living novelist in English."[58]

In 1962 he died, and the encomium had to be changed to the greatest American novelist of the twentieth century. He did not merely tell a story; he painted a picture, and projected a philosophy. He saw his country as a biopsy of life—a piece of tissue taken from a living body for clarification and diagnosis; he looked without blinders, but with sympathy, at its fauna and flora, its men, women, and children, its blacks and whites; he studied intently their shape, touch, taste, sound, and smell, their bodies and minds and secret hearts, their hopes and fears, loves and hates, sufferings and crimes; he put them all down on paper, laboriously and obscurely but bravely and honestly; and he found through them a philosophy of patience and fate. He left us deepened.

CHAPTER II

Ernest Hemingway*

I KNOW of no other author in whom life and letters have been so intimately and persistently united as in Ernest Hemingway. A woman in "The Snows of Kilimanjaro" tells her husband, "You're the most complete man I've ever known."[1] Someone—perhaps Hemingway—gave Hemingway that compliment, and it never left his memory. He wanted to be a writer, but he was secretly ashamed to be so unnatural a freak; he longed to redeem authorship with deeds, to enliven meditation with virile action and the speech of physical men. He was the victim of a hundred accidents, a hero of two world wars, a victor over sharks and lions; and he wrote the most influential fiction of his time.

He was born in a quiet suburb of Chicago—Oak Park, Illinois—in 1899. His father was a moderately successful physician, who taught him a fondness for outdoor life and sports. His mother had been brought up in strict piety, which she graced as director and soloist of a Congregationalist church choir. Contrary to Freud, the boy loved his father much more than his mother, and took to woods and streams more readily than to hymns and prayers. On his twelfth birthday his grandfather gave him a shotgun; soon the boy rivaled his father, who was "a beautiful shot."[2] He learned to fish, sail, ski, and box. His ideal was a mixture of William Shakespeare and John L. Sullivan. All through his life he challenged people to put on the gloves, and he seldom failed to knock respondents down. When he won a fishing contest at Bimini (1935) he appeased his defeated rivals by offering two hundred dollars to any of them who could survive four rounds in the ring with him; several tried, not one lasted.[3]

Ernest did not enjoy schooling, but succeeded in getting through Oak Park High School, apparently with ease, for he found no difficulty with Latin. "Cicero is a pipe," he wrote; "I could write better stuff with both hands behind me."[4] His ego was burgeoning. He composed short stories

* This chapter is especially indebted to Carlos Baker's scholarly *Ernest Hemingway: A Life Story*.

for the high-school magazine. He read Ring Lardner, and liked his short sentences and proletarian speech. In October, 1917, he was taken on as a cub reporter by the Kansas City *Star*. That first-class journal issued to its staff a style book which recommended "short sentences, . . . short first paragraphs. . . . Be positive, not negative."[5] The Hemingway style took form.

Journalism fitted his flair for combining writing and doing, but he lusted for a larger arena. A defect in his left eye disqualified him for service in the Army, but he enlisted with the American Red Cross (April, 1918), and served as ambulance driver at the French, then at the Italian, front in World War I. He relished danger, though he knew and acknowledged fear. On July 8, still two weeks short of nineteen, he was severely wounded at Fossalta—while carrying a wounded man to safety through the line of Austrian fire—by a trench-mortar shell that deposited in his legs hundreds of small pointed steel rods. Twenty-eight of them were soon removed; about two hundred were cut out in Milan hospital, some by himself with a pocket knife; several remained *in situ* till his death.

This was one slice of life that went to vitalize *A Farewell to Arms*. The other was Agnes von Kurowsky, his nurse in Milan. Naturally he fell in love with her, for men are more lastingly moved by tenderness than by beauty; and she gave him just enough encouragement to warm his convalescent gratitude to proposal pitch. When able to walk steadily he returned to the Italian front, but there he developed jaundice, and was sent back to the Milan hospital. The war ended in November, and in January, 1919, Ernest sailed from Genoa for New York.

He was welcomed by his family and Oak Park as a hero, but he soon grew lonesome for Italy, or for Agnes. "We only half live over here," he said; "the Italians live all the way."[6] When he received word from Agnes that she had accepted a rival he consoled himself with so many American girls that his mother mourned that he was lost to Satan. She was appeased when (September 3, 1921) he married Elizabeth Hadley Richardson of St. Louis. "Hadley" was twenty-nine and Ernest was twenty-two, but she had an income of some $2,500 a year.[7] (Her father had committed suicide; Ernest's father would shoot himself in 1928; Ernest . . .)

In December, 1921, he sailed with his bride to France as correspondent for the Toronto *Star*. In Paris he worked hard, seeking to add some enduring masterpiece to his ephemeral reports. Armed with letters of introduction from Sherwood Anderson, he made friends with Gertrude Stein, John Dos Passos, Scott Fitzgerald, and James Joyce. Gertrude called them and their contemporaries "the lost generation"—which had shed its gods and ideals in the First World War's revelation of human nature, and was now seeking revenge in satire, solace in sex, and forgetfulness in drink. Ezra Pound, Ford Madox Ford, and Scott Fitzgerald gave the newcomer a helping hand. Pound proclaimed him "the finest prose writer in the world."[8] Fitzgerald wrote to Scribner's in 1924: "This is to tell you about a young writer named Ernest Hemingway, who lives in Paris . . . and has a brilliant future. I'd look him up right away. He's the real thing."[9] Horace Liveright took a chance, and published a collection of Hemingway's early short stories under the title *In Our Time* (1925). It did not sell. When Liveright rejected a second set of stories—*The Torrents of Spring*—Max Perkins, the alert and helpful editor at Scribner's, took the volume on the understanding that his firm would have first choice on the novel that the author was writing. So began a lifelong association between Scribner's and Hemingway.

The Torrents of Spring (1926) was generally chastised as a tasteless and meatless satire of Sherwood Anderson's style. But when *The Sun Also Rises* appeared later in that year, Perkins' foresight was rewarded: the critics agreed that a new novelist had appeared, with a fresh skill in dialogue and rapid narrative. The book was not well constructed: it began—and for a hundred pages continued—as a sketch of life, love, and liquor in the foreign colony in Paris; then it moved over the Pyrenees to a firsthand account of the bullfight fiesta in Pamplona; the two parts did not make a united and harmonious whole. Members of the colony recognized themselves in the characters of the tale: Lady Duff Twysden became Lady Brett Ashley, Pat Guthrie became Mike Campbell, Harold Loeb was renamed Robert Cohn, and Harold Stearns was Harold Stone. Lady Duff, Guthrie, and Loeb had joined Ernest and Hadley at the fiesta in 1925; it was Hemingway's third visit to Pamplona, and it confirmed his ardor for the bullfighters and their art.

The book was published in Europe as *Fiesta*. The title of the American edition was taken from the first chapter of Ecclesiastes:

> One generation passeth away, and another generation cometh; but the earth abideth forever.
> The sun also ariseth, and the sun goeth down, and hasteth to his place where he arose. . . .
> The thing that hath been, it is that which shall be, . . . and there is no new thing under the sun. . . .
> I have seen all the works that are done under the sun; and behold, all is vanity and vexation of spirit.

So this first success of Hemingway as a writer announced not only his mastery of vivid narrative and his penchant for rapid-fire conversation but also his pessimistic philosophy.*

I pass over, and have not read, a third volume of short stories—*Men without Women* (1927). This title too is characteristic: in Hemingway's books the women are subsidiary to the men, the men to the events, and the events to the philosophy. He was all man, preferred the company of men, and concerned himself with women only as lovers, nurses, and conveniences.

In 1926 he began to notice, then to welcome, the advances of Pauline Pfeiffer, an Arkansas girl with a rich uncle. Hadley, who had been a model of fidelity, industry, and patience, left him, taking their son, John, and obtained a divorce decree on January 27, 1927. He married Pauline on May 10, took her to Havana, Kansas City (where she gave birth to a son, Patrick), and Sheridan, Wyoming. There, in September, 1928, he finished the first draft of *A Farewell to Arms*, which Scribner's published twelve months later.

He found the title in a poem in which the Elizabethan dramatist George Peele had pictured an old warrior exchanging war for prayer;[10] it does not quite fit Hemingway's novel, in which a young ambulance driver exchanges war for love. He described it as "my long tale of transalpine fornication including the entire war in Italy and so to BED."[11] Here again the book was composed of two successive stories. The first was a classically restrained description of the Italian Army's retreat from Gorizia after defeat by the Austrians at Caporetto in 1917. Those fifty pages are Hemingway's best—a quiet, matter-of-fact narrative of incompetence, chaos, cowardice, suffering, and courage; there is no appeal to emotion, there is only the impartial, almost *sotto voce* account of small events totaling a doubly moving scene. Then, *in mediis rebus*, the novel leaves the war; the American ambulance driver, badly wounded, falls in love with an English nurse, makes her pregnant, and escapes with her from Italy into Switzerland. The tone passes from classic severity to romantic sentiment; the conversation of the lovers is idyllic and delightful; the agony of first childbirth is tenderly described; and the romance and the book are suddenly ended by the death of the child and then of the mother. The "separate peace" by which Lieutenant Henry and Catherine Barkley turned their backs upon the war (like the Russians at Brest Litovsk in 1917) reflected Hemingway's revolt against

---

* I am reminded of Clarence Darrow's remark: "Anyone who is an optimist after thirty is a fool, and anyone who is a pessimist before thirty is too damned smart."

Western civilization and its periodic holocausts. He thought now of leaving the United States and Europe, and living in Cuba or Africa. America reproached him by acclaiming the book, pardoning its soldierly profanity, making it into a motion picture, and enabling the author to send financial aid to his widowed mother.

In April, 1929, he returned with Pauline to France, and in September he took her to another fiesta at Pamplona. In Madrid he met Sidney Franklin, a Russian-Jewish *torero* from Brooklyn. The friendship that they developed heightened his interest in bullfights; he visited Pamplona repeatedly, and became so familiar with the rules, rituals, and tragedies of the *corrida* that in 1932 he felt justified in issuing an enthusiastic treatise called *Death in the Afternoon* (1932). A kind of thanatotropism, or turning toward death, lured him; "the only place where you could see life and death, i.e., violent death, now that the wars were over, was in the bull ring, and I wanted very much to go to Spain where I could study it."[12] He passionately admired the matadors because they faced mortal danger a dozen times a day without a whimper, and with that economy of motion in which Herbert Spencer saw the anatomy of grace. Yet he confessed that it was not a fair fight. "It is one hundred to one against the *matador de toros*, or formally invested bullfighter, being killed unless he is inexperienced, ignorant, or out of training, or too old and heavy on his feet."[13] How, then, could the ethics of the sport be defended? Hemingway gave a strange reply:

> About morals I know only that that which is moral is what you feel good after, and what is immoral is what you feel bad after . . . The bullfight is very moral to me because I feel very fine while it is going on, and have a feeling of life and death and mortality and immortality, and after it is over I feel very sad but very fine.[14]

He saw nothing unreasonable in the preliminary weakening of the bull by the thrusts of the mounted picadors, nor was he disturbed when the bull ripped open the belly of an inoffensive horse; he thought it quite comic when a gored horse ran around the arena with its entrails hanging out.[15] The bullfight, he argued, should be seen not as a sport but as a tragic drama and aesthetic spectacle. "Killing cleanly and in a way which gives you esthetic pleasure and pride has always been one of the greatest enjoyments of a part of the human race." A scribbler hiding in an ivory tower may be startled by this frank brutality, but a hunter bringing down his prey, a fisherman harpooning a whale, a soldier destroying a dangerous enemy, will agree with Hemingway; survival must come before civilization. Hunting was once a way of preserving and supporting human life; the sport is a vestige of a past necessity; and the stockyard slaughter is a substitute for the hunt.

In a cruel review of Hemingway's book Max Eastman described it as "Bull in the Afternoon," and ridiculed the novelist's infatuation with matadors, his pose of "red-blooded masculinity," and his "literary style of . . . wearing false hair on his chest."[16] The criticism was warranted, but Eastman went on to suggest that the infatuation indicated Hemingway's lack of "serene confidence" (which Max unquestionably had) that he was "a full-sized man." Hemingway, then fishing lustily off the Cuban coast, could hardly refrain from flying to New York to "beat the shit out of" Eastman and sundry other reviewers.[17] Geography detained him till August 11, 1937, when he came upon Eastman in Max Perkins' office in the Scribner headquarters on Fifth Avenue. "What do you mean," he asked, "accusing me of impotence?" Eastman protested that he had not meant this literally, and he handed Hemingway a copy of the book *Art and the Life of Action*, in which he had reprinted the article. "Here," he said, "read what I really said." Hemingway pushed the open book into Eastman's face. Eastman grappled with him; caught off balance, Hemingway fell to the floor. Perkins helped him to his feet, and stood between the gladiators; Hemingway laughed, and took no further action. "I didn't want to hurt him," he later explained.[18] Eastman was fifty-four at the time, Hemingway was thirty-eight. Despite its critics *Death in the Afternoon* is still an eloquent introduction to the art of dodging and puncturing bulls.

For good measure it offered a reasoned exposition of Hemingway's ethical philosophy. This was frankly, pugnaciously individualistic. Our author would have ridiculed as weak-kneed and tenderfoot my definition of morality as the cooperation of the individual with the group; he had no feeling for any group larger than the hunting pack. Like the ancient Romans he interpreted virtue as *virtus*—virility, manliness; and like Nietzsche he identified goodness with bravery. He divided men into those who have *cojones* (testicles) and those who have not; the matador, he felt, had *muchos cojones*. He despised the mere intellectual, who prefers to deal with ideas rather than with persons and life; he admired the man of action, who excels in sport, war, and bed. He looked upon the Christian ethic of returning good for evil as a confession of cowardice. "It is in defeat that we become Christian."[19]

Between each book and the next there had to be either an accident or an adventure. He denied that he was accident prone, but his eyesight was poor, and he repeatedly stumbled into mishaps. In 1927, while Hemingway was suffering from grippe, toothache, and hemorrhoids, his four-year-old son stuck an inquisitive finger into his father's one good eye, leaving him nearly blind for several days. A month later Ernest went skiing, challenged the worst turns, and took ten spills in a week. Two months later he pulled the chain on an overhead toilet box in his Paris apartment; the box fell upon his head, knocking him out and causing a gash that required nine stitches. Further accidents reopened his scalp and necessitated more needlework. In 1930, after a summer of hunting and fishing at a ranch in Montana, he started south in an open Ford; blinded by the lights of an oncoming car, he ran into a ditch; the car turned over, and Hemingway suffered a broken arm and such deep cuts that for seven weeks he remained impatiently bedded in a Billings hospital.

He was not deterred. In the fall of 1933 he led a motorized hunt in East Africa. The party bagged gazelles, antelopes, leopards, cheetahs, lions. In January Hemingway developed amoebic dysentery; he continued to hunt, but soon he was so weakened that he had to be flown to Nairobi in Kenya for treatment. Later he rejoined the expedition. He told its story at length in *The Green Hills of Africa* (1935). In the course of the book he defined critics as the lice that crawl over literature, and he compared most New York authors with "angleworms in a bottle," which seek nourishment from mutual contact. Most of the critics gave *The Green Hills* a low mark, but Carl Van Doren praised its "easy, intricate, and magical prose."[20]

In 1934 he settled down for a while with Pauline in Key West, but he spent much of his time deep-sea fishing in the Caribbean. He reveled in catching marlin, because they were "fast as light, . . . strong as bucks," had jaws like iron, and might weigh up to twelve hundred pounds. In 1935 he landed a 785-pound shark. He liked the company of fishermen, coastguardsmen, stevedores, manual laborers in general; and they reciprocated by admiring an author who could hit like a blacksmith. In 1920 he had voted for Eugene Debs, but in 1935 he condemned the Soviet system as just another czarist autocracy. "I cannot be a communist now because I believe in only one thing: liberty. . . . The state I care nothing for. All the state has ever meant to me is unjust taxation. . . . I believe in the absolute minimum of government."[21] This eighteenth-century liberalism shocked the liberals of twentieth-century America; they joined in attacking Hemingway for ignoring the crimes of capitalism and the plight of the poor in those dour thirties; it seemed to them a disgrace that the former Socialist should be spending his time fishing, hunting, skiing and hiring or buying expensive boats. He may have sought to appease his critics with his next novel, *To Have and Have Not* (1937), but they joined in rating it his least successful book, and he concluded that they had "ganged up . . . to put him out of business."[22]

In 1936, when civil war divided Spain, Hemingway declared his sympathy for the Loyalists, and raised forty thousand dollars, on his personal note, to buy ambulances for their troops. To pay off this obligation he agreed to go to Spain as war correspondent for the North American Newspaper Alliance. There he showed his usual courage in facing danger, and his usual sensitivity to the nearest young woman; a fellow journalist, Martha Gellhorn, shared his perils, and soon his bed. Called back to New York, he addressed a mass meeting at Carnegie Hall (June 4, 1937) in behalf of the Loyalists, and enjoyed the applause of liberals and radicals. He pleaded with Franklin Roosevelt to allow the export of arms to the Spanish republicans, and predicted that if Mussolini and Hitler were not defeated in their efforts to enthrone Franco they would soon get control of nearly all Western Europe. He returned to Spain and Martha. When Pauline began action for a divorce, he left the unfinished war, went to Cuba (1939), and took with Miss Gellhorn a ranch in San Francisco de Paula, some fifteen miles from Havana.

His finest book, *For Whom the Bell Tolls*, came from the press on October 21, 1940. Its title was taken from John Donne's parable about the interdependence of all human beings in one common responsibility and fate: "Any man's death diminishes me, because I am involved in Mankinde; and therefore never send to know for whom the bell tolls; it tolls for thee." The background of the tale was the Spanish Civil War; its hero was an American volunteer commissioned by the Loyalists to blow up a bridge and so delay the advance of the pro-Franco troops. The Book-of-the-Month Club took it as a selection, and Paramount Pictures paid for the motion-picture rights the highest price ever given, till then, for the film rights to a book—$136,000. Almost as gratifying were the reviews. Only the radicals entered some reservations: they complained that the author recorded with outrageous impartiality the atrocities committed by both sides, instead of explaining that Loyalist atrocities were necessitated by a noble cause. Hemingway had warned Scribner's against sending advance copies to the "ideology boys," for he "would sooner make cracks about religion to a nun than deprive the leftists of their ideology."[23]

He dedicated the book to Martha Gellhorn, and on November 21,

1940, he made her his third wife. She was an author and personality with a mind of her own, and she soon tired of Hemingway's assumption that women should take their orders and color from their men. When their quarrels came close to blows, wherein she acknowledged his superiority, she left him to resume her work as foreign correspondent. He took to heavy drinking at this declaration of independence, and was hardly happy again until World War II enabled him, as a reporter, to forget his grief in the zest of danger and the smell of battle.

He flew with several British and American bombing missions over Germany. In 1944 he worked for a time with Patton's division; then, disgusted with dust and mud, he joined the Fourth Infantry Division of the United States Army, and earned the respect of the troops by his apparent immunity to fear. "He was an imposing figure," we are told, with his six-foot stature, his "leonine head," tanned face, broad shoulders, swelling biceps, hairy chest, and immense fan-shaped beard.[24] The American soldiers took readily to calling him "Papa," a title that his beard had already won him from his entourage. He often advanced ahead of the infantry in his jeep; he was in the van in the liberation of Paris. There, however, he relaxed in style at the Ritz, delighting in the company of Mary Welsh. Late in 1944 he flew back to the United States in an army bomber, and retired to his ranch in Cuba. Mary joined him there in May, 1945. When Martha divorced him (December 21, 1945) he took it as "a Christmas gift," and three months later he made Mary Welsh his fourth wife.

In June, 1946, while driving her to Havana, he crashed his car against a tree and suffered fresh head wounds, four cracked ribs, and a hemorrhage of the synovial membranes in the left knee. Three months later, while he and Mary were driving to Sun Valley, Idaho, she had a nearly fatal miscarriage in a motel at Casper, Wyoming. Hemingway rushed her to a hospital, but the only doctor available there was an interne who gave Mary up as beyond saving. Hemingway ordered him to give Mary two blood transfusions and four bottles of plasma. She recovered. "As always in emergencies," says his biographer, "Ernest behaved admirably, drinking little" during Mary's convalescence. From these events Hemingway concluded that "fate could be fucked" rather than be accepted unresistingly.

Through all the event-full years of his life he had kept at least one eye open for incidents and faces that pointed to the ironies of human existence or confessed the secret thoughts and character of men; and he had described such sights and subtleties in the most striking and accomplished short stories of his time. Nearly all of these were etched in acid, incisive and bitter, at once describing life and questioning its sense and worth. In one of the best, "The Snows of Kilimanjaro" (1936), he told of a writer who, dying of gangrene in Africa, mourned that the temptation to lead the idle life of the rich had ruined him as an artist; it was a fear that Hemingway himself, often surrounded by moneyed friends, must sometimes have felt amid his yachts and cups.

He proved himself with *The Old Man and the Sea* (1952), the ecstatic product of six weeks' devoted concentration. Too long to be a short story, too short to be a novel, it was printed in full in one issue of *Life*, and became the literary event of the year. I approached it skeptical of the high rating accorded it; I finished it seconding Faulkner's handsome praise: "Time may show it to be the best single piece of any of us. . . . Praise God that whatever makes and loves and pities Hemingway and me kept him from touching it any further."[25]

The story, told with classic simplicity and clarity, takes a lead from Melville's *Moby Dick*, but it is most indebted to Hemingway's own battles on the sea. An old fisherman, after gently refusing an admiring boy who asked to accompany him, rows out alone into the Gulf Stream to make a last great catch, to set a mark for youth to match, and to test his aging strength of body and soul. The drama is shared by a giant marlin, which takes his bait, pulls him far from sight of land, and gives him a full day's fight before dying. "You are killing me, fish," the old man muses, "but you have a right to. Never have I seen a greater or more noble thing than you, brother. Come on and kill me. I do not care who kills who. . . . Man is not much beside the great birds and beasts."[26]

Night falls on the struggle. "The moon affects the sea as it does a woman."[27] His hands are deeply cut by the line tugging on them, " 'but man is not made for defeat,' he told himself. . . . 'A man can be destroyed but not defeated.' "[28] He wins and loses. The marlin surrenders, but it is too heavy to be pulled into the boat; he can do no more than lash it to the side. Sharks come and feed on it; he kills one after another of them till all his harpoons are gone. More sharks come; he battles them with a club; they elude his blows and proceed with their feast. Exhausted, the old man rows through the night. He reaches shore, but by that time hardly anything remains of the marlin but its bones. Astonished fishermen compliment him. With his final strength he climbs the beach to his cabin and into his cot, uncertain whether he has achieved victory or defeat.

Critics interpreted the story as a parable of man's struggle with the challenges of life; the author disclaimed any intent of symbolism, but the allegory stood out, and raised the book to significance by expressing

again Hemingway's chosen motto: *"Dans la vie il faut (d'abord) durer.*
In life the first obligation is to endure," to hold on.[29] The little volume
well deserved the Pulitzer Prize awarded it in 1953.

Otherwise those were not lucky years. In June, 1953, Hemingway
took Mary to another fiesta at Pamplona, and then to four months of
hunting in Africa. He had to wear glasses, but he was still a good shot,
and faced danger as a daily routine. On January 23, 1954, the Cessna
plane in which they were approaching Murchison Falls, Uganda, struck
a telegraph wire and crashed; they escaped with nothing worse than
Ernest's sprained right shoulder. The next day another plane undertook
to get them to Entebbe; it ran into a rut in trying to take off, and broke
into flame. Mary received severe damage to a knee; Hemingway broke
his head butting his way through a jammed door; he suffered concussion of the brain, a ruptured liver, kidney, and spleen, damage to the
sphincter muscle and the lower vertebrae, loss of vision in the left eye,
loss of hearing in the left ear, a sprained left leg, and first-degree burns
of face, head, and arms. The concussion made him maudlin at times but
even in his suffering he wrote a pretty letter to Bernard Berenson com-
plimenting him on having achieved a "lovely and fragile" old age. He
remarked that he had inhaled fire twice in the second disaster, and that
this had never helped anybody but Joan of Arc.[30] Meanwhile reports
had appeared in almost every major city that he and Mary had been
killed. After some days of rest they were flown to Nairobi, and thence
they retired to Cuba, where Hemingway set himself bravely to regain
his health.

On October 28, 1954, he was awarded the Nobel Prize, but he was
still too weak to go to Stockholm. In 1956, however, he led a television
crew into the Pacific off Peru, and hooked several mighty marlin before
a camera filming *The Old Man and the Sea*. Later that year, and again
in 1959, he and Mary revisited Spain to see more bullfights. In 1960 increasing tension between Washington and Cuba, and dangerous hypertension in Hemingway himself, reconciled him to residence in the
United States.

Perhaps this essay has lingered too long over the turbulence of Hemingway's life, too little over his books; but was any of these as rich in
incident and character as his life? Excepting *The Old Man and the Sea*
his novels were too timely to be timeless; they were usually immersed
in historical events, and these slip out of man's memory as new events
rush in. The persons in his novels seldom take body or living form; the
hero of *For Whom the Bell Tolls* disappears in his hiding places, or in

his sleeping bag; the men and women in *The Sun Also Rises* are confused memories of Paris wastrels and their sexual moltings and repartee;
the hero of *A Farewell to Arms* comes to life only because he is Hemingway himself.

He was fascinating because he was totally alive, and had vitality
enough for a dozen matadors. His courage was all the deeper for having
to fight fear. Though half blind, he let a wild beast come to within a
dozen paces of him before depending upon his marksmanship to save
his life. We smile at his egotism, but it was the natural consciousness of
his achievements, and of his physical and mental resources. Only the
greatest men can quiet, as well as hide, the ego, and I have doubts of
them; for the ego is the backbone of personality, courage, and accomplishment. Hemingway never forgot the importance of being Ernest.

He failed in the civilized art of widening the ego to leave room for
other egos to find play. Too often he displayed his muscles, his strength,
his endurance of stress and pain, and usually he added a touch of fiction
in reporting his feats. We are told that "he seldom lied when he was
sober,"[31] but he was often drunk. His days were so strenuous that he
had to have three Scotches before dinner to revive his energies and dull
his nerves.

He was so self-centered that he suffered from seeing excellence in
others. He remarked too tellingly upon the faults of his friends, even of
those who, like Sherwood Anderson or Scott Fitzgerald, had gone out
of their way to help him. He told James T. Farrell "that Faulkner was
a far better writer than either himself or Farrell";[32] but later he reassured
a correspondent that Faulkner was "a no-good son-of-a-bitch," and that
Faulkner's *A Fable* was not even worthy of a place at Ichang (where
human offal was collected).[33] He could be cruel, as in leaving Hadley
and Pauline for new contours; yet he could hardly have been so exciting
a writer had he not tingled with a sensitivity that knew no morals. He
was always on his toes, on his mettle, on his guard, always ready to
pick a quarrel; he enjoyed knocking people down, if not out. The other
side of the ledger contains many kindnesses. He helped several persons,
especially if he had quarreled with them. He sent a thousand dollars to
Ezra Pound in need, and another thousand to John Dos Passos down
with rheumatic fever. When he heard that Margaret Anderson, editor
of *The Little Review*, was stranded penniless in Nazi-occupied Paris, he
sent her four hundred dollars to pay for her passage to the United
States.

His conversation was sometimes illuminating with fresh phrases,
sometimes shocking with a coarse brutality. He could curse like a

stevedore, and call his mother (who was then still alive) an "all-time, All-American bitch."[34] He used four-letter words in his books as well as in his daily speech, because he found them inextricably mingled with the force and color (perhaps with the odor) of their native habitat. His humor had a scatological flavor, even in his description of himself as "Old Ernie Hemorrhoid, the poor man's Pyle."[35] (Ernie Pyle had won fame by his correspondence and his death at the front.)

His books may not last as long as his own saga, but they were written with greater care than we should expect from so crowded a life. "Isn't writing a hard job, though?" he wrote to Gertrude Stein; and he told Charles Scribner that "he always had to ease off on making love when he was working hard, because the two things were run by the same motor."[36] He could not compose by dictation. "Anything meant to be read by the eye," he said, "must be written out by hand and checked by the ear and the eye in the process."[37] His career as a journalist formed his style to directness and simplicity, to short paragraphs, short sentences, and short words. He was proud that *For Whom the Bell Tolls* contained no loose writing but was all of a piece, with "every word depending upon every other word," from beginning to end.[38] He presented the nature of man through no theoretical discourse or abstract formulations but through narratives of incidents intensely and thoroughly perceived and felt, but told without stress or rhetoric or bias or sentiment; the facts themselves should be left to bring the reader not to identification with a character but to participation in the scene, the feeling, and the thought. There should be no preaching.

Nevertheless his interpretation of life emerges clearly enough. He respected religious belief when it molded conduct to nobility, as in the modest and kindly priest in *A Farewell to Arms*. He soon discarded his mother's Congregationalist Protestantism, but after marrying Pauline Pfeiffer he accepted the Catholic theology, and knelt in prayer, until he joined the Loyalist forces in Spain and noted how the Catholic prelates were importuning God to support Franco. Sometimes his books, more often his letters, spoke of religion, even of Christ, with scant sympathy. He thought that Christ had "yellowed out on the Cross" by complaining that the Father had apparently deserted him; after all, said Hemingway, Christ was "only successful because they killed him."[39] One of his characters recites a bitter parody of the Lord's Prayer.[40] When Hemingway heard of Mungo Park's proof of God from the growth and beauty of a flower he countered by describing the agony of persons dying in an epidemic, or the stinking corpses of men on a battlefield.[41] He resented the application of terms like "sacred," "glorious," and "sacrifice" to such deaths. "Now for a long time I had seen nothing sacred, and the things that were glorious had no glory, and the sacrifices were like those of the stockyards at Chicago."[42] In 1945 he described his religion as "life, liberty, and the pursuit of happiness."[43] But like so many ex-Christians, he carried a load of superstitions to the grave.

Religion, says a speaker in "The Gambler, the Nun, and the Radio," is not the only opium of the people; so are patriotism, ambition, music, radio, gambling, alcohol. Even bread is opium, for it dulls the eater to the futility of life. "The world breaks everyone. . . . Those that will not break it kills. It kills the very good and the very gentle and the very brave impartially. If you are none of these you may be sure that it will kill you too, but there will be no special hurry."[44] An early death is a blessing; anyone who dies soon after a happy childhood is fortunate, since he will be spared the discovery that life is brutal and meaningless.[45] Here are the "anguish" and "absurdity" that Sartre and Camus would soon express in existentialism. Only courage could redeem man from the stupidity of life and the ignominy of death.

Premonitions of death had often come to Hemingway, and as early as 1936. By 1960 his beard and receding hair were completely white; his once mighty arms and legs were thin and weak; he was physically, sexually, mentally used up, and he despaired of ever writing well again. Spells of anxiety sometimes raised his blood pressure to 250/125. At times he feared that he was becoming insane.

On November 30, 1960, his friends took him to the Mayo Clinic in Rochester, Minnesota. Examination found evidences of diabetes and an enlarged liver—"the result," says his biographer, "of heavy ingestion of alcohol over many years."[46] Through dieting, light exercise, electric-shock treatments, and his humble submission to orders, he improved sufficiently to warrant his discharge on January 22, 1961. He was flown to Hailey, Idaho, where Mary kept him under loving surveillance. He resumed writing, but the hypertension returned, and Hemingway despondently relinquished the pen. One day in April Mary found him sitting alone with a shotgun in his hands and shells on a nearby window-sill. He was persuaded to hand over the weapon, but a few days later he found another gun, loaded it, and was aiming it at his throat when a friend intervened.

On April 25 he was flown back to the Mayo Clinic. He responded to treatment, and was released on June 26. A friend drove him and Mary seventeen hundred miles to Ketchum, Idaho. There, on July 2,

1961, he searched and found the keys to the gun rack in the basement. He chose a double-barreled shotgun, loaded it, rested the butt on the floor, pressed the two barrels against his forehead, and blew his brains out.

He left behind him a frothy wake of imitators who used his tricks of tough talk and staccato dialogue, of flashbacks and symbolism and stream of consciousness, but who never rivaled the simplicity, clarity, and verve of his style, or the stimulating challenges of his thought. The imitators fade away, but the figure of Ernest Hemingway remains, rising out of newspaper offices and Parisian attics, shrugging off the terrors of theology, molding himself through a mysterious resolve and meticulous work, facing the lords of the forest and the giants of the sea, and finally defying the Life Force itself by an act of will that chose the mode and moment of his death. *Voilà un homme!*

John Steinbeck and Upton Sinclair

TWO men have just died (1968) who were a credit to America and the human race. Each of them fought throughout life against the cruelty of man to man or beast; each struck a lusty blow for justice by writing a book that stirred the nation; each learned to be grateful for the many advances that America made in his time. They were not supreme geniuses, but if literature should be a criticism of life they deserved well of mankind.

John Steinbeck was born in 1902 at Salinas, California, of a German father and an Irish mother; that duplex heritage gave him strength and wit, six feet of height and Celtic whimsy and sentiment; and the half-Latin people of his native terrain gave him fond memories for his early pen. He went through public school, and not quite through Stanford University. He was fascinated by biology as a science that ruthlessly put man in his place and left little room for a benevolent God; now he began to shed that Christian faith, lovely and terrible, whose loss he never ceased to mourn.

Eager for experience, he shipped on a freighter down the West Coast, through the Panama Canal, and up the East Coast to New York. There he earned his bread by working as a painter's apprentice, then as a brick carrier in the construction of Madison Square Garden in one of its avatars. He soon had his fill of the metropolitan scramble; he hurried back to California, took a wife, and settled in Pacific Grove, near Carmel. He wrote books, saw them drop dead in manuscript or in print, continued with desperate persistence, and at last, in 1935, he struck gold with *Tortilla Flat*.

It is unique. Steinbeck took from his fused recollections six hoboes—Danny, Pilon, Pablo, Jesus Maria Corcoran, Joe Portagee, and the Pirate—and made of them a Round Table of rugged knights dedicated to just enough thieving to maintain them in dignified leisure and philosophical peace. They gather in Danny's shack on "that uphill district above Monterey, called Tortilla Flat, although it isn't a flat at all."[1]

They thrive on wine, adding, occasionally, some chicken snatched from
its yard. They are skeptics except in religion, and there they ignore
the doctrines and live on the legends. In the gem of the string—Chapter
XII—the Pirate, through occasional work, has earned a thousand
quarters; he takes them to Father Ramon and asks him to buy with them
a golden candlestick to burn candles for a thousand days before a statue
of Saint Francis. At the installation of his gift he attends Mass, but
grieves that his five dogs—his most faithful and understanding friends—
are not allowed to enter the church and worship with him; later he
bids the dogs sit at attention before him while he recites to them all that
he can remember of the padre's sermon; they say amen with their tails.
Then Danny dies, his aged house burns down, and the sorrowing
knights take to their individual roads. Steinbeck overdoes the wine
drinking to a tasteless dilution, but he lifts the story to literature by his
whimsical humor and the sly simplicity of his style.

He protested, in a post-factum preface, that he had not, as critics
supposed, written the book out of pity for these penniless sages; he had
written because he liked them. "They had merged successfully with
their habitat; for men this is called philosophy, and it is a fine thing."[2]
But when he lived for a time among the migrant agricultural laborers of
California he went beyond their own resentment of the condition in
which they worked and lived, and he told the story of their strike with
a grim restraint more eloquent than passion; *In Dubious Battle* is a
classic of the class struggle in America. Those were depression years,
and half the nation was desperate with poverty. Steinbeck himself, however, was prospering enough to buy a car and drive with his wife to
Mexico.

In 1937 he scored again with a little tale *Of Mice and Men*. His heroes
now were two migrant workers: George, who dreams of saving enough,
from his fifty dollars a week, to buy a little land of his own; and Lennie,
an affectionate giant whose hands are so strong, and his mind so weak,
that he kills a succession of beloved mice by fondling them too zealously.
A skeptical worker laughs at George's dream: "I see hundreds of men
come by on the road and on the ranches, . . . an' every damn one of
'em's got a little piece of land in his head. An' never a God damn one
of 'em ever gets it."[3] "Guys like us that work on ranches," George tells
Lennie, "are the loneliest guys in the world. They got no family. They
don't belong no place. They come to a ranch an' work up a stake, and
then go into town and blow their stake, and the first thing you know
they're pounding their tail on some other ranch. They ain't got nothing
to look ahead to. . . . They ain't got nobody in the worl' that gives a

hoot in hell about 'em."[4] But Slim the boss adds an enlightening word: "They work a month and then they quit and go out alone. Never seem to give a damn about nobody."[5] No woman redeems the tale except a slut who dies of suffocation when Lennie embraces her with unrestrained enthusiasm. Film makers loved that denouement, and made a successful picture of the story; the drama critics gave the picture their award. Steinbeck might now forget that he had ever been poor.

He did not; on the contrary, in *The Grapes of Wrath* (1939), he redoubled his attack upon the agricultural employer in California. Millions of Americans and Europeans warmed to his comic-tragic account of how the Joad family, dispossessed of their Dust Bowl farm in Oklahoma, packed themselves and their salvaged belongings into an ailing car and drove through a thousand miles of tribulation to the grape vineyards of California, only to find the conditions of labor there just as back- and heartbreaking as in the arid acres on which they had nearly starved. The book sent a wave of indignation rolling across the land from Boston to Salinas, where it met the plea of the growers that their helplessness before organized middlemen, and the perishable character of agricultural products, made it ruinous for them to pay higher wages to migrant unreliable and inefficient labor. The bitter argument continues today, and the struggle to unionize and humanize those fragrant fields is as violent as it was thirty years ago.

"Fleeing from publicity," Steinbeck went back to Mexico (1940) to film a documentary, *Forgotten Village,* and to collect specimens of marine life with Edward Ricketts—who was to serve as model for Doc in *Cannery Row* (1945). The novelist collaborated with the scientist in writing *The Sea of Cortez* (1941), which described their explorations and mused upon the philosophical implications of nature's neutrality in the struggle for existence in the waters and the sky.

Meanwhile the United States entered World War II. Steinbeck wrote *The Moon Is Down* (1942) to celebrate the Resistance movement against the Nazi occupation of France. In 1943 he served as war correspondent for the New York *Herald Tribune.* After the war he crossed America in *The Wayward Bus* (1947)—which served both to reconcile him to his country and to symbolize man's rough passage through life. A visit to Russia, recorded in *A Russian Journal* (1948), furthered his acceptance of the United States.

And so I come to *East of Eden* (1952), which moved me more than any other of his books. It is an ambitious allegory, for California is Eden, turning from gold to lettuce and grapes; Adam is a good man, suffering patiently blow after blow; his wife, Kate, is a temptress who lures men to sin and crime; and Aron and Caleb, like Abel and Cain, represent the good and evil in man's nature and history. The characterizations are too sharply drawn; Steinbeck forgets that in *Tortilla Flat* he proclaimed "it a fact verified . . . in many histories that the soul capable of the greatest good is also capable of the greatest evil," and "the belly of every black and evil thing is as white as snow," and "the concealed parts of angels are leprous."[6] These are rather strong generalizations, and Steinbeck himself describes "the ability for generalization" as something which "only the inexperienced can have."[7] I find it hard to believe in the unmitigated viciousness of Kate after she has shot and left her husband.[8] Almost equally unbelievable is the mature psychology ascribed to the seventeen-year-old girl Abra.[9] Along with the incongruities are sentences worthy of Heracleitus: "Some people exude their fortunes, good or bad"[10] (or, as Heracleitus said, "A man's character is his fate"). "Laughter comes late, like wisdom teeth, and laughter at yourself comes last of all, in a mad race with death, and sometimes it isn't in time."[11]

Once, in this most basic of his books, Steinbeck steps out of the wings onto the stage, and declares his philosophy in the first person:

> Our species is the only creative species, and it has only one creative instrument, the individual mind and spirit of man. Nothing was ever created by two men. There are no good collaborations. . . . Once the miracle of creation has taken place, the group can build and extend it, but the group never invents anything. The preciousness lies in the lonely mind of a man.
>
> And now the forces marshaled around the concept of the group have declared a war of extermination on that preciousness, the mind of man. . . .
>
> And this I believe: that the free, exploring mind of the individual human is the most valuable thing in the world. And this I would fight for: the freedom of the mind to take any direction it wishes, undirected. And this I must fight against: any idea, religion, or government which limits or destroys the individual. This is what I am and what I am about. I can understand why a system built upon a pattern must try to destroy the free mind. . . . I hate it [such a system], and will fight against it to preserve the one thing that separates us from the uncreative beasts. If the glory can be killed, we are lost.[12]

Hence he could not accept the omnipotent Soviet state, and he could even see some excuse for a national policy that sought to restrict the spread of such a form of government. His son served in Vietnam.

Hence, too, his hostility to organized religion as a potential threat to free minds. But even in discouraging it he recognized its gifts to man:

> The church and the whorehouse arrived in the Far West simultaneously. And each would have been horrified to think that it was a different facet of the same thing: . . . they took a man out of his bleakness for a time. . . . They brought music, . . . conscience. They built the structure of social life in the Salinas Valley.[13]

He saw that while religion sometimes hardened the soul into harsh doctrine or harsh judgments, it enabled the old to meet old age with some hope mingled with their fear.[14] And he strove to find for his own comfort a new god for a forlorn universe: an experimental, struggling, evolving creator. "Can you think that whatever made us would stop trying?"

I liked Steinbeck. I resented the backbiting that greeted the award of the Nobel Prize to him in 1962. I should have wished, too, that the Swedish Academy had similarly crowned the life of Upton Sinclair. I remember being moved to vegetarian fervor by his exposé of the Chicago stockyards in *The Jungle* (1906). Theodore Roosevelt too was stirred, and brought his "big stick" down upon the packers in a glancing blow. Some improvements were made in the daily massacre of snorting bulls and patient cows, and I understand that the odor of the sacrifice has been somewhat refined and contained.

A year later I met Sinclair briefly at the "Helicon Hall" which he had founded as a socialist colony in Englewood, New Jersey, with the proceeds of his book. I have never forgotten his handsome, almost girlish face, his modest manner, his quiet voice; here, I felt, was an honest and dedicated man. Through all his ninety years he remained steadfast: faithful to his first wife till she left him for my wild friend Harry Kemp; faithful to the death to his later consorts; faithful to his vegetarian creed; and faithful to the socialism that inspired nearly all of his more than eighty books.

He loved America enough to castigate its spendthrift and rich in *The Metropolis* (1908), its industrial exploitation in *King Coal* (1917) and *Oil* (1927), its Elmer Gantrys in *The Profits of Religion* (1918), its biased press in *The Brass Check* (1919), its commercialism of beauty in *Mammonart* (1925), and its legal processes in *Boston* (1928)—a passionately partisan report of the Sacco-Vanzetti tragedy. His criticisms were one-sided but beneficent; it was good that we were made to study our sores; and many of the remedies he prescribed were later adopted by the Democratic Party and were finally accepted by the Republicans. Indeed, the Democrats of California almost elected him governor in 1934 on his EPIC platform to End Poverty in California—a generation before Lyndon Johnson began his heroic attempt to end it in the United States. He valued democracy enough to reject any socialism that negated it; he preferred Franklin Roosevelt to Joseph Stalin, and wrote a dozen novels to celebrate the jovial President in war and peace.

I believe Upton Sinclair has been more widely read in Europe than any other American author of our century. None of his books is a literary masterpiece; each of them will be too soon forgotten because too closely tied to its time; but all of them constitute a silent monument to a nobleman without pedigree and a Christian without creed.

CHAPTER IV

Eugene O'Neill

IF I were writing a history of contemporary literature, instead of merely the notes that I made from my recent reading, I should take time here to do honor to Sherwood Anderson, Thomas Wolfe, Thornton Wilder, Erskine Caldwell, William Saroyan, and others who, in my lifetime, have placed American fiction on a high level of honesty, vitality, and courage, though not yet on a level of form and style with the novelists of France. And were I to do justice to the American theater of today I should commemorate the achievements of Saroyan and Wilder, Arthur Miller, Tennessee Williams, and Edward Albee. I am especially guilty in not having kept up with the drama, its probes into philosophy and psychology, and its experiments in dramatic technique. But in my mental youth (aged thirty-five) I looked once into the tense and somber face of Eugene O'Neill, and him I have followed, as auditor or reader, from the night when I saw *The Emperor Jones* in 1920 until this very week in September, 1967, when I shall see *More Stately Mansions* in its American premiere.

I know of no one who paid a heavier price for being a genius. His greatest plays are his autobiography, and they are tragedies of lifelong suffering. His ancestors were Irish, bringing him poetry, fantasy, and alcohol. He never ceased to be Irish, never learned to bear Anglo-Saxons cheerfully; he was pleased when Sean O'Casey told him, "You write like an Irishman, you don't write like an American."[1] He inherited the Catholic faith, lost it, and longed for it; he disliked Protestantism, and despised Puritans, to the end.

His father was among the most famous Irish-Americans of the nineteenth century. James O'Neill, born in Ireland in 1846, came to America in the steerage at the age of eight, took up acting at twenty-one, and played *The Count of Monte Cristo* some six thousand times. (I saw him, from the twenty-five-cent gallery, in one of those performances in Newark, New Jersey, about 1905.) Later he complained that this long enslavement to one role had kept him from binding his name to *Hamlet* in the memory of mankind. He was a good man, a hard worker, a loving husband, a tolerant but parsimonious father; he knew how much labor had gone into his savings, and he hoarded them in fear of an old age in which his shiftless sons would need, rather than offer, support.

He had married Ella Quinlan in 1877. Their second son, Eugene Gladstone O'Neill, was born on October 16, 1888, in a family hotel at Forty-third Street and Broadway, New York. The middle name reflected an Irish patriot's gratitude for the Home Rule Bill of 1886. Mother and child followed *The Count of Monte Cristo* from town to town for several years; sometimes she nursed Eugene in the wings. He received his education at Catholic schools in New York, at Betts Academy in Stamford, and at Princeton University for one year (1906–7); there he followed the boys to girls and drink.[2] In the summer of 1909, not yet twenty-one, he married Kathleen Jenkins; in October, leaving her behind, he sailed for Honduras to make his fortune by mining gold. He made no money, and caught malaria; but his memories of a tropical jungle gave him background and mood for *The Emperor Jones.*

Returning penniless to New York (May, 1910), he found that his wife had borne him a son, Eugene II. James O'Neill refused Eugene I anything more than token sums, partly through disapproval of his marrying an Episcopalian, partly through fear that substantial help would accustom him to irresponsible dependence. The disappointed youth took a room at "Jimmy the Priest's," a waterfront saloon at Fulton Street and the North River; there he drank heavily and studied such human wrecks as those he would portray in *The Iceman Cometh.* Desperate, he served as seaman on vessels sailing to South America, Africa, and Europe; those laborious days and mysterious nights toughened his spirit and language, let him see life from the stoker's room or near the top of a mast, and provided the realistic foundation of the many plays that he was to write about the sea. So he made a dying stoker say, in *Bound East for Cardiff,* "I ain't never took much stock in the truck them sky-pilots preach. . . . but I know whatever it is comes after it [death], it can't be no worse'n this."[3] The only solace of these men was in drink and dreams; they had fled from marriage but they longed for women. For O'Neill there were many moments of poetry in that hard life.

> When I was on the Squarehead square rigger, bound for Buenos Aires. Full moon in the Trades. The old hooker driving fourteen knots. I lay on the bowsprit, facing astern, with the water foaming

into spume under me, the masts with every sail white in the moon-light, towering high above me. I became drunk with the beauty and singing rhythm of it, and for a moment I lost myself—actually lost my life. I was set free! I dissolved in the sea, became white sails and flying spray, became beauty and rhythm . . . I belonged, without past or future, within peace and unity and a wild joy, within some-thing greater than my own life, or the life of Man, to life itself![4]

Meanwhile his deserted wife obtained a divorce, and Eugene, home from the sea, found a grudging shelter in the spacious mansion of his parents, at New London, Connecticut (1911). Many years later he pictured those days and heartbreaks in his greatest play, *Long Day's Journey into Night:* the father, at sixty-five, "still remarkably good-looking—a big, finely shaped head, . . . a simple, unpretentious man," loving his children but hugging his savings; the mother white-haired but still beautiful, with painfully arthritic hands, a secret addiction to morphine, "the unaffected charm of a shy convent girl"; older brother "Jamie" a tipsy wastrel at once romantic and cynical, who reproached himself for introducing Eugene to the world of glamorous whores;[5] and Gene himself (here "Edmund Tyrone"), "tall, thin, wiry," with "big, dark eyes, . . . long, narrow, Irish face," nervous hands (like his mother's), and a frequent cough suggesting tuberculosis.

There were at least two bookcases in James O'Neill's home at New London, and Gene remembered them especially for novels by Stendhal, Balzac, and Zola, plays by Ibsen, Strindberg, and Shaw, poems by Swinburne, Rossetti, Wilde, and Kipling, radical classics by Marx, Engels, Stirner, and Kropotkin, sets of history by Hume, Smollett, Gibbon, and Thiers, and volumes by Schopenhauer and Nietzsche. O'Neill steeped himself in the pessimism of Schopenhauer, the individ-ualism of Stirner, the misogyny of Strindberg, and the amoralism of Nietzsche. He told Benjamin De Casseres that *Thus Spake Zarathustra* had had more influence upon him than any other book in his first forty years.[6] Marx and Nietzsche competed for the soul of twentieth-century man.

In 1912 he was sent to a sanitarium, from which he was dismissed a year later as practically cured of his tuberculosis. He returned to the New London mansion, where he shocked his parents by radical tirades against capitalism and religion. His father urged him to study law; instead he wrote plays, usually of one act, hot with violence and death; his father, supposedly stingy, put up a thousand dollars to have some of them published. In 1914 Gene went to Harvard and took George

Pierce Baker's famous course "47, Drama Workshop"; father paid his tuition and allowed him ten dollars a week for all other expenses. He startled the professor with his plots, and his fellow students with his cynicism; one of them described him as "a sarcastic bastard."[7]

In 1915 he took a room at 38 Washington Square West; there he earned some fifteen dollars a week by writing scenarios. His favorite resort now was a tavern popularly known as the Hell Hole at Sixth Avenue and West Fourth Street. He liked the inebriated philosophers who meditated there, and who in their cups revealed the secrets of their lives; these men, he said later, were the best friends he had ever had. He grew particularly fond of Terry Carlin, who had graduated from the I.W.W. (the International Workers of the World) and the anarchist movement into a blend of cynical disillusionment and beery benevolence.

In 1916 Carlin accompanied O'Neill to Provincetown, on the tip of Cape Cod, and introduced him to the Provincetown Players, a group of dramatists and actors who were undertaking to rescue the American theater from superficial stories of violence and sentiment (e.g., *The Count of Monte Cristo*), and from the drawing-room trivialities imported or imitated from England; they called for new subjects, new methods, new settings, and a braver facing of the actualities in American life. The Players agreed to hear O'Neill's one-act play, *Bound East for Cardiff*, read to them in an old building built on a wharf where the rhythmic noises of the surf, and the hoarse calls of the foghorn, gave a realistic and somber obbligato to the evocation of a sailor's death at sea. O'Neill was hailed as just the man to carry the campaign of the Players to public acceptance. In 1917 they opened their "Playwrights' Theatre" at 139 (later 133) Macdougal Street, where they produced several of O'Neill's plays; and by 1925 they had set up nineteen hundred similar "little theaters" in the United States. With their help, and with the acclaim of the *Smart Set* magazine of Mencken and Nathan, and later with the enthusiastic support of the Theatre Guild, O'Neill established himself as the most powerful and popular dramatist in America.

He remained poor till 1920, for the Players, till then, paid him no royalties. In 1918 he pooled his poverty with a second wife, Agnes Boulton. She bore him a son, Shane, who fought a lifelong battle with drug addiction, and a daughter, Oona, who became Charlie Chaplin's lovely, modest, fruitful mate. O'Neill's second marriage was not much happier than the first; he was too nervous and irascible to bear other egos patiently. "He wore," she wrote, "the mask or echo of a sardonic laughter, at times ribald and again becoming painful, etched on his restless face." Occasionally "he went at her with his fists, but afterwards he would suffer terrible remorse."[8] When his father died he and his brother went on a protracted drunk.

Meanwhile his volcanic genius broke out in a rapid and remarkable series of plays. *Beyond the Horizon* (February 2, 1920) was his first financial success; it ran for 204 performances, and earned him $7,600 plus the Pulitzer Prize, which brought him $500 more. On November 3 of the same year he aroused the mental elite of New York with *The Emperor Jones*, eight short, powerful scenes of pride, greed, and terror: the flight of the bogus ruler through forest and jungle, pursued by rebel natives and the fearful acceleration of their tom-tom; his fevered visions of Negroes tossing helplessly back and forth in the hold of the ship rolling them to slavery in America, and of an auction of Negro flesh there; his return, after a night of almost blind wandering, to the same spot at which he had entered the forest, his capture and death in a classic revenge of merciless gods upon human pride. Seeing Paul Robeson in this role was one of the most stirring experiences of my life.

Gold (June 1, 1921) was a failure, but *Anna Christie* (November 2) brought O'Neill back to his waterfront memories of "the old devil sea," and redeemed an improbable plot with vividly realized characters. The happy ending shocked the Provincetown reformers, but may have helped to win a second Pulitzer Prize. (Is it our secret conscience that makes us men take to tales of reformed prostitutes?) More original was *The Hairy Ape* (March 9, 1922). A rich young woman visits the stokehole of an ocean liner, is frightened by the size and grime of the head stoker, "Yank"; she calls him a "filthy beast," and flees. His pride in his physical strength is shaken; he becomes class conscious, and swears vengeance on millionaires. In port he tries to join the I.W.W.; it repudiates him as too violent. He finds more satisfaction in talking to a gorilla in the zoo; he pries open its cage, releases it, offers it his hand as a fellow hairy ape; it hugs him so forcefully that his ribs break and his lungs burst; the gorilla puts him in the cage and locks the door; there he collapses and dies. When I saw it I took it as a proletarian manifesto; reading it now I note that all but one of the stokers ridicule the Socialist gospel. Yank himself, before being insulted, asks merely that the manual worker be accepted as a vital element in the economy; he wants to be respected, to "belong." The conclusion of the play seems to satirize revolutionary violence as a return to savagery.

On March 17, 1924, O'Neill offered, in *Welded*, a merciless picture of marriage as immature idealization passing through boredom and mutual recrimination to one or more "affairs," and ending at best in a weary compromise; apparently O'Neill was not enjoying his second marriage. The play proved too disagreeable, and was withdrawn after twenty-four performances. Another, *The Ancient Mariner* (April 6, 1924), ran to thirty-three, and died. But in that same *annus mirabilis* the Provincetown Players presented three more dramas by O'Neill: *All God's Chillun Got Wings* (May 15), *S. S. Glencairn* (August 14), and *Desire under the Elms* (November 11). The first of these studied the tragedy of a Negro who befriended a persecuted white girl, won her in marriage, and was made desolate by her inability to accept his relatives. Many auditors were offended when they saw a white actress kiss the hand of the Negro Paul Robeson. The play was denounced by Irish Catholics, by the Ku Klux Klan, and by the Society for the Suppression of Vice; it was soon withdrawn. Now we recognize O'Neill's courage in facing, so soon in our racial debate, the ultimate question and test in race relations, just as he had faced the problem of class relations in *The Hairy Ape*. In 1925 he joined Max Eastman, Sherwood Anderson, Van Wyck Brooks, and Carl Sandburg in launching a Socialist magazine, *New Masses*. But he was too strongly individual to remain long attached to any group or doctrine, conservative or radical; and in *Desire under the Elms* he returned from economic debates to study the overriding nature of man.

Like nearly all his plots the story here exaggerates a point and outstretches credibility. Ephraim Cabot is consistently to the end the New England nineteenth-century puritan: laborious, thrifty of words and pence, hard and merciless, and firmly believing in a hard and merciless God. Abbie Putnam, his second wife, suddenly changes from a cold woman loving money more than love into a passionate woman killing and dying for love. Eden Cabot is a vacillating youth who finds in his stepmother an economical substitute for whores, and then bravely accompanies her to the scaffold after she has killed their child: Freud would have been pleased to see the Oedipus complex so dramatically staged. Brooks Atkinson, philosopher among critics, thought that *Desire* "may turn out to be the greatest play written by an American."[9]

By this time O'Neill had become a rich man, partly through royalties, partly through death. In 1922 his mother died, and he received $56,000 as his share of her estate. A year later his brother "Jamie" died in a Paterson sanitarium, leaving him $73,000 more. Wealth did not make him happy; as late as 1923 he still ran off, now and then, to the Hell Hole to seek the euphoria of drink; his wife had to find him there and bring him home. In 1924 he moved with her to an estate in Bermuda. Thence he sent to New York *The Great God Brown* (January 23,

1926). Convinced that every individual has contrary characters competing in one soul, O'Neill presented each person of the drama sometimes as wearing, sometimes as discarding, a mask expressing one side—usually the more presentable side—of his personality. (Masks were used in the ancient Greek and Roman theater, and in the Italian *commedia dell' arte*, to identify and characterize the *personae dramatis*—the "persons," literally the "through-sounding" masks, of the drama.) Dion Anthony, to all appearances a happy and poetic idealist, is, when without the mask, a bitter and ruthless cynic. William Brown wears the mask of a successful and honorable businessman, but secretly he cheats Dion and aspires to Dion's wife. In the end each reveals his real character, and everybody is ruined. Despite some absurdities in the plot the play received 283 performances.

Leaving his family in Bermuda, O'Neill came to New York in 1927 to supervise the production of two plays. *Marco Millions* (January 9, 1928), an echo of Sinclair Lewis' *Babbitt*, did not do well, but *Strange Interlude*, staged three weeks later, set three records for O'Neill: in the number of performances (426), in royalties earned ($275,000), in winning his third Pulitzer Prize, and in the time each performance required—it began at 5:30 P.M. and ended at 11 P.M. with eighty minutes' intermission.

The story is one of O'Neill's acid analyses of women and love. The central and consuming character, Nina Leeds, like so many women, thinks she is a bicycle built for two. She begins as the lover of Gordon Shaw, a soldier who perishes in World War I; she marries Sam Evans, commits adultery with Edmund Darrell, and lets Evans believe that the consequent child is his own. She names the child Gordon, and transfers to it all her love. When this second Gordon grows up she burns with jealousy of his fiancée. Left stranded by their departure, and her husband's death, she falls back upon the paternal love of an old friend. She concludes, in her declining years, that "our lives are merely strange dark interludes in the electrical display of God the Father"[10]—whom Darrell describes as "deaf and dumb and blind."[11] The inevitable hypocrisy of civilized humanity is here displayed not by the use of masks but by a combination of the old-fashioned aside with the stream-of-consciousness technique; each character speaks his real thoughts in words heard only by the audience, though not addressed to it. The play is too long and complicated, but it stands as a landmark in the history of the American theater.

An interlude as strange as any in his dramas was meanwhile changing the course of O'Neill's life. He had on several occasions met an alluring actress who went by the stage name of Carlotta Monterey. Born in San Francisco in 1888, she was now (1927) wedded to a third husband, Ralph Barton, a caricaturist for *The New Yorker* magazine. O'Neill fell deeply in love with her, and pleaded with her to join him, saying, "I need you, I need you." She yielded, left Barton, and accompanied the dramatist on a tour of England, France, and the Far East. O'Neill's second wife went to Reno and secured (July 2, 1929) a divorce decree awarding her from six to eight thousand dollars a year for herself and her children. On July 23 O'Neill and Carlotta were married in a civil rite in Paris. On May 17, 1931, they returned to New York. On May 20 Ralph Barton killed himself.

The plays moved on. *Lazarus Laughed* (April 9, 1928) puzzled and disappointed its audiences with its masks, its mysticism, its message: "Are you a speck of dust dancing in the wind? Then laugh dancing! Laugh yes to your insignificance! Thereby will be born your new greatness!"[12] —an echo of *Thus Spake Zarathustra*. O'Neill brooded over a famous line in that book: "God is dead! Long live Superman!" He thought of composing a trilogy entitled "God Is Dead! Long Live —What?"[13]

Dynamo (February 11, 1929) opened the series. Reuben Light, son of a puritan clergyman, replaces religious belief with worship of science and machinery. "There is no God!" he cries, "no God but Electricity." He concludes, like Dostoevski's Ivan Karamazov, that now there is no sin, and that every natural impulse is beyond reproach. He seduces Ada, and refuses to marry her. His real love is for the whirling, humming dynamo in the local powerhouse; he kneels before it, prays to it, goes insane. Ada seeks him amid the machines; he kills her. He touches the carbon brushes of the giant generator, and is electrocuted. The play, crowded with improbabilities and atheistic blasts, proved too much for the public stomach; after fifty performances it closed. O'Neill complained that the critics had paid more attention to Claudette Colbert's legs than to the theme. In a clumsily composed comment basic to understanding his philosophy—and the twentieth century—he described *Dynamo* as a

> symbolical and factual biography of what is happening in a large section of the American soul right now. It is really the first play of a trilogy that will dig at the roots of the sickness of today as I feel it—the death of an old god and the failure of science and materialism to give any satisfying new one for the surviving, primitive, religious instinct to find a meaning for life in, and to comfort its fears of

death with. It seems to me that anyone trying to do big work nowa-
days must have this big subject behind all the little subjects of his
plays or novels, or he is simply scribbling around on the surface of
things . . .[14]

O'Neill, obsessed with the complexity of our contemporary problems,
seems to have been thinking of trilogies; no single play could present
his themes. *Mourning Becomes Electra* (October 26, 1931) studied the
nemesis of heredity and crime in three plays designed for consecutive
performance between 5 and 11 P.M. of one day, allowing an intermission
for dinner. O'Neill boldly attempted to rival the *Oresteia* trilogy of
Aeschylus—*Agamemnon, Choephoroi,* and *Eumenides*—by depicting
two generations of the Mannon family moving through pride, puritanism, lust, and hate to murder and suicide; again, as in Heracleitus, character predestined fate. An old general is poisoned by his wife and her
paramour; her son and daughter, to avenge their father, drive her to
suicide; add Freud to Aeschylus and you find the son loving his mother,
the daughter loving her father, and also the son loving his sister. The
love is sexual, and reasons that extramarital sex is no sin; even the dourly
puritan daughter Lavinia is secretly charmed by Captain Bryant's report
that the women of the South Pacific "had found the secret of happiness
because they had never heard that love can be a sin."[15] (Was this an
apologia pro vita sua?) To all this O'Neill added a mystic sense of
heredity as fate: each generation of the Mannon family rebels against
its predecessor, replaces it, and becomes like it in a modification of
Nietzsche's "eternal recurrence." By describing the decline and fall of
the Mannons O'Neill revenged himself against the Calvinist New Eng-
landers who had snubbed the Irish O'Neills in New London. — Despite
its length, improbabilities, and horrors the triple play was well received,
and was hailed by the critics as the author's best.

He rewarded his public with a cheerful interlude between his
tragedies. *Ah, Wilderness!* (October 2, 1933) was frankly a comedy of
surface sentiment; it ran for 289 performances, and the critics praised
it despite its popularity. But only the Catholics relished *Days without
End,* which O'Neill offered on January 8, 1934, as a foil to *Dynamo.*
The protagonist, John Loving, is represented by two persons: one,
called John, is tender-minded, flirts with socialism, anarchism, and philosophy, but feels some nostalgia for the religion he has lost, and welcomes the visit of his former teacher and friend, Father Baird; the other,
called Loving, seen only by the audience, but also heard by the other
persons of the drama, is a cynic who misses no chance to satirize the

Catholic Church; this is another of O'Neill's ways of representing on the stage the conflict of moods and views in the same soul. The priest is pictured as a good and tolerant man with "an unshakable inner calm and certainty, the peace of one whose goal in life is fixed by a goal beyond life."[16] In the finale John, tortured over remorse for having once committed adultery, goes to church, kneels before the crucifix, seeks reconciliation, and sees forgiveness when, as he prays, the sun comes through a window and shines upon the face of the Crucified. The play received only fifty-seven performances in New York; it was acclaimed in Dublin; it was banned in Russia for violating the prohibition of religious teaching.

Presumably O'Neill had hoped to expound a *via media* in a third play, but this was never written, or never given to the public. Many of O'Neill's friends concluded that his third wife, a Catholic, had won him back to the faith; doubtless she had tried,[17] convinced that only religion could give peace of mind to the tortured dramatist. However, both O'Neill and Carlotta denied that he had ever accepted conversion,[18] and three years after his death she declared to the New York *Times:* "He never thought of returning to religion, never at any time."[19]

Thinking to benefit by a better climate, and by escape from city crowds, O'Neill and his wife moved from New York to Sea Island, Georgia (1932), and four years later to a place near Seattle on Puget Sound. He was awarded the Nobel Prize in 1936, but could not go to Stockholm to receive it, for in that year he was stricken with appendicitis; he was taken to a hospital in Oakland, California; the appendix burst before it was removed, poisoning his whole system and adding to his rich variety of ailments. By the age of forty his nervous disorder had so progressed that when he raised a drink to his lips his hand shook the ice so hard (reported George Jean Nathan) as to make him sound "like a Swiss bell-ringer."[20] In 1937 the wandering couple built a Chinese "Tao House" on a mountain overlooking the San Ramon Valley, some thirty-five miles north of San Francisco. There Gene worked on several plays at once. Carlotta served as his secretary and typist, and, during the servantless war years, did the housework herself.

Oona complained that Carlotta was becoming a barrier between O'Neill and his children. When Oona married Chaplin (1943) her father condemned the marriage, and he never saw her or communicated with her again.[21] Shane found Carlotta likable, but when he married Cathy Givens (1944) his father disapproved, and refused to see them. By 1948 Shane was hopelessly addicted to heroin; he was arrested for possessing the drug, and spent time in a hospital for the mentally ill;

his hands trembled like his father's. Eugene O'Neill, Jr., son by the dramatist's first wife, killed himself.

In 1943 O'Neill and his wife moved to a three-room apartment in San Francisco. There Carlotta had a nervous breakdown, and Gene suffered a paralytic stroke; now he could no longer write, and was usually too excitable to dictate. In 1945 they returned to New York to stage _The Iceman Cometh_. All who saw him were shocked by the spread of trembling from his hands to his arms. The gloomiest and most successful of his plays had its premiere on October 9, 1946, to an advance sale of $262,000. It ran to 136 performances, and when José Quintero revived it in 1956 it had 565 more. It offered a dismal spectacle of some twenty ruined men in the saloon of "Harry Hope,"—O'Neill's recall of the Hell Hole and Jimmy the Priest. The theme was the role of illusion in human life: these wastrels still dreamed of some windfall or success, and kept themselves inspired with drink until that triumph arrived, or until the Iceman—their name for death—should come to fetch them. The most consistently drunk of all is Hugo Kalman—in real life Hippolyte Havel, a jolly anarchist whom I knew in 1912. (Arrested for "committing a nuisance" on Fifth Avenue, he berated the judge for the uncivilized lack of _pissoirs_ in New York.) Awakened by some uproar in the saloon, he denounces all and sundry as "capitalist swine! Bourgeois stool-pigeons! Have the slaves no right to sleep, even?"[22] The philosopher among them is Larry Slade—O'Neill's old friend Terry Carlin, an ex-"Wobbly" with "the face of a pitying but merry old priest." "Forget the anarchist part of it," says Larry; "I'm through with the movement long since. I saw men didn't want to be saved from themselves, for that would mean they would have to give up greed, and they'll never pay that price for liberty.... So I took a seat in the grandstand of philosophical detachment." Larry is the one quite disillusioned man among these delusionees, but he sympathizes with their hopeful fantasies. "Don't mock the faith.... To hell with the truth! As the history of the world proves, the truth has no bearing on anything. It's irrelevant and immaterial.... The lie of a pipedream is what gives life to the whole misbegotten mad lot of us, drunk or sober. And that's enough philosophic wisdom to give you for one drink of rot-gut."[23] It is a depressing scene, but in O'Neill's opinion it "strips the secret soul of a man stark naked." Spoiled though it is by too much palaver, repetitions, drunken quarrels, and tearful reconciliations, _The Iceman Cometh_ nevertheless is surpassed in power, among American plays, only by a drama just as long and terrible.

O'Neill began to write _Long Day's Journey into Night_ at Tao House in California in 1939 because, Carlotta said, "it was a thing that haunted him"; because, he said, there is "an ache in our hearts for the things we can't forget."[24] The writing was an ordeal that consumed him; after a day's work on it he would come out of his study gaunt and weeping, and looking ten years older than in the morning. He finished the play in 1941; Carlotta typed it; he revised it; she typed it again; he dedicated it to her on the twelfth anniversary of their marriage, July 22, 1941.

It reports one day in the life of the Tyrone family. We have already borrowed from that play as really a memory of the O'Neill home in New London. Everybody in it drinks heavily except the mother, who takes morphine. (Mother O'Neill conquered that habit in her later years, as Eugene overcame his love of alcohol.) Jamie is nearest to a villain: drinking, whoring, and scolding his father for not engaging the most expensive doctors to treat Edmund's tuberculosis. To which the father replies: "And what could the finest specialist in America do for Edmund [Eugene], after he's deliberately ruined his health by the mad life he's led ever since he was fired from college? . . . playing the Broadway sport to imitate you, when he's never had your constitution to stand it. . . . he's always been a bundle of nerves like his mother."[25] When Jamie absents himself and the father says, "He's probably in the whorehouse," Edmund retorts, "What of it if he is? Why not?"[26] The father reproves Edmund for "your damned Socialist anarchist sentiments," and for having "flouted the faith you were born and brought up in—the one true faith of the Catholic Church—and your denial has brought nothing but self-destruction!" Edmund replies curtly, "God is dead."[27]

O'Neill never forgot such scenes; he wrote of them in the vain hope of dulling their sting in his memory. Probably he knew that his picture exaggerated the stinginess of his father and the poverty of their home. He sent the typescript of the play to Random House in New York with instructions that it should not be published or produced until twenty-five years after his death. But when his parents and his brother were dead Eugene (according to his wife) withdrew the prohibition. An enterprising Swedish producer staged its premiere in Stockholm on February 10, 1956, two and a half years after O'Neill's death. New York saw it for the first time on November 7, 1956, and gave it a run of 390 performances; it won for its author his fourth Pulitzer Prize. I should rate it O'Neill's greatest play.

About 1931 he had planned a cycle of nine dramas, which would picture the history of America in the nineteenth century as the corrosion of a nation's soul by material greed. The titles exist; most of the sketches were burned by O'Neill and his wife at Tao House in 1943; two of the plays remain to us, in uncorrected form. *A Touch of the Poet* was produced in New York in 1958. *More Stately Mansions*, much abbreviated, was staged in Stockholm in 1962; still more curtailed, it had a gala American premiere on September 12, 1967, when the prosperous citizens of Los Angeles gathered to applaud the bitter critic of American wealth.

Hatred was the theme and tone of the play. Simon Harford begins as a Rousseauian idealist, scorning economic materialism; he is disinherited by his tycoon father for marrying the daughter of a tavern keeper; his wife, Sarah, urges him to forget his dreams and improve his income; by Act II he is as rich and hard as his father has been. He tells his brother Joel, "Your right has no power, so you have no right. The only moral law here is the strong are rewarded, the weak are punished. All else is an idealistic lie."[28] He regrets his marriage as taking too much of his time from business; he advises his brother to "shun marriage and keep a whore instead."[29] Meanwhile his wife and his mother fight each other to insanity for his love and his money. — These speeches of hatred, filling a hundred pages, seem to have erupted in spontaneous profusion from a mind which was itself consumed with hatred—of America, of woman, of life. As we read them we wonder was O'Neill himself going insane.

Sick in body and soul, he left New York in 1948 and moved with Carlotta to a cottage in Marblehead, on the Massachusetts coast. His intense concentration upon his work, his self-centered irritability, combined with her own failing health and passionate spirit to generate many disputes. In February, 1951, in a legal document, she charged him with "cruel and abusive treatment." Late that year O'Neill fractured his knee in a fall; he was taken to a hospital in Salem; he developed pneumonia but recovered; he was sent to New York for an operation on his knee. Amid these troubles Carlotta was removed to a hospital for the mentally ill. Released, she sued for separation and support. Convalescence cooled tempers; husband and wife made up, and moved to an apartment in Boston. Now O'Neill signed a will leaving everything to Carlotta and cutting off from "any interest in my estate my son, Shane O'Neill, and my daughter, Oona O'Neill Chaplin, and I exclude their issue now or hereafter born."[30] Carlotta joined him in burning the drafts and notes for unfinished plays. He died of pneumonia in the Shelton apartment hotel, Boston, November 27, 1953. His widow reported, "He wished nobody to be at his funeral but me and his nurse. He wished no religious representative of any kind."[31]

He was the chief of many victims of his genius. Physical or social heredity gave him his father's poetic spirit and dramatic flair, and his mother's nervous disorder; the hectic environment of a traveling theatrical company affected his boyhood; Broadway and his brother and Nietzsche corrupted his youth; tuberculosis weakened his lungs, and drink helped to shatter his nerves; add to these a passionate ambition for literary fame, and the excitement of producing plays and reading critiques, and we get the background and whip of an uncomfortable, uncompromising, unsocial man. He was too tense to be lovable, too alert to beauty to be a faithful husband, too absorbed in his work to be a good father. "Why was I born without a skin, O God?" asks Dion in *The Great God Brown.* "I will always be a stranger who never feels at home," says Edmund in *Long Day's Journey into Night,* "who does not really want and is not really wanted, who can never belong, who must always be a little in love with death!"[32] "I'm extremely bashful," O'Neill told Lawrence Langner. "In my younger days I used to drink in order to get up the nerve to meet people. Since I've quit drinking it's become worse."[33] So he withdrew into himself, and was accused of selfishness. Having suffered years of desperate poverty, he clung to money when it came to him, and drove hard bargains with producers and publishers[34] while he condemned America's acquisitive regime.

His plays conveyed a philosophy rooted in his character. A passionate individualist, he soon broke away from Christianity and its moral code; he became an atheist, and gave his desires a loose rein. He wondered how God could forgive himself for all the misery he had caused or permitted on the earth.[35] Seeking a natural substitute for religion to give meaning and dignity to man's existence and career, he thought for a while to find this in socialism, and to the end of his life he retained and dramatized the socialist critique of American civilization. But he did not relish the governmental omnipotence which he feared that socialism would bring. He saw in Russian Communism only a new despotism, a new oppressive orthodoxy: "God with a change of whiskers becomes the state—and then there is always a Holy Book—dogmas—heresy trials—an infallible Pope—etc.—until you become sick."[36] Like any artist, he aspired to freedom and novelty rather than to order and discipline; "I am a philosophical anarchist," he declared.[37] Besides, he believed, the acquisitive and competitive nature of man frustrates any basic reform. "The material the ideal society must be constructed from is men themselves, and you can't build a marble temple out of mud and manure."[38] Instead of seeing history in terms of class war, O'Neill saw it as a conflict of individual against individual, of generation against generation, of environment against heredity, of man against fate, of life against death. He thought that heredity is usually stronger than environment, and fixes a man's character, history, and fate. "It's all there at the start," says Hickey in *The Iceman Cometh.* Or, as Mary Tyrone puts it, "The past is the present, isn't it? It's the future too. We all try to lie out of that, but life won't let us."[39] So there is a constant, perhaps an eternal recurrence in history; in any case the basic fact of life is the endless chain of birth, growth, love, suffering, and death;[40] and "what is the use of bearing children, . . . of giving birth to death?"[41] Men are all doomed to defeat, and their sole nobility lies in the courage of their struggle.

One faith alone sustained O'Neill—confidence in the power and lasting fame of his plays. Upon them he lavished all his force, into them he poured all his experience and his hopes, all the dramatic art and technique that he had learned from his father's career and the theaters of Broadway; only in writing them did he find a more than momentary joy. He took for his all-embracing subject man's conflict with fate; everything else seemed to him superficial, subordinate. Therefore nearly all his plays were tragedies, rich in crime, violence, vengeance, and despair, and almost totally lacking in humor. He agreed with Aristotle that the contemplation of tragedy as an aesthetic or dramatic spectacle could partly cleanse the spectator of his own violent emotions, and confer an inspiring sense of human grandeur in battling with destiny.[42] But he rejected the "Aristotelian" unities of place, action, and time; one of his plays covered seventeen, another thirty, years, and one could roam from New England to Poughkeepsie. He offended probability in almost every play—like Shakespeare. He tried now and then to rival the Greek dramatists in poetry; sometimes he made unlikely characters soar into purple flights. (E.g., toward the end of Act IV, Scene ii, of *The Great God Brown;* and in the prologue to that play he made Margaret muse, "The moon is drowned in the tides of my heart.") He lacked the finish of a disciplined artist, but he was a master of dialogue, dialect, and the evocation of character.

He left no labor undone, no trick unturned, to give reality and force to his plays. His stage directions and character descriptions were almost as explicit and detailed as in a novel. He studied history to find material that would point the time or place of the story, like the square dance in *Desire under the Elms,* or the horsecars in *All God's Chillun Got Wings.* He removed the front of a house to show several rooms and actions at once. He symbolized the inhuman continuance of machinery by the hypnotic throb and hum of a dynamo; he conveyed the presence and terror of the sea by the recurrent blast of the foghorn, and he made fate audible in the tom-tom sounded by the pursuers of Emperor Jones. He employed soliloquies and asides to display the secret thoughts of his characters, and masks to reveal their contradictory selves. Few dramatists have so well exposed the perceptions, feelings, intuitions, suspicions, attractions, repulsions, and aspirations hidden behind the words and faces of men.

Looking back upon this wild career and its profuse product, we marvel that a man could rise out of a misspent adolescence to the highest place in the American literature of our age, and to such international fame as no other dramatist but Shaw has enjoyed before death. His plays are more stimulating than Shaw's, more varied in their portrayal of life, more basic in their themes; and they excel in power any English plays since John Webster's. They effected an invigorating revolution in the American theater, releasing it from bondage to bourgeois parlors and badinage, and rising sometimes to the level of Greek drama in picturing the confrontation between man and fate.

CHAPTER V

Robinson Jeffers and Ezra Pound

I HAVE given up the attempt to understand contemporary poetry. I am too old, too bound to prose, to puzzle over the built-in obscurity of twentieth-century verse. The mobility and insecurity of our lives, the absorption of energy in maintaining income and status, and the rising importance of science and economics, have predisposed most of us to facts and figures, and has left us doubtful of dreams, dull to rhymes, and unimpressed by lack of punctuation and capitals. We are willing to be stirred by intelligible and pertinent drama, but we resent the august ritual by which so many poets clothe the trite in mystery.

Nevertheless I have enjoyed the gentle and lovable spirit of Robert Frost (1874–1963), whose verses run as clear and musical as a mountain stream. I like especially "My November Guest,"[1] for previously I had agreed with Thomas Hood's gloomy estimate[2] of my natal month. And though I could not share the somber mood of Robinson Jeffers (1887–1962), I respected it, and his aloof and ascetic personality. One of his prefaces, dedicating a volume to his wife, touched a responsive chord: "She never saw any of my poems until they were finished and typed, yet by her presence and conversations she has co-authored every one of them. Sometimes I think there must be some value in them, if only for that reason."[3] We visited him at Carmel about 1960, after the death of his wife, and found him a man absorbed, quiet, living with his memories and his natural surroundings, bearing intrusions patiently, and hoping for their early end. It seemed to us that he had buried himself with his wife.

That same preface voiced a conviction very congenial to my mood: "Modern poetry was becoming slight and fantastic, abstract, unreal, and eccentric. . . . It must reclaim substance and sense, and physical and psychological reality. This feeling . . . led me to write narrative poetry, and to draw subjects from contemporary life, . . . to attempt the expression of biological and scientific ideas in verse." Ariel agreed with me in liking the generally acclaimed *Roan Stallion*, but we were moved still more by the sixty-page *Tamar*, despite its assortment of incest, murder, and insanity. No rhyme and no rhythm here, but intense feeling and dark imaginings, vivid, original, often abnormal; we did not relish the picture of worms eating dead Helen's breasts.[4]

Like so many sensitive spirits in our time, Jeffers mourned his loss of religious faith, and replaced it with socialistic hopes. He rejected all saviors—Lao-tse, Confucius, Buddha, even Christ, whose "personal anguish and insane solution / Have stained an age; nearly two thousand years are one vast poem drunk with the wine of his blood."[5] He welcomed the Russian Revolution; he reproved Woodrow Wilson for not recognizing the greatness and vision of Lenin;[6] and with a fury like O'Neill's he condemned America's rush toward wealth, empire, and power:

> *While this America settles in the mold of its vulgarity,*
> *heavily thickening to empire,*
> *And protest, only a bubble in the molten mass, pops and*
> *sighs out, and the mass hardens,...*
> *Shine, perishing republic.*[7]

He expected that the passage from republic to empire would be followed by a deterioration of democracy into dictatorship.[8] He advised his children to "keep their distance" from the centers of political power as foci of corruption and moral decay, and to seek peace and prosperity in rural scenes or on mountain slopes far from "the cities [that] lie at the monster's feet."[9]

His socialistic hopes waned as he studied the nature of man and the savagery of states. He saw cruelty everywhere. Of all Greek plays he chose Euripides' *Medea*, red in tooth and claw, for his powerful translation. He did not deceive himself into deifying nature; there he found an impartial mixture of what we prejudiced animals call evil and good, and an infinite variety of ways in which organisms suffer and die. He liked nature nevertheless. He celebrated the swift directness of the birds, the calm endurance of mountains under assaults from the sky, the stern resistance of rocky coasts to the obstinate attacks of the sea. He acknowledged the sovereignty of death over all the things that he loved; even those stony cliffs would atom by atom crumble, and those proud mountains would be leveled with the plains in the patient pertinacity of time. An inescapable determinism rules every choice and fixes every fate: "Today plays on last year, and the inch of our future / Made the first morning of the world."[10]

Despite his morbid emphasis upon deviltry, decay, and death I liked Robinson Jeffers more than Ezra Pound, both as poet and as man; yet I found Pound's career so absorbing a panorama from world-shaking youth to finger-shaking age, so graced by a hundred generosities, so illuminated by its contacts with literary lights, that I forgot space and time in pursuing him from our Northwest plains to an asylum near Washington and a final retreat in the Tirol.

He was born at Hailey, Idaho, October 30, 1885, of an old and lusty American family; two hundred of his forebears had fought in the Revolution, and he itched to follow their example. His parents moved to Wyncote, near Philadelphia. Ezra passed through Hamilton College (now Colgate University), received an M.A. degree in Romance languages from the University of Pennsylvania, and was appointed "graduate fellow and scholar" (1906), with a stipend of five hundred dollars. Most of this he used for a trip to Europe; he walked through Spain, south France, and Italy to Venice, picking up en route much lore of Provençal poetry. Returning in January, 1907, he was given an instructorship at Wabash College, Crawfordsville, Indiana, but after a few months of teaching French and Spanish he was dismissed for letting a stranded burlesque queen spend a night in his room.[11] With money saved from the full year's salary paid him, and with moderate help from his father, he sailed again for Europe. In that year 1908 his first published poems appeared at Venice under an Italian title, *A lume spento* (*With Lights Extinguished*). After some wandering he settled down in London at 10 Church Walk, Kensington. John Gould Fletcher described the "general shabbiness" of Pound's single room as revealing "a state of poverty bordering upon indigence," but he admired "the real generosity with which Pound, a poor man, was ready to help a well-to-do poet like myself to get a hearing."[12] Ezra earned his bread, and not much more, by teaching a course in "The Development of Literature in Southern Europe" at the Polytechnic Institute in Regent Street. There he fell in love with a pupil, Dorothy Shakespear. In 1910 he returned to the United States; he remained for a while in New York, relishing the "surging crowd on Seventh Avenue"; but he deplored the lack of interest in poetry, and the domination of letters by conservative editors like William Dean Howells. Early in 1911 he took ship for Italy, soon moved on to London, and did not see America again till 1939.

In 1909, in a London restaurant, he startled friends and waiters by reading, with all the gusto of a young American, a poem celebrating the Provençal soldier-troubadour Bertran de Born, whom Dante had placed in hell for loving battle as well as love. It began:

Damn it all! all this our South loves peace. . . .
You whoreson dog, Papiols, come, let's to music!
The man who fears war . . . hath no blood of crimson,
But is fit only to rot in womanish peace.[13]

Pound called this poem *Sestina altaforte*—i.e., "six-line stanzas high and strong"; he remained *altaforte* to the end. This and three other of his poems were accepted by *The English Review.* Elated by their reception, he published (1909) a little book of verse entitled *Personae of Ezra Pound.* He proclaimed his modest enterprise:

I would shake off the lethargy of this our time, and give
For shadows—shapes of power,
For dreams—men.

This call was heard in Chicago by Harriet Monroe, who was preparing the first number (October, 1912) of *Poetry: A Magazine of Verse.* For this historic venture she had persuaded one hundred subscribers to pledge fifty dollars annually for five years. In that inaugural issue she recorded Ezra Pound's promise that "such of his poetic work as receives magazine publication in America will appear exclusively in *Poetry.*" He agreed to serve as *Poetry*'s foreign correspondent; in that capacity he secured for it poems by William Butler Yeats, Richard Aldington, and Rabindranath Tagore. At this time he was optimistic about American literature: "What I believe in the end to be inevitable, our American *Risorgimento,* is dear to me."[14] Soon afterward came the Chicago outburst with Carl Sandburg and Vachel Lindsay, and the American invasion of Europe with Scott Fitzgerald and Ernest Hemingway. Later Pound quarreled with Miss Monroe, who wanted T. S. Eliot to make "Prufrock" more intelligible—"Most emphatically I will not ask Eliot to write down to any audience whatsoever"[15]—and in 1919 he severed his connection with *Poetry.* In 1917 *The Little Review* of Chicago, and in 1920 *The Dial* of New York secured his services as their European representative.

He was very moderately paid for these services, but his marriage with Dorothy Shakespear in 1914 ended his poverty. After a honeymoon in Provence they took what Eliot described as "a small dark flat" at No. 5 Holland Place Chambers in Kensington. There he gathered his own group of poetic enthusiasts, while he and Dorothy joined the larger circle that assembled in the rooms of Ford Madox Hueffer, who was to become Ford Madox Ford. There they could meet H. G. Wells,

Hilaire Belloc, D. H. Lawrence, Wyndham Lewis, T. S. Eliot, and May Sinclair, and could hear the latest "neo-Nietzschean clatter."[16] Pound's special friend in those days was William Butler Yeats, whom he served as secretary and fencing instructor.

The Irish poet, who was turning toward aristocracy, must have smiled at the American's bohemian costume: jacket of corduroy or velvet (pearl buttons), tieless shirt open at the neck. His handsome face was bounded by flaming red hair, heavy sideburns, mustache, and pointed beard. His high-pitched, almost feminine voice was in amusing discord with his proud carriage and challenging virility. Until Mussolini awed him he was an unalloyed individualist, demanding liberty of body and mind, and conceited beyond his due. Englishmen found him too assertive for their proud reserve, but nearly all who knew him forgave his braggadocio for his open purse and heart. "He was one of the kindest men that ever lived," said John Cournos, and T. S. Eliot testified: "No one could have been kinder to younger men, or to writers who . . . seemed to him worthy and unrecognized."[17] Some of these he fed, some he clothed. Said Percy Wyndham Lewis: "Ezra is not only himself a great poet, but he has been of the most amazing use to other people."[18] We shall soon see how he arranged for the publication of Eliot's first volume of verse, and how, later, he secured financial aid for James Joyce at a critical point in the composition of *Ulysses*. He introduced Amy Lowell to London, and gave her letters that smoothed her reception in Paris. "My problem," said Pound, "is to keep alive a certain number of advancing poets, and to set the arts in their advancing place as the acknowledged guide and lamp of civilization."[19]

He himself was writing verse that moved Eliot (with a modesty that only a well-established author can master) to rate him, in 1933, as "probably the most important living poet in our language."[20] Eliot was thinking of the *Cantos*, but in addition he gave special praise to *Hugh Selwyn Mauberley*, which Pound published in 1920. This commendation was all the handsomer since *Mauberley* anticipated the mood, and some ideas, of Eliot's "Prufrock" and *The Waste Land*.

Mauberley is a sequence of eighteen poems belaboring America and England. "Seeing he had been born / In a half-savage country, out of date; / Bent resolutely on wringing ladies from the acorn" while "his true Penelope was Flaubert," Hugh Selwyn, scorning tenses, mourns that

> *Christ follows Dionysus,*
> *Phallic and ambrosial [rites]*

> *Made way for macerations;*
> *Caliban casts out Ariel.*
> *All things are a-flowing,*
> *Sage Heracleitus says;*
> *But a tawdry cheapness*
> *Shall outlast our days.*

In one of the series ("Brennbaum") the poet satirized the Jews of England, apparently thinking of Max Beerbohm; in "Mr. Nixon" he lashed an author (presumably Arnold Bennett) for writing with a main eye to money; in Poem X he intoned an elegy to his London (Church Walk?) room, with its leaking and sagging roof; in XII he made fun of the purring tea-pouring ladies of the social afternoon. And in a melodious "Envoi" he frankly imitated Waller's "Go, lovely rose":

> *Tell her that goes*
> *With song upon her lips*
> *But sings not out the song, nor knows*
> *The maker of it, some other mouth*
> *May be as fair as hers,*
> *Might, in new ages, gain her worshipers,*
> *When our two dusts with Waller's shall be laid,*
> *Siftings on siftings in oblivion,*
> *Till change hath broken down*
> *All things save beauty alone.*

Mauberley rejects England as well as America. World War I had killed some English poets, maimed others, left nearly all the rest exhausted in spirits and hope. Pound, still restless and eager, began to yearn for "new friends, new faces, places,"

> *And you,*
> *Love, you the much, the more desired!*
> *Do I not loathe all walls, streets, stores,*
> *All mire, mist, all fog,*
> *All ways of traffic?*
> *You I would have flow over me like water,—*
> *Oh, but far out of this!*
> *Grass, and low fields, and hills,*
> *And sun,*
> *Oh, sun enough!*
> *Out, and alone, among some*
> *Alien people!*[21]

So, in 1921, he and Shakespear left England, and for a while courted the sun in Italy. Soon they turned back to look for genius in Paris. They met a lively dozen of them—Jean Cocteau, Georges Bracque, Constantin Brancusi, Man Ray, Alfred Kreymborg, E. E. Cummings, Gertrude Stein, Alice Toklas, Scott Fitzgerald, Ernest Hemingway, George Antheil, Wyndham Lewis, Harriet Monroe, William Carlos Williams. To all of them Ezra preached his gospel: that poetry should be realistic, contemporary, imageful, and that poets should rescue Western civilization from Mammon and guide it to a life of understanding and art. According to Hemingway, Pound spent most of his time in Paris helping friends. "He gets them into magazines and out of jail. He loans them money. He sells their pictures. He arranges concerts for them. . . . He advances them hospital expenses and dissuades them from suicide. And in the end a few of them refrain from knifing him at the first opportunity."[22] He revised much of Hemingway's early work, deleting adjectives imperiously. He found an "angel" for Joyce. *En passant* he wrote an opera, which Hemingway considered "very fine";[23] and some of his music was performed in the chambers of the Salle Pleyel. He authored a book on Antheil, in which he praised the composer so superlatively that Antheil felt ruined.[24]

In 1921 he published the first of the *Cantos* which were to be his principal contribution to American letters. They were a Greek gift, for they denounced America and contemporary civilization, and added injury to insult by encasing each ounce of sense or beauty in a pound of jagged obscurity. Dante had put a hundred cantos into *The Divine Comedy*; resolved to equal that number, Pound added to his *Cantos* in 1928, 1930, 1932, 1935, 1937, 1940, 1949, 1956, and 1957. As these emerged they became a receptacle for whatever seethed in the author's brain—notes from his reading, eruptions from his memory, images from his fancy, irritations from his daily life, utopias from his dreams; they were his stream of consciousness flooding the world. Here, amid professed poetry, appeared long stretches of prose pilfered from Confucius, Jefferson, John Adams, John Quincy Adams, and Benedetto Varchi's *Storia Fiorentina*. Enamored of the Greek and Roman classics, Provençal poetry, and Chinese philosophy, Pound poured helpings of them into his cantos. Scorning the addiction of well-behaved English poets to iambic pentameter (which he ridiculed as "whakty, whakty, whakty, whakty, whak") he discarded rhyme, and offered no rhythms except those based upon successive stresses of significant words. He took no time or care to forge his phrases into clarity; he stifled half his pages with untranslated quotations, with learned allusions to remote events in history, with esoteric references to incidents in his own life. Reading him becomes a game of hide-and-seek, in which even a quondam student of classic tongues gives up the game as not worth the chase; little wonder that Joyce found the *Cantos* as unintelligible as Pound found *Finnegans Wake*. Perhaps Ezra had heard Joyce's remark on the uses of obscurity— that it would keep a book alive by providing problems for professors indefinitely; so we now have several books on what those meandering cantos mean. Art ceases to be a communication in significant form, and becomes a crossword puzzle for the leisure class.*

Wandering through the *Cantos,* I noted salient items. Cantos VIII–XI tell the story of Sigismondo Malatesta, Lord of Rimini, lover of art and the female form, who said that he was "neither Christian, Jew, Gentile, nor any sect pagan, *nisi forsitans epicureae*" (unless, perhaps, the Epicurean).[26] Canto XI disposes truculently of "that nick-nosed s. o. b. Feddy [Federigo de Montefeltro, Duke of] Urbino" (recklessly praised in *The Renaissance*). XII is a rollicking tale of a drunken sailor. XIII celebrates Confucius, and quotes some sober advice from the (in China) superannuated sage. XIV–XV take Pound to hell, which he finds crowded with politicians, and "perverts who have set money-lust before the pleasures of the senses"; these cantos are littered with usurers, slum landlords, orators, preachers, and monopolists, in an ambiance of human offal and gas, all peppered with the most obscene, sticky, and odorous words at the poet's command. XV immerses imperialists, bishops, Fabians, newspaper owners, and lady golfers in a lake of excrement. XVI, forgetting Bertran de Born and his excoriation of peace, is a blast against war, especially bedeviling "that son of a bitch Franz Josef of Austria, and . . . that son of a bitch Napoleon III Barbiche [goateed]," who sent to their death (in wars against beloved Italy) "a lot of kids of sixteen howling and crying for their mamas." XVIII begins with Marco Polo and Kublai Khan, and leaps to an attack upon oil barons and munitions makers. XXI roams from the Florence of the Medici to the Virginia of Jefferson and back to the Milan of "Galeaz Sforza Visconti"—all in lines full of color, poetry, and vituperation. XXV is Venice and Titian. XXVI tells how the dignitaries of the Greek Orthodox Church came to Florence in 1438, and how Florence made fun of their theology and beards. XXXI quotes letters of Jefferson, one of which declared that "there is not a crowned head in Europe whose talent or merits would entitle him to be elected a vestryman by any American parish;" how-

---

* In 1913 Pound wrote: "If I were a painter . . . I might found a new school of painting, of 'non-representative' painting, a painting that would speak only by arrangements in color."[25]

ever, the next three cantos reek with descriptions—from Jefferson and the Adamses—of corruption in American officialdom. XXXV berates European politicians and moneylenders, with a hot page against the Jews for their "intramural, almost intravaginal warmth of affections in the family." XXXVIII recurses the munitions makers. XXXIX sings the glory of reproduction, in language ranging from Homeric Greek to privy monosyllables. XL commemorates the rise of the Morgan banking firm from "inferior arms sold to the government . . . at an extortionate profit" during the Civil War. LII–LXI are snatches from Chinese history, Confucius, and the story of the Jesuits in China. LXII–LXXI are gleanings from the papers of John Adams. Most of these cantos read like Socialist pamphlets, and become poetry only through typography.

All in all, the *Cantos* are the epic of a disordered soul in search and recall of civilization, honoring high moments in China, Greece, Rome, the late Middle Ages, and the early Renaissance; damning industrial bourgeois regimes as a degradation, and crying out for a return to the heroic spirit of pioneering days. "The more I see of nations," he wrote in 1919, "the more I loathe them; the more I learn of civilization the more I desire that it exist"[27]—i.e., that the world be made safe for poets, artists, philosophers, and saints. He symbolized present and past by noting a beer bottle on a statue's pediment.[28] He thought for a time that socialism would cure most social ills; he hailed the Russian Revolution joyfully; he read John Reed and Scott Nearing with relish as Yankees worthy of 1776. But in 1917 he met Major C. H. Douglas, and heard him expound a plan for "social credit"—a system of paper money by which a state would issue monthly to its citizens "social dividends" promoting their power to purchase goods and backed by their ability to produce them. Pound became an apostle of the new idea as a way to replace a price system controlled by manipulations of bank credit. Following Douglas in the assumption that the most powerful bankers were Jews, he declared war upon the Jewish people, and so prepared himself for his Fascist entanglements.

In 1924 the Pounds traveled in Italy and Sicily, and in 1925 they settled down in Rapallo. In that year a new periodical appeared in Paris; it was dedicated to "Ezra Pound, who by his creative work, his editorship of several magazines, his helpful friendship for young and unknown artists, his many untiring efforts to win better appreciation of what is first-rate in art, comes first to our mind as meriting the gratitude of this generation."[29] (The editors later retracted this dedication.) In 1928 *The Dial* gave Pound its annual award for services to literature; this brought two thousand dollars. About 1929 Yeats joined Pound, Antheil,

Gerhart Hauptmann, and Franz Werfel in Rapallo's foreign colony. He spoke of Pound as "a man with whom I should quarrel more than anyone else if we were not united by affection . . . Anyone must like Ezra who has seen him feed the stray cats at Rapallo. . . . He thinks Confucius the perfect man."[30]

From Italy, in a short-lived magazine called *The Exile*, and in later essays later collected as a *Guide to Kulchur*, Pound sallied forth again upon America and England as irremediably ruined by the triumph of middle-class manners, morals, and wealth. Echoing Mencken, he described America as "the most colossal monkey-house and prize exhibit that the astonished world has yet seen;"[31] and in 1934 he added, in his delicate scatological way, that "American *vie intellectuelle* sits patiently under the British bum, carefully collecting and cataloguing the droppings."[32] (Hemingway and Faulkner had already issued several major works, in which said droppings show only microscopic traces.) To an Englishman Ezra wrote (1933): "There is only one thing to do with an Englishman—kick him in the teeth."[33] He had by this time quite succumbed to Spengler's *Der Untergang des Abendlandes*, which had meticulously diagnosed "the decline of the West," and had predicted the coming of new Caesars. "This conception," said Pound, "freed me from British liberalism and all its dreams."[34] Now he could love Mussolini with the sanction of the latest philosophy.

He accepted the "corporate state" as a successful and antiseptic amalgam of capitalism and socialism. He liked its fiscal system as drawing the fangs of the bankers. He was impressed by Mussolini's vigorous restoration of social and economic order; in 1926 he compared him very favorably with recent American Presidents (Harding and Coolidge).[35] Given an audience by Il Duce in 1933, he fell in love with him at first sight of *A Draft of XXX Cantos* on the great man's desk. In 1936, in *Jefferson and/or Mussolini*, he praised the Italian leader's statesmanship. He had no love for Hitler or Germany, but he hoped that National Socialism might rescue Central Europe from Spengler's inclusion of it in his diagnosis of decay.

He expressed nothing but contempt for Franklin Roosevelt and the New Deal (Canto XLVI), though this too was an attempt to modify capitalism with socialistic measures. In a private letter (February, 1939) he gave his vocabulary free rein: "Is it possible to BE American in America today? Doesn't one have to live out of the god-damn bankslime, the high-piled shit of Barney Baruch and his brother (Frankie R[oosevelt]) to get any view of what our forebears intended, and what we damn well OUGHT to create (the whole of it having slopped and slithered increasingly from 1866 to the criminal Hoover, and still wallowing in judea hysteria)?"[36] In April, 1939, he came to the United States in the royal suite of the *S.S. Rex*. On arrival he gave an interview in which he defended Mussolini and predicted that there would be no war. He went to Washington, met Henry Wallace and Senators Borah, Bankhead, and Byrd, and urged upon them a policy of peace; Roosevelt was too busy to see him.

Back in Italy, he began in January, 1941, to broadcast from the Rome radio a defense of the Axis powers. Startled by Pearl Harbor and the consequent entry of America into the war (December, 1941), he and his wife sought to return to the United States, but they were refused an American visa. They tried again in 1942, and were again refused. In March Pound began to broadcast from Rome, twice a week, attacks upon America; for each of these addresses he received 350 lire. The broadcasts were recorded (1941–43) by the Federal Communications Commission, and in July, 1943, Pound was indicted for treason by the District of Columbia District Court of the United States. He countered by accusing Franklin Roosevelt of treason, and questioning his sanity. He ascribed America's entry into the war to a conspiracy of bankers led by Henry Morgenthau, Herbert Lehman, and Bernard Baruch.[37] In a pamphlet published in Venice (1944), *America, Roosevelt, and the Causes of the Present War*, he declared that "usury is the cancer of the world, which only the surgeon knife of Fascism can cut out of the life of nations."[38] Meanwhile his son, Omar, who had been in Paris since his birth there in 1926, enlisted in the United States Army.

When the German and Italian forces retreated before the Allied invasion of Italy, they turned Rapallo into a citadel of defense, and the Pounds retired to the suburb of Sant' Ambrogio. The triumphant Americans arrested him in the spring of 1945 and took him to Genoa. There he defiantly called Hitler "a Jeanne d'Arc, a saint, and a martyr," called Stalin "the best brains in politics today," and mourned that Hitler and Mussolini had "failed because they did not follow Confucius more closely."[39] From Genoa he was moved to a military detention camp near Pisa, where he was put in solitary confinement in a roofless barbed-wire cage; he was allowed no reading matter except Confucius; searchlights trained upon him at night made sleep difficult; after three weeks he collapsed. He was transferred to a tent, still excluded from communication with friends; but on October 3 his wife was allowed to visit him; and thereafter she stood by him through all his troubles. Now he was permitted access to books and magazines, and wrote part of what came to be known as the Pisan Cantos. In November he was flown to Washington, and was put in a District of Columbia jail.

On the eve of his trial for treason he was examined by a medical board, which declared him "insane and mentally unfit for trial."[40] In December he was transferred to St. Elizabeth's Hospital in a suburb of the capital. There he remained for thirteen years, in relatively humane conditions. His wife saw him daily, and spent the remains of her modest fortune in trying to secure his release; his son and daughter joined her in comforting him. After the first eighteen months he was given a small private room, a typewriter, some writing materials; soon he was pouring forth more cantos. Distinguished visitors came to him: T. S. Eliot, H. L. Mencken, Edith Hamilton, Robert Lowell, Witter Bynner, Thornton Wilder . . . In 1949 Eliot, Lowell, W. H. Auden, and Conrad Aiken, as judges for the Fellows in American Letters of the Library of Congress, voted him the Bollingen award ($1,000) for the Pisan Cantos (LXXIV–LXXXIV), which had been published in 1948. Finally an appeal by Robert Frost, Archibald MacLeish, T. S. Eliot, and Ernest Hemingway secured his release (April, 1958). After enjoying acclaim in several American cities he and his wife sailed for Italy. When they reached Naples he gave the Fascist salute, and told reporters, "All America is an insane asylum."[41] His daughter took him to her husband's Schloss Brunnenberg near Merano, in the Italian Alps.

Such is the story of Ezra Pound. He was not a great poet, but he influenced a host of poets by his experiments in versification, mystification, and imagery; he was one of the prime imagists in English, communicating by images rather than by sentences. Gradually his poems became prose in all but typography, and his writings became as undisciplined as his mind. He was often absurd, even as you and I; but we forget our blunders and hide our sins, while Pound spread his follies over the mercuries of the air, and suffered resilient storms. It is easy now to forgive him, for he sought out new talent eagerly, and helped it like some ministering angel divinely appointed to succor genius in need. Across our alien moods and a thousand leagues we send him greetings and wish him peace.

CHAPTER VI

James Joyce

I HAVE sometimes thought how high Ireland would stand in the world of letters if all her literary sons had stayed on her soil: Swift, Burke, Goldsmith, Wilde, Shaw, Joyce . . . The land was fertile, the moist cold air put blushing roses in the cheeks of the girls, and lusty sons were eager to plant new life in willing wombs. But the spiritual atmosphere was deadly: a government Irish in name but foreign in humiliating fact; an Anglican Church more intolerant in Ireland than in England; a Catholic Church that loyal Irishmen could not criticize or reform since she had suffered in fighting for Irish liberty. And just across the water was a Britain with a larger and more literate public, a freer press, a taste for Irish eloquence and wit. So Erin's genius crossed the Irish Sea, and left the lovely island to destitute peasants and Joyce's Dubliners.

William Butler Yeats (1865–1939) was an exception: he stayed or returned home, explored Irish legends, turned them into melodious verse, and appealed so loyally to his countrymen that he never found an international audience. I, who swallowed Shaw whole in my thirty years of adolescence, never read a line of Yeats till my old age. I traveled through Ireland (1912) before I had even heard of Yeats, and I knew the Abbey Theatre before I learned that Yeats had been one of its founders and the most frequent contributor to its repertoire. As late as 1923, when he received the Nobel Prize, I barely knew his name. And now when I try to relish his poetry I find it mystical and sad, alien to a mind pledged to reality and reason, and gastronomically gay.

I. AN IRISHMAN'S ODYSSEY

James Joyce left Ireland, though in his books he could seldom get away from its capital. He was born in a Dublin suburb in 1882 to a kindly, pious mother and a jovial, shiftless father. As our own story is the clearest drama known to us, he began his literary career by recording his youth in a thousand-page fragment entitled *Stephen Hero*. Part of this was published after his death, since posterity is curious about the sins of genius; Joyce, with a common sense uncommon in genius, destroyed most of it after compressing and polishing it into *A Portrait of the Artist as a Young Man*—his finest work of literary art.

He disguised himself in the tale as Stephen Daedalus—which might be interpreted as Stephen of the Airy Flights, for Stephen was a poet soaring hopefully above reality. The first pages recalled a riotous argument, at the family's Christmas dinner, about the role of the Catholic Church in Ireland's struggle for independence. The father could not forgive the prelates for having turned against Parnell, who had softened the hardships of politics with a mistress; and he called the Irish "an unfortunate priest-ridden race," doomed (he thought) to remain such "till the end of the chapter."[1] Joyce's picture of his father surpasses any portrait in *Ulysses*.

His account of Stephen's schooling under the Jesuits describes them as strict but humane—excepting a slightly sadistic Father Dolan. The boy "felt his body small and weak, and his eyes were weak and watery" (these frailties stayed with Joyce till his death); but he stood up bravely for Byron as superior to Tennyson, and held his ground when assured that Byron was roasting in hell. Soon he passed on, in hesitant admiration, to the atheist Shelley. One night, when Stephen, aged sixteen, was wandering in a dark street, a gay voice accosted him. Lusting for experience more than for pleasure, he followed the woman into her room and surrendered his youth. Back in the college chapel he heard a lurid sermon on the eternal physical and spiritual sufferings of hell. He trembled at the thought of his secret depravity, and decided to confess his sin—not to one of his teachers but to an old village priest. He was astonished to receive absolution and kindly counsel. His faith revived in gratitude for such gracious cleansing, and for a time Stephen was the most pious lad in University College. His teachers invited him to enter a novitiate in preparation for admission to the Society of Jesus. But the sight of a comely girl wading barelegged into an inlet of the sea unnerved him; the ancient war between sex and Christianity, between woman and the Virgin, rose in his soul, and his faith withered as desire bloomed. Soon he was so fanatically atheist that he refused to do his Easter duty, to the horror and desolation of his mother. To a friend who reproved him for his cruelty he replied, "I will not serve that in which I no longer believe, whether it call itself my home, my fatherland, or my church; and I will try to express myself in some mode of life and art as freely as I can, using for my defense the only arms I allow myself to use—silence, exile, and cunning."[2] So ends the *Portrait*.

In October, 1904, after borrowing every detachable sum from his friends, Joyce left Dublin for London. Secretly he took with him his latest sweetheart, Nora Barnacle, who was to live with him in angry patience and apparent fidelity to his end. (Resenting all Catholic sacraments, he did not marry her till twenty-seven years later.) From cold London they moved hopefully to Paris. Leaving Nora on a park bench, Joyce hunted up acquaintances and borrowed enough to take him and his consort to a promised job in Zurich. Disappointed there, they passed down to Trieste, then under Austrian rule. He found a place as teacher of English in a Berlitz school at eighty pounds a year; this he supplemented with private lessons which he gave at home at tenpence an hour.[3] Nora bore him a son, George, in 1905, and a daughter, Lucia, in 1908. His younger brother Stanislaus joined him in Trieste, and helped, by his steady industry, to keep the family alive. James tried to blur tribulation with alcohol, but Nora won him to temporary temperance by threatening to have the children baptized if he ever came home drunk again.

In those troubled years at Trieste (1904–14), amid lessons scholastic and domestic, Joyce wrote *Dubliners*—sketches of Irish characters and scenes; *A Portrait of the Artist as a Young Man*; and, in 1914, the beginnings of *Ulysses*. *Dubliners*, after heart-searing delays, reached publication in London in 1914. *A Portrait* appeared first in the British periodical *The Egoist* (1914–15), through the intercession of Ezra Pound; it was given book form by B. W. Huebsch in New York (1916). Miss Harriet Weaver, who in 1914 had assumed editorship of *The Egoist*, now began her remarkable career as Joyce's financial nurse by sending him enough money to give him food and confidence. Since no one in England would yet publish *A Portrait* as a book, she bought 750 copies from the American edition for sale in Great Britain. H. G. Wells wrote a laudatory review in *The Nation*, but other reviewers were unsympathetic; one of them hoped that no "clean-minded" person would allow the book within reach of his family.[4]

When World War I reached Trieste James, Nora, George, and Lucia Joyce moved to Zurich (June, 1915). For a time they were almost destitute, despite some private pupils. Soon, however, help came in a succession of benefactions deserving a place in history. In July Yeats sent specimens of Joyce's writings to Edmund Gosse with a letter:

> I have just heard that James Joyce, an Irish poet and novelist of whose fine talent I can easily satisfy you, is in probably great penury

through the war. . . . If things are as I believe, would it be possible for him to be given a grant from the Royal Literary Fund? . . . If more particulars are needed you would perhaps get them from Mr. Ezra Pound.

Seven weeks later Joyce was given seventy-five pounds. Pound sent him twenty-five pounds, and induced the Society of Authors to allot Joyce one pound a week for thirteen weeks.[5] In 1916 Yeats and Pound persuaded Prime Minister Asquith to grant Joyce a hundred pounds from the Civil List. In 1917 an anonymous donor contributed two hundred pounds. In 1918 Mrs. Harold McCormick, then living in Zurich, settled upon Joyce an annuity of twelve thousand francs ($2,400?); this was ended after two years. In 1919 Harriet Weaver transferred to him five thousand pounds in British bonds yielding five percent. These gifts made *Ulysses* possible, for it was chiefly in Zurich that this highly seminal volume was written.*

In July, 1920, Joyce and his family went to Paris for a week's stay; they remained there twenty years. Pound welcomed them and found an apartment for them. Joyce was then thirty-eight, tall, thin, bespectacled, at once aggressive and shy, with a tuft of beard on his chin and tennis shoes on his feet.

Meanwhile the manuscript of *Ulysses* was rivaling Odysseus in wanderings and vicissitudes. In February, 1918, Pound forwarded Episode I to Margaret Anderson and Jane Heap in New York; they published it in the March issue of their *Little Review*, and printed further sections despite Pound's warning that they might get into trouble with the censorship. In 1920 John S. Sumner, secretary of the Society for the Prevention of Vice, charged the *Review* with publishing obscene material, and served a summons upon the Washington Square Bookshop for selling a copy of the magazine. The United States Post Office confiscated all obtainable issues containing episodes of *Ulysses*. The censors had been particularly excited by Episode XIII ("Nausicaa"), which described obscurely the expansive effect of Gerty McDowell's lingerie upon the imagination and glands of Leopold Bloom. The case was tried (February, 1921) by three judges in the state Court of Special Sessions in New York. My late beloved friend John Cowper Powys testified for the de-

---

* The first episode ("Telemachus") was completed in November, 1917; the second ("Nestor") and third ("Proteus") in December; the fourth ("Calypso") was sent to Pound in March, 1918. Apparently these four extensive sections were written in heat, and in pain, for in 1917 Joyce began to suffer from glaucoma and other diseases of the eyes. Part XVIII and last ("Penelope") was completed in Paris by February, 1921.

fendants that the novel was "a beautiful piece of work, in no way capable of corrupting the mind of a young girl."[6] The verdict was guilty, and the two editors of the *Little Review* were fined fifty dollars each.

This setback deterred Huebsch and other publishers from presenting *Ulysses* in book form. A solution was found by Sylvia Beach, who kept the "Shakespeare and Company Bookstore" at 12 Rue de l'Odéon in Paris. She had no capital, and no experience as a publisher, but she advertised for advance subscriptions at 150 francs a copy, received subscriptions from Shaw, Yeats, Pound, Hemingway, Gide . . . , and sent *Ulysses* forth, February, 1922, in an issue of one thousand copies. Harriet Weaver, using Miss Beach's plates, brought out an edition of two thousand copies for the Egoist Press in London in October; five hundred copies of this issue, sent to New York, were confiscated by the U. S. Post Office, and in 1923 all circulation of the book in Great Britain was forbidden. The ban against it in America was removed by U. S. District Court Judge John Munro Woolsey on December 6, 1933, on the ground that "whilst in many places the effect of 'Ulysses' on the reader undoubtedly is somewhat emetic, nowhere does it tend to be an aphrodisiac."[7]

II. ULYSSES

The book is not an emetic, but it is a maze of such varied contents and forms that Joyce must have been puzzled to find a title for it. He found it by pretending to see, in the passage of Leopold Bloom through one day in Dublin (June 16, 1904) a loose correspondence with the wanderings of Homer's Odysseus (in Latin, Ulysses) from his leaving his wife, Penelope (Molly Bloom), and his son, Telemachus (Bloom's spiritual protégé Stephen Daedalus), through his conflict with the Trojans (the Dublin anti-Semites), his flirtation with the nymph Calypso (Bloom's restless eye for Dublin girls), his dallying with the Lotus Eaters (Bloom's taste for the sensual delights of life and his distaste for steady work), his struggle with Aeolus and the cave of the winds (a Dublin newspaper office), his fascination with Nausicaa (Gerty McDowell) . . . , and his return to his wife after exhausting experiences in battle and love. Joyce took a boyish delight in finding other analogies between his epic and Homer's; we need not take them too seriously.

He outdistanced the author(s) of the *Odyssey* by running Bloom's one day to 735 pages (edition of 1926), and by recording not only events and speech but also the "interior dialogue," or unspoken thoughts and feelings, of the principal characters. This was not the first, it was only the most striking, appearance of the "stream of consciousness" technique; Tolstoi had used it in *Sebastopol Sketches* (1855) to describe Praskukhin's random thoughts on the verge of death; Joyce claimed to have derived it from Édouard Dujardin's *Les Lauriers sont coupés* (1886). He acknowledged no debt to the free-association method used by Freud in exhuming the secrets of a patient's mind and past; he rejected Freudian psychoanalysis as depending too much upon arbitrary and often absurd symbolism—interpreting a fire as a phallus and a house as a womb.[8] Joyce was attempting to describe "normal" minds in their unexpressed ideas, feelings, and memories, free from logic, grammar, or moral control. In this way he restored "reality" to the chaos of thought; he did not so much "shatter the realistic novel" as turn its camera upon the interior as well as the visible or audible world. The result was a new depth, breadth, and force in the portrayal of character.

The personages in *Ulysses* are a complex motley, apparently fictional, but "keys" have identified many of them with Dubliners living in Joyce's day. Some were so factually described, under transparent pseudonyms, that, like Cosgrave and Gogarty, they resented their new fame. When the book appeared it was common for Dubliners to ask one another, "Are you in it?" or "Am I in it?" Nearly all the characters were Irish patriots, fighting conversational battles against England; all but one were bibulous, soaking their fertility in drink; and nearly all were proud anti-Semites. Hence the unhappy day of the tale's protagonist.

Joyce individualizes Leopold Bloom not so much by perceivable peculiarities of body, features, dress, or speech as by letting us eavesdrop upon his secret motives, feelings, and thoughts. The resultant picture is unheroic, but it is sympathetic. Joyce knew the faults of the Jews, but, himself an outcast, he could understand something of their sufferings. He admired their quick and subtle minds, their faithful and cohesive family life, their patient persistence under every adversity. "The oldest people. Wandered far away over all the earth, captivity to captivity, multiplying, dying, being reborn everywhere."[9] He had met many Jews in Trieste, and had taken a liking to some of them—especially his amiable pupil Ettore Schmidt, and Leopold Popper, father of another pupil, and Teodoro Mayer, a local newspaper publisher. From Mayer Joyce derived Bloom's mustache and Hungarian parentage; from Schmidt a mass of Hebraic lore; from Popper the name Leopold. Bloom was the name of several Jews whom Joyce had known in Dublin. Some of them, like the new Ulysses, had accepted Christian baptism as a precondition to commercial life in a Christian city.

Bloom is presented as a canvasser for newspaper advertisements and publicity. He is too easygoing to be a financial success, but Joyce describes him as "holder of a modest substance in the funds"[10]—a trustful investor in government bonds. He is "the meekest man and the kindest";[11] he feeds his cat, some sea gulls, and a dog; he gives to charity, visits the sick, buries the dead, helps a blind man across a street, and protects the drink-stupefied Daedalus. He is "passing grave, . . . by cause he still had pity of the terror-causing shrieking of shrill women in their labour."[12] He gently reproves his Irish friends for their intense nationalism and religious bigotry; he meets their anti-Semitic needling with a timid reminder that Christ was a Jew. They teach him to drink.

Only one Dubliner is consistently his friend—the young poet and apostate Stephen Daedalus, who passes from *A Portrait of the Artist* into *Ulysses* still haunted by the memory of a sorrowing mother to whom he had refused even one day's conformity to Catholic ritual. He represents the rebel, agnostic, alcoholic, word-loving side of Joyce. He bores the Dubliners with learned discourses, and lapses into drink and venery when he finds no answers to his questions about man, woman, and God. Bloom, who has reconciled himself to a universe without answers (and whose only son died in infancy), takes an almost paternal care of Stephen, reproves him for "living riotously with wastrels, and murdering his goods with whores."[13] In the "Night town," or brothel alleys of Dublin, Leopold and Stephen share in the central incidents of the book.

These occur toward the end of the "Circe" episode—a wild fantasia of 163 pages composed of urination, onanism, masochism, sadism, copulation, and suicide; here Joyce's scatology and vocabulary run quite out of bounds (e.g., pages 502, 559). Bloom wallows in memories of his past—his father, his loves, his people and their tribulations—and suffers unbelievable indignities from hilarious prostitutes. Stephen gets into an argument with officers of the law and is about to be jailed when Leopold rescues him, gives him food to soak up his alcohol, and takes him to the Bloom home. He invites him to stay there through the night; Stephen refuses and departs, but not before Mrs. Bloom has caught a stimulating glimpse of his handsome, poetic face. Leopold, exhausted, dressed and unwashed, falls into bed beside his wife, and ends his odyssey in a heavy sleep.

Now Molly Bloom, lying awake beside her unconscious mate, begins the "Penelope" episode which ends the book—the most amazing and unprecedented chapter in the literature of the twentieth, perhaps of any, century. For forty-one pages, with hardly a stop for punctuation, she silently speaks her mind in an "interior dialogue" which only Joyce hears, and which no virgin should read. It is obscene but magnificent. T. S. Eliot, who had the puritanism of both Old and New England in his soul, asked, "How could anyone write again after achieving the immense prodigy of the last chapter?"[14] Molly, according to her creator, was intended to represent "perfectly sane full amoral fertilizable untrustworthy engaging shrewd limited prudent indifferent *Weib*"[15]—or, more simply, the average woman of the European lower middle class. She is probably no worse and no better than the woman next door. She is a Catholic, with more creed than piety: "As for them saying theres no God I wouldnt give a snap of my fingers for all their learning why dont they go and create something?"[16] She has had twenty-five lovers (according to Bloom), and remembers some of them fondly, but she has limited herself to two since her marriage; and her excuse for these is that her husband has given her too little passion for her Irish temperament. She gives herself to "Blazes" Boylan, but, surfeited with fire, she creeps back in spirit to her husband, forgives his flirtations, recognizes his virtues, and ends her meditations—and the book—by affectionately recalling how, long ago in Gibraltar, he proposed to her:

> when I put the rose in my hair like the Andalusian girls used or shall I wear a red yes and how he kissed me under the Moorish wall and I thought well as well him as another and then I asked him with my eyes to ask again yes and then he asked me would I yes to say yes . . . and first I put my arms around him and drew him down to me so he could feel my breasts all perfume yes and his heart was going like mad and yes I said yes I will yes.

Is that breathless chapter an accurate mirror of a woman's mind? Joyce's wife said of him, "He knows nothing at all about women";[17] but there is no evidence that she had read *Ulysses,* or even its brightly burning end. After all, Joyce was describing Molly Bloom, not Madame de Sévigné, not even the Marquise de Pompadour. He knew the Circes of the cafés better than the goddesses of the salons. Nevertheless he tried to imagine the idealizing meditations of a girl; he saw the look of wonder and love in the face of a young mother just recovering from her childbirth agony and receiving into her arms her cleansed and simian babe. He wrote to his wife letters of romantic fervor and adoration.

Perhaps Joyce took from the bragging banter in Dublin barrooms, and from the cynical jests of expatriates in Paris restaurants, an undue emphasis on the physiology of love. Mr. Malachi Mulligan's card announces his profession as "Fertilizer and Incubator" extraordinary; Alf Bergan carefully describes the doubly erectile effect of hanging; the police derive their favorite adjective from a four-letter synonym of coitus; episode "Virag" analyzes that conjunction in unromantic detail. To all this Joyce adds some fond odors and the congealed detritus of the nose. These privia, as the good judge said, are more calculated to turn the stomach than to raise desire, and they constitute a modest fraction of the whole.

Joyce, like two of my favorite authors, did not know when to stop. He emptied into *Ulysses* nearly every scrap of history, literature, bawdry, and sacred ritual that had lodged in his merciless memory. Here, burying brilliants, are teeming mounds of trivia, of bootless badinage between nobodies, of Latin tags and scholastic shreds, of barbs that have lost their point in the wear of time, and of sly allusions that only dead Dubliners can understand. "I've put in so many enigmas and puzzles," said Joyce, "that it will keep the professors busy for centuries arguing over what I meant, and that's the only way of insuring immortality."[18]

III. IN THE WAKE

For a year or two Joyce rested after the seven years of gestation and delivery given to his masterpiece. He worried his wife and coddled his children; he frequented the haunts of the scribblers of Paris; he fomented reviews of his novel; he collected, consciously or not, heaps of ideas, stories, fancies, quips, and puns for his next indictment and augmentation of life's absurdities. In 1922 he attended the funeral of Marcel Proust, who had also written an unforgettable or interminable book. In 1923 he received an additional gift of £1,500 from Miss Weaver, which raised her subsidy to £8,500. In July, 1931, he married his wife to legalize his estate and effectuate his will. In December his father died, after outdawdling and outborrowing Micawber; and in that year his beloved daughter, Lucia, began to go insane. Carl Jung infuriated her father by diagnosing her condition as a more violent form of the author's mania for jumbling incongruous words and ideas. Joyce tried every plan and friend to care for her; Saint Harriet Weaver took the task and spent on it sleepless nights and countless pounds; finally Joyce put Lucia into an institution. His relapses into alcohol became so frequent that his wife twice left him; but she loved the helpless madman, and always returned.

The vision of a new chef-d'oeuvre sustained him. *Ulysses* had been published in book form in February, 1922; thirteen months later Joyce began *Finnegans Wake*. The longer volume had taken him seven years; the shorter one consumed sixteen. Eye trouble delayed him; he submitted to six operations; for months he was nearly blind. His vision returned, but never completely. The new book was finished in 1938, and was published in 1939, in both London and New York.

The form of the book cooperated with World War II in damaging its reception. Here was a new language, born of Joyce's frolicsome imagination and polyglot vocabulary; no dictionary could explain it, no grammar gave it structure, no story gave it sequence, no ascertainable philosophy gave order to the jumble and riot of ideas. Wife Nora again complained: "Why don't you write sensible books that people can understand?" Brother Stanislaus rejected the first installment as a "driveling rigamarole, . . . unspeakably wearisome." Ezra Pound, who was composing *Cantos* meticulously obscure, wrote (November 15, 1926) that "nothing short of divine vision or a new cure for the clapp can possibly be worth all that circumambient peripherization." H. G. Wells, who had helped *Ulysses*, now inquired: "Who the hell is this Joyce who demands so many waking hours of the few thousands I have still to live for a proper appreciation of quirks and fancies and flashes?"[19]

Joyce felt that all these plaints were unwarranted because they ignored his explicit aim—to record the inconsequential sequence of ideas, feelings, actions, words, and syllables in a *dream*. "One great part of every human existence," he argued, "is passed in a state which cannot be rendered sensible by the use of wide awake language, cut and dry grammar and goahead plot."[20] *Ulysses* had described the vagaries of the conscious mind during a waking day; *Finnegan* tried to reproduce the chaos of an unconscious mind during a night of uncontrolled fancies. In dreams the mind not only ignores the bounds of possibility and the restraints of morality, it also transcends the relations of past, present, and future, the limits of time and space, the barriers of matter, and it is utterly without respect for the rules of logic, grammar, or punctuation. It takes words apart into their syllables and recombines the syllables, it takes memories and persons apart and recombines their elements, according to marginal resemblances or fortuitous association. To find some sense in the phantasmagoria of dreams had challenged Freud and now tempted Joyce; both undertakings were faulted by the tendency of the conscious mind, recalling a distorted dream, to distort it further by unwittingly remolding it according to canons of logic, sequence, and significance. (Compare the "Heisenberg effect" in atomic physics.)

The title of the book is itself a play on words: with an apostrophe it would mean the mourning of a dead Finnegan by his convivial relatives; but the title has no apostrophe, and can mean "Finnegans wake up"; furthermore, it could mean *fin* (the end) plus again; so the insatiable prankster suggests not only indestructible generations of Finnegans, but the rhythmic recurrence of life, death, life, death, life . . . The mythology of the volume stems from Tim Finnegan, a building laborer, who, too fond of the bottle, falls drunk from his ladder, and dies; but at his wake some spray or fragrance of whiskey brings him rushing avidly back to life. He is told to lie down like a good corpse, and await a proper resurrection in due theological time. He obeys, and resumes his interrupted dream. It transforms him into Finn MacCool, the giant leader of the Fenians in Ossianic legend; then, leaping over centuries, it reshapes Finn into H C E—i.e., Humphrey Chimpden Earwicker, keeper of a public house at Chapelizod (a suburb of Dublin). "I always write about Dublin," said Joyce, "because if I can get to the heart of Dublin I can get to the heart of all the cities in the world."[21]

Having read Giambattista Vico, Joyce followed him in conceiving history as a cycle of four stages: (1) theocratic, in which government is by priests, (2) aristocratic, in which government is by an elite of birth, (3) democratic, (4) anarchic, in which democracy crumbles into chaos; thereafter, in a grand *ricorso*, society seeks order through religion, theocracy is restored, and the cycle begins anew. Joyce divided *Finnegans Wake* into four sections corresponding to Vico's stages in history; so in the final section Saint Patrick comes to Ireland (A.D. 432), establishes Christianity, ends disorder, and sets Ireland upon another turn of the Viconian wheel.

On this wheel Earwicker is Everyman, and represents all men. His sons Shem and Penman (=James Joyce) and Shaun the Post (=Stanislaus Joyce) represent the opposite and conflicting principles of thought and action, which are finally reconciled and unified (Joyce had read Giordano Bruno, and perhaps a little Hegel too). Their mother, Anna Livia Plurabelle, is all women—daughter, wife, mother, widow; she is also the stream of life, bearing all humanity and its woes; she is one with the river Liffey, which carries all its soiled and burdened waters into extinction in the sea, where they will be lifted up as mist to fall as rain into the rivers in another cycle symbolizing the resurrection of life and the eternal recurrence of history. Here, as in *Ulysses*, woman has the last word. In a lyric chapter that almost forgets puzzles and puns, Joyce pictures Anna Livia as looking back forgivingly upon life, accepting death without resistance, hoping that she will be cleansed of her sins as the oceans purify the effluvia of the streams, and dreaming of being reborn as fresh as water from the skies. The final sentence is cut short, suggesting both death and continuance; to complete it we must turn back to the beginning, as life does with each new birth; the last line of the book is finished by the first; the cycle is renewed.

Sometimes, as I hurried through this maze of philosophy, etymology, and history, I asked myself, Why couldn't Joyce say all this intelligibly, instead of hiding it under a hundred bushels of dreams, word mutilations, and puns? He could have replied that by presenting ideas through symbolic persons and events he might give them the dramatic power to penetrate and endure. Actually he answered: I was reporting a dream, not a Ph.D. thesis, and I had to use the confused memories, irrational combinations, and mangled speech of dreams. But do we mangle speech in our dreams, and do we then summarize summaries of history and cosmology?

In truth Joyce was drunk with dictionaries, and bursting with pilferings; he was infatuated with philology, and aspired to philosophy. He suffered from—enjoyed—an autoerotism of words, manipulating them, fondling them, squeezing every drop of juice out of them, in the ecstasy of imagination and privacy. It delighted him to break up a word into its components and varied meanings; to throw these pieces into the air, and to watch them fall into new and hilarious combinations. He was a man of sardonic humor, bearing pains and indignities impatiently, and revenging himself upon life by pricking its inflated actors, from prostitutes to popes, with the acid point of his impish pen. Oliver St. John Gogarty called *Finnegans Wake* "the most colossal leg pull in literature since Macpherson's *Ossian*." Joyce agreed; the book, he said, is "a great joke, and is meant to make you laugh."[22] In any case, he felt, it sounded well; read it aloud, and you will find some music in it; "Heaven knows what my prose means, but it is pleasing to the ear."[23] In many ways it corresponded to the abstract painting that was beginning to rear its disheveled head.

IV. OBITUARY

"I don't know whether my husband is a genius," said his wife, "but I am sure of one thing, there's nobody like him."[24] Frail, rheumatic, half blind, tortured with sciatica, fighting Church and state, dismembering dictionaries, watching his daughter go insane—no wonder

Joyce drank himself to sleep nearly every night, after working intensely almost every day. No wonder that he became absorbed in his writing as the only consolation of his life; that he became self-centered, and shamelessly dependent upon gifts; he felt confident that his gifts to posterity would far outweigh these drafts upon his contemporaries. He put on a proud face to the world. Usually somber and silent, he would flare up at the slightest slight, and was apt to break out suddenly with a caustic limerick or an irrepressible pun.

He offered a relatively new literary art, but no new philosophy, nor any clear political creed. He followed Vico's cyclical conception of history to a dour conclusion that the future would endlessly repeat the past.[25] He stood aside from Ireland's fight for freedom; he was afraid that those Dubliners would make a mess of liberty. He damned the French, the "Prooshians," and the British with all his heart.[26] The British could forgive his application of a four-letter obscenity to the pope, but could never forgive his use of the same description for their king.[27]

One thing was clear to him—that the Catholic Church was the enemy of mankind. "To hell with the pope!" resounds in *Ulysses*.[28] Episode "Circe" frolics with satirical imitations of Catholic ritual in picturing the capers of whores; the litany of the Virgin is parodied by the "Daughters of Eros,"[29] and a papal nuncio recites the ancestry of Bloom in terms of the Gospel's genealogy of Christ.[30] Intermingled with such travesties and pasquinades are Catholic symbols and phrases, fragments of Scholastic philosophy, and kindly memories of the Jesuits who had borne with his youth.[31] There is some flippant praise of the deity,[32] and a savage, wistful description of Europe's twentieth century as "an age of exhausted whoredom groping for its god."[33]

The despondent quest for meaning was further darkened by the Second World War, which, like the First, made Joyce a fugitive. When Hitler's troops advanced to Paris (December, 1939) the harassed family fled to St.-Gérand-le-Puy; and when France surrendered they took refuge in Zurich. Exhausted and bewildered by these repetitions of history, Joyce lost all interest in life, and offered little resistance to death. On January 10, 1941, suffering from severe pain, he was taken to a hospital. An X ray showed a perforated duodenal ulcer. An operation failed to save him, and on January 13 he died. Faithful Nora survived him for ten years, idealizing "my poor Jim," and consoled by her proud confidence that she had "been married to the greatest writer in the world."[34]

CHAPTER VII

T. S. Eliot

I. THE POET

ONE of his ancestors, Andrew Eliot, was among the judges at the Salem witch trials. One of his cousins was Charles W. Eliot, who for forty years (1869–1909) was president of Harvard University, and incidentally begot the "Five-Foot-Shelf" of "Harvard Classics." This New England ancestry brought T. S. puritanism, Unitarianism, and a good style. His grandfather moved to St. Louis, and there Thomas Stearns Eliot was born in 1888.

His name drew him to Harvard, where he spent eight years (1906–14) as undergraduate and graduate student, interrupted and followed by two years of study in France and Germany. At Harvard he took courses under Irving Babbitt, and agreed with the professor in opposition to Rousseau's romanticism and President Eliot's elective system. He followed the lectures of George Santayana, but did not take to the Spaniard's skeptical, amiable, pagan view of life as a spectacle to be enjoyed. Even in those Harvard days he took the dress and tone of an Englishman, and signed himself distinctively "T. Stearns-Eliot."

When World War I disturbed his studies in Germany he moved to Oxford. In 1915 he married an English girl, and settled down in London as teacher and book reviewer. He had some lapses into gaiety, chiefly literary, as when he wrote to Conrad Aiken (1915): "Come, let us desert our wives, and fly to a land where there are no Medici prints, nothing but concubinage and conversation."[1] Generally, however, he was a model husband and citizen, careful of his appearance, his morals, and his speech—a natural foil to his friend Ezra Pound. Ezra forgave his virtues for his poetry. Eliot, in the September, 1946, issue of *Poetry*, recalled:

> I had kept my early poems . . . in my desk from 1911 to 1915—with the exception of a period when Conrad Aiken endeavored, without success, to peddle them for me in London. In 1915 (and through Aiken) I met Pound. The result was that "Prufrock" ap-

peared in the summer of that year; and through Pound's efforts my first volume was published by the *Egoist* press in 1917.

The little book was entitled *Prufrock and Other Observations*. It began with "The Love Song of J. Alfred Prufrock," the musings of a mild and hesitant fellow who repeatedly goes—but never makes up his mind—to propose to a lady. Prufrock silently addresses an imaginary friend, somewhat in the manner of Browning:

> *Let us go then, you and I,*
> *When the evening is spread out against the sky*
> *Like a patient etherised upon a table;*
> *Let us go, through certain half-deserted streets,*
> *The muttering retreats*
> *Of restless nights in one-night cheap hotels*
> *And sawdust restaurants with oyster-shells:*
> *Streets that follow like a tedious argument*
> *Of insidious intent*
> *To lead you to an overwhelming question . . .*
> *Oh, do not ask, "What is it?"*
> *Let us go and make our visit.*

He finds the lady immersed in a chattering crowd whose elegant gossip jars with those dull tenements:

> *In the room the women come and go*
> *Talking of Michelangelo.*

Prufrock feels a symbol of his uncertainty in "the yellow fog that rubs its back upon the window-panes"; how can he intrude his life-and-death question into their sparkling inanity of "toast and tea" and art?

> *And indeed there will be time*
> *To wonder, "Do I dare?" and, "Do I dare?"*
> *Time to turn back and descend the stair,*
> *With a bald spot in the middle of my hair . . .*

Yes, he is getting on in years; he must ask her soon; but how could he bear the dilettante life she leads?

> *For I have known them all already, known them all:—*
> *Have known the evenings, mornings, afternoons,*
> *I have measured out my life with coffee spoons;*

> *I know the voices dying with a dying fall*
> *Beneath the music from a farther room.*
> *So how should I presume?*

He keeps his peace, returns to his solitude, dreams of lovely women, and waits for death:

> *I have heard the mermaids singing, each to each.*
> *I do not think that they will sing to me . . .*
> *We have lingered in the chambers of the sea*
> *By sea-girls wreathed with seaweed red and brown*
> *Till human voices wake us, and we drown.*

A companion piece, "Portrait of a Lady," is the distaff side of the diptych. "I have saved this afternoon for you, prepared for all the things to be said, or left unsaid." They attend a concert together, each sinking silent into lonely thought. She feels that she has grown old between teas:

> *But what have I, but what have I, my friend,*
> *To give you, what can you receive from me?*
> *Only the friendship and the sympathy*
> *Of one about to reach her journey's end.*
> *I shall sit here, serving tea for friends.*

Instead of proposing, he tells her he is going abroad. "Perhaps you can write to me," she suggests. The last glimpse shows him writing to her and wondering if she is alive.

The publication of *Prufrock and Other Observations* brought Eliot into the circle of London's literati. While he earned his living as a genteel clerk in Lloyd's Bank he became assistant editor of *The Egoist*, the avant-garde magazine that was publishing Joyce's *Ulysses*. From his own retrospective viewpoint he joined the radicals in condemning bourgeois civilization, British and American; they struck at it from below as mostly impecunious intellectuals, he looked down upon it from a pedigreed perch in the Anglo-Saxon gentility. He was dismayed to find England becoming more and more like the United States—a democracy exalting number, replacing class with mass, subjecting landed property to industrial wealth, and submerging old graces, guidance, and beliefs in a rising flotsam of commercialism, crudity, and petty purposes erased by death.

In that mood—and during a convalescence from a nervous break-down—he wrote the most famous poem of our time. He submitted the manuscript of *The Waste Land* to Pound, who performed upon it what he called a "Caesarian operation," cutting out almost half the lines. Then the lusty surgeon sent the torso to various editors, calling it "a masterpiece, one of the world's most important nineteen pages in English."[2] When it appeared in print (1922) it was dedicated by Eliot to "Ezra Pound, *il miglior fabbro*" (the better workman). Some of its obscurity may be due to Ezra's elisions; most of it, apparently, was born of Eliot's fond erudition, which he tried to clarify in appended notes. The poet deliberately teased the reader by multiplying assumptions and curtailing transitions, challenging him to recall or supply them, and so cooperate in the composition. In Part V he darkened the obscure by omitting punctuation. He described objects and ideas by sly indirection; he chose startling adjectives, incongruous combinations, recondite metaphors; he preferred to establish a mood rather than to state a fact. Like the abstract painter he felt that art need not convey meanings; it need only stir the imagination with suggestive imagery. "It is a test," he wrote, "that genuine poetry can communicate before it is understood."[3] Connoisseurs of verse recognized in Eliot's experiments a legacy from the French Symbolists, from Baudelaire, Mallarmé, and Rimbaud; Eliot himself traced the subtle irony and conversational tone of his lines to the poems of Jules Laforgue.[4]

The theme of *The Waste Land* was that in contemporary civilization all standards of beauty and taste, all incentives to moderation or nobility, all encouragement of far-sighted statesmanship, had been lost in the pursuit of size, number, production, wealth, success, and popularity. Eliot, a timid and sheltered spirit, breathing with difficulty the sooty fog and chaotic crowds of London, longed for what he imagined England had been—an orderly rural regime in which the peasant respectfully accepted rule by the squire, the squire by his lord, the lord by his king. He felt (as Carlyle had felt eighty years before) that he would have been happier on a medieval farm than in an industrial society noisy with cobblestones and noisome with slums. "What are the roots that clutch, what branches grow/Out of this stony rubbish?"[5] In the "Unreal City" surrounding him nearly all souls seemed dead:

> *I see crowds of people, walking round in a ring . . .*
> *A crowd flowed over London Bridge, so many,*
> *I had not thought death had undone so many.*[6]

And as this last line, taken from Dante,[7] suggested to the literate that London was hell, so in Section III Eliot took a line from Spenser's *Prothalamion* to describe, by contrast with its current pollution, the cleanness of the Thames in Elizabethan days:

> *Sweet Thames, run softly till I end my song.*
> *The river bears no empty bottles, sandwich papers,*
> *Silk handkerchiefs, cardboard boxes, cigarette ends*
> *Or other testimony of summer nights.*
> *By the restless waters of Leman I sat down and wept.*[8]

The Waste Land delighted the literary world from London to San Francisco. The annual *Dial* prize was given to Eliot in 1922 chiefly for this poem. The "lost generation," which had forfeited its religious faith through science and its democratic faith through war, accepted the poem as its theme song; radicals hailed it as the death knell of capitalism; tired souls found in it a threnody of their fatigue; religious spirits welcomed it as a repudiation of this lamentable world. Eliot himself, in 1931, questioned this interpretation. "When I wrote a poem called *The Waste Land* some of the more approving critics said I had expressed the 'disillusionment of a generation,' which is nonsense. I may have expressed for them their illusion of being disillusioned, but that did not form part of my intention."[9] Nevertheless, three years after *The Waste Land*, he echoed it in "The Hollow Men," an unpunctuated litany of decay:

> *We are the hollow men*
> *We are the stuffed men*
> *Leaning together*
> *Headpiece filled with straw. Alas! . . .*
> *This is the way the world ends*
> *Not with a bang but with a whimper.*

Meanwhile the atomic scientists, without a whimper, prepared a bang.

II. THE CONSERVATIVE

There is a note of consolatory superiority in Eliot's whimper: the world and its struggling souls fell so lamentably far beneath genteel taste and wistful hope. Perhaps *The Waste Land* is the jeremiad of a bank clerk walking daily, wearily to his work, swinging his umbrella or dodging the rain, and warming himself with visions of Elizabethan courts or feudal halls. Contemporaries described the new poet as "tall, lean, and hollow cheeked, dressed in the formal manner appropriate to his daytime occupation in Lloyd's Bank; . . . generally silent but with a smile that was as shy as it was friendly."[10] "His strong-set aquiline features and his well set-up figure were observed to advantage in the traditional costume of bowler [derby] hat, black coat and striped trousers."[11] He considered his own features to be "of clerical cut," and Pound in the *Cantos* called him "the Rev. Eliot."

Finding his daily dealing with pounds, shillings, and pence a discouragement to poetry, Eliot, as he advanced in years, reconciled himself to prose and punctuation, and determined to answer the question that his admirers were putting to him: How shall we cure this bourgeois hollowness, this cosmic weariness, this vain whoring with the gilded goddesses of decay? He met the challenge in a series of brilliant essays that phrased in classic style a conservative philosophy; he rose like another Burke to oppose with eloquence the Foxes and revolutions of his day. In October, 1922, he assumed the editorship of a new magazine, *The Criterion,* and made it an influential organ of his creed.

He took his lead from Charles Maurras, a French Catholic who had written: "The ideas stemming from the [French] Revolution—democracy, liberal Protestantism, and Romanticism—degraded the three fundamental characteristics of French civilization: monarchy, Catholic sentiment, and the classical spirit." Eliot frankly acknowledged his debt: "I have been a reader of the work of Maurras for eighteen years." Hence, in his 1928 preface to an essay "For Lancelot Andrewes," he summarized his point of view as "classicist in literature, royalist in politics, and anglo-catholic in religion." Liberals and radicals, shocked by this candid reaction, now mourned him as a lost leader. In a reissue (1936) of "For Lancelot Andrewes" Eliot omitted the disconcerting preface on the ground that it had "more than served its turn," and had misled many readers into supposing that in his mind "all these three [positions] are inextricable and of equal importance."[12] Now he wished to stress religion.

Meanwhile he spoke his mind forcibly on literature. In an extreme reaction against Romanticism he rejected Byron as "uninteresting," Shelley and Keats as overrated, Tennyson and Swinburne as sentimental. He called *Hamlet* "an artistic failure," rejected Milton as unsatisfactory," and rated Goethe as a mere dabbler in poetry and philosophy;[13] however, he commended Dryden, who had embraced the Catholic faith (the most romantic epic of all). He defined the classic mood as "the adult mind, thoroughly realist—without illusions, without daydreams, without hope, without bitterness, and with an abundant resignation"[14]

Feeling that the foundations of social order were cracking under his feet, Eliot called for a moratorium on individualism and revolt, and for a better understanding of the saving role played in history by tradition and leadership. He admitted that reason must reserve the right to question tradition, for "in even the very best living tradition there is always a mixture of good and bad, and much that deserves criticism."[15] But tradition is the vital trunk of the tree of life; it is the center and source from whose sap and fibers experimental branches can venture unsupported into space; branches may survive or perish, but the trunk must be preserved if the tree is not to die. Tradition is not mere repetition or imitation; it does not mean standing still; it is a living continuity, a sound and orderly growth, "a means by which the vitality of the past enriches the life of the present."[16]

Culture is the cultivation of a plant or a garden, not the eradication of its roots; it is an understanding of the roots and the seeds, their patient care and instructed nourishment, the removal of the weeds that would impede or distort development. Culture is not knowledge, nor is it art; still less is it "knowledge *about* culture"—acquaintance with literature and art. "By culture I mean first of all what the anthropologists mean: the way of life of a particular people living together in one place. That culture is made visible in their arts, in their social system, in their habits and customs, in their religion."[17] It is an aggregate of customs, institutions, manners, standards, tastes, morals, and beliefs. Now, these are transmitted rather by the family than by the school; hence "when family life fails to play its part we must expect our culture to deteriorate."[18] It is "a delusion [to think] that the maladies of the modern world can be put right by a system of instruction";[19] on the contrary, universal education, by lowering morals, standards, and tastes to a common denominator, and by sharpening the wits rather than disciplining character, tends to break down existing checks and balances, "destroying our ancient edifices to make ready the ground upon which the barbarian nomads of the future will encamp in their mechanized caravans."[20] Education should be the drawing forth of potential values; it should not be the destruction of the safeguards that tradition places around young egos naturally inclined to willful and precarious flights.

The resurgence of barbarism has been made possible by the triumph of the industrial middle class over the landed aristocracy. "We are being made aware that the organization of society on the principle of private profit, as well as public destruction, is leading both to the deformation of humanity by unregulated industrialism, and the exhaustion of natural resources; and that a good deal of our material progress is a progress for which succeeding generations may have to pay dearly."[21] When Socialists concluded that industry should be regulated or operated by government, Eliot replied that more government would be no cure, since the evils of industrialism are due to a human nature tainted by original sin. He preferred the plantation culture of the Southern United States to the industrial civilization of the North, and called the Civil War "the greatest disaster in the whole of American history."[22]

He expected no long duration of democracy, for he thought of it as government by middle-class leaders hampered by the intellectual immaturity of their constituents; "at the moment when public interest is aroused, the public is never well enough informed to have the right to an opinion."[23] This defect can be mitigated, but never cured, by general and secular education, for this sharpens the intellect far more than it trains character. Moreover, superior ability is not always superiority of intellect; it may be due to better heredity or a favorable environment; hence "a happy combination of privilege and opportunity" is preferable to a system of equal opportunity for all. Equality of opportunity is an "ideal which can only be fully realized when the institution of the family is no longer respected"—i.e., when the natural inequality of ability or wealth among families is artificially prevented from resulting in inequality of opportunity among children.[24] But such prevention is seldom practicable, and never permanent.

Aristocracy of some kind, Eliot believed, is natural and desirable. He rejected caste, but he considered it inevitable that a society would group its manual workers, its farmers, its scientists, its artists, its men of letters, its men of public affairs, in loosely distinguished classes, each with its own culture, its own virtues, capacities, and needs. Classes should mingle at will, and there should be "constant additions and defections" to or from the dominant minority; but "on the whole it would appear for the best that the great majority of human beings should go on living in the places in which they were born"; only so can the family function as an institution for the formation of character and the maintenance of social order. Government should be guided by a trained and privileged minority, it should be headed by a king, and it should be supported by a national church.

The radical error of the radical is his failure to understand the role

of religion in giving supernatural sanction to our frail moral code, and
in buttressing that social order which, in almost every hour of our days,
is assailed by the deep-rooted unsocial instincts of mankind. Eliot sig-
nalized his own convictions in 1927 by assuming British citizenship and
being confirmed in the Church of England. In 1930, in a poem called
"Ash Wednesday," he offered to the Virgin Mary his penitence for
years of addiction to worldly interests; and in a fuguelike litany
counterpointing lauds and griefs, he proclaimed his conviction that only
religion could save man from insignificance, and civilization from death.

In 1934 he delivered at the University of Virginia three lectures
which were later published as *After Strange Gods*. Deeply influenced
by Pascal's *Pensées*, he accepted as his basic premise that only a belief
in God could uphold man in his conflict with sin and his terror of
death. A philosophy founded upon rationalism or science can never
satisfy mankind, for it reveals death as the final fact in biology and
history. Machiavelli properly assumed the baseness of human nature;[25]
man is by nature inclined to actions that violate and sap social order;
this is what Christian theologians have meant by original sin. The
Church met this condition by teaching that a soul can be cleansed of
sin by divine grace conveyed by priestly ministrations and awesome
ritual. Those who believed were comforted and were encouraged to
decency.

Eliot saw no likelihood that Protestantism would revive sufficiently
to serve as a savior of civilization. "Liberal Protestant theology . . . is
Protestant theology in its last agonies";[26] its doctrine of predestination
had lost the power to convince, and its remnant of ritual had ceased
to awe. The Reformation, according to Eliot, was a mistake; that
"rending of the seam of the garment of Christ" (the division of
Christianity into sects) brought "the disintegration of European culture."[27] "I prefer the culture which produced Dante to the culture
which produced Shakespeare."[28] The Anglican convert so often quoted
Roman Catholic ideas, hymns, ceremonies, prayers that we suspect in
him a secret longing to join the Roman Church as the strongest spiritual
bulwark against social chaos, aesthetic barbarism, and mental despair.
(Why, then, so many Communists in Catholic Italy and France, so few
in Protestant England?) He agreed with the Roman Church that "the
virtue of tolerance is greatly overrated, and I have no objection to
being called a bigot."[29] "Every effort must be made to instill orthodoxy."[30] Education should be restored to the Church, for "education
is from top to bottom religious, or it is not education," and "the universities are too far gone in secularization."[31] "Unless by civilization

you mean material progress, cleanliness, etc., . . . if you mean a spiritual and intellectual co-ordination on a high level, then it is doubtful whether civilization can endure without religion, and religion without a church."[32] "I do not believe that the culture of Europe could survive the complete disappearance of the Christian faith. . . . If Christianity goes, the whole of our culture goes. . . . The world is trying the experiment of attempting to form a civilized but non-Christian mentality. The experiment will fail."[33]

III. THE DRAMATIST

Eliot reaffirmed his religious faith in two plays that showed not only a subtle and versatile wit but considerable and successful dramatic art.

Murder in the Cathedral was written for the Canterbury Festival of 1935, which commemorated the assassination (1170) of Saint Thomas à Becket by four knights of Henry II's court. The form of the play united Catholic history and feeling with Greek theatrical technique; it allowed the Archbishop to expound his theology and philosophy in speeches too long for drama, but it achieved unusual dramatic effect by using the nave, as well as the sanctuary, of the great cathedral as the scene of the action. The armed knights force entry at the portal, make their way up the aisle through the spectators, and desecrate the altar with their language and fury. The assassination, however, is not represented on the sanctuary stage; it is narrated with horror, and in classic style, by a chorus of women; "human kind cannot bear very much reality."[34] These choral odes contain some of Eliot's best poetry, unwontedly intelligible.

The Cocktail Party (1949), written in prosaic verse, elevates to drama the most wearisome of modern spectacles; polite society, using whiskey to ease strange animals, cutely dressed, down cultured throats, is here titillated with scandal and alarmed by sanctity. Lavinia Chamberlayne, tired of twaddle and the pursuit of wealth, walks out from her husband's life into a promiscuous and disintegrating world. Edward, abandoned and brooding, gives a definition of hell wisely antipodal to that which we shall find in Sartre's *No Exit:* "What is hell? Hell is oneself, hell is alone." One of the cocktail guests, Celia Coplestone, thinks hell is a life of sophisticated skepticism, cautious hypocrisy, and meaningless futility; she feels a sense of sin, of selfish alienation from other souls and their sufferings; she longs for a dedication that will give her existence some excuse and significance; "I could do without everything, put up with anything, if I might cherish it."[35] She enlists for service as a nurse in Central Africa; the natives kill and mutilate her. The news of this finale leaves the cocktail party with a moment's awareness of itself as the absurd symbol of a superficial life.

Eliot does not seem to have found much comfort in the religion that he professed, for his final productions were obsessed with a sense of helplessness and death unrelieved by any perceivable hope of an after and lovelier life. In 1943 he issued *Four Quartets*, in which peaks of poetry were separated by depressions of verse distinguished from prose only by the printer. In the first of these quadruplets, "Burnt Norton" (a manor in Gloucestershire), he delved into a Proustian mysticism of time, and emerged with a determinism and fatalism echoing *The Rubaiyat* and *Finnegans Wake:*

> . . . the end precedes the beginning,
> And the end and the beginning were always there
> Before the beginning and after the end
> And all is always now . . .[36]

In "East Coker" (a family estate) Eliot visioned time as a mercilessly destructive force. He saw houses and cities crumbling and burning, he contemplated people eating, drinking, marrying, breeding, dying, and he saw nothing in the human condition except "dung and death." He found no wisdom in old age, but wisely reckoned that love is wiser than wisdom. In "The Dry Salvages" (a group of rocks on a Massachusetts coast beaten by the wind) the dirge continued:

> There is no end of it, the voiceless wailing.
> No end to the withering of withered flowers,
> To the movement of pain that is painless and motionless,
> To the drift of the sea and the drifting wreckage,
> The bone's prayer to Death its God.[37]

And in number four, "Little Gidding" (an Anglican parish), the final message is: "You are not here to verify" or to know the answers to your questions; "you are here to kneel"—to respond to the mystery with love, humility, and prayer.

This harping on pain, grief, death, and happiness beyond the grave does not appeal to a man whose stomach is flourishing, whose heart is pumping steadily, and who has found that outgoing love brings love in return. Some lines in *The Cocktail Party* suggest a narrowing, astringent self-absorption:

> *Can we only love*
> *Something created by our own imagination?*
> *Are we all in fact unloving and unlovable?*
> *Then one is alone.*[38]

He could not have been quite alone, or very thorough in his pessimism, for after the death of his first wife he married again, taking at sixty-eight a lady of twenty-nine.[39] He mourned the Americanization of Europe, but he was glad when American industry, producing planes by the minute, saved Western Europe in World War II. He became an air-raid warden and served faithfully on civic committees; he forgot himself and enlarged himself into a citizen. In 1948 he received the Nobel Prize for Literature; thereafter he lived seven years to enjoy his select but spreading fame. Prosperous poets in England and the United—especially the Southern—States accepted him as their leader, and some of them declared proud war upon commas, capitals, and commoners. But his quondam impresario, Ezra Pound, rejected his summons to lords and altars, and the new generation of writers that survived the Second World War looked rather to the *Communist Manifesto* than to the Westminster Confession or the Apostles' Creed. The God of his fathers had preceded Eliot to the grave.

CHAPTER VIII

Somerset Maugham

DURING his ninety-one years William Somerset Maugham wrote almost a hundred novels, short stories, and plays. I have read only three of the novels and two of the short stories, and have seen none of the plays except a filmed *Quartet*. I find it hard to tramp through every page of a novel; the actual world seems to me so inexhaustibly interesting that I grudge the time required for exploring the imaginary scenes and characters invented by novelists, unless these creations add to my understanding or appreciation of reality—as with Fielding, Dickens, Thackeray, Stendhal, Flaubert, Balzac, Dostoevski, Tolstoi, Goethe, Mann. I enjoyed *Of Human Bondage* mostly because it was a disguised picture of Maugham's youth, and *The Moon and Sixpence* because it offered one side of Paul Gauguin; but I found *Cakes and Ale* to be petit fours and small beer, and *The Razor's Edge* remains unread. However, when I opened *The Summing Up*—the mirror of a modest mind—I felt that I had hold of a man, and I read every word. Here, as with Gide and Mann, the author was more fascinating than his books.

He had the advantage of belonging to a distinguished family, which traced itself back to a brother of King Edward I. It had produced noted churchmen and barristers; William's brother Frederick became a viscount and a lord chancellor of England; and Frederick's son Robin is a successful author. William's father was a prosperous solicitor attached to the British Embassy in Paris; his mother was a woman of culture, who entertained half the dignitaries of the French capital. She was beautiful, consumptive, and extravagant; her husband was ugly, industrious, and economical; William took after his father.

He was born on January 25, 1874, in Paris but in the British Embassy —so ensuring his British citizenship. His native tongue was French; he received English lessons from a tutor; his mind was European. He saw little of his father, much of his mother; he loved her intensely; and when she died (1882) in giving birth to her sixth child her disappearance left upon "Willie's" spirit a cloud that never cleared. Till his death he kept a picture of her on a table beside his bed, as if, like Proust, he needed her benediction before he could sleep. Perhaps, like Proust, he loved his mother so much that he could never really love a woman again.

In 1884 the father died. So much of his earnings had gone to supporting a luxurious home that little remained to be divided among his children; each received £150 a year. William, aged ten, was sent to live with his stern, pious, self-absorbed uncle, the Reverend Henry Maugham, Anglican vicar of Whitstable, near Canterbury. From this point onward Somerset told his own story in *Of Human Bondage*. He changed Whitstable to Blackstable, Henry Maugham to William Carey, and himself to Philip Carey. William suffered to the end of his life from a stammer that poisoned almost all his social relations; the novel changes this handicap to Philip's clubfoot. In *The Summing Up* Maugham recorded his childhood disabilities, and their psychological results:

> I was small; I had endurance but little physical strength; I stammered; I was shy; I had poor health. I had no faculty for games, which play so great a part in the normal life of Englishmen; and I had, whether for any of these reasons or from nature I do not know, an instinctive shrinking from my fellow men. . . . I have loved individuals; I have never much cared for men in the mass. . . . I have never liked anyone at first sight; I do not think I have ever addressed someone I did not know in a railway carriage, or spoken to a fellow passenger on board ship unless he first spoke to me. . . . I do not think I was a likable boy.[1]

After three years of fretting under the severity and sermons of the vicar, William was sent to King's School at Canterbury. There he failed as a student and suffered from the teasing and bullying of the boys. He persuaded his uncle to let him study for a year at Heidelberg (1891), where at last he found tolerance and some happiness. He took a course in philosophy under the famous Kuno Fischer, discovered a soul kindred to his own in Schopenhauer, and began a lifelong love of Spinoza.

Returning to London, he faced unwillingly the choice of a career. He could not, like his relatives, go into the church or the law; these professions were closed to him by his stammer. In 1892 he entered the medical school attached to St. Thomas's Hospital in Lambeth, South London. There, for five years, he studied medicine, learned scientific method, adopted materialism and determinism,[2] read a multitude of books, and had a bitter view of poverty in the capital of British wealth. "I had to attend a certain number of confinements to get a certificate, and this meant going into the slums of Lambeth, often into foul courts that the police hesitated to enter, but in which my black bag amply protected me. . . . I do not know a better training for a writer than to spend some years in the medical profession."[3] There he might see with objectivity the poverty underlying opulence, the waste product of the social organism, the battle of life against hunger, ignominy, and death.

In 1897 Maugham received his medical certificate and published a novel. *Liza of Lambeth* described the slums and tragedies that environed the hospital and the school, and did so with such fidelity that his readers were unwillingly fascinated and his relatives were shocked and appalled. Did not this twenty-three-year-old stammerer know that those slums were the natural result of the incompetence of their denizens, and that no civilized person would bring up such subjects in a decent book or home? *Liza* was denounced as obscene because it revealed the loose sexual relations of the slum dwellers, and the unhygienic conditions and avoidable sufferings of childbirth. So the novel sold, and Somerset Maugham decided to be a writer instead of a physician.

Now, though already a success, he carefully trained and disciplined himself for authorship. He studied the sciences and history to learn more of the world and man. He read the most acclaimed novelists and analyzed their methods of structure, characterization and style. But he failed for many years to repeat his initial triumph. Between 1897 and 1914 he wrote ten novels, none of which paid the cost of its composition and publication. He had better fortune with plays; the cleverness of their plots and the vivacity of their dialogue pleased the public; after six failures he turned up a trump with *Lady Frederick* (1907); thereafter he scored so frequently on the stage that at one time he had four comedies running simultaneously in London theaters. A cartoon in *Punch* showed William Shakespeare biting his fingers in envy before a billboard advertising these simultaneous plays. They received no critical acclaim, and found no lasting place in the history of literature, but they kept Maugham in comfort while he strove to polish his art as an author of fiction. "I did not take to writing seriously till I had had much experience as a dramatist, and this experience taught me to leave out everything that did not serve the dramatic value of my story."[4]

World War I threatened to end his literary career. He volunteered, served as an ambulance driver, and then became a secret agent for the Intelligence Department. A winter in Switzerland brought him down with consumption. Thinking to find health in the South Pacific, he crossed the Atlantic, assisted in producing two of his plays in America, and sailed from San Francisco (1916) for Tahiti, where he laid up impressions for *The Moon and Sixpence.*

And yet it was not that book that now simmered in his brain. He could dash off elegant short stories about incidents in his travels, but he found that he could write most vividly about the basic situations that had molded his own career and character. Many of his experiences had left him bitter memories; perhaps he could reduce their sting by viewing them as the mishaps of another soul, or of a self that had been outgrown and replaced. So he wrote *Of Human Bondage* (1915). The title was lifted from the heading of Book IV in Spinoza's *Ethics*, where it meant the enslavement that man suffers by letting emotion dominate reason in responding to events. The novel was essentially an autobiography except for Philip Carey's brush with art in Paris, and his sudden, happy marriage. Maugham could not put his wounded heart into that cheerful finale, and it hangs precariously on the tail of the tale. The book is not high literature; it does not hold attention through depth of thought, nobility of feeling, or excellence of style; it is, however, a faithful and unpretentious record of a soul's development.

Maugham's own marriage was not idyllic. He appears to have had sexual relations, on and off, for eight years with a young woman portrayed as Rosie in *Cakes and Ale,* but when he proposed marriage she rejected him. In 1913 he took as mistress Mrs. Syrie Barnardo Wellcome, a sprightly divorcee; in 1915 she bore a child which he accepted as his; in 1916 he married her. Thereafter, till 1927, he spent half of each year with her in London, and the other half in travel or diplomatic service; we do not know whether she resented or enjoyed these annual separations.

In 1917 he was sent by the British government on a secret mission to St. Petersburg "with unlimited money at my disposal," and with instructions "to keep Russia in the war, and prevent the Bolsheviks, supported by the Central Powers, from seizing power."[5] The Bolsheviks were too much for him; "I failed lamentably." Tuberculosis gripped him again, and he was sent to a sanitarium in Scotland (1917–18). Meanwhile the success of his plays had given him economic independence. Eager to study diverse nations and men, he traveled to China (1919), and, between 1920 and 1930, wandered deviously over half the globe. Twice he nearly died of fever, once he was shot at by bandits, once he was nearly drowned. Though these adventures confirmed his morose view of human nature, they enriched his memory with a hundred places and faces that were later to lend life and color to his books. "I have been interested in men in general not for their own sake but for the sake of my work. I have not, as Kant enjoined, regarded each man as an end in himself, but as material that might be helpful to me as a writer"[6]—though here perhaps he exaggerated his selfishness. Usually in these travels he was accompanied by his young American cousin, Gerald Haxton, as secretary. Gerald arranged transportation and accommodations, and his amiable, volatile disposition solaced Maugham's melancholy moods. Maugham learned to love him, perhaps beyond accepted mores, and became almost dependent upon him. When England banned Haxton from its shores for some obscure fracas, Somerset went with him, and lived the remainder of his life abroad.[7]

Turning reality into fiction, he loosely united, in his next outstanding novel, his adventures in marriage and in the South Pacific. The first part of *The Moon and Sixpence* (1919) describes the desertion of a charming and popular wife by a husband tired of London society and enamored of art; the second tells the story of Paul Gauguin under the name of Charles Strickland. He is described as completely selfish, insulting, and cynical; he shows no remorse for taking his best friend's wife from him, nor for soon thereafter driving her to suicide; his standard greeting is "Go to hell," and his philosophy of anything but art is "I don't give a damn." His strong aesthetic sense does not include cleanliness. He goes for months without a woman, and then erupts in an explosion of unscrupulous sexuality. But there is an heroic side to him. He is devoted to painting, and makes no concession of his tastes, principles, or methods to academies or popularity; he hardly bothers to sell his pictures. He works hard, lives near starvation, and cannot bear the noise, materialism, hypocrisy, and human exploitation in European civilization. Suddenly he turns his back upon Paris and goes off to Tahiti. There he lives like a native, paints like a madman, and dies of leprosy. We can hardly believe that Gauguin—or anyone—was as hard and coarse as Strickland, but Maugham insists. "It seems strange even to myself, when I have described a man who was cruel, brutal, and sensual, to say that he was a great idealist. The fact remains."[8] And, sympathizing with Strickland's sexual periodicity, Maugham writes:

> After a strong abstinence from sex, all of a sudden you can't stand
> any more. . . . You find some woman, coarse and low and vulgar,

some beastly creature in whom all the horror of sex is blatant, and
you fall upon her like a wild animal. You drink till you are blind
with rage. . . . I'll tell you what must seem strange, that when it's
over you feel so extraordinarily pure. You feel like a disembodied
spirit, immaterial. . . . You feel like God.[9]

It is a comfort to know that so clever a man can talk such nonsense.

We excuse him, for he was prevented by his nature or his development from experiencing the full rewards of lasting heterosexual love.
He was uncomfortable with women, and, in the second half of his life,
he beat them back with an almost savage discourtesy. To one who gave
him an unwelcome kiss he publicly expressed his profound sorrow
at learning that she had lost all her money (she had not); to another
he demanded, "If you don't take off your clothes I shan't come to
lunch";[10] these stories, however, we have on the sole authority of his
nephew Robin. Maugham was probably expressing his own view when
he made Strickland say:

> Because women can do nothing except love they've given it a
> ridiculous importance. They want to persuade us that it is the whole
> of life. It is an insignificant part. I know lust. That is normal and
> healthy. Love is a disease. . . . When a woman loves you she is not
> satisfied until she possesses your soul. Because she's weak she has a
> rage for domination, and nothing less will satisfy her. She has a
> small mind, and she resents the abstract which she is unable to
> grasp.[11]

To which the narrator adds: "There are few men to whom love is the
most important thing in the world, and they are not very interesting
ones; even women, with whom the subject is of paramount interest,
have contempt for them."[12]

Somerset tried to the end of his life to conceal from the public his
preference for young men, but his homosexuality became obvious to
his intimates. "In Siam they're sensible," he told his nephew. "They
don't regard homosexuality as anything abnormal. They accept it as
something perfectly natural. . . . And I believe that one day people
will realize that there are people who are *born* homosexual. And there's
nothing whatsoever that they can do about it."[13]

We cannot say, though it is very likely, that his sexual deviation
caused the breakup of his marriage; nor do we know how just was his
suspicion that the daughter whom he had accepted was another man's
child. In any case Syrie divorced him in 1927, and he retired to the

French Riviera. There, a year later, he bought for £7,000 the Villa Mauresque, on a promontory reaching out to the Mediterranean between Monte Carlo and Villefranche; the house and gardens were valued at £500,000 at his death.[14] He found a new secretary, Alan Searles, who took care of him with loving patience; and there principally Maugham remained till his death, except for World War II, during which he found refuge in a home provided for him in South Carolina by his American publishers.

His basic solace was his work. He produced two more successful novels—*Cakes and Ale* (1930) and *The Razor's Edge* (1944). I did not appreciate the earlier of these, because I did not have a "key" to the living characters it satirized. In those days Maugham's chief rival in British fiction was Hugh Walpole, whom he demolished under the name of Alroy Kear. "I could think of no one among my contemporaries who had achieved so considerable a position on so little talent."[15] However, it is not pleasant to hear a man belittle his competitors.

The short stories are more delectable, for in that field Maugham was for a generation accounted supreme. He described the form carefully: "The short story [is] a narrative of a single event, material or spiritual, to which, by the elimination of everything . . . not essential to its elucidation, a dramatic unity could be given."[16] He derived his art in this field from Maupassant; he refused to follow a current trend toward the Chekhov style of story, which pictured a mood rather than an event. I found "The Alien Corn" interesting, except for its improbable ending; and the same demurrer would apply to "Rain."

This famous piece first appeared in 1921 as "Miss Thompson" in a volume called *The Trembling of a Leaf*. Sadie is a boisterous woman who runs through men as Maugham ran through stories. She is one of a group of Caucasians stranded by persistent rain in Pago Pago, in the Samoas. Another among the wayfarers is the Reverend Mr. Davidson, a missionary returning from the Solomon Islands. He has found the natives there "so naturally depraved that they could not be brought to see their own wickedness." "We" (he and his devout wife) "had to make sins out of what they thought were natural actions. We had to make it a sin not only to commit adultery, and to lie and thieve, but to expose their bodies, and to dance, and not to come to church. I made it a sin for a girl to show her bosom, and a sin for a man not to wear trousers. . . . When we went there they had no sense of sin at all."[17] He resolves to convert Miss Thompson to virtue. He comes to her room night after night with a new sermon; his wife warns him not to go too near the fire; he persists, and is thrilled by the rising warmth; he dreams of twin mountains in Nebraska, which someone in his hearing had likened to a woman's breasts. He comes to Sadie one night too often. The next morning he drowns himself.

Of all Maugham's books I like best *The Summing Up* (1938). Here, with delightful candor and simplicity, he reviewed his history as an author, and the development of his philosophy. He was sixty-three when the volume was published; he wrote "in expectation of death"; it never occurred to him that he would live twenty-eight years more. He warns us not to expect a full exposure: "I know that if I set down every action in my life and every thought that has crossed my mind, the world would consider me a monster of depravity."[18] He makes a few doubtful statements ("The common idea that success spoils people by making them vain, egotistic, and self-complacent is erroneous"[19]); but he comforts prisoners of the pen with a revealing paragraph:

> The disadvantages and dangers of the author's calling are offset by an advantage so great as to make all its difficulties, disappointments, and maybe hardships, unimportant. It gives him spiritual freedom. To him life is a tragedy, and by his gift of creation he enjoys the catharsis, the purging of pity and terror, which Aristotle tells us is the object of art. For his sins and his follies, the unhappiness that befalls him, his unrequited love, his physical defects, illness, privation, his hopes abandoned, his griefs, humiliations, everything is transformed by his power into material, and by writing it he can overcome it. Everything is grist to his mill, from a glimpse of a face in the street to a war that convulses the civilized world, from the scent of a rose to the death of a friend. Nothing befalls him that he cannot transmute into a stanza, a song, or a story, and having done this be rid of it. The artist is the only free man.[20]

He did not quite shed his aches by putting upon them the amalgam of his imagination and his memory; those handicaps and griefs survived and wrote their history upon his face. In his later years he was cursed not only with deep wrinkles, sallow cheeks, and sad, tired eyes, but with lines that accentuated the bitterness of his memories and the cynicism of his views. He was too short to redeem his physiognomy with his stature, but he graced his figure with elegant dress and velvet shoes bearing his monogram in gold braid.[21] Behind the hard features was a man capable of tender feelings and sentimental tears as well as of undying resentment and morose misanthropy. A face can be a mask as well as a revelation.

He was proud of his achievement, tended to snobbery, and liked to tell—with some envy—of his rich acquaintances. "You see," he told his nephew, "though I am a millionaire, I am a *very poor* millionaire compared to some of my millionaires here at the Cap."[22] He tried to observe, rather than to judge, mankind, but "I have no natural trust in others. I am more inclined to expect them to do ill rather than to do good."[23] He did not soon forgive injuries; he could keep a hatred burning till and beyond death. He never absolved his wife for the harm he believed she had done him; when he heard that she had died (1955) he sang, "Tra-la-la-la; no more alimony."[24] He made no claims to good humor. "My sympathies are limited . . . I am not a social person. I cannot get drunk and feel a great love for my fellow men. Convivial amusement has always somewhat bored me. . . . I have never sung a hymn. I do not much like being touched, and I have always to make a slight effort over myself not to draw back when someone links his arm in mine."[25] "I find social intercourse fatiguing. . . . To me conversation has always been an effort. When I was young and stammered, to talk for long . . . exhausted me, and even now that I have to some extent cured myself, it is a strain. It is a relief when I can get away and read a book."[26] He was usually courteous, but he had many moments of hot temper. He confessed "an irascibility that was a defect of nature."[27] In his old age he told his nephew, "I've been a horrible and evil man. Every single one of the few people who have ever got to know me well has ended by hating me";[28] but again we have only Robin's word for this extreme self-abasement. Those who, like Gerald Haxton and Alan Searles, could adjust themselves to his sexual orientation, learned to see the suffering behind these faults.

His homosexuality, probably more than his stutter, was the root of his asperity and unhappiness. "My greatest mistake" was that "I tried to persuade myself that I was three quarters normal and that only a quarter of me was queer—whereas it was the other way round."[29] He struggled almost every hour against the bitterness that his handicaps and humiliations had bred. The same sensibility that intensified his slights and pains made him keen to the music of words, and enabled him to rise to sympathetic emotions. He often wept at pictures.[30] He longed for the affection that his face and mood repelled. He counted his pence carefully, but he gave substantial sums to that King's School where he had been so miserable in his youth, and he left bequests for aid to struggling authors.[31] He treasured his wealth as a prop to intellectual and social independence, but "I could part without a pang with every possession I have."[32]

His reading of Schopenhauer, at Heidelberg and afterward, gave him

a philosophical theory to fit his temper. He read all the major philosophers, and, like so many of us, felt especially the impact of Spinoza's
simple sincerity, clarity, and force. "I look upon my first reading of
Spinoza as one of the signal experiences of my life,"[33] but he never
attained Spinoza's equanimity and tolerance. He deplored the obscurity
that, since Kant, had muddied the stream of philosophic thoughts. "The
philosopher who will not take the trouble to make himself clear shows
only that he thinks his thoughts of no more than academic value."[34]

He became an atheist because he studied biology, medicine, and the
London slums, and because he felt upon his own flesh and spirit the
sting of unmerited misfortune. He could not, like Spinoza, transfer his
worship from God to Nature, for he found the new deity too ingenious
in devising calamities that multiplied man's griefs; indeed, she seemed
to "take sometimes a terrible delight in torturing her children."[35] Men
are the helpless victims of a universal determinism in which the ruling
trinity is not God the Father, the Son, and the Holy Ghost, but
heredity, environment, and circumstance. "I do not suppose men in past
centuries were any different from the men we know."[36] He could
discover no meaning in life,[37] but he thought there had been some
progress in history."[38] Whatever changes might come on the surface
of life, the permanence of man's basic drives and nature's incorrigible
propensities would leave the basic realities as before. So as early as 1918
he described the turmoil of today:

> Youth has turned to gods we of an earlier generation knew not,
> and it is possible to see already the direction in which those who
> come after us will move. The younger generations . . . have done
> with knocking at the door; they have burst in and seated themselves
> in our seats. The air is noisy with their shouts. Of their elders some,
> by imitating the antics of youth, strive to persuade themselves that
> their day is not yet over; they shout with the lustiest, but . . . they
> are like poor wantons attempting, with pencil, paint, and powder,
> with shrill gayety, to recover the illusion of their spring. The wiser
> go their way with a decent grace. In their chastened smile is an
> indulgent mockery. They remember that they too trod down a sated
> generation, with just such clamor and with just such scorn, and
> they foresee that these brave torch-bearers will presently yield their
> places also. There is no last word. The new evangel was old when
> Nineveh reared her greatness to the sky. These gallant words which
> seem so novel to those that speak them were said in accents changed
> a hundred times before. The pendulum swings backwards and for-
> wards. The circle is ever traveled anew.[39]

So Maugham took no part in movements for social reform. "I cannot doubt that the proletariat, increasingly conscious of its rights, will eventually seize power in one country after the other";[40] but he trusted that this deluge would be deferred till he had left the scene.

He did not enjoy life, but he was resolved to make himself comfortable while it lasted. At the Villa Mauresque he had six servants, four gardeners, and Alan Searles. In his old age he made a will leaving almost everything to Searles, and nothing to his presumptive daughter, Liza, who had always sided with her mother in the family quarrels. (The court later overruled the will.) At the age of ninety, Robin tells us, the world-famous author "suddenly buried his head in his hands. 'I've been a failure,' he stammered. 'The whole way through my life I've made mistake after mistake. I've had a wretched life. And I've made a hash of everything.' "[41] Time and again he thought of imitating his brother Harry, who had killed himself; but the instinct of self-preservation proved stronger than the lure of death. "If you believe in prayer," he said to his nephew, "then pray that I don't wake up in the morning."[42] The prayer was answered on December 16, 1965.

He was not such a failure as he supposed. He did not quite reach that summit of literary excellence which once may have been his dream; he recognized that he had remained in the second rank;[43] but in the short story his sharp skill and resolute fertility raised him to a generally acknowledged supremacy. He had talent, industry, and pertinacity, which in his view, and in sum, are close to genius.[44] He considered the elements of a good style to be simplicity, clarity, and euphony;[45] his own style had all these, but he lacked the kindly humor and tolerance that might have given his works a nobler excellence. He had to live without happiness because nature had punished him in advance of his sins, and it was not given him to learn that love and forgiveness are wiser than bitterness and revenge.

CHAPTER IX

Marcel Proust

WHEN T. S. Eliot first came to Paris in 1910 he was astonished by the "exciting variety of ideas" in the bubbling *pot au feu* of literary movements and magazines. The poets were still manufacturing symbols in the wake of Mallarmé, Romain Rolland was completing *Jean-Christophe*, Anatole France was feasting his old eyes on stereopticon nudes, the Sorbonne was warm with *la ferveur bergsonnienne;* "the predominance of Paris was incontestable."[1] The First World War diverted that energy from the cafés and salons to the rostrum and the battlefield, but when France emerged victorious the poets and proseurs broke out anew, though chastened by reality and bewildered by the death of God; the Bergsonian *élan* receded before existentialist *Angst*. Gide, Valéry, Claudel, "Céline," Cocteau, Camus, and Sartre raised their heads so that all the world could see. James Joyce was sending out from Paris flaming fragments of *Ulysses*, and Marcel Proust was publishing the strangest novel of the century.*

---

* *À la Recherche du temps perdu* ("In Search of Times Lost") appeared in sixteen volumes between 1913 and 1927. The admirable English translation (*Remembrance of Things Past*) appeared in eleven volumes, here listed with the original titles and dates in parentheses.
>   I, II. *Swann's Way* (*Du Côté de chez Swann*, 1913–14), Vols. I and II.
>   III, IV. *Within a Budding Grove* (*À l'Ombre des jeunes filles en fleurs*, 1919), Vols. I and II.
>   V, VI. *The Guermantes Way* (*Le Côté de Guermantes*, 1920–21), Vols. I and II.
>   VII, VIII. *Cities of the Plain* (*Sodome et Gomorrhe*, 1921–22), Vols. I and II.
>   IX. *The Captive* (*La Prisonnière*, 1924).
>   X. *The Sweet Cheat Gone* (*Albertine disparue*, 1925).
>   XI. *The Past Recaptured* (*Le Temps retrouvé*, 1927).

This essay will refer to the volumes of the English translation by their Roman numerals.

I. THE AUTHOR

Proust was born at Auteuil, Paris, July 10, 1871. He was baptized Valentin-Louis-Georges-Eugène-Marcel—some relatives had to be appeased, some saints had to be invoked. His father, Achille-Adrien Proust, was a distinguished physician, who was received into the Legion of Honor for his work in an epidemic of cholera, became inspector of public health, and taught that subject at the University of Paris. Marcel took from his father only an external acceptance of Catholic faith; he saw little of the busy surgeon, administrator, and professor. He grew up in the love and nearness of his mother, Jeanne-Clémence Weil, daughter of Nathé Weil, a wealthy Jewish broker. She had received considerable education; she knew English and German, read Shakespeare in the original, and played the piano well. Apparently Marcel derived from her his sensitivity, his sense of humor, his interest in literature and art. Almost until her death in 1905 he remained bound to her psychologically and financially. His novel begins with the story of his childhood dependence, for sleep and happiness, upon receiving his mother's good-night kiss; the remembrance of that ritual recurs again and again in his books. She in her turn was strongly and piously attached to her own mother, Madame Nathé Weil. Marcel followed her in this devotion, so that the death of his grandmother (1890) became a central event in his narrative. Often he visited, at Auteuil, his uncle Georges Weil, whose mistresses may have contributed to form Odette de Crécy. Marcel's boyhood friends were mostly Jewish; later his associates were predominantly Catholic, but he never forgot his Hebrew heritage. Though he satirized some unlikable Jews like Bloch, he supported the campaign for Dreyfus. He wrote letters of thanks to people who spoke well of Jews.

His adolescence was harassed by severe attacks of asthma and hay fever; after his tenth year he had to avoid all contact with nature during the spring. Digestive and other ailments weakened him. He needed and demanded attention and affection, and craved these from his mother especially. Often she slept in his room to quiet his fears; if she left home overnight he wept hysterically. He wrote long letters to her, and left them in the hall so that she would come upon them in the morning. Living mostly indoors, he read a great deal, and spent lonely hours in brooding introspection; at an early age he became adept in the analysis of sensations and feelings.

We can imagine the discomfort, almost desolation, of this frail, well-

mannered, well-dressed, almost girlish boy in his seven years of schooling at the Lycée Condorcet. The other students scorned him as a sissy
ripe for sexual inversion. One boy, whose hand he had seized in a
moment of ardor, shrank from him in revulsion; others repelled his
friendship with insults.[2] He fared better with the teachers, who recognized his painful sensitivity, his intellectual gifts, and his excellent
literary style. He bore those years bravely, and received his baccalaureate in 1889. In November he entered the Army as a volunteer, which
entitled him to leave after a year. He studied law, passed the examinations, and later received a degree in philosophy. He was now a handsome youth, with thick, unruly hair, dark and melancholy eyes, at once
proud and timid, jealous and kind. His associates admired his wit, but
were suspicious of the orchid that fluttered in his buttonhole. His
father urged him to establish some economic base for his life, and
Marcel appeased him by serving for six months in the Bibliothèque
Mazarin; but he avoided work as long as he could, being absorbed in
psychology, philosophy, literature, and sex.

He tried manfully to lose his virginity to the opposite sex, and
claimed to have succeeded at an early age;[3] however, no sexual autobiography is to be trusted. As a boy (he tells us) he fell in love with
Marie de Benardsky, and announced his readiness to die for her. Volume II of the *Remembrance* relates in fond introspective detail an
adolescent passion for "Gilberte," but we do not know how much of
that ecstasy was history, how much of it imagination. We may guess
that in those awakening years he passed through an idealistic heterosexual attachment (our "calf love"), before discovering that he was
increasingly attracted by boys. To a questionnaire received when he
was turning twenty, he replied: "The quality you most like in a man?
Feminine charm. The quality you most like in a woman? A man's
virtues, a frankness in friendship. What is your dream of happiness? I
really haven't the courage to say what it is, and if I did I should
probably destroy it by the mere fact of putting it into words."[4] He was
particularly attracted by Comte Robert de Montesquiou-Fazensac, who
perfumed his perversion with poetry. For a time Proust took him as a
model, and used him as a door to aristocratic salons. Later, having tired
of the Comte's poses and his appetite for flattery, he transformed him
relentlessly, through eight volumes, into the rich, cultured, and degraded homosexual Baron de Charlus.

These divagations created oppressive problems at home. Proust's
notebooks contain touching passages about the anguish and terror of a
homosexual youth struggling to conceal his condition, and his secret

adventures, from his parents and his normal friends. His play at love affairs with women may have been devices to disarm suspicion, especially by his mother. Inverts, he wrote, "are sons without mothers, because to their mothers they must lie their whole life long."[5] He postponed the writing of his masterpiece till both his parents had died, lest it should make desolate their old age by revealing his tragedy.

He pleased his parents by finding access, through his friends, his good manners, his culture, and the wealth of his family, to the most exclusive homes in Paris. He became enamored of the surviving aristocracy of France, among whom one's essence was his lineage; and the aura of ancestry, with finery of costume, ease of manners, and grace of carriage, took the place of physical beauty, moral courage, and intellectual power. Marcel, while praising solitude as the nurse of genius, left no wire unpulled to get invitations to exalted gatherings. The upper bourgeoisie, to which he belonged, recognized the class system as a prop of social order; his own father drew a careful line between those to whom he would talk and those "to whom he would never have dreamed of speaking."[6]

His parents had the distinction, in 1892, of entertaining a young professor named Henri Bergson, who had become a nephew by marriage, and therefore a cousin of Marcel. The youth took eagerly to the rising philosopher, and accepted the *élan vital* as a redeeming feature of a Nature often red in tooth and claw. He read the philosophical classics from Plato to Kant. He took from the German idealists a conviction that the objective world had no meaning or worth except through man's responses to it in feeling and thought; and he made this theory the cornerstone of his literary practice and creed. He loved literature more than philosophy, because it could dress philosophy with elegance and brighten it with imagination; he loved beauty more than truth, though he keenly felt its tragic brevity. He especially cultivated British authors. He relished Ruskin above the rest, for he knew enough English to catch Ruskin's aesthetic frenzy and the color of his prose. From him he learned to appreciate medieval art; he longed to visit Venice and Rouen, where he might check Ruskin's descriptions with every commemorated stone. With some help he translated two of Ruskin's volumes. He cherished the hope that someday he himself would be an author acclaimed by the educated world.

So in 1896 he arranged for the publication of a series of stories called *Les Plaisirs et les jours* (*Pleasures and Days*). It was a sad book, which almost pre-summarized Proust's life and art: its theme was the fading of pleasures and the disillusionment of the years; the best plan, said the

young pessimist, is to shun action, reject reality, and live in the ideal—
in our sensations, feelings, memories, ideas, hopes, and dreams. Here for
the first time appeared his mother's indispensable good-night kiss, with
stories of precipitate seductions, tortured romances, dull adulteries, consuming jealousies, and desperate suicides; add flowery descriptions, and
much psychology of love. — At the salon of Madame de Caillavet he had
met Anatole France (who was to become the Bergotte of *À la
Recherche*[7]); at Marcel's urging Madame asked her lion to write a
preface for *Les Plaisirs;* Anatole sampled the pages, detected decadence,
and protested against a rambling and formless style quite opposed to his
own forms of clarity, simplicity, precision, and melody; in the end
Madame de Caillavet wrote the preface herself, Anatole added a line
here and there, and signed his name, perhaps on the theory that a lie
told for a lady is a sacrament of grace.

The sale of *Plaisirs* was not encouraging to the author or his parents.
They urged him to enter the business world; he pleaded his ailments
as excuse for staying at home, half the time lying in bed; a dozen times
a day he took drugs, or measured his temperature or his pulse. Even
so, he risked his life by sallying out now and then to fashionable parties,
or by receiving into the privacy of his room young people of lower
estate who met his needs for love.[8] He himself entertained, giving lavish
dinners to famous or titled friends, including Anatole France. His
parents complained of his associates and his extravagance; his mother
tried to reduce his allowance to the level of his necessities; his once
passionate devotion to her was soured with monetary disputes. Nevertheless she provided funds for his visit to Venice and Padua (1896).

Meanwhile he had begun the first form of the book that was to justify
his existence. He called it *Jean Santeuil*, and described it as "the very
essence of my life." It "has not been manufactured; it has been
garnered"[9]—his secret notebooks had provided its theme and incidents.
After years of occasional work on the manuscript he became dissatisfied
with it, concluded that it was beyond repair, and left it unfinished. It
was published thirty years after his death.

In 1903 his father died, leaving him a liberal annuity. In 1905 his
mother died; now he was independently rich, and could publish his
private problems and feelings without fear of causing her grief. Shortly
thereafter his asthma came so near to choking him that he entered a
suburban sanitarium. On returning to Paris he took an apartment at
102 Boulevard Haussmann (1906), and resumed his apparently aimless
and unproductive life of medication and entertainment. Actually he was
again enriching his notebooks with events, recollections, and observa-

tions that were to serve as the raw material of the masterpiece that he was still resolved to write. It should not be just another concoction of imaginary adventures or amours, sauced with evanescent badinage; "I sought a philosophic theme for some great literary work."[10]

He found it in making time the master and substance of his tale. He would show the evolution of a soul from wondering and timid childhood through experimental loves, moral puzzles, social conflicts, and philosophical debates to the maturing of the mind and the rotting of the flesh; at the same time he would show the evolutions of the French aristocracy from its pomp and elegance in 1880 to its political, moral, and intellectual decay in the early twentieth century; he would watch the impartial action of time in removing human rubbish from the path of life. He drove through Paris again and again to get impressions of scenery, buildings, sunsets; he frequented museums to study Manet and other Impressionists for his description of his fictional artist Elstir; he leafed through decaying volumes to gather authentic details of French dress, speech, manners, ideas, and conveyances about the time of his birth. And at last he felt prepared.

Agreeing with Goethe that "a talent builds itself in quietness," he abandoned most of his social life, closed his doors to all but a few intimates, isolated himself in his room, and lined its walls with cork to deaden the noise. "I subordinated all my pleasures to an object which I judged to be infinitely more important than these—that of becoming strong enough to be able to bring into being the work which possibly I had within me."[11] "I had lived a life of idleness and dissipation, of sickness, invalidism, and eccentricity. I was embarking on my work when already near death, and I knew nothing of my trade."[12] He was obsessed with doubts "either that I was wholly devoid of talent or that, perhaps, a malady of the brain was hindering its development."[13] At last— probably in 1909—he began his book.

In 1911 he brought his chauffeur, Alfred Agostinelli, to live with him and type his manuscript. Gossip suggested that the handsome Italian served additional purposes, but Alfred's wife came with him. Even so, Proust fell in love with him, and suffered keen bereavement when Agostinelli left (1913)—to be drowned in the Mediterranean a year later. Some have seen him, sexually transformed, in the charming Lesbian, "Albertine," who, in Volumes IX and X, lives for a year with "Marcel," leaves him, and is shortly thereafter killed by a fall from a horse.

In September, 1912, Proust submitted Volume I to various publishers. It was rejected by Le Figaro, by Ollendorff, by the Nouvelle Revue *française*—on Gide's report that it was long-winded and jejune—and by the firm of Fasquelle, which also pronounced it tiresomely prolix; we can imagine the consternation of the publishing fraternity, when the author intimated that Volume I was only an eighth of the projected whole. Finally Proust had the manuscript printed at his own expense by Bernard Grasset (November, 1913).

II. THE BOOK

All of it is written in the first person by one who calls himself merely Marcel, and who, in the concluding pages of the whole, becomes clearly identical with Marcel Proust himself. Volumes I and II were entitled *Du Côté de chez Swann*, which in English became *Swann's Way*—the neighborhood and story of the amiable and cultured Mr. Swann, wealthy Jewish stockbroker, a long-time friend of the narrator's family and of the Prince of Wales, and "one of the men most sought after in the aristocratic world of the Faubourg Saint-Germain."[14] The initial locale, "Combray," is Proust's idealized recollection of his father's ancestral town, Illiers, near Chartres. The first page sets the tone by describing the thoughts, fancies, wonders, and fears of a nervous boy trying to sleep. Soon we hear of his mother, the soul of tender solicitude, so devoted to her son that she spends half her days and nights treating his illnesses, assuaging his pains, comforting his griefs, allaying his dreads. Then we are introduced to the indispensable ceremony which brought her nightly up the stairs to soothe the anxious boy with an assuring kiss. Here is the bathos of sentiment and the summit of feeling; for the love between mother and child is deeper than the love between man and woman, which is only a prelude and instrument to that maternal love which preserves the higher species of life. By page 45 the charm is on us, and our cynicism is stilled; we cease to look for events or dialogue; we yield to the flow of feeling, the mood of meditation, the music of the language, the careless, unhurried meandering of the style. This book, we perceive, is to be the history and exploration of a man's mind, which, in Proust's philosophy, is the only reality that man can ever know.

Several critics complained that Volume I was a windy compilation of impressions rather than a novel. Anatole France said: "I don't begin to understand the book. . . . I used to know Proust, . . . but I long ago lost sight of him."[15] Proust defended his offspring by asking influential friends to write favorable reviews. Jean Cocteau and Lucien Daudet complied, and Maurice Rostand assigned to Proust a place beside Dante and Shakespeare in the history of literature. Marcel himself wrote some congratulatory pieces about *Du Côté de chez Swann;* to conceal his authorship he had them copied by another hand before sending them to the literary journals.[16] The sweetest laud came from André Gide, who wrote: "Sorrow and remorse will torture me to the end of my life" for having rejected *Swann;* that rejection, he added, "will always be the greatest blunder made by the *Nouvelle Revue française.*"[17]

When Volume II of *Du Côté de chez Swann* was completed, Proust sent the manuscript to the publisher of the *Revue,* Gaston Gallimard, who accepted it (1914). The author had promised it to Grasset, but begged to be released from his contract on the ground that Grasset's firm was new and uncertain of continued life. "I have no idea," he wrote to Grasset, "whether I shall live long enough to see it [the entire *Recherche*] published, and it is only natural that, with the instinct of an insect whose days are numbered, I should be in a hurry to find some sure refuge for the child born of my entrails, who is destined to be my sole representative on earth."[18] With Gide's *Nouvelle Revue française* behind the new volume, some measure of success was assured.

It was one of the most readable in the series, for it told the love stories of Swann with Odette de Crécy and of the narrator, Marcel, with their budding daughter Gilberte. Each romance has its detailed background: Swann meets Odette at the salon of Madame Verdurin, where Proust begins his picture of the French aristocracy; and Marcel, in his teens, meets Gilberte among her playmates in the gardens of the Champs-Elysées. Odette (modeled on Madame Laure Hayman) is an ex-courtesan who has made her way into the Verdurin circle by her musical accomplishments and her beauty and charm. Her exquisite dresses and hats open male eyes on the boulevards; Proust himself dilates on her gowns, even on her corsets, with all the ardor of an invert for the other sex's finery. But Odette catches Swann particularly by her playing of Saint-Saëns' Sonata in D Minor for Piano and Violin; one phrase of it haunts Swann for many years.

The love interest quickens the tempo of Proust's narrative, brightens its color, raises its warmth. He calls love "that blessed bane," a glorious and consuming disease, the most frightful of sufferings (*le plus affreux des supplices*); he studies its stages, refinements, cruelties, absurdities with classic precision and romantic fascination. Swann is mature and experienced; he has had a Frenchman's assortment of mistresses; yet he becomes a willing prisoner in Odette's arms, pursues her breathlessly when she strategically retreats, and trembles with jealousy when she flirts with Forcheville. He furtively opens the letter which she has addressed to this rival; love knows no morals and no etiquette. His creator spares him no torture, even to letting him discover that Odette was once the Lesbian mistress of Madame Verdurin. She marries him, but cheats, and there is no certainty Gilberte is his as well as hers.[19] Perhaps Proust, who may never have known a woman "carnally," exaggerated the amorous pains of so practiced a gallant as Swann; and in his acid etching of Odette he may have yielded to the invert's hatred of women as socially advantaged competitors.

After diagnosing the lovesickness of the aging Swann, Proust skipped back to adolescence, and wrote an idyl of Marcel's calf love for Gilberte. Still too young and frail to be let loose without an attendant, Marcel, in his daily gambol on the Champs-Elysées, sees with envy a band of girls and boys playing games. One of them he recognizes as the Gilberte of whom he once caught an entrancing glimpse through some flowering shrubbery at Combray; "already the charm with which her name, like a cloud of incense, had filled that archway in the pink hawthorn . . . was beginning to conquer, to cover, to embalm, to beautify everything with which it had any association."[20] Now she is a frolicsome girl of thirteen or fourteen, ready to flirt with him, to draw him with a smile and then take laughing flight on prancing feet. One day she asks him to team with her in a game; thereafter he lives only when with her; her gay spirit, her winged body, even her pretty dresses, fill him with a zest and joy that his mother's kiss no longer gives. Happy weeks run by. Then boy and girl quarrel; Marcel stays at home, nursing a misery different from all the others that he has known. Separation, sickness, and distractions slowly cool the fever; that ethereal love fades, and Eros prepares other allurements, other passions, in other scenes.

World War I (1914–18) kept Proust's next volume in long gestation. All France was busy defending itself against German invaders; "Big Berthas" were bombarding Paris and scarring Notre Dame; this was no time for idyls. Proust, too frail to handle guns, found in his absorbed writing the best relief from the alarums of war. When the conflict was over he sent to his publishers Volumes III and IV, which appeared in 1919 under the title *À l'Ombre des jeunes filles en fleur* ("In the Shadow of Girls in Flower," which the English translator changed to *Within a Budding Grove*).

Now Marcel (the narrator), to ease his asthma, was spending a summer with his grandmother in "Balbec"—a Channel resort compounded in Proust's imagination from Trouville, Cabourg, and Dieppe. There

Proust's Marcel began a long friendship with the Marquis de Saint-Loup, who had everything—youth, health, wealth, beauty, manners, wit, grace, and a brothel girl for a mistress. There, too, Marcel became acquainted with the personality and art of the Impressionist painter Elstir. And there he met the heroine-to-be of many volumes, Albertine Simonet, then the liveliest of the girls who daily romped on the beaches or lawns of Balbec. At first Marcel fell in love with all of them, in their collective apotheosis of fresh, happy, wistful, dreamy girlhood. "When I was lying on the grass among all these girls, the plenitude of what I was feeling infinitely outweighed . . . the infrequency of our speech, and brimmed over from my immobility and silence in floods of happiness, the waves of which rippled up to die at the feet of these young roses";[21] then, if ever, silence was golden. Perhaps in the precarious equilibrium of erotic development a "period of indifference," of hesitation or oscillation between heterosexual and homosexual inclination, allowed Marcel to appreciate in all his organs the delights which these girls offered to sight, hearing, smell, and touch—the dreamy depth and seductive tenderness of their eyes, the music of their voices and the peal of their laughter, the fragrance of their perfumes or their flesh, the enticement of their hair, the smooth texture of their skin, the electric contact with their hands. Andrée's hands, "warmed at the fire, with the light behind them," had "the golden transparency of two autumn leaves."[22] Albertine was not so beautiful, but she multiplied her charms by her modesty and restraint, and by some mystery in her past which it would take seven volumes (III–IX) to resolve. Marcel privately lingered in fond fascination over her attractions of body, character, and mind, analyzing them with subtlety and magnifying them with sensuous desire. "Our love becomes immense," says Proust; "we never dream how small a place in it the real woman occupies."[23] Seldom had love been described with so complex a mixture of realism and imagination, of classic skepticism and romantic abandon.

For these two volumes (III–IV) Proust won the Goncourt Prize; and though there was some critical discontent with the award, the author received almost eight hundred letters of congratulation. Arnold Bennett and John Galsworthy declared Proust to be the Dickens of the age; Middleton Murry announced a "new era in the history of great novel-writing"; Henry James ranked Proust with Cervantes and Balzac.[24] He would never be so happy again.

In June, 1919, he moved from the Boulevard Haussmann to an apartment in the Rue Laurent-Pichat; and in October he moved again to 44 Rue Hamelin. He must have accumulated manuscript during the war, for in 1920 he published Volume V, and in 1921 Volume VI, as together constituting the third unit of his work. So far he had described his own development, and the upper middle class as seen in his entourage; now he moved on to describe the nobility—Bourbon or Bonapartist—which, though it had lost the government, still ruled French society. The new volumes were called *Le Côté de Guermantes* (*The Guermantes Way*), from the road in Combray leading to one of the estates of that aristocratic clan. There had been a family by that name in French heraldry, but it was almost extinct when Proust wrote, and he could enrich, extend, and impoverish it as he pleased.

He pictured the fictional Marcel, at the outset of Volume V, as inhabiting a spacious flat that formed part of the Hôtel (town mansion) de Guermantes. From one window Marcel could see "Oriane"—the Duchesse de Guermantes—moving at stately pace from her door to her carriage. She was still attractive with her cosmetics and finery, and the odor of her pedigree penetrated walls and windows to intoxicate Marcel with an awe that he came to identify with love. For a while, to her pleased amusement, he frequented streets where he expected her to pass. Her husband, the Duc de Guermantes, "was formidably rich in a world where everyone was steadily growing poorer."[25] He passed gracefully through a succession of mistresses, but he served as host at Oriane's parties. She ignored his adulteries, and he praised her wit.

"Marcel" and other rich members of the upper middle class were admitted to "society," for their fortunes could be absorbed into titled families by marriage. Nevertheless the nobles regretted such unions as bringing inferior qualities not only into their stock but also into their manners; aristocracy seemed to them a matter of careful rearing and training as well as of select genes; Baron de Charlus, a man of homosexual tastes but of immaculate genealogy, held that "there is such a thing as social as well as physiological eugenics."[26] Hence Marcel found that class distinctions and barriers were still strong in France a century after the Revolution. They were usually respected by the lower classes; these untitled folk had less fear of the seigneur than before, but seem to have felt almost as much awe. Marcel observed that many nobles responded to this deference by treating the commonalty with an unaffected geniality and simplicity not generally accorded by the bourgeoisie to its inferiors.[27]

Within the aristocracy itself, however, there was a ridiculous amount of jealousy, backbiting, snobbery, and arrogance. The entire nobility was divided into camps or cliques, each scorning and excluding some other. The liveliest debates in "society" concerned who could be introduced to whom, who would be invited to which gathering; Proust gives page after page to such agitation.[28] Near the end of Volume VI the Duc and Duchesse de Guermantes spend ten pages discussing titles and invitations while waiting to enter their carriage. Marcel affects a philosophical superiority to such stratifications, but he expands to three pages his ecstasy on being introduced to the Princesse de Parme, who "was richer than any reigning princess."[29]

Most of the two Guermantes volumes, and a dreary part of the later ones, are taken up with a meticulous description of aristocratic receptions. These were generally held in splendid mansions in the Faubourg St.-Germain, which had been Proust's particular area of circulation. He adored the aristocracy even while writing its obituary; he deployed his army of adjectives in picturing the splendor of the Duchesse de Guermantes; he transformed the precious raiment of noble ladies into reams of paper and streams of ink; and when he attended the opera he rhapsodized over the "goddesses" in the boxes;[30] nothing on the stage could compare with them in their silks and furs and stately grace. And yet when he records the conversation of these divinities, in the theater or the salon, they seem incapable of anything but trivialities, personalities, conceits, and badinage. Marcel reports through 135 pages[31] the gossip at a party given by the Marquise de Villeparisis; they are unforgivable pages unless taken as a satire, and as such they are overwhelmingly *de trop*. He writes fifteen pages[32] about the Duchesse de Guermantes' wit, but not one of her many *bons mots* remains in the memory. The outstanding repartee in these volumes is that of Madame Leroi, who, being asked "What are your views on love?" replies: "Love? I make it constantly, but I never talk about it."[33] Probably these lords and ladies had learned, with their A B C's, that a mixed gathering is no place for a serious idea.

To pass from these volumes to VII and VIII is to step from a drawing room of duchesses into a brothel of perverts. Proust gave this fourth installment a startling title—*Sodome et Gomorrhe*, which the genteel translators softened into *Cities of the Plain*. By "Sodome" Proust meant the male inverts of Paris; by "Gomorrhe" he meant the Lesbians. He asked his publishers to advertise the books as "not to be read by young girls," and he frankly hoped that this attractive warning would bring him many readers of any age or sex.[34] Perhaps the horrors of war and the waning of his energies (he was fifty years old in 1921, when Volume VII was published) had deepened his youthful pessimism, and possibly his own abnormal pursuits had brought him into wider contact with the secret vices of the capital.

Volume VII opens by telling how Marcel eavesdrops on the sexual transactions of Baron de Charlus with his tailor and procurer Jupien. The Baron is of the upper aristocracy, a brother to the Duc de Guermantes. He is pictured as "a stout gentleman with gray hair, black mustache, his lips reddened with a salve"; a man of great wealth, cheap pride, violent temper, and open purse. Homosexuality "had produced in him a feminine refinement of sensibility and mind."[35] He describes some of his homosexual forays to Jupien, and asks him to "act as my agent" in securing fresh playmates.[36] Marcel assures us that "my discovery of the sort of malady in question dated from that afternoon."[37] Charlus comforts himself by believing that nearly everyone in Paris is in some way morally tarnished; "for every evil reputation that is unjustified there are hundreds of good ones which are no less so."[38] He wins the violinist Morel to be his sexual accompanist, enriches him, and is exposed by him at a party given by the Lesbian Madame Verdurin.[39] Later he sinks so low as to let it be known that during the funeral rites of his wife he took the opportunity of asking an acolyte for his name and address.[40]

Marcel does not admit that he was one of the homosexual fringe. He stresses his love for his mother, and Albertine. We do not know whom Albertine represented in the life of Proust; she may have been a transvested image of Proust's chauffeur Agostinelli, or some transient object of ambisexual desire. She confesses her love for Marcel; he tells her (falsely) that he prefers her friend Andrée. He loves her only when he is jealous, and especially when he suspects her of having Lesbian associates. He takes her as his mistress, and at the same time he plots to win the versatile embraces of Madame Putbus' maid.[41] He discusses with Saint-Loup the comparative attractions of diverse brothels.[42] A tender-minded reader concludes that Marcel is a heartless rake; a critic may acknowledge the author's candor in revealing the coarser features of his namesake and other self.

In Volume IX Marcel, while his mother is staying at Auteuil, takes Albertine to live with him in Paris. He gives her his late father's study as her own room, and allows her a daily outing, but he keeps jealous watch over all her movements; Proust frankly entitled this volume *La Prisonnière*. (The fact that her living with a bachelor is accepted by Marcel's relatives with no audible objection has indicated to some sympathetic biographers[43] that "Albertine," in actual life, was a boy kept for homosexual purposes.) Marcel goes into surprising detail about his captive: her body, her services, her mind. He is entranced by the color and flow of her garments, and spends freely to garb her radiantly.

A passage of great beauty describes Albertine asleep (in his bed) when he returns to his room:

> She reminded me of a long blossoming stem that had been laid there. . . . Her life exhaled toward me its gentle breath. I listened to this murmuring, mysterious emanation, soft as a breeze from the sea. . . . So long as her sleep lasted I was free . . . to look at her, and, when her sleep grew deeper, to touch, to kiss her. . . . Her hair, falling all along her rosy face, was spread out beside her on the bed.[44]

On another occasion he is allowed to undress her. He enthuses over her "little upstanding breasts," and "her belly, . . . closed at the junction of her thighs by two valves of a curve as hushed, as reposeful, as cloistral, as that of the horizon after the sun has set";[45] who but Proust would have thought of a cloister and a vulva in one line? But also there are ethereal interludes:

> We left our motor-car and walked a long way together; indeed for some moments I gave her my arm, and it seemed to me that the ring which her arm formed around it united our two persons in a single self, and linked our separate destinies together. At our feet our parallel shadows, where they approached and joined, traced an exquisite pattern.[46]

All in all, Volume IX is a subtle and merciless description of one man's love—feverish, possessive, selfish, deceitful, transitory. On the same day that Marcel enjoys Albertine's caresses he thinks of taking into his arms some stray woman whom he has seen from his window or passed in the street; yet he cannot bear that another man, much less a woman, should look upon Albertine with more than casual and superficial interest. He accuses her of going to Lesbian friends; she denies it; he puts her down as "by nature a liar";[47] meanwhile he lies to her repeatedly. She has given herself in hopes of marriage; he does not offer it. "I asked myself whether marriage with Albertine would not spoil my life, as well by making me assume the burden, too heavy for my shoulders, of consecrating myself to another person, as by forcing me to live in absence from myself because of her continual presence, and deprive me, forever, of the delights of solitude."[48] After a year of her services her "presence weighed upon me, and so I regarded her sullenly, feeling it . . . a pity that we had not had a rupture."[49] Other women attract him because he has not yet possessed them, and his imagination can glorify them; "of Albertine, on the other hand, I had nothing more to learn."[50] "Gradually Albertine had lost her beauty"[51]— i.e., she has satisfied his desire. Now he can perceive her mental limitations, and he is bored by her conversation. He gives vent to "my vacillating, nagging disposition."[52] He feels himself imprisoned by his imprisonment of Albertine; he longs to be free. Sometimes he thinks, "What a pleasure it would be if . . . she should take it into her head to ride off somewhere, . . . and never return to my house!"[53] The volume ends when Françoise, the faithful, grumbling, loving old servant of the family, brings him the news that Albertine, in the early dawn, has fled.

Volume X, *Albertine disparue*, is the drooping tale of Marcel's efforts to get his mistress to come back to him, of her death by being flung against a tree by her horse, of his slowly subsiding remorse, of his gradual absorption in other women and affairs. He engages a friend to investigate rumors of Albertine's past in Balbec and Touraine; the reports confirm his suspicions, and he concludes that "what I had possessed of her, what I carried in my heart, was only quite a small part of her."[54] "Each one of us," he reflects, "is not a single person but contains many persons, who have not all the same moral values."[55]

He invites Albertine's former comrade Andrée to come and be his mistress, and he importunes her to tell him of Albertine's Lesbian loves. Andrée confesses that she herself has had sexual relations with many girls, some of whom were brought to her by Charlus' catamite, Morel. "Once he had the nerve to bring one of these girls, with Albertine, to a brothel, . . . where four or five of the women had her at once, or in turn. . . . She hoped that you would rescue her, that you would marry her."[56] Marcel descends to the point of telling Andrée that "it would be of great interest to me to see her—even if she simply confined herself to caresses which would not embarrass her unduly in my presence—performing such actions with those of Albertine's friends who shared her tastes."[57] She refuses, but she "now had relations with me," though "we can't do quite the same things as I used to do with Albertine."[58] Who would believe all this, if it were not all there, Gomorrah piled upon Sodom, in Proust's delicate and immaculate style?

In these concluding volumes there is not much to choose, in taste or morals, between Marcel and the persons whose deterioration he now records. Swann is the most decent figure in the social whirl; everybody, however anti-Semite, has a good word to say for him, and his patient courtesy holds out to the end. His wife, Odette, whom he rescued from promiscuity, deceives him, and when he dies she marries his rival, the

Marquis de Forcheville. His (?) daughter Gilberte takes the name of her stepfather, and tries to "hide the fact that her father was Jewish."[59] She marries the Marquis de Saint-Loup, who in Volume III was a model of manhood (allowing for a mistress); but soon he leaves Gilberte desolate in her wealth and finery while he replaces Charlus as the homosexual mate of Morel.

The story seems to have reached nadir, but there are deeper depths to explore. The eleventh and final volume, *Le Temps retrouvé* (*The Past Recaptured*), describes the heroism and shattering of France in the First World War. Marcel comes back to Paris in 1916 after "long years . . . in a sanitarium." His picture of the unswept snow covering the boulevards and gleaming in the moonlight[60] shows the author's literary skill surviving time and slime. He finds the people facing the oncoming Germans with feverish courage and a patriotism so ardent that any soldier who returns from the front with less than a disabling wound feels ashamed to survive. Many Parisians, says Charlus, "declare that they will never be able to go through with this war, that their hearts will never stand it; that they can think of nothing else, that they will die suddenly one day—and the most extraordinary thing about it is that this actually does happen!"[61]

The most astonishing scene in the eleven volumes has for its background the inn where Jupien collects inverts for the sexual service of Monsieur de Charlus.[62] Marcel, for reasons open to doubt, enters this hostelry, and climbs to a perch from which he sees the Baron, in a masochistic frenzy, receiving with delightful pain a beating by a boy wielding chains.* In another scene Charlus, temporarily blind, draws into his room a child of ten.[63] This same Baron, according to Jupien, is "too kind-hearted; he would give everything he possesses";[64] he turns his home into a military hospital, and is famous for his care of responsive soldiers. However, he is resolved to kill his rebellious ex-lover Morel, who further shocks him by making love to women; but Morel eludes him, and the Baron dies unrepentant and unavenged. Of all the personages in Proust's 2,500 pages, Charlus is the most completely and most mercilessly portrayed.

Almost as macabre is Marcel's account of the party at which he looked for the last time upon his assembled aristocratic friends. He

---

* Maurice Sachs, in *Witches' Sabbath* (New York, 1964, pp. 193–200), claimed that Jupien was Proust's footman Albert; that this Albert presided over just the kind of homosexual brothel that Proust here described; and that this house was partially furnished with pieces which had once belonged to Proust.

shows them no longer in the brilliance of their prewar display, but in various stages of physical or mental debility. The men have blotched skin, their bald heads are dotted with liver spots, their legs cannot sustain them for more than a few steps at a time. The goddesses whom Marcel worshiped twenty years before are now fat and formless or parched and thin; the rosy complexions of the past are now vermilion noses emerging from rice powder and rouge; the Duchesse de Guermantes, whose wit once charmed even her philandering husband, now with effort enounces platitudes. Madame de Villeparisis, formerly "the most beautiful woman of her generation," has become "a little hunchbacked, red-faced woman, quite hideous."[65] One stout lady accosts him; he cannot recognize her, but guesses she may be the Odette whose raiment he once admired; no, it is Odette's daughter Gilberte, the same that romped along the Champs-Élysées. "You took me for mama," she says, and "it is true that I am beginning to look very much like her."[66] She is already a widow; her husband, Saint-Loup, has atoned for his bisexual infidelities by dying bravely in battle. Odette herself has best covered the imprints of time: at the age of seventy she has become the last of the Duc de Guermantes' mistresses. Her granddaughter, Mademoiselle de Saint-Loup, aged sixteen, is the bright inheritor of the spirit and fortunes of Swann, Odette, Gilberte, and Saint-Loup. Marcel, sadly contemplating her youth and beauty, sees in her another bubble on the stream of time. So, through three generations, life, while confessing its mortality, professes its permanence. Time is the only hero of the tale.

It was at that somber party that Marcel, retreating from the noise and perfume into the peace of the Guermantes library, found in the touch of a book the redemption of his shiftless career. An old dream of writing something memorable reawoke in him. Instead of spending his days and nights passing from one party to another, one liaison to another, one sex to another, why should he not devote the years remaining of his frailty to recapturing the past, holding it steady for study and understanding, picturing the pride and passing of that gilded generation whose career he had intimately seen? But not merely to record events; rather, to feel them through the hearts and flesh of men and women; to seek in them, if not some worth and meaning of human life, at least the satisfaction of giving form to chaos, and some modest duration to vanishing scenes and souls. "Happy the man who could write such a book, I thought to myself; what a mighty task lay before him!"[67] "If there were granted me time enough!"[68]

So Proust ended and began his book.

III. THE ARTIST

It is, of course, the outstanding novel of the twentieth century, superior in artistry and depth to its only rivals, *Jean-Christophe* and *Ulysses*. It bears one vital feature of a work of art—that through the particular it illustrates the general, perhaps illuminates the universal; for here, in describing one individual man and one class, it portrayed an age and mirrored the life of man.

À la Recherche du temps perdu is not so much a narrative as a kaleidoscope of representative figures caught in diverse stages of development and decline. The road of the procession is time, and its marshal is memory. Proust was fascinated by the pervasive operations of time—destroyer and preserver, elastic and indestructible, subjective but obstinately real: discarding the old and insinuating the new; varying the surface and maintaining the base; lengthening or shortening the hour according to the number of events and the character of moods; multiplying every person into a succession of different—even opposite —personalities (as with Saint-Loup); changing every year the map of the world. Proust admired the Papacy because it "reckons in centuries."[69] Like the new physicists, he added time to the three dimensions of space as an indispensable element in the description or measurement of any reality. "I would not fail, above all else, to describe man as having the length not of his body but of his years, which he must drag about with him from place to place, an ever-increasing burden which overcomes him in the end."[70] "I would try to make this dimension of Time continuously perceptible in a transcription of human life necessarily very different from that conveyed to us by our senses."[71] Far deeper, richer, and more pervasive than our sensations are our memories.

Through memory we both circumvent and implement time. We evade in some measure the eroding acids of forgetfulness. We carry cargoes of the past with us, stored in our conscious or unconscious or involuntary memory, stored perhaps in every part of our flesh and bones and blood. Unconscious memories reappear in dreams, and sometimes in our waking states. Involuntary memory operates when a present experience recalls not only an event in our past, but some of its accompaniments—forms, colors, sounds, odors, pressures, tastes—which, though not then consciously felt, were imprinted in our unconscious memory. Through memory we can reverse the flow of time and move backward in our history. So Proust emancipated himself from time's domination; his minute and swelling recollections recaptured old scenes, old sensations, wonderments, tendernesses, and anxieties. Such resurrections do not come in any temporal sequence; the mind, like a motion picture, can flash back from present to past; it can make time go slowly or fast; occasionally, in the remembrance of things past, we can have the illusion that time has been standing still. (Pictorial art is in one aspect the technique of making time stand still—for a time.)

Through sensations barnacled with memories, we enrich and deepen our perceptions, and so transform the "reality" which we might have supposed to be an external object or event. Every reality is subjective: it is our present sensations plus the relevant remembered past. "Without that relationship"—without that subjective accretion—"there is nothing."[72] Hence realism in literature or art is a delusion; it supposes that by describing the "object" it is depicting reality; but the deepest reality is the memories, imaginations, purposes, desires, and feelings with which living beings clothe and interpret the object or the incident.[73] It is these subjective conditions and reverberations that the artist must portray if he would make his subject live. And the historian must remember that events happen to persons, and are otherwise meaningless; history must not be immobilized into statistics, but should be seen through souls.

So at times Proust's book reads like psychology interrupted and illustrated by autobiography or social history. A page of events can generate a dozen pages of analysis; the smell of a flower in a room can permeate a paragraph. Persistent ailments, recurrent pains, and a secretiveness compelled by sexual deviation sharpened Proust's senses, and inclined him to introspection, reminiscence, and to a meticulous dissection of the motives and feelings underlying—and of the words and pretenses covering—the actions of his enemies, his friends, his mistresses, and himself. He felt, from his own case, how "self-centeredness enables every human being to see the universe spread out in descending scale beneath himself who is its lord."[74] He saw the protective layer of lies with which each ego approaches a world of worried, competing, hostile egos. "Falsehood is essential to humanity," at least in polite society; "we lie all our life long, especially . . . to those who love us";[75] even while enjoying Albertine's caresses he suspected her of prolonged and tortuous mendacity.[76] He recognized the subservience of intellect to instinct; "each time I wrote that 'Albertine was pretty' I crossed the words out, and wrote instead that I felt a desire to kiss Albertine."[77] He reduced love to a bodily hunger casting "an evil spell" over the soul.

This finesse of analysis is the chief excellence and defect of the book.

À la Recherche has great value as a self-revelation, a study of human conduct, a dissection of a class, by a highly perceptive mind; but it carries the anatomy of feeling to such lengths as to become at times a cliché and a bore. Marcel spins out to three pages his agony at saying au revoir to his mother at a railway station.[78] He asks Albertine may he kiss her; she raises no objection, but before kissing her he considers for seven pages the physics, chemistry, physiology, and psychology of a kiss.[79]

Proust likes to describe rather than narrate; he leaves narration to the storytellers; thereby he defies Lessing's advice[80] to the novelist to leave description to the artist, and to the artist to leave narration to the historian or the novelist. So Proust joins Joyce in effecting a revolution in the form of the novel. He describes everything because he sees everything. He is keenly aware of sensations that others might ignore. He notices "the transpositions to another octave that occur in the breathing of a sleeper."[81] He is sensitive to, and records, every change in the weather, the moments or stages in a sunset, or "that inconceivable marvel, a morning in spring."[82] He follows for half a page the leisurely creeping of the sunlight along a balcony rail. He lets us know just what trees and flowers grow along his road. He is a woman, and perceives significant minutiae in dress, manner, features, and speech. This descriptive ecstasy is carried to excess; sometimes it becomes a display of trivialities—the furniture in the room at Balbec, the door-boy at the Grand Hotel whose whole function is to tip his hat to every entering or leaving guest.[83] We wonder by what devious course the blood of Juliet's nurse came into Marcel Proust. Amid these descriptions and meditations we lose the thin thread of the narrative, even the locality of events. We learn of a pivotal event like Swann's marriage only indirectly, and as if by chance; this is a favorite trick by which Proust puzzles and chastises the reader who has dared to skip. We sympathize with Gide's complaint that Proust left so much scaffolding around his building that the structure becomes almost invisible.[84]

Even so, as Gide recognized, the structure is there, subtle, pervasive, and remarkable. It is composed of stages in the social history of France in Proust's lifetime: of the middle class in *Swann's Way*, of the aristocracy in *The Guermantes Way*, of the moral deterioration of Paris in *Sodome et Gomorrhe*, and in the final volume, of the collapse of a culture through unsound moral foundations and the bite of time. The flow of the narrative lies not so much in the succession of events as in the evolution of character. Proust studied men and women with almost malicious intensity, and perhaps he made his *dramatis personae* degenerate too uniformly. Of course we change in body and character as the years pass over us, and we can readily believe that the frolicsome Gilberte grew matronly fat, but we are reluctant to acknowledge that the courtly, generous, and loyal Saint-Loup could have become a rude, faithless, and tasteless fool.[85] There are a few cases in which Proust forgets the relationships previously established among his personages.[86] Nevertheless we must admire the consistency—probably through careful affiliations in his notebooks—with which he led his complex stable of characters through so many paces and crises from the first of his pages to the last. He seems to meander, but he never loses his way.

Unquestionably his style meanders, and is unique. Many a sentence contains a clause within a clause inside a clause; and often the subject has been forgotten when the verb appears.[87] Some sentences wind leisurely through a page. ("I have been told," said Joyce, "that a single sentence of Proust would fill a whole magazine.")[88] However, we feel a certain quality of conscience in these serpentine proliferations; Proust likes to pause and complete every sensation or feeling, and thinks himself obliged to convey it thoroughly, in every aspect and nuance. You can read any of these volumes in an hour if you dispense with all subordinate clauses; but then, of course, you are not reading Proust. If you cease to hurry, forget the merciless tick of time, and accept his pace, follow his wandering but penetrating gaze, relish with him the sound and savor of his words, you will find yourself enveloped in an exotic charm, as if some perfume of the style had bewitched you into love. The slowly multiplying details have their effect at last, like the passes and incantations of a hypnotist. You feel an uncanny realism in this painstaking evocation of the feelings and memories that give life to things, souls to flesh, and significance to events. You stop to catch the melody of a sentence, the structure and flow of a paragraph, the tenderness of a sentiment, the revelation of a metaphor. He pictures his mother at his grandmother's death: "At the foot of the bed my mother —convulsed by every gasp of this agony, not weeping but now and then drenched with tears—presented the unreasoning desolation of a leaf which the rain lashes and the wind twirls on its stem."[89] And this is a translation; imagine the music of the French.

IV. HIMSELF

Let us look at Proust in his later years. Edmond Jaloux described him in 1917 as "a mixture of apparent strength and femininity," with "thick black hair," and eyes "so dark, excessively large, that they gave to the whole face a look of passion and ill-health."[90] Arthritis increasingly disabled him, and asthma always threatened to choke him. He was an invalid, weak in body and disturbed in mind; "Marcel" speaks of "my excess of tortured sensibility and intellectuality,"[91] of "my morbid tendency to melancholy, to solitude."[92] He preferred solitude to friendship,[93] and used his ailments as an excuse for discouraging would-be visitors. So isolated, he became careless in his dress, sometimes wore soiled collars and shirts.[94] He was upheld by a conviction of his genius, and of the unique quality and lasting value of his work. When he was photographed among recipients of Legion of Honor awards, he wrote to the editor of *Le Gaulois:* "Unfortunately, I am grouped with people whose literary merit is slight. Could you not publish a little note mentioning me apart from the others?"[95] We are not all so frankly vain.

"Marcel" confesses, or professes, an especial sensitivity to women. He tells us that he was thrilled to ecstasy by the touch of a woman's skirt.[96] He takes pains to assure us that he loved normally; at Doncières he had a "few days" of "physical pleasure" with a servant girl;[97] "I began to frequent houses of prostitution."[98] But he shunned and resented monogamy. A man should have "not one woman only but several," for if you "live with a woman altogether you will soon cease to see any of the things that made you love her."[99] The love of a man for a woman, he believed, is entirely the production of imagination stimulated by unsatisfied desire; let the desire be satisfied, and imagination will be crushed by realization; then love will fade except when revived by jealousy. Proust was denied the love that ripens with fidelity and children.

He described Marcel's affairs with women in such detail, and with such intimacy of observation and feeling, that at times we begin to doubt his homosexuality. He inveighed against Lesbians, and mourned the apparent multiplication (or increased visibility) of sexual inverts in the cities of Europe. "They form in every land an Oriental colony, cultured, musical, malicious, which has certain charming qualities and intolerable defects."[100] Now and then, to offset rumors about his boys, he sent word to his friends that he was planning marriage.[101] Yet his lengthy preoccupation with the subject of inversion, his detailed discussion of Charlus' adventures and character, his generous sympathy with Oscar Wilde,[102] his expert discussion of the expedients to which inverts resorted for finding or attracting a mate, his familiarity with homosexual coteries, assemblages, and rivalries, suggested to many deviates that this brilliant writer was secretly one of their own.

One of them, André Gide, praised Proust's volumes *Sodome et Gomorrhe*, but resented as unbearably dishonest his condemnations of inversion. Proust invited him, sent a car for him; Gide came, bringing with him a copy of his unpublished *Corydon*, which defended homosexuality. Gide's *Journal* noted, under May 14, 1921: "Spent an hour yesterday with Proust. . . . Far from denying his homosexuality, he exhibits it, and I could almost say boasts of it. He claims never to have loved women save spiritually, and never to have known love except with men." But he urged Gide to avoid any public confession of inversion. "You can tell anything, but on condition that you never say 'I.'" Gide's report continues: "Proust blames himself for that 'indecision' which made him, in order to fill out the heterosexual part of his book, transpose, in *À l'Ombre des jeunes filles en fleur*, all the attractive, affectionate, and charming elements contained in his homosexual recollections, so that for *Sodome* he is left nothing but the grotesque and the abject." Gide asked Proust would he "ever present that Eros in a young and beautiful guise"; Proust would not commit himself.[103]

It was too much to ask of an aging invalid with so many attachments in polite society. He had much diminished these external contacts, but he did not propose to limit them to inverts like Charlus. Despite his satire of snobbishness, and his claim "I had never made any distinction between the classes,"[104] he was keenly class-conscious, and prided himself on his aristocratic connections. He deplored "the mediocrity of even the most splendid plate in a middle-class household."[105] He frowned upon the use of expressions current only among commoners, and admitted that "we are always less at our ease in the company of one who is not of our station."[106] A title of rank seemed to him almost a sacrament—an outward sign of an inward grace.

A similar concession to prevailing ways marked his attitude to racial divisions. He muted the Hebraic half of his parentage. He defended Dreyfus, but he avoided the subject in aristocratic circles, which were patriotically sure that the French Army was *sans peur et sans reproche*. He presented at great length the unattractive characteristics of the Jews whom he brought into his volumes.[107] Like many Jews, he was fond of telling stories that made fun of Jews.[108] He added now and then a favorable comment: the Jews "had plenty of intelligence and spirit, and were men to whom, in the long run, one could become closely attached."[109]

Generally he was too observant to see only one side of any vital question. His spirit was additionally embittered by the evil that World War I had exposed in individuals, classes, and states; yet he had observed many instances of kindness, generosity, and self-sacrifice, and he suggested that "the part played by disinterested motives in people's ✓ lives is greater than we are inclined to think."[110] He was skeptical of religious creeds, but he feared that the spread of unbelief was sapping the supports of French morals and character.[111] He would have been happy to recapture at least the promises of his childhood faith, and at times—as when he heard of Bergotte's death—he dallied with the idea of transmigration;[112] but generally the most he would let himself hope for was survival of the soul through the endurance of its living work. "They buried Bergotte, but all through the night of mourning, in the lighted windows, his books, arranged three by three, kept watch like angels with outspread wings, and seemed, for him who was no more, the symbol of his resurrection."[113]

Some such hope was his chief support in his final years. His soul became his books, and in that form it might surmount his body's death. Contemplating his notebooks,

> I understand that all these materials for literary work were nothing else than my past life, and that . . . I had stored them up without foreseeing their final purpose, or even their survival, any more than does the seed when it lays by all the sustenance that is going to nourish the seedling. Like the seed, I might die as soon as the plant had been formed, and I found that I had been living for this seedling without knowing it, without any indication whatsoever that my life would ever witness the realization of those books I so longed to write. . . . I felt myself pregnant with the work which I was carrying within me, like a precious fragile object which had been entrusted to me, and which I desired to transmit intact.[114]

He was haunted by the fear that an external mishap, or some internal disorder, or a "cerebral accident" would kill or cripple him before he could complete his task. (Only eight of the eleven volumes appeared during his life.)

So, after 1919, he lived only for his book. He wrote during the quiet solitude of the night, and slept fitfully during the day. He had a servant, Céleste Albaret, who sometimes brought in her sister and her niece to help take care of him. He did not ask much of them, and he seldom allowed them into his room. He, aesthetically so sensitive in his writings, let his room fall into an ungainly disorder. Jean Cocteau described "the table crowded with phials, with a theater-phone (a device enabling one to listen in on certain theaters), a pile of exercise books, and—as on the rest of the furniture—a pelt of dust which was never brushed off. . . . smell of anti-asthmatic powder, a sepulchral smell."[115] Arthritis was crippling his neck and hands. Gide reported, May 14, 1921: "Proust is really seriously ill. He says he spends hours on end without being able even to move his head. He stays in bed all day long, and for days on end."[116] René Boylesve, in that year, wrote of Proust's bluish face, sunken eyes, hair uncut for two months past, badly frayed collar unchanged for a week; he seemed "young, old, sick, feminine."[117] In the summer of 1922 Proust wrote to Gallimard: "I fall down whenever I try to walk, and . . . I can no longer speak properly." But he wrote, in his last volume: "Let us allow our body to disintegrate, since each fresh particle that breaks off . . . adds itself to our work to complete it."[118] And finally: "When we understand that suffering is the best thing we can encounter in life, we contemplate death without dismay as a sort of emancipation."[119]

It came, November 18, 1922.

CHAPTER X

André Gide

PROUST not only buried himself in the past; he belonged to the past in his art. He labored to produce a psychological—almost an epistemological—novel just when French prose literature was turning from psychology to philosophy, from the minute study of motives and character to the bewildered consideration of man's place in the universe, of evil and good, of fate and freedom, of life and death, of absurdity and significance. And while most philosophers, particularly in England and America, retreated from such problems into the safe obscurities of logic and linguistic analysis, the major novelists and dramatists of America and France risked their royalties by writing of first and last things. In France, led for a while by André Malraux, they came out of the boudoir into the arena, and dared to face and explore the condition of man in an age that had lost God and was seeking the bomb, that had abandoned tradition for experiment in morals and art, and was setting the planet dizzy with multiform revolutions. These men—Gide, "Céline," Cocteau, Camus, and Sartre—deepened the problems by their answers, but they lit some candles in the darkness if only by the questions they asked; and half the world listened.

André-Paul Gide was born in 1869, two years before Proust, and published thirteen books before the appearance of *À la Recherche du temps perdu* (1913). Nevertheless he belonged to a later age in mind and mood; not merely because he survived Proust by twenty-nine years (1922–51), but because Proust lived mentally and peacefully with a dying class, while Gide actively experienced the changing present and strove to mold the future. They resembled each other in their inherited wealth, their mastery of French style, and their addiction to boys; but Proust expressed little concern for the disinherited of the earth, while Gide compelled reforms in the colonies of France, traveled to Russia, and won laurels from the Soviets.

Like Proust he came of a divided religious ancestry. His father was a Protestant, his mother was a Catholic, more puritan and dogmatic than her mate. The father died soon after André's birth; the boy was brought up by two austere women, and learned womanly ways. In the family estate at Cuverville-en-Caux (near Le Havre) he grew up in semisolitude, sheltered from life and associates. His sensitivity made him feel keenly the awakening of sex, and he suffered spasms of guilt over his inability to control the impulse to masturbate.[1] "Until the age of twenty-three I lived completely virgin and totally depraved, so crazed that I sought everywhere some bit of flesh on which to press my lips."[2] In this condition of alternating congestion and detumescence he wrote— and published at the age of twenty-two—his first book, *Les Cahiers d'André Walter*, the records of a youth who was transparently Gide himself.

In 1891 he traveled to Algeria, and surrendered his virginity to a prostitute. Four years later, again in Africa, he met Oscar Wilde, and was moved by Oscar's example to take the plunge into homosexual re- lations.[3] Nevertheless, on returning to France, he married his cousin, Madeleine Rondeaux (1895). He loved "Em," as he called her (for Emmeline), but as a woman of fine character rather than physical charm; so far as we know, he never consummated the marriage.[4] Mean- while, we are told, he begot a daughter by his niece.[5] His wife consoled her sexual solitude with intense Catholic piety, just as André was be- ginning to lose his religious faith.

In his secret journal Gide laid down two definitions and one con- fession:

> I call a pederast the man who, as the word indicates, falls in love with young boys. I call a sodomite the man whose desire is addressed to mature men. . . . The pederasts, of whom I am one, . . . are much rarer, and the sodomites more numerous, than I first thought. . . . That such loves can spring up, that such relationships can be formed, it is not enough for me to say that this is natural; I maintain that it is good. Each of the two finds exaltation, protection, a challenge in them.[6]

Like most of us, Gide found a philosophy to sanction his desires in ✓ the face of religious prohibitions. In 1897 he issued a passionate defense of pleasure and instinct entitled *Les Nourritures terrestres* (*Fruits of the Earth*). All natural desires are wholesome (ran the argument); without them life would lose its savor. "The pleasure I feel in an action I take as a sign that I ought to do it." Therefore "satisfy your joy while it gladdens your soul—and your desire of love while your lips are still sweet to

kiss."[7] Lead "a life open to adventure, free from the fear of consequences and the restraints of formal ethics."[8] However, Gide warned
his readers against the dangers of self-indulgence, and bade them, at
the end: "Throw away my book; do not let it satisfy you. Do not
✓ think *your* truth can be found by anyone else. . . . Tell yourself that my
book is but *one* of the thousand possible postures for confronting life.
Seek your own."[9] This moral afterthought was forgotten in the welcome warmth of the central argument; Gide became for many years
an idol of the avant-garde, while conservatives denounced him as a
corrupter of youth. He retorted that Socrates, who was now one of
their gods, had suffered a similar charge.

Living part of his time in Paris, Gide joined the circle of Stéphane
Mallarmé, who, with Paul Verlaine, had led a Symbolist movement
pledged to subordinate sense to symbol and sound. Gide soon freed
himself from this pose, but he learned from Mallarmé some secrets of
style, and loved the music of words as much as their significance. He
had acquired excellence as a pianist, and this reacted on his writing. "The
exactingness of my ear . . . was such that I should have warped the
meaning of a sentence for its rhythm."[10] He wrote prose that rivaled
the best poetry of his time.

He did not feel, in his twenties, that he had either the fullness of
experience or the reach of artistry to write a novel; besides, he said, he
had a "fierce hostility to prolixity, rhetoric, and eloquence."[11] So he
experimented with what he called *récits* or *soties*—novelettes midway
between novels and short stories. Nor had he much skill in drawing
character. Most of the persons described in these *romans* (to use
Voltaire's term) were Gide himself in diverse disguises, expounding
through these masks his favorite views or revealing his ambivalent
moods. "One would say that my own thought frightened me, and this
is the source of the need I felt for attributing it to the heroes of my
books in order the better to separate it from me."[12]

Oppressed by a need to defend his ethic of release and his practice of
homosexuality, he published in 1902 (aged thirty-three) a venturesome
tale called *L'Immoraliste*. The title echoed Nietzsche's phrase "I am the
first Immoralist," and his volume *Beyond Good and Evil;* both titles
meant not an addict of "immorality," but a philosophical rejection of
Christian ethics. Like nearly all the radical writers of his time in Europe,
Gide had been strongly influenced by Nietzsche's "transvaluation of
all values." He read *Thus Spake Zarathustra* "seven or eight times,"
though he later reacted against Nietzsche's exaltation of bravery and
strength. Michel, the narrator of Gide's first *récit*, says, "I fell ill, I

traveled, I met Ménalque, and . . . I was born again." How? Because Ménalque expounded to him the relativity of moral codes, the mundanity of their origin, and the limits and area of their force. Michel was relieved to learn that the homosexual urges which were frustrating his marriage with Marceline were accepted as legitimate in Islam and Asia. He took his wife to Africa, and enjoyed the embraces of Arab boys, while his neglected wife faded in the heat and died.

The legitimacy of revolt against established authority and traditional norms found another expression in *Le Retour de l'enfant prodigue* (1907). Here, like Thomas Mann, Gide tried to retell a Bible tale. The Prodigal Son, after exhausting adventures in strange lands and ways, comes back in humility to the ancestral home; presumably he symbolizes the return of the extra-*vagant* mind, after willful wanderings amid forbidden ideas, to the intellectual moorings and charted ways of its youth. His younger brother joins their father in welcoming him. The brother assumes that he should learn from this disillusionment the wisdom of unventurous stability. The Prodigal tells him, No, no; you too should go out into the world, make your own experiments, mistakes, and discoveries—even if you are to be shattered by your trials. A door must always be left open to the new.

That Gide himself missed the security and warning trustfulness of his childhood faith appeared in the tenderness, touched with satire, with which in *La Porte étroite* (1909; *Strait Is the Gate*) he told the story of a saint immured in the native creed. Alissa Bucolin, daughter of an epileptic mother, is a pretty girl just turning puberty; but her beauty is fenced with piety, and when her cousin Jérome Pélissier, all of fourteen, falls in love with her, she gently reproves his advances, and bids him await the maturing of their years. She reads Pascal, and adopts all the terrors of his theology; she shrinks into a fearful love of God that dissuades all human attachments. Jérome waits in vain for her to feel the "nourishments of the earth"; year after year she holds him off, while she wastes away in ascetic practices and lonely meditation. "Her thinness, her paleness smote me horribly,"[13] and soon after this meeting she dies.—This, the longest of Gide's *récits*, struck me as exaggerated and unreal, but the author, twenty years later, still considered it his best.

Gide was a dedicated writer, working many hours daily, threading idea after idea on his tenuous lines, and hoping somehow, however tardily, to bring the world—or France or Paris—to greater tolerance of inverted souls. With only a brief rest after *La Porte étroite*, he turned from fiction to tell sympathetically (1910) the story of Oscar Wilde. He did not dare yet to proclaim his own homosexuality, but he was now writing, with all the intensity of a man pleading for his life, that strange volume which he would publish in 1924 as *Corydon*, defending his kind against the world.

After a decade of success with novelettes, he ventured upon a longer narrative, which reached print in 1914 as *Les Caves du Vatican*. The *caves* are the cellars in which, says a rumor, the current Pope has been imprisoned by Freemasons, who have raised a false pope to the papal throne. A conspiracy of criminals, led by one Protos, has manufactured the rumor, and is now using deluded priests to collect funds from rich Catholics for the liberation of the true Pope. (A like false rumor had actually circulated in 1893 about an alleged kidnaping of Leo XIII.) The central character of Gide's tale is Lafcadio Wlacki, a young Romanian who has followed Nietzsche in throwing out the Christian ethic along with the Christian theology. Sharing a railway compartment with Amédée Fleurissoire, Lafcadio takes a distaste for him, and plays with the idea of pushing him from the swiftly moving train. He leaves the decision to an accidental succession of ideas in his imagination; the fatal idea comes, and the crime is committed. Protos discovers Lafcadio's guilt, and blackmails him into joining the antipapal cabal. The conspiracy is foiled, and Lafcadio is arrested. An incidental character, Count Julius, in discussing the murder, expounds the notion of *l'acte gratuit*, a gratuitous act—one that springs from the pure play of fancy, free from external compulsion and from self-seeking calculation; "there is no reason," argues the Count, "why a man who commits a crime without reason should be called a criminal."[14] Critics condemned this casuistry as nonsense, and churchmen added that the story showed far less than due respect for His Holiness.

Gide did not appease the clergy with *La Symphonie pastorale* (1919). A Protestant minister takes into his home a blind girl, teaches her, and falls in love with her, so alienating his wife and children. The girl recovers her sight, sees that the pastor is aging and that his son is handsome and vigorous; she goes off with the son; the pastor consoles himself with Beethoven's Sixth Symphony. The story was beautifully written, became a best seller, and was made into a successful film. Perhaps it reflected Gide's estrangement from his wife. She had refused to read his books, believing them to be subtle apologies for his diverted love; now she burned all his letters to her, and withdrew into increasing silence and solitude till her death.

In 1924 he made the apology more boldly direct by publishing *Corydon*. Jacques Maritain, having learned of its trend, had begged him not to print it; Gide persisted, feeling that he could no longer bear the pretense of heterosexual conformity, and that the case for his minority had never been intelligibly presented. Corydon—named after a shepherd in Theocritus—expounds this case to a visitor, presumably Gide. He describes the frequency of homosexuality in animals, in classic Greece, and among the Moslems; outside of Christendom the practice was widely condoned, perhaps as a check to overpopulation; it was so widespread that we should admit its deep roots in animals and human nature, and should cease to treat its practitioners as criminals. How much fine literature and art has been inspired by homosexual love! "Had not Socrates and Plato loved young men, what a pity for Greece, for the whole world!"[15] Gide thought *Corydon* his most important book; certainly it was his bravest. The campaign against him as a corrupter of youth redoubled its intensity.

He fought back by issuing (1926) *Si le Grain ne meurt* (*Unless the Seed Dies* it will not sprout into a developing life). It was one more autobiography, revealing the early repressions and youthful tensions that may have led to his inversion. Paris admired his style, and deplored his morals.

Meanwhile he had been working, with more industry than passion, at what he felt would be his supreme literary test: Could he write a successful full-length novel? The implicit thesis of *Les Faux-Monnayeurs* (1926; *The Counterfeiters*) was that most human beings, at least in "civilized" society, pretend to a quality and value they do not have, and that most of our institutions are tarnished with a like dishonesty, with fiction and appearance disguising reality.[16] Nearly every urban husband has a mistress, nearly every wife has a lover, and all alike descend the slope from passion to ennui. The explicit theme of the book is the rebellion of youth, in each generation, against hypocrisy and pretense, against the parental authority, the religious traditions, and the social restraints, that seek to cover the truth and to cool desire. The story describes the vicissitudes of three young men—Bernard, Vincent, and Olivier—in their diverse moves from psychological repression to hectic liberty and moral chaos. The narrative is interrupted—and the illusion of reality is destroyed—by Gide's comments on his characters, and by the puzzling pretense that one of them, Édouard, is writing a novel entitled *The Counterfeiters*. Édouard, like Olivier and Passavant, is a homosexual; Olivier's mind is "filled with impure visions which he did not try to banish";[17] and there is much talk of self-abuse.[18] Altogether it is an unpleasant performance: lacking in taste, order, and clarity; cluttered with incidental discussions and irrelevant ideas; failing to make its too numerous characters stand out as living individuals rather than bloodless copies of Gide in various phases or moods. Yet he was so proud of this volume that he wrote a *Journal of "The Counterfeiters,"* describing his methods, experiments, difficulties, and progress in composing "the only novel and final book I shall write. I want to pour everything into it, without reservation."[19] He succeeded, and failed.

He made no further attempt at fiction. After 1926 he confined himself to plays, essays, travel impressions, editing his influential magazine *Nouvelle Revue française* (1909–40), and jotting down incidents and reflections in a diary. These *Journals*, published by installments during his lifetime (1939, 1946, 1950), are his most interesting legacy, partly because they show an active and sensitive mind in its disturbed and diffident growth, partly because they record contacts with distinguished contemporaries, partly because they convey, sometimes with eloquence, Gide's views on literature, philosophy, and art. They reveal him as a completely self-centered man, analyzing his motives, professing his sincerity, defending his morals, countering accusations of vanity and stinginess,[20] living on his nerves, fighting insomnia, answering his enemies, and cultivating his friends. His enemies made his faults forgivable.

In 1921 a leading critic, Henri Massis, assailed him as a "demonic" influence. Others attacked him as a degenerate, morally bankrupt, philosophically sterile, theologically at sea. In 1940 *Le Temps* charged him with weakening French character with his youthful gospel of pleasure, and held him partly to blame for the collapse of France before Hitler's troops.[21] Gide replied that the defeat of France was due not to amoralism in its literature but to "disorder, incompetence, negligence, internal divisions, and decay" in its government.[22] In 1952 his books were placed on the *Index of Prohibited Books* by the Catholic Church, and the *Osservatore romano* alleged that "Gide's work from beginning to end is altogether orchestrated on a note of equivocal seduction, so consistent that it eventually bores and nauseates. Generations of young people came under his treacherous fascination; things which before him would scarcely have been whispered among mature people became through Gide's fault a sort of boast—a filthy boast of adolescents."[23]

The Church might have overlooked these offenses if Gide had followed some of his friends into the Catholic fold. In 1916 he learned of the conversion, at the front, of his friend Henri Ghéon. At first he ridiculed it; then he thought of imitating it. He wrote some religious meditations, which he published (1922) under the Scriptural title *Numquid et tu?* (*And you too* are a Galilean—i.e., a Christian?). He wrote tender descriptions of youthful piety, even amid the irreverent *Caves of the Vatican.*[24] He echoed confusedly, as late as 1935, the question that de Musset had asked of the *philosophes* a century before.

> To all outcasts, the bent under a yoke and the heavy laden, the thirsty, the sore at heart, the aching—assurance of a compensatory after life! However fanciful it may be, would you dare rob them of that hope? Yes, if it is to tell them: even "here below" [there could be Paradise]. Leave them eternal life, or give them revolution. Or, rather, rob them of eternal life, and you will have revolution.[25]

Time and again he returned to the idea of God. In 1941 he defined religion as "a state of effort . . . toward something indefinable and adorable, toward a higher condition in which the individual is lost and absorbed—to which I see no other name to give but the very name of God."[26] For a year or more he thought that this vague conception might provide a new religious basis for morality: "As soon as I had realized that God was not yet but was becoming, and that his becoming depended upon each one of us, a moral sense was restored to me."[27] Finally, in 1947, he declared himself an atheist, and called for an ethic independent of religion:

> Man must learn to get along without Providence . . . We have not yet reached this point. It requires much virtue to achieve that state of total atheism; even more to remain there. The "believer" will probably see in it nothing but an invitation to license. If this were so, hooray for God! Hooray for the sacred falsehood that would preserve humanity from collapse, from disaster. But cannot man learn to demand of himself, through virtue, what he believes demanded of God? Yet he must nevertheless get to that point; some, at least must, to begin with; otherwise the game would be lost. That strange game that we are playing on earth . . . will be won only if the idea of God, on withdrawing yields to virtue, only if man's virtue, his dignity, supplants God.[28]

He hoped, like so many other denuded souls, to compensate the death of God with the imitation of Christ; only so, he thought, could Christianity be rescued from its "pitiful bankruptcy."[29]

He was not quite clear about the morality with which he hoped to replace religion. In *The Counterfeiters* he made his mouthpiece, Édouard, attack the family as a tyranny of authority over children "born to freedom";[30] he was then still in his individualistic stage. But as his knowledge of men and history widened he saw the seeds of chaos in the doctrines he had preached. In 1942 he deposed his old goddess: "I do not believe in *Liberty*," he wrote; "we are dying of its idolatrous cult; and I am ready to accept many a constraint."[31] Now, struggling to free himself from the prison of self, he saw the secret of happiness in an ever-widening love; "I doubt whether there is any other virtue than love . . . , to love as much as possible, and continually more and more."[32] However, he continued to forage for boys, and in one mood (May 13, 1937) he interpreted ever-widening love in a novel way: "As soon as I am not absorbed by some precise occupation I feel vague, wandering idly. I should like to forget everything; live for a long time among naked Negroes, people whose language I didn't know and who didn't know who I am; and fornicate savagely, silently, at night, with anyone whatever, on the sand."[33]

In 1925 and again in 1926 Gide traveled in the Congo, enjoying the sturdy figures of Negro youths, and resenting the treatment of the natives by European colonials. Back in France he published two long articles (1927–28) exposing the malpractices of French and other commercial companies operating in Africa. The pieces caused a stir; a governmental investigation followed, and some abuses were mitigated with all the leisureliness of justice.

Long accustomed to a sheltered and physically comfortable life, Gide came slowly to awareness of poverty and class rule. His rebellion against the heterosexual moral code inclined him to sympathize with rebels against religious obscurantism, economic exploitation, and political tyranny. He welcomed (May 13, 1931) the news that Spanish crowds were "burning convents more ferociously than did ever the land of Voltaire," though he saw in such outbreaks "something spasmodic that might well not last."[34] Soviet Russia's war against religion moved him to favor the Communist experiment. He was eager "to see what can be produced by a state without religion, a society without the family. Religion and the family are the two worst enemies of progress" (July 27, 1931).[35] And yet "what leads me to Communism is not Marx, it is the Gospel."[36] He recognized in the Russian Revolution the most basic economic or political event of the century. "How can one still write novels when around us our world is crumbling, when something unknown is being elaborated?"[37] "Never have I bent over the future with a more passionate curiosity. My whole heart applauds that gigantic and yet entirely human undertaking."[38] "I have come to wish most heartily for the upset of capitalism and everything that lurks in its shadow."[39] In his enthusiasm he transferred his worship from individual liberty to group cooperation. "The notion of liberty, as it is taught to us, seems to me singularly false and pernicious. And if I approve the Soviet constraint, I must likewise approve the Fascist discipline" (October, 1931).[40] Here was a novel note for the quondam apostle of youthful freedom.

Nevertheless he refused the invitation of French Communists to join the party. He called himself "unfit for politics," and begged his new admirers to excuse him (June 13, 1932).[41] He still clung to intellectual freedom. By June, 1933, he was again a skeptic.

> Like the conversion to Catholicism, conversion to Communism implies an abdication of free inquiry, submission to a dogma, recognition of an orthodoxy. It happens that all orthodoxies are suspect to me. . . . Whether the text invoked be by Marx or Lenin, I cannot abide by it unless my heart and my reason approve it. I did not escape from the authority of Aristotle or Saint Paul to fall under theirs. Yet I recognize the necessity of a credo to bring together individual wills; but my adhesion to that credo has no value unless it is freely consented to.[42]

Eager to see the vast change in actual operation, he set out in 1936 to visit Soviet Russia. He was received as a famous convert, enjoyed every honor, and traveled under discriminating guidance. He liked the spacious landscape and the openhearted people. When he was safely back home he wrote an account of his expedition—*Retour de l'U.R.S.S.* (1936), applauding the enterprise but regretting the regimentation of thought. The Communists accused him of having lost courage. He comforted himself in his *Journal* (summer of 1937):

> In the little unfinished book of Lenin, *The State and the Revolution,* . . . there is a sentence that holds my attention. "Until now," he says, repeating an idea dear to Marx and Engels, "there has not been a revolution that in the long run has not led to a strengthening of the administrative mechanism." . . . That was twenty years ago. And now what is the status of the U.S.S.R.? Dreadful bureaucracy, administrative mechanism, has never been stronger.[43]

Moreover, he had read Marx's *Das Kapital,* all four volumes,

> with no other desire than to let myself be convinced, to yield even, and to learn. And each time I came away aching all over, my intelligence bruised as by instruments of torture. . . . What especially

bothers me here is the very theory, with everything if not exactly
irrational, at least artificial, . . . fallacious and inhuman, it contains.
I think that a great part of Marx's prestige comes from the fact that
he is difficult of access, so that Marxism involves an initiation, and
is generally known only through mediators. It is the Mass in Latin.
√ When one does not understand one bows down.[44]

Finally (February 24, 1946), aged seventy-six, he reaffirmed his youthful nonconformity, and remembered his class:

> Catholicism or Communism demands, or at least advocates, sub-
> mission of the mind. Worn out by yesterday's struggle, young men
> (and many of their elders) seek, and think they have found, in that
> very submission, rest, assurance, and intellectual comfort. . . . Thus
> it is that, without being really aware of it, or becoming aware of it
> only too late, . . . they are going to contribute to the defeat, to the
> retreat, to the rout of the spirit, to the establishment of some form
> or other of "totalitarianism," which will be hardly any better than
> the Nazism they were fighting.
>
> The world will be saved, if it can be, only by the *unsubmissive*.
> Without them it would be all up with our civilization, our culture,
> what we loved, and what gave to our presence on earth a secret
> justification.[45]

After his sally into Communism Gide withdrew from *la littérature
engagée*. The death of his wife (April 17, 1938), though they had been
so long divorced in spirit, intensified the loneliness that he had always
felt in a world that calls upon every man to take sides and shoulder
arms—and love women. Now that Emmeline was gone he longed for
her, if only for her silent presence: "Since she has ceased to exist I have
merely pretended to live, without taking any further interest in anything or in myself, without appetite, without taste, or curiosity, or desire,
and in a disenchanted universe; with no further hope than to leave it"
(August 21, 1938).[46]

A year later the outbreak of World War II deepened his despair. He
shuddered at the thought that "a bomb can do away with a museum."[47]
He drugged himself by memorizing long passages of Racine or La
Fontaine. He refused to contribute to French military ardor by speaking on the radio. "I will not contribute to pumping oxygen into the
public," he told himself (October 30, 1939); "the newspapers already
√ contain enough patriotic yapping."[48] He had so many connections with
Germany, so many readers there, so much acquaintance with German

literature and philosophy; he had often visited those admirably ad-ministered German cities, whose audiences had been the first to applaud his plays; he found it hard to think of the Germans as the enemies and destroyers of civilization. He himself, a Protestant in a Catholic coun-try, was almost a German mind vainly struggling to be Latin. After the surrender of France he took refuge in Tunisia, and remained there till the end of the war. He inclined to think that Pétain had made the best of a bad bargain; in any case, he felt (March 7, 1943) France had by its decadence invited a war of German revenge against the Treaty of Versailles.[49] French patriots denounced him as a traitor.

In February, 1940, he had predicted, in effect, the coming of de Gaulle to power. "One must expect that after the war, and even though victors, we shall plunge into such a mess that nothing but a determined dictator-ship will be able to get us out of it. One can see the soundest minds gradually progressing in that direction."[50] In June, 1943, de Gaulle in-vited Gide to visit him in Algiers. Gide came, and proudly noted in his journal: "De Gaulle's welcome has been very cordial and very simple, almost deferential toward me, as if the honor and pleasure of the meet-ing had been his."[51]

This is believable, for at that time de Gaulle had not made his mark upon history, while Gide was probably the most famous writer in Europe. The young acclaimed him, the old deplored him, and when he returned to France after the war there was no warm greeting for him; it was felt that he had deserted his country in her darkest hour. But all educated Frenchmen read him, and he had a wide audience in Germany and America. In 1947 the Swedish Academy awarded him the Nobel Prize for Literature. He was then seventy-eight; "Constantly," he wrote, "I hear the eldest of the Fates whispering in my ear, you haven't much time left."[52] Till his death (February 19, 1951) he was surrounded by debate as to his character and his influence, and an "onslaught of criticism" from Right and Left, from Catholics and Communists, fol-lowed him to the grave.[53] France still wonders whether he was the Devil incarnate in his effect upon morals, or the finest writer of French prose since Anatole France. He was a great artist, but only those can love him who have shared his problem and his harassment.

CHAPTER XI

The Philosophers

I. WITTGENSTEIN

A T this point in our literary travelogue we come face to face with Jean-Paul Sartre, who dominates the living scene of France in both literature and philosophy. We shall not understand his ideas, or his novels, or his plays unless we venture from our *diritta via*[1] and spend an hour with the philosophers of our time. The prospect is a bit disturbing, for the kind of philosophy most honored in American universities today continues a timid retreat from the actual problems of life into the mammoth caves of metaphysics and epistemology—that same retreat which I raged at in the initial chapter of *The Mansions of Philosophy* forty years ago. It was an uneven contest; I emerged from it unbowed but bloody. Professorial philosophy still hides itself from the world, lost and secure in the labyrinths of logic, the mysteries of mathematics, or the meticulous, anesthetizing analysis of words.

Bertrand Russell is a lusty exception to this norm; he soon broke out of the cave to face bravely what seem to me the real problems of philosophy: nature and mind, morals and character, liberty and order, violence and law, youth and age, love and marriage, beauty and ugliness, Communism and democracy, war and peace, religion and secularism, progress and decay, the lessons of history, the meaning of life and death.[2] But before he dealt so recklessly with these vital issues, Russell had felt the fascination of mathematics. In 1910–1913, with Professor Alfred North Whitehead, he reformulated the propositions of mathematics in forms of symbolic logic; and in 1915 he declared, "I am convinced that all fundamental work in philosophy is logical."[3] It was during that ecstasy that he discovered and befriended the strangest figure in contemporary thought.

Ludwig Wittgenstein (1889–1951) was the son of a rich Viennese Jew. Too familiar with money to be enamored of it, he gave his love to logic and mathematics, and went to Trinity College, Cambridge, to study under Russell (1912). "He was," Russell recalls, "the most perfect example I have ever known of genius as traditionally conceived, passionate, profound, intense, and dominating."[4] When war broke out, the young philosopher joined the Austrian Army; he fought on the Italian front, and was taken prisoner (1918). From his bondage in Monte Cassino he sent to Russell the manuscript which reached print in 1921 as *Tractatus logico-philosophicus*.

I have studied it manfully, but I am so innocent of logic that I am sure I have merely skimmed the surface of its significance. It was a comfort to note, in his subsequent *Philosophical Investigations*, a humble admission: "I have been forced to recognize grave mistakes in what I wrote in that first book."[5] Even the later work was a sorrowful compromise between desire and accomplishment: "I should have liked to produce a good book. This has not come about, but the time is past in which I could improve it."

All propositions about the world or the mind are (1) elementary— in which things directly known are represented by "names" originally pictorial; or (2) significant propositions, which are "truth-functions" or derivatives of elementary propositions. Hence the *Tractatus* is a series of numbered elementary propositions, each followed by derivatives decimally numbered (e.g., 6.1, 6.2, etc.), these often followed by their own secondary derivatives (e.g., 6.11, 6.12 . . . , 6.21, 6.22 . . .). Wittgenstein, like Spinoza, took mathematics as his ideal, and dreamed of reducing all philosophy to mathematical form. "The logic of the world, which is shown by the propositions of logic, is shown in equations by mathematics."[6] (Recall Einstein's search for an equation that would express all the operations of nature.)

But first all philosophy should be reduced to logic. "The exploration of logic means the exploration of everything that is subject to law."[7] "Logic pervades the world; the limits of the world are also the limits of logic. . . . Logic presents an order, in fact the a priori order of the world: that is, the order of possibilities, which must be common to both world and thought. . . . Logic is not a body of doctrine but a mirror image of the world."[8]

Despite this adoration of logic, Wittgenstein came to realize that logic is a man-made convenience of thought, and that nature may have irregularities and absurdities not allowed for in our philosophies. "People today stop at the laws of nature, treating them as inviolable, just as God and Fate were treated in past ages."[9] We can perceive and formulate regularities of succession in events, but sooner or later an exception appears; a certain whimsicality in nature makes conclusions provisional; and science, abandoning explanation, confines itself to description.[10] This malleability of events warrants our reluctance to accept complete determinism. "The freedom of the will consists in the impossibility of knowing actions that still lie in the future. We could know them only if causality were an *inner* necessity like that of logical inference."[11] But "belief in the causal nexus is superstition."[12] Here, evidently, Wittgenstein is combining Hume and Kant.

Wittgenstein not only gave up hope of finding in logic the very structure of the world, he went near to despair of ever clearing logic and philosophy of absurdities in their terms. In *Philosophical Investigations* he called for, and exemplified, a painstaking analysis of the language used in philosophy. "Philosophy is a battle against the bewitchment of our intelligence by means of language."[13] How much nonsense has been talked about infinity—which is a word without any positive significance. How many moralists have written about virtue without defining it. "Most of the propositions and questions of philosophers arise from our failure to understand the logic of our language."[14] All philosophy henceforth should be "a critique of language."[15] "A philosophical work consists essentially of elucidations. Philosophy does not result in 'philosophical propositions,' but rather in the clarification of propositions. Without [such] philosophy thoughts are, as it were, cloudy and indistinct; its task is to make them clear and give them sharp boundaries."[16] In these sentences is the fountainhead of that placid stream of "analytical philosophy" which now waters the ivy of academes in Great Britain and the United States.

The final step in the intellectual peregrinations of Wittgenstein was his conviction that language, however chastened and clarified, could not express the deepest thoughts. "There are things that cannot be put into words. They *make themselves manifest*. They are what is mystical. . . . What can be shown cannot be said. . . . Those who have found, after a long period of doubt, that the sense of life became clear to them have been unable to say what constituted that sense."[17] Words can at best serve as hints to understanding. "My propositions serve as elucidations in the following way: anyone who understands me eventually recognizes them as nonsensical, when he has used them as steps to climb up beyond them."[18]

"Whether Wittgenstein's theories are true," wrote Bertrand Russell, "I cannot know; I devoutly hope they are not, as they make mathematics and logic almost incredibly difficult."[19] I am relieved to learn that one of the clearest minds of this century finds Wittgenstein difficult to comprehend. I have quoted some sentences that seemed within my grasp, and have tried to link them in some order and sequence; but I suspect that there is a vision here beyond my ken. And I remember

Wittgenstein's proud warning to Russell himself: "Don't suppose that everything that you won't be able to understand is a piece of stupidity."[20]

Russell might have answered that obscure language is sometimes due to unclear and vacillating thought. Instead he helped to get Wittgenstein a teaching post at Cambridge. There the passionate logician attracted some devoted followers. But he was so absorbed in his ideas, so careless of social graces and conformity, so proud of his propositions and impatient of opposition, that he soon became uncomfortable among these calm and courteous Englishmen. He returned to the Continent, and, having given to his brother and sister his share of the paternal legacy, he earned his bread by teaching school in Austria (1920-26). In 1929 he resumed his lectures at Cambridge, and he taught philosophy there till 1947. At a date unnamed, William Gass heard him take an excited part in a discussion at Cornell University. "Old, unsteady, queerly dressed, . . . uncomfortable in space, he struck me as some atheistical, vegetarian nut who'd somehow found his way to this meeting of the Cornell Philosophy Club, and would, at any moment, heatedly, endlessly support and denounce, with wild irrelevance, whatever simple, single thought was burning him up."[21]

I do not know what happened to him afterward, except that he died in 1951, at the age of sixty-two. Probably his flame burned itself out through its own intensity. Perhaps he erred in taking logic and philosophy so seriously; modesty and humor—seeing the part in the light of the whole—are good vaccines against metaphysical madness. It is a blessing that his inheritors, the analytical philosophers, have led his madness into a private pasture, and tamed it into a harmless game.

II. THE FORERUNNERS OF EXISTENTIALISM

Existentialism is more interesting, but who will dare define it? Martin Heidegger, most prominent of the German school, repudiated the term; so did Karl Jaspers; so did Camus; so did Sartre,[22] until general usage compelled him to accept it; and Gabriel Marcel, who gave it currency, rejected the most characteristic idea of Heidegger and Sartre. The word had appeared in Kierkegaard's "existential dialectic"; it was applied to Heidegger's insistence on the meaning of being, or existence, as the fundamental problem of philosophy; and it described the emphasis, in Heidegger and Sartre, on the priority of existence over essence in time and significance. Against the notion that the essence or nature of man determined the character and fate of every man, the existentialist believes that each individual's existence is a unique and primary fact, and that his essence or essential character is the gradual and ever-changing product of his existence in the flux of time.[23] A man's essence is formed by his total past, to which he adds in every moment of his life. In Heidegger and Sartre existentialism is additionally the study of human existence after the "death of God": the loneliness and anguish of the individual in a world bereft of divine guidance and moral worth. Usually the existentialist rejects the naturalistic approach to the study of man through biology and history, and prefers the "phenomenological" approach through the study of consciousness, and of objective reality as phenomena appearing to consciousness. Obviously existentialism is too multiform and mutable to be compressed into a line, but we shall provisionally define it as the philosophy of the individual mind confronted by the changing contemporary world.

Many ideas converged to form it. Heracleitus, five hundred years before Christ, emphasized the fluidity and ubiquity of change. Nothing *is*, everything *becomes*; everything at every moment is ceasing to be what it was, and is becoming what it will be; where, in this *panta rhei*, or universal flow, is the essence? In this flux all things are in conflict with their opposites; but the conflict produces the fertile union of the opposites in tensile and mounting strength; strife (*polemos*) is the father of all things, the source of all development. Sartre concluded that in Heracleitus, and in all reality, everything is a combination of being and nonbeing, of "being and nothingness."

From Descartes' *Cogito ergo sum* (1637) Kierkegaard, Heidegger, and Sartre inferred that man's consciousness is the prime datum and logical starting point of philosophy. Since thought is the reality most directly known to us—and since external realities are known only indirectly and uncertainly through their *appearance* to thought—it follows that the proper study of mankind is mind; and theories like materialism and determinism, which originate from the study of external things, lose their force when applied to the immaterial world of consciousness, will, and thought.

Pascal (1623–62) believed in free will, and it terrified him; it was God's ominous gift to man, making sin possible, and therefore responsibility, guilt, anxiety, and damnation. Thought seemed to Pascal a tragedy; it found itself crushed and stupefied between two unintelligible infinites—the limitless expanse of the universe and the endless divisibility of the atom. What sense or worth could these infinites have if there were no God to give their being some significance in a drama where every soul would play a leading and possibly fatal role? What an absurdity this life of inescapable pains and baffling mystery would be if it had to end in meaningless annihilation. Why had existence been forced upon us helplessly contingent and dispensable mites?[24]

And then Hegel, plunging into the Heracleitean flux, found there again eternal Becoming, the present ever rising out of the past and vanishing into the future. Pure Being, indeterminate and unparticularized, said Hegel, is the same as Nothing; they are indistinguishable abstractions; only when Being becomes *something*—a particular object or mental state—does it achieve existence. So we should say not "Being is," but "Being becomes." Becoming is a dialectical process—an orderly, logical movement—in nature, history, and thought: each stage develops logically through an antithesis and merger which in turn become the thesis or starting point of a further development in the growth of consciousness and reason.

It was in reaction against Hegel that Kierkegaard proclaimed the first form of existentialism. It was in the path of Hegel that Sartre mated Being and Nothing to produce a universe.

III. SØREN KIERKEGAARD

Michael Kierkegaard was a Copenhagen wool merchant who was compelled to marry Anne Lund (as his second wife) because he had gotten her with child. When she was forty-five and Michael was fifty-six she gave birth (May 5, 1813) to her seventh child, Søren, who paid for parental exhaustion by his hunched back and uneven legs.[25] The father, in his declining years and growing piety, was oppressed by recalling the sexual sins of his youth, and a fit of rage in which he had cursed God; now he lapsed into lengthening moods of melancholy under the weight of his guilt; and he sought vicarious atonement by giving his children repeated injections of Lutheran theology, stressing the inborn depravity of man. When Søren learned of his father's sins he felt that he had inherited the paternal guilt, and that only a lifetime of religious devotion could wash it away. For ten years (1830–40) he studied—chiefly theology—at the University of Copenhagen. In 1836, on a drunken carouse, he visited a brothel, "and there lay with a harlot."[26] The consciousness of this lapse filled him with shame and despair, and led him to thoughts of suicide.

A better side of life was opened to him a year later by his meeting Regina Olsen, a wholesome girl of fifteen. He won her away from another suitor, and in 1840 she pledged herself by giving him a ring. His happiness was haunted with secret anxiety about his physical and moral fitness for marriage. Had he a right to bind this healthy young woman to a hunchback weak in the legs and of undependable virility? "He sometimes declared himself no full man, since the animal element was lacking."[27] He feared that the guilt which he thought had come down to him from his father was attached to the sexual act, and would be thereby passed on to his wife and children. "Because of the resultant spiritual bashfulness and dread, Kierkegaard felt incapable of entering into marriage."[28] In August, 1841, he returned Regina's ring and ended the engagement, declaring himself unworthy of her. When she begged him to reconsider he went to Berlin and wrote a major work, *Either/Or*, which recounted his love affair through fictional characters; the hero, to ease the pain of his broken engagement, pretends that he is a mean scoundrel who could not make a good woman happy. Regina recovered with disconcerting rapidity, married Friedrich Schlegel, and repulsed Søren's efforts to be accepted as a friend of the family. He never married. His will left all his possessions to "Madame Regina Schlegel," but they hardly sufficed to pay for his funeral.[29]

He had inherited most of his father's fortune, which enabled him to live a life of study and authorship. He issued many books, usually under various noms de plume; he took an impish pleasure in playing hide-and-seek with his readers. His starting point was expressed in a volume called *Repetition* (1843), in queries recalling Pascal and often repeated in existentialist philosophy: "My life has been brought to an impasse. I loathe existence; it is without savor, lacking salt and sense . . . Where am I? Who am I? How came I here? What is this thing called the world? . . . What does the world mean? . . . How did I come into the world? Why was I not consulted?"[30] He wished he could ask God these questions and get an authoritative answer.

The divine silence did not discourage his preoccupation with religion. In *Stages on Life's Way* (1845) he suggested that a developing mind evolves from aesthetic to literary to religious interests. When he contrasted the Christianity of Christ with the state-supported Lutheran Church of Denmark, he was roused to anger by the worldliness of the clergy, and by the ridiculous attempt of the divines to rationalize Christian theology on the basis of Hegel's philosophy. He attacked the Danish Church in a series of passionate and reckless volumes; he challenged the clergy to forgo their creature comforts and live in strict conformity with the ethics of Christ. He advised his readers to take no part in public worship, to make their piety private and familial, and to repudiate a religious establishment which seemed to him to be a shameful departure from New Testament Christianity.[31] He complained that Hegelianism had forgotten the individual soul in the theoretical and abstract Absolute, and had ignored the heart in an idolatry of reason. He proposed to abandon intellectual generalities, to explore the inner self, and to ask, "What does it mean to be a human being?"[32] The Lutheran leaders denounced him as an upstart egotist; he retorted; the controversy continued, and contributed to his death.

In *Either/Or* (1843) he bade his readers choose definitively between the world and Christ. He scorned the Hegelian legerdemain of tossing up opposites in the hope that they would come down merged; life is not both-and, but either-or; "either/or is the key to heaven, both-and is the way to hell."[33] He admitted that the doctrines and divinity of Christ could not be proved by reason; no matter; experience is surer than logic; and our innermost experience tells us that without belief in God and salvation life is a brutal struggle full of suffering, injustice, sickness, defeat, and death, unintelligible and unbearable if there is no Son of God to redeem us from the guilt of our sins. Kierkegaard joined the Romantics of Germany and France in reaction against the rationalism of the Enlightenment: "It is the duty of the human understanding to understand that there are things which it cannot understand."[34] All propositions that make for a good life are to be held true; all that make for sin or grief are false; "only the truth that edifies is truth for thee."[35] Let us seek the truth from our inward spiritual conviction, not from a science based upon observation of matter and its operations, and not from a logic based upon science. "Subjectivity, inwardness, is truth";[36] the testimony of consciousness is superior to any science. And since science fails us, we must determine our existence by our own free choice, by a "leap into the dark." But because we are free to choose, we are responsible for the results. Because we are free to sin and we do, we feel ourselves guilty in the sight of God. Sometimes we despair of ever winning divine forgiveness; and a secret anxiety, generated by our liberty, harrows our hearts.[37]

Either/Or is of high literary quality, comparable with the best German literature of the time. Strangely, and yet in accord with Kierkegaard's ambivalent self, the most brilliant pages of the book record "The Diary of a Seducer," who gives a detailed description of woman's beauty as so desirable that "God may keep Heaven if I may keep her."[38] The seducer gets his way with the maid, deserts her, and meditates mercilessly: "I hope never to see her again. When a girl has given away everything, then she is weak, then she has lost everything. For a man guilt is a negative moment; for a woman it is the value of her being. . . . I do not wish to be reminded of my relation with her; she has lost the fragrance."[39] There may be memories of Regina Olsen here; in any case, if she read *Either/Or* we can understand why she could not bear to see Kierkegaard again.

The book brought the author new enemies and wide fame; he came to be known in Copenhagen as "Either/Or Kierkegaard." He knew that the journalists of the capital would laugh at his theology, but he proposed to let them croak in their swamps undisturbed.[40] Though he kept a *Journal* (*Papirer*), he declared that "the lowest depth to which ✳ people can sink before God is defined by the word *Journalist*," and he recommended abstention from newspapers as more important than avoidance of alcohol.[41] His controversies exhilarated and exhausted him.

On October 2, 1855, he was stricken with paralysis of the lower limbs while carrying from a bank the final installment of his patrimony. He was taken to a hospital, where he soothed his sufferings with celestial visions. "I have had a feeling," he told a visitor, "of becoming an angel, getting wings; and that indeed is what will come to pass—to sit upon the clouds and sing Hallelujah, hallelujah, hallelujah! . . . I am glad to die."[42] His happy torture ended on November 11, 1855. He was forty-two. He had dispensed with the last sacraments because he would not receive them from a clergyman, and no laymen volunteered;[43] but the Danish Church, as one of death's little ironies, gave him a formal funeral.

Kierkegaard presents an ambiguous figure to a twentieth-century prejudice. He received all the education then available in Copenhagen, and yet—a century after Holberg had brought the Enlightenment to Denmark—he professed belief in a personal Devil, and in the full verbal inspiration of the Bible by God. He emerged a bit scathed from his romance. He preached the imitation of Christ while living on inherited money. He attacked his opponents with something less than Christian charity. In the face of these debits stand his brave struggle against physiological disabilities and theological terrors, and his stimulating legacy of ideas to existentialist philosophers. From Pascal's bewilderment and anguish, and Descartes' rediscovery of the self, he formulated conceptions of guilt and anxiety, and of consciousness as the supreme source and test of truth. He felt that any existence worthy of a man is one which, however helplessly begun, can be guided and formed by a free and responsible choice.

His influence remained negligible until his works were translated into German in 1909–14; and by that time his basic assumptions had been called in question by the course of European thought and events. In 1859 Darwin replaced divine design in nature by natural selection; in 1883 Nietzsche's Zarathustra announced that "God is dead"; and in two world wars God seemed to vanish from history. After this hundred years' flood of doubt and disaster Søren Kierkegaard appeared antediluvian, and existentialism fell to the infidels.

IV. HUSSERL AND HEIDEGGER

Some tributary incidents fed the existentialist stream. In Dostoevski's *The Brothers Karamazov* (1880) Ivan offered a startling challenge to philosophy: "If there is no God, everything is permitted" (except detection); that is to say, a moral code unbuttressed by belief in a surveillant and retributive deity would be ineffective, unless every second man became a policeman—which would be intolerable; here is a problem which atheistic existentialism has not solved. — In *L'Évolution créatrice* (1906) and other works Bergson rejected mechanistic science, reaffirmed free will, and proclaimed consciousness as the citadel of philosophy. Heidegger was moved by Dostoevski, Sartre by Bergson, both of them by Edmund Husserl.

As professor at Göttingen and Freiburg, Husserl expounded what, after Hegel, he called phenomenology. The study of consciousness is the most basic of all sciences, for nothing is known to us except as a condition or content of consciousness—i.e., as phenomenon. But consciousness is never an independent and empty awareness; it is always a consciousness of *something;* it is *intentional*—it tends, or is directed, toward an object. Without the object (which may be a thing, a relation, a person, or a mental state) consciousness would have no content; without consciousness the object would have no significance.[44]

At Freiburg one of Husserl's most fervent scholars was Martin Heidegger. Born at Messkirch in the Black Forest in 1889, Heidegger was brought up as a Roman Catholic, and received a strong infusion of Scholastic philosophy from the *Summa*s of Saint Thomas Aquinas; later he abandoned belief in God, but kept a passion for metaphysics. His conversations with Husserl, he said, "provided the immediate experience that led to *Sein und Zeit*" (1927),[45] and in that first classic of existentialist philosophy he affirmed that his investigations had "become possible only on the ground that had been laid by Edmund Husserl."[46]

Being and Time is in the Kantian tradition of subtle epistemology, and, like the *Critique of Pure Reason*, adds to its impenetrability by discarding much of the traditional terminology for a vocabulary of novel and ponderous compounds. The simplest of Heidegger's terms is *Sein* itself—*being* in its largest, vaguest, emptiest sense, the *is*ness of anything that is; it is bare existence devoid of any distinguishing mark or specific form; it is the being of all entities, but "is not itself an entity."[47] "In *Sein und Zeit*," says Heidegger, "the question of being is raised and developed as a question for the first time in the history of philosophy."[48] Man is the metaphysical animal; no other organism, so far as we know, ever rises (or falls) to the depth of asking, "What is being?"

We know being, says Heidegger, most directly through our own consciousness as the vague but pervasive *am* in Descartes' "I think, therefore I am." Husserl is right: all philosophy must be phenomenological—it must be the study of the mind, or of other realities as appearing to the mind. The individual consciousness is the most immediate and inescapable of all realities. To the individual man, and above all to his consciousness, Heidegger gives the name *Dasein*—"existence." Each of us knows of his existence before he ever learns of his essence, for a man's essence as an individual is created accumulatively, minute by minute, by his experiences and his reactions; his essence is his history, his total past.

But we cannot understand ourselves as purely individual. "The basic state of *Dasein*" is "Being-in-the-World."[49] Each consciousness is aware of an external reality; it is "intentional" in Husserl's sense; it points outside itself; and without such content it is nothing. But, so filled, it has unique powers. For the purpose of thought it can distinguish an object from its surroundings by "nihilating"—reducing to nothingness—all that is irrelevant to the object in hand. It can contract or expand the sense of time; it can think of past and future as if they were present. But consciousness is subject to time, to change, decay, and death.

Each of us is oppressed by a sense of his contingency. There is no reason why we should have been born; we are mere happenings, not indispensable to any ascertainable scheme of things. We are thrown into existence without our permission, and snuffed out of it without our leave. We resent this "thrownness" (*Geworfenheit*); we fret over our pitiful helplessness in the flux of forms; the thought of inevitable death darkens our lives. And though we feel ourselves in some measure free,[50] that freedom adds to our burdens, for it makes us responsible for what we do. Care (*Sorge*) is almost the essence of consciousness. Anxiety (*Angst*) haunts us because we can look ahead; "we look before and after, and pine for" assurance and security. We live surrounded by others, but each of us feels essentially alone, and ultimately helpless. And our condition is worse than in earlier centuries, for now—for many of us—"God is no longer a living God";[51] the "ground of being" has become impersonal, no longer a haven of refuge or a promise of salvation.

Faced with the certainty of individual extinction, our wisest response is a quiet acceptance of our fate as part of the natural order and common to all men; we can solace our loneliness by solicitous "Being-with-Others," by accepting responsibilities and sharing care. We can reduce our guilt by a stoic adherence to a self-imposed morality. "To give oneself a code of laws is the highest form of freedom." ✓

That high counsel distinguished Heidegger's address on being installed as rector of the University of Freiburg on May 28, 1933.[52] A year later he resigned to give all his time to teaching. He joined the National Socialist Party, and called upon his students to accept Adolf Hitler as "the current and future reality of Germany, and his word as your law."[53]

Between Heidegger and Sartre two minor figures appear in the development of existentialism. Karl Jaspers (1883–1969), professor of philosophy at Heidelberg, issued in 1931 *Die geistige Situation der Zeit* (translated as *Man in the Modern Age*, 1933), and in 1938 *Existenzphilosophie*. He rejected both the positivism or behaviorism that had tried to bypass consciousness, and the idealism that had dismissed the external world as merely a state of mind. He described man as a compound of mind and body, with a free will limited by heredity and environment. Today, Jaspers felt, man is especially subject to domination and standardization by masses of population in the cities and by the demands of technology in industry. Sufficient individual freedom remains to give us a sense of responsibility, guilt, and alienation; and these, added to the fear of death, incline us to seek supernatural aid. We should not discourage popular belief in God; and indeed the incompleteness of our knowledge points to some "transcendent" ground-of-being which is the philosopher's vague substitute for deity. — In 1937 Jaspers was dismissed from his professorship by the National Socialist government; he lived in obscurity for eight years, until the collapse of the Hitler regime restored him to his post.[54]

Gabriel Marcel returned to Kierkegaard's conception of the philosophical problem as the search for a God to give meaning and support to human life. Born (1889) of a French father and a Jewish mother, he went through years of ill health, cured himself, worked as a Red Cross volunteer in the First World War, and never recovered from its sights of savagery and suffering. In his *Journal métaphysique* (1927) he recorded the steps by which he had come to a faith that seemed to make evil and absurdity bearable. François Mauriac, author of pro-Catholic novels and essays, asked him, "Why are you not one of us?" In 1929 Marcel was received into the Roman Church. Six years later, in *Être et avoir* (*To Be and to Have*), he ascribed the pessimism of current philosophy to the replacement of religion by a race for material goods; character was sacrificed to possessions, and the soul of man was crushed in a maze of machines which made him a tool attached to a tool. How much wiser is "love as the breaking of the tension between the self and the other,"[55] enlarging our being by widening our concern and cooperation. When Sartre published *L'Être et le néant* (1943), affirming conflict as the natural relationship between man and man, stressing the absurdity, suffering, and futility of life, and assuming the evanescence of God, Marcel assailed him as recklessly destroying the religious supports of social order and individual character; only through the acceptance of an authoritarian church and a fortifying creed could modern civilization save itself from collapse through debilitating doubt, class struggle, expanding war, and chaotic revolution. Sartre stood his ground; and in him, as in Heidegger, existentialism became the "phenomenological" study of human existence bereft of God.

CHAPTER XII

Jean-Paul Sartre and
Simone de Beauvoir

I. ADOLESCENCE

SARTRE is a rare bird, of no entrancing plumage, but capable of varied and exciting flights. The world recognized him first as a novelist, then as a philosopher, then as a dramatist, then as a political activist; and it reluctantly acknowledged his importance, if not his preeminence, in all these fields but the last. It is difficult to describe him, or to give unity and continuity to his career, for he has changed character and place almost as frequently in life as he leaps from one person and scene to another in a page or a paragraph of his deliberately chaotic novel, *The Reprieve*. Add to this that since 1929 he has been intimately associated, in love and letters, in philosophy and politics, with the most brilliant Frenchwoman of our time, Simone de Beauvoir. We shall not divorce them in this essay.

Sartre's unfinished autobiography, *Les Mots* (1964; *The Words*), is almost as puzzling as his *Being and Nothingness*. Narrative is mingled with fantasy; simple facts are stated with all possible complexity; poetic dreams are salted with startling phrases plucked from the depths ("My grandfather takes pleasure in being a pain in the ass to his sons"[1]) —though the corresponding French may have some aesthetic overtones. Altogether *The Words* is a disappointing performance, as if written in a careless weekend when disorder was the order of the day.

We gather that Sartre was born in Paris in 1905, son of a French Catholic naval officer and an Alsatian Protestant mother. When the father died (1909) the mother took Jean-Paul to live with her parents. For the next seven years the formative force in the boy's life was his grandfather Karl Schweitzer, uncle to the musician-physician-theologian-philosopher Albert Schweitzer of Lambaréné. Karl was a skeptical Lutheran "who never missed an opportunity to ridicule Catholicism"[2]; meanwhile the mother, following her marriage vows, brought up her son as a Catholic. Buffeted between two mutually critical faiths, Jean-Paul, aged twelve, found it convenient and painless to discard both. "As I was Protestant and Catholic, my double religious affiliation kept me from believing in the Saints, the Virgin, and finally in God himself. . . . He tumbled into the blue and disappeared. . . . Never have I had the slightest temptation to bring Him back to life."[3] In 1916 the mother married again, and took the boy to live with her in La Rochelle. He was apparently unhappy there, and was glad to get back to Paris in 1925. He entered the École Normale Supérieure, and prepared to become a teacher.

Simone de Beauvoir's autobiography* is a substantial and pains-taking account of a bourgeois girl's evolution from Catholic piety to a carefree atheism, Socialist devotion, and literary fame as a novelist and a philosopher. There is no Sartrean obscurity here. "I was born at four o'clock in the morning on the ninth of January, 1908, in a room fitted with white enameled furniture and overlooking the Boulevard Raspail."[4] Her maternal grandfather was a banker, her father was a lawyer. Her mother coddled her with unrequited love. "Sheltered, petted, and constantly entertained by the endless novelty of life, I was a madly gay little girl," cross when crossed, and guilty of "a lack of all moderation which I have never outgrown completely."[5] Menstruation clouded her gaiety for a time. She went through passionate friendships with other girls. She developed an Oedipus complex. "My real rival was my mother. I dreamed of having a more intimate relationship with my father."[6] He failed to respond.

She was at first charmed by the fragrant beauty of Catholic ritual, and the tender story of the Marys in Jesus' life. "I found it sweet to kneel at the foot of the cross and dream vaguely of the cup of chocolate awaiting me at home."[7] "I imagined that I was Mary Magdalene, and that I was drying Christ's feet with my long hair."[8] But she developed a fondness for books, read Maupassant, Bourget, Colette, and lost her sexual and theological innocence. She had seen her father smile at stories of the cures at Lourdes; she mused over his remark that "the greatest miracle at Lourdes is Lourdes itself."[9] Suddenly, one day when she was fourteen, she said to herself, "I no longer believe in God."[10]

Her moral and social inhibitions melted after her religious faith. She fell in love with a wastrel philanderer, Jacques Laiguillon, and thought of living with him without benefit of clergy or law. "I didn't care a bit about being respected; living with Jacques and marrying him were all one to me."[11] Jacques did not return her devotion; he preferred short-term investments properly diversified. Simone consoled herself

---

* Vol. I, *Mémoires d'une jeune fille rangée* (1958; translated as *Memoirs of a Dutiful Daughter*); Vol. II, *La Force de l'âge* (1960; *The Prime of Life*); Vol. III, *La Force des choses* (1963; *Force of Circumstance*).

with cafés, literature, and philosophy. She met Romain Rolland and became a pacifist; she read Schopenhauer and became a pessimist; she read Leibniz and became a metaphysician; she read Nietzsche "with passionate enthusiasm," and rejoiced in being confirmed in her individualism.

Meanwhile her father had suffered a blow to his finances and morale by the collapse of czarist Russia, in whose bonds he had invested much of his savings. His law practice declined. The family moved to a cheap apartment with no bathroom or running water or central heating. Soon Simone left the parental home, and took a private room. Resolving to support herself, she enrolled at the École Normale Supérieure, seeking a teacher's degree. There she met Sartre.

She was overwhelmed by his energy, his wide knowledge, his sharp wit, his skill in debate, and his readiness to help her and his other friends. She was only briefly shocked by their heresies. They "had all explored much more fundamentally than I the consequences of the non-existence of God."[12] "They made fun of bourgeois law and order; . . . they jabbed a pin into every inflated idealism; . . . they set out to prove that men are not rarefied spirits but bodies of flesh and blood, racked by physical needs, and crudely engaged in a brutal adventure that was life."[13] Sartre liked her courage in the face of their freedom of speech and the smoke with which they filled his room. "From now on," he told her, "I'm going to take you under my wing." Soon she was convinced that "time not spent in his company was time wasted."[14] "How cramped my little world seemed beside this exuberantly abundant universe!"[15]

Simone does not tell us when she and Sartre merged their sexual lives. Like her he "hadn't a good word to say for marriage,"[16] or for parentage. "There is no good father, that's the rule," he would write in *The Words;* "the bond of paternity is ruthless. To beget children, nothing better; to *have* them, what iniquity!"[17] Simone had no desire for motherhood; "maternity seemed incompatible with the way of life upon which I was embarking." She was shocked when her girl friend Zaza "declared that having babies was just as important as writing books."[18] When she saw a friend pushing a baby carriage "it was my ardent hope that my own future would have no place for that sort of thing."[19] "Whatever happened, I would have to try to preserve what was best in me: my love of personal freedom, my passion for life, my curiosity, my determination to be a writer."[20] And some years later she wrote: "I remained faithful to my declared intent of turning all that life imposed upon me to my own purposes."[21]

Simone and Sartre carried their love of liberty so far as to give each other the right to have "contingent loves" as occasional relaxation from their entente. "Sartre was not inclined to be monogamous by nature; he took pleasure in the company of women, finding them less comic than men. He had no intention, at twenty-three, of renouncing their tempting variety."[22] Soon after agreeing to live together he engaged for two years, on and off, in an intimacy with an actress-singer called Camille. Simone suffered pangs of jealousy, but later she had love affairs apparently more intense and intimate than her relations with Sartre. The young philosophers thought to ease these digressions by vowing to tell each other everything.[23]

They did not make a home for themselves, but almost always lived apart; sometimes in the same hotel but in separate rooms; only on special occasions did she prepare a meal for him. Usually they ate in restaurants or cafés—the Dôme, the Flore, the Deux Magots; these half–open-air places became their informal academy, where they preached their doctrines and, in some part, wrote their books. Simone in particular liked to wander among the night clubs and bars of Paris, with or without Sartre; sometimes she found relief from her teaching assignments by making "a round of the more or less shady dives that Marco [a homosexual friend] ferreted out"; once he escorted her through a brothel.[24]

Her character was quite different from Sartre's. He was pledged to thought, with love as an occasional diversion; she "was an impetuous creature, with more passion than subtlety."[25] She liked to go off, with or without him, on long walks, even into unfrequented mountainous terrain. Both were interested in foreign lands, and they toured Europe together, sometimes on bicycles, sleeping (in the early years of their romance) on decks or in mountain huts. They bore their semipoverty cheerfully because they were young and strong, and felt that the world was theirs to study, enjoy, and overcome. In those halcyon days they preferred anarchism to socialism, resenting any impediment to individuality. "Our love of freedom, our opposition to the established order of things, brought us close to the anarchist position. . . . We were anti-capitalist, yet not Marxists. . . . We were attracted by any sort of extreme; . . . any sort of upheaval gratified our anarchistic instincts."[26]

In 1931 Sartre and Simone received assignments to teach in *lycées* (high schools)—he at Le Havre, she at Marseille. Simone tramped the Maritime Alps while Jean-Paul fretted amid the dull bourgeoisie and tough prolétaires of the northern port. In the fall she was transferred to Rouen, an hour's ride from Le Havre. Now she enjoyed many weekends with Sartre, but he marred her happiness by falling in love with one of her pupils.

In 1933 he went to Berlin, and spent nine months as a student in the French Institute there. He saw the rise of Hitler, he took a fancy to Husserl's phenomenology, he read Heidegger and Jaspers;[27] all these experiences left their mark on him. Back as teacher in Le Havre, he took an injection of mescaline to induce hallucinations (February, 1935), as an experiment in psychology; in consequence he was disturbed for several months by illusions of crabs, lobsters, and vultures pursuing him wherever he went, even to Venice, where he stopped for a while with Simone on their way to a tour of Greece. At times he came close to a nervous breakdown, and thought he was going insane.[28] The anxiety and depression that he suffered in that half year may have darkened his philosophy.

On their return to France Simone was given a teacher's post in Paris. "It mattered little to me that I had only one room, and that not a particularly attractive one, when all Paris was mine—its streets, its squares, its cafés."[29] She must have impressed her pedagogical superiors, for she was appointed one of the examiners for the baccalaureate in Caen. Meanwhile Sartre was shifted to Laon, which he disliked so much that in *The Reprieve* he made Ivich flee from it as from a fate worse than death. Twice a week he traveled to Paris to see Simone. She recalls: "We set up our General Headquarters, as it were, in the Café du Dôme . . . A whole crowd of artists and writers gathered there . . . Every night tall American girls could be seen getting themselves majestically stewed."[30]

In 1938 Sartre was transferred to the Lycée Pasteur in Neuilly, so close to Paris that he could live in the same hotel with Simone, though on separate floors. Now they moved their café séances to the Flore. "Sartre and I were the only two who turned up regularly every night at the Flore," to eat, drink, talk, and write. Each was working on a novel and searching for a publisher. Sartre found one for the book that was to set all literary Paris wondering who was this somber upstart who announced, in the city that he loved, that life made him puke.

II. NAUSEA, 1938

The manuscript was refused, then accepted, by Gaston Gallimard, publisher of Gide and the *Nouvelle Revue française*. Sartre had entitled his novel "Melancholia," but he accepted Gallimard's suggestion

to rename it *La Nausée*—hardly a lure to buyers, but a whet to curiosity. The locale of the story is "Bouville" (Mudville, presumably Le
Havre); half the volume is Sartre's vengeful description of the stodgy,
money-grubbing, conformist middle class amid which he had lived for
years as a secret anarchist and atheist; his favorite term for these dreary,
law-abiding, self-righteous, law-skirting bourgeois was *salauds*, "the
dirty ones." In form the book is the diary of Antoine Roquentin, a
lonely bachelor of thirty, blessed with an income, cursed with melancholy, fretting over the defects of his neighbors and the general absurdity of human life. He seeks to forget the meaningless repetitiousness
of existence by writing the biography of the Marquis de Rollebon, a
Frenchman living at the court of the czars in the eighteenth century.
Meanwhile, on his walks through the town, Roquentin is depressed by
the types of human futility that he encounters, by the crimes, per-
versions, cheatings, hypocrisies and tyrannies, by the physical deterioration of men and women in their descending years. He sees nothing in
women except uncleanness, and finds no charm in their charms.[31]

> I dined at the Rendezvous des Cheminots [railwaymen]. The
> Patronne [proprietress] was there, and I had to kiss her, but it was
> merely out of politeness. . . . I played distractedly with her sex
> under the covers; then my arm went to sleep . . . I let my arm run
> along the woman's thigh, and suddenly saw a small garden . . . Ants
> were running everywhere, centipedes, and ringworms. The Velleda
> [a statue] in the public park pointed a finger at her sex. "This park
> smells of vomit." I shouted. "I didn't want to wake you up," the
> woman said, "but the sheet got folded under my back."[32]

In the town library Roquentin becomes acquainted with a zealous
middle-aged student who has resolved to read every book on the
shelves, in alphabetical order. However, this "Self-Taught Man" is
caught in mid-alphabet making homosexual approaches under the table
to a boy in the reading room. The librarian pounces upon him, drives
him out of the library, and forbids him ever to return. Roquentin muses
on what "this gentle, baited soul" could have done had he completed Z;
and he answers, "Nothing."

He concludes that the future will be like the past, that history is
meaningless, and that life is ridiculous. He is oppressed by his sense
of universal contingency, by which he means that nothing and no one
is necessary, and that there is no reason why anything or anybody
should exist. Indeed, why does the world exist, instead of plain in-

nocuous nothingness?[33] Formerly these questions were met by saying that God had created all things, and knew the reason for them, and their value and significance; but now that God is no more what need is there for so many—or for any—cockroaches, fish, lions, men?[34] Where are they bound for, in such confusion and haste? Only to death. Everything dies—every organism, every city, every civilization. And no one can know the date when death will come; that uncertain certitude hangs over everything, as the ignominious culmination of a hundred thousand struggles, illnesses, anxieties, and defeats. What a colossal absurdity!

And so Roquentin comes to that upset stomach and belching mind which gives the book its name: no merely metaphysical distaste but a retching, seismic desire to vomit reality, to throw up the world.

> I hated this ignoble mess mounting up, mounting up as high as the sky, spilling over, filling everything with its gelatinous slither. . . . I knew it was the World suddenly revealing itself, and I choked with rage at this gross and absurd being. . . . I shouted "filth! what rotten filth!" and shook myself to get rid of this sticky filth, but it held fast, and there was so much, tons and tons of existence, endless. I stifled.[35]

In this philosophical dyspepsia everything lost savor. The beauty of woman, which caused so much commotion in male gonads, was only a male imagination, a snare to reproduction, and a promise of decay. Children were not delights, they were a mess, a nuisance, a mutiny, and a blighted hope. The sky was not an inspiring panorama but an overpowering and treacherous immensity. And no thinking, sensitive person could escape these sour realities by losing himself in a symphony, a museum, or a book. "To think that there are idiots who get consolation from the fine arts!"[36] And these lovers of humanity—can they really love such an abstraction?

It is an unhealthy but powerful book. Sartre wrote it at thirty, when he was weary with teaching neophytes and cramped by the commanding hypocrisies of life. Perhaps he was choking not with metaphysics but with the fogs of Le Havre; what he needed was to join Simone on her lusty walks over hills and plains, feeling the pagan joy of arms and legs, breathing in vitality gratefully from the rural air and the smiling sun. Sartre rarely speaks of the countryside; he is a city man, crushed by crowds, and burdened with the books he has read. Above all, in those groping Le Havre days he was too absorbed in his ambitious, fretting self, too much (despite his cautious love) a "simple separate person"; he had not yet heard the words *"en masse."*

Critics sensed in *La Nausée* a certain whimpering over a dead God. Camus thought that Sartre had exaggerated the ugliness of life.[37] Some were shocked at the erotic passages, or such macabre metaphors as of a woman with "the thin mouth of a dead snake."[38] But most critics acknowledged the force of Sartre's indictment of life, and the novelty and acuteness of his observations, as of the distinctive smells of persons and streets; they too had felt or seen the dulling tread of captive souls through undistinguished days. Here, they agreed, was a new voice that would insist on being heard. Sartre sipped the praise, and dreamed of philosophy.

In January, 1939, he reread Heidegger's *Being and Time*,[39] and plotted his rival *Being and Nothingness*. World War II intervened; he was called to the Army, and served as meteorologist for an artillery group. After the collapse of the French forces at Sedan (May, 1940) he was captured by the advancing Germans, and was held in a prison camp till March, 1941. For two months Simone received no word of him. "Death stalked among us daily," she recalls, "and it was impossible to think of anything else."[40] She took Hegel's *Phenomenology of Mind* as a sedative, but could "scarcely make head or tails of it"; however, she found it "the most soothing occupation." Then (July 11, 1940) a note came assuring her that her semi-husband was alive and well. In March, 1941, Sartre escaped, found his way back to Paris, and to his professorship at the Lycée Pasteur. He and Simone took rooms at opposite ends of a corridor in the Hotel de Louisiane near the Café de Flore, and joined in the Resistance to the German occupation.

Their war experiences modified their individualist, almost anarchistic sentiments. When Sartre organized a Resistance group he gave it for motto "Socialism and liberty."[41] Simone noted the change: "What Sartre used to call my 'divided mind' had finally yielded before the unanswerable arguments that reality had brought against it. I was at last prepared to admit that my life was . . . a compromise between myself and the world."[42]

Those years when Paris was governed by Germans were an exciting time for Jean-Paul and Simone. They took part in plots against the German officials; they flirted with detection, torture, and death. In 1944 Camus warned Sartre that an arrested Resistant, under torture, had given Sartre's name to the police; Sartre went into hiding till the liberation.[43] Later he startled his readers by declaring, in an essay, "The Republic of Silence" (1947), "We were never more free than during the German occupation"; it was a typical Sartrean paradox, meaning that in those days Frenchmen had an opportunity to declare themselves as free human beings—free and compelled to make decisions risking and molding their lives. "The choice that each of us made of his life and his being . . . was made face to face with death. . . . All those among us . . . who knew any details concerning the Resistance asked themselves anxiously: "If they torture me, shall I be able to keep silent? So they constituted the Republic of Silence."[44] But in 1942 the Communists of France charged Sartre with having earned his release from captivity by agreeing to work for the Germans as an *agent provocateur*.[45] Sartre poured his bitterness into his masterpiece.

III. BEING AND NOTHINGNESS, 1943

Ever since his year of study in Berlin he had tried his hand at applying phenomenology—the study of consciousness—to psychology. In 1936 he published *L'Imagination;* in 1939 *Esquisse d'une théorie des émotions;* in 1940 *L'Imaginaire, psychologie phénoménologique de l'imagination;* they were fledgling flights. At last, in 1943, he issued *L'Être et le néant (Being and Nothingness)*, a volume of 722 pages, in which Sartre, half German, succeeded in rivaling the Germans in obscurity and subtlety. "It sold very few copies," Simone tells us, "and was very little discussed."[46] France, pledged to clarity, passed it by, and waited till other nations praised the book; now it is the most renowned of all French works on philosophy since Bergson's *L'Évolution créatrice* (1906).

Its subject, like that of Heidegger's *Sein und Zeit,* is Being—that largest and thinnest of all abstractions. "I want to describe in an exhaustive manner the relation of man to being."[47] Above all, what is that most intimate, and yet indescribable, form of being—consciousness? Do objects exist independently of our awareness of them? What is the vast Nothingness that surrounds, limits, and defines every perception, and that seems to be all that we find when we try to look at consciousness itself?

We cannot, like Descartes, assume that there is a good God who has created this mind of man, and who might guarantee the validity of its perceptions. "Today," says Sartre, "God is dead even in the heart of the believer."[48] "Existentialism is nothing else than an attempt to draw all the consequences of a coherent atheistic position."[49] There are metaphysical consequences: there is no a priori necessity in things—all are contingent and dispensable, including ourselves; and there is no divine omnipotence to make human free will illogical. There are moral consequences: there are no God-given Ten Commandments, and man will have to build a moral code independent of religious belief.

Sartre is almost as skeptical of science as of theology. He does not believe that we get a just view of what the human mind is by studying external nature or our bodies; he prefers to study mind and conscious-ness at first hand—i.e., from within; he follows Husserl and Heidegger into "phenomenology." So we are back to Kant and epistemology; it is another German occupation of Paris. Sartre may have been envious of Kant's obscurity; in any case he achieved a style so tenebrous as to as-sure his fame. He disliked Heidegger's play on words, and surpassed it.* He had struggled with Heidegger's novel terminology; he invented another of his own; at every second line we must translate him into our own humdrum language. Yet he was no mere word juggler or phrase monger; he was dealing manfully with the most complex of all prob-lems—sensation and consciousness, determinism and free will, body and mind, life and death. I am not sure that I understand him, and the reader should be warned that he proceeds here at his own risk. I have an obligation to follow this man into his labyrinth.

Sartre gradually defines his terms:

I. *Being* is the reality of all things and thoughts as distinguished from these things and thoughts themselves. It takes chiefly three forms: (1) *Being-for-itself* (*être-pour-soi*)—the subjective being of human consciousness; (2) *Being-in-itself* (*être-en-soi*)—the objective being of the external world; and (3) *Being-for-others* (*être-pour-autrui*)—our being in relation to other consciousnesses.

II. *Existence* is being particularized in an individual form—this thing, this man, this feeling, this idea . . .

III. *Essence* is the defining qualities of a particular existence at a particular time. Since every existence develops—and may change—its characteristic qualities in the course of its growth or history, it fol-lows that in everything existence precedes and forms essence. A soul or a thing, as Hegel said, becomes rather than is; at each moment it is the sum of its growing past; my essence will not be complete until

---

* "The being of consciousness is a being such that in its being, its being is in question."[50] "The For-itself [consciousness] . . . must at the same time fulfill these three requirements: (1) to not-be what it is, (2) to be what it is not, (3) to be what it is not and to not-be what it is—within the unity of a perpetual refer-ring."[51] "The body is the In-itself which is surpassed by the nihilating For-itself, and which reapprehends the For-itself in this very surpassing."[52] Some allowance must be made for such acrobatics as being torn from their context.

I am dead. And this is true of the species as well as of the individual; human nature is always changing, however slightly, with every new experience; the essence of the species *homo* will not be definitely definable until the species has completed its history.

IV. *Nothingness* is the opposite of being; it is all that is not. In that sense it is merely an idea, an abstraction;[53] but in specific situations it becomes a positive experience, and takes on a vague yet influential reality. Sartre goes to a café expecting to see Pierre; he does not find him; he feels the nothingness of Pierre's absence; and in that nothingness all irrelevant existences—customers, waiters, tables, lights, smoke, sounds —are included, and give substance to his disappointment. Again he gets the feeling of an active nothingness when he looks into his purse for the ten francs he supposed were there, and finds them gone; their absence is no mere idea, it is an effective force, and therefore a reality. Besides such nothingness of absence or lack, he can feel nothingnesses of change (the temperature has fallen), of destruction (Hannibal's Carthage is no more), of limitation (color has no sound). All these forms of nothingness result from the power of consciousness to "nihilate" (*néantir*)—to deny reality to an idea, and to wrap external realities in a coating of denials (this jar is not of jade, not heavy, is not Chinese . . .) that give them boundaries and character.

V. *Being-for-itself*, or *Consciousness*, is itself and by itself a nothingness; when we look for it we find nothing. Yet through this nothing all that we know is known. It is the most immediate of all realities, obscure but undeniable, immaterial but real. It occurs at certain points in space, and is limited in duration, but in many ways it transcends space and time. It can think of things as near or far, large or small, above or below, in or out; and these spatial relations exist only in the mind It can think of things past or present or future; it is in a sense a union of all three; hence Sartre loves to say that man is a being who is not that which he is, and who is what he is not: i.e., man at any present moment is not that past whose sum he is, and he is potentially that future which he is not yet.

Consciousness is Being-for-itself because through it being becomes aware of itself, can question itself and the world. Man, including his consciousness, is a natural product, like any animal;[54] but, so far as we know, he is the only being that inquires into its origin, nature, and destiny, and can plan and mold its life.

Consciousness exists only when it is consciousness of *something;* it is, in Hegel's term, a negative plate upon which experience is printed; but it distinguishes itself as a nothingness, a dependent reality, from the positive and independent something which it mirrors or perceives.

VI. *Being-in-itself* is the external world; it is, for each of us, everything outside of our own consciousness and body. That it exists is evident from the fact that all consciousness is of something. As perceived by us, the external world (including all other human beings) is a medley of sights, sounds, pressures, temperatures, tastes, and smells. These phenomena are the total of external reality as known to us, and we need not, like Kant, presume that there is any noumenon behind them.

The In-itself is so termed because its existence does not depend upon consciousness, whereas consciousness depends upon the In-itself for its existence; nevertheless, without a consciousness to perceive it and differentiate it into specific objects, the In-itself or external world would be mere indiscriminate and meaningless being. So Sartre unites idealism and realism; his philosophy is idealist in its starting point and realist in its development. Like William James he suggests that reality is a structure in which subject and object, the observer and the thing observed, cannot be disassociated, and have no significance apart from each other.[55]

VII. *Body and Mind* are one inseparable reality. At times the body seems distinct from the mind, as when I think of my feet, my hair, my pains; generally, however, the body [as in Spinoza] is the external aspect of what internally appears as mind; the two act as one in sensation, perception, desire, and volition. Sartre is a bit uncertain here: he explicitly rejects materialism, but, "without being materialists, we have never distinguished soul from body, and we know only one indecomposable reality."[56] "The body is nothing other than the For-itself"; when we say that consciousness is always of something, and is nothing without this something, we necessarily imply that "the very nature of the For-itself demands that it be body."[57]

VIII. *The Self.* Though fusing body and mind, Sartre distinguishes the self, or ego, and the personality from consciousness. The ego is the total of our mental states, past and present; it is the individual person formed by the addition of individual experiences to hereditary influences. It can be the object of consciousness (I can think of myself), and therefore it is not identical with consciousness; Sartre places it in the In-itself, the objective world.[58] (How the body, which can also be the object of thought, can belong to, or be one with, the For-itself or consciousness, while the self belongs to the In-itself as an external reality is a puzzle for which I have found no solution in Sartre.) However, he repeatedly uses "self" as a variant expression for the For-itself.

IX. *Being-for-others* is consciousness that for other consciousnesses I am an object, a part of the external world. We do not like to be an object, to be the target of the look (*le regard*) which the Other directs upon us; now we become conscious of our self, self-conscious; we feel that the Other is considering us as victims of his study, as tools for his use, as possible enemies of his purposes. To him we are means, while to ourselves we wish to be ends. So he limits our freedom, which is our very essence. Unconsciously, but by the very nature of this confrontation of souls, each looks upon the other as a nuisance, a hindrance, a danger, or a potential foe.*

Wonder first, and then hostility, are the basic relations we feel toward others. Each of us tries to make the other an object, a means to our ends. "One must either transcend [dominate] the Other or allow oneself to be transcended by him. The essence of the relations between consciousnesses is not *Mitsein* [togetherness], it is conflict."[60] Desire —even the desire for knowledge—is usually a wish to dominate. Generosity is superiority; to give is to subject. Sex is a duel, coitus is conquest, marriage is war. Usually, in such conflicts, one party yields, or pretends to. Sometimes the submissive one takes a masochistic pleasure in being overcome; conversely, the dominant one may take a sadistic delight in inflicting humiliations, as in deflowering, rape, or fellatio. All men, all lovers, are potential enemies.

X. *Freedom*, like desire, is one of the constituents of consciousness. It is possible because consciousness is not a part of the objective world, and so may escape the causal "laws" that Sartre recognizes there.[61] (Here he follows the lead of Kant.) He calls it freedom of choice rather than freedom of will; every man chooses what kind of man he wishes to be, what basic ends he proposes to pursue; this is his "life project," and every later choice he makes will depend upon it. Every man is compelled to make such a choice by the fact that he is a human being; in this sense he is "condemned to be free."[62] Since existence precedes essence, since consciousness precedes the formation of specific character, that character cannot determine the fundamental choice; it is the choice that molds the character, and only thereafter does character mold choice; *then* "the will is determined within the compass of motives and ends already posited by the For-itself in transcendental

* This hostile "look" appears in Sartre's plays (notably in *No Exit*) and novels (*The Age of Reason, The Reprieve*) and in his *Baudelaire*, where he speaks uncomfortably of "the tyranny of the human face," which "would be much less frightening if there were not planted in each of the faces two eyes spying upon you."[59]

projection of itself towards its possibles."[63] Doubtless my past, my environment, and my circumstances enter into the determination of my actions; but behind and beneath all these is that upsurge of my inherent self which fixes my life project, and of which I am conscious as an immediate reality of my innermost being.

XI. *Bad Faith*. It is because of this ineradicable sense of our essential moral freedom that we feel responsible for our actions. Only the coward denies his responsibility, and tries to use determinism as an excuse for his transgressions. This is a form of "bad faith" (*mauvaise foi*), which consists not so much in lying to others as in lying to oneself. Even faith in God may be bad faith, for the believer relies upon God for protection, for resolution of his problems and the forgiveness of his sins. A real man accepts responsibility for his deeds, whatever his heredity or his milieu may be; he admits that his offenses share in making the world what it is, and he willingly eats the fruit of the tree that brings knowledge of good and evil.

XII. *Anguish* (*angoisse*) is part of the price we pay for responsible freedom. That mood, so stressed by Kierkegaard and Heidegger, has many constituents. It is the painful hesitation before the necessity of choosing between possible responses to a situation. It is a fearsome recognition that our basic choices mold the destinies of others besides ourselves. It is a sense of guilt for our offenses. It is a feeling of shame before others, before their "look," however silent, of accusation or scorn. Finally, it is a recognition that we are unnecessary in the scheme of things, that to many of those around us we may seem uncalled for, *de trop*. Nor can we dignify our lives by any feeling that we are players in a massive drama which will have a noble or heroic significance and a redeeming end; there is no guidance or purpose in the cosmos or in history; and the only certainty is that every organism will suffer and die. Each of us is alone, helpless and doomed.

XIII. *Absurdity and Nausea*. Seen in this perspective (says Sartre) life is absurd and in many ways revolting. This endless parade of babies, monkeys, insects—born, struggling, breeding, dying, generation after generation after generation—what is the sense of it, or the use? Man is impelled by passion from desire to desire, but "man is a futile passion" (*l'homme est une passion inutile*); the end is always the same. Consequently life has no meaning in itself; only the individual can give meaning to his life—by the free choice of his project and goal, and by recognizing his responsibility for the results.

XIV. *Morality* is in flux. God-given commands are no more, and moral codes vary so much in place and time, and have suffered so much from economic change and technological devices, that they are losing their force. The individual is free, as never before, to accept or reject the ethical code offered him by his civilization or his community. Moreover, life is now so complex that old moral principles do not always meet the situation; the individual must then make his own morality. Sartre realized that his reduction of human relations to suspicion, hostility, and conflict, and the reduction of morality to the individual's free choice of principles, came close to anarchism and anarchy. These ideas may have pleased the young professor jealous of his intellectual freedom and fretting under theological dogmas and social norms; but he was already conscious that no social order could rest on his individualistic principles, and in the final pages of his book he promised a further volume that would face the problems of morality.

I cannot offer an expert judgment on this majestic tome. I respect the range of Sartre's studies, the subtlety of his analysis, and the courage of his enterprise in dealing with almost inexpressible complexities. I have never been at home in the recesses of epistemology, and I cannot overcome a Gallic prejudice against a book so painstakingly obscure. However, I will venture some casual comments.

The title is a mystic marriage of abstractions. "Being" is a word for the *idea* of existence in general, abstracted from all existing realities; "Nothingness" is a word for the *idea* of the absence of beings; objectively, only specific things exist. You see that I am an old-fashioned conceptualist like Abélard, or an obdurate nominalist like William of Ockham; six centuries ago these men taught us not to mistake concepts or words for objective entities. If I go to the Café de Flore to look for Pierre, and do not find him, I do not perceive nothingness, I merely perceive that Pierre is not there. Sartre was right when, in *Nausea*, he made Roquentin say, "Nothingness was merely an idea in my head."[64]

Does existence precede essence? I should define essence as the *general* qualities by which a normal individual entity belongs to its class; so the essence of water is H_2O, and the essence of any normal man is that he is a thinking biped. In this sense the essence of man logically precedes, and is independent of, every individual man except the first, and is the test of his man-ness. This verbal dispute hardly deserves to provide a definition of existentialism.

I rejoice that Sartre stressed the primacy of consciousness in philosophy; it is of course the only reality that we directly know. But whereas he calls it a nothingness except when it is consciousness of something, I should rather say that it exists only as specific mental states checked by sensation. (Mental states not so checked can exist without consciousness, as in dreams.) His assumption that man alone has reflective consciousness, or can plan his life, may be unjust to some animals: I believe that a dog, a chimpanzee, an elephant, and other "beasts" can think, reason, plan the future, and meditate; I have heard of elephants hesitating to cross an untested bridge, of dogs interpreting complex signs, of squirrels hoarding nuts; and I see no unbridgeable gap between Jean-Paul Sartre contemplating nothingness and a lion calmly viewing his realm. Sartre does not pretend—and no one has been able —to explain how (as he believes) consciousness arose in the course of evolution; consciousness is the *datum primum* of philosophy, but it is the *datum ultimum* of nature.

Assuming such a natural origin of consciousness (or, as Sartre puts it, the derivation of the For-itself from the In-itself), it is difficult to see how he can let consciousness escape the determinism—the unbroken rule of cause and effect—which he recognizes in the objective world. At what point in the chain of being did freedom arise? Certainly many of us feel that within severe limits we have some freedom of choice and will; but we must allow to heredity, environment, indoctrination, and circumstance far more influence in determining our responses than Sartre concedes in *Being and Nothingness*. (Seventeen years later, in his *Critique of Dialectical Reason*, he will withdraw to a more moderate position.) Logically, of course, free will is indefensible; we are "condemned" to determinism by the logic in which we have cast our thought through our conception of invariable natural laws; we can't logically believe in free will unless we believe that the world is not quite logical. Perhaps it is not.

I think Sartre was bravely right in seeing conflict as the basic relation of my self to other human selves. Every "Other" is a potential competitor and enemy. There are exceptions—through an enlargement of the self—in a mother's love for her child, or possibly in a lover's devotion to the beloved; but even in those cases a potential hostility may develop in time. We have social as well as selfish instincts, but they are weaker, and require persistent reinforcement by preachments and police. Sartre found it discouragingly difficult to build a viable ethic upon so egoistic a psychology, but our need for it is made imperative by the continued decline of the economic and religious conditions that buttressed the old moral code. Conceivably the great majority of our grandchildren may be made to understand that the survival of the individual depends upon the survival of his group, which depends upon the cooperation of the individual with the group—which is a definition of morality. Sartre soon (1946) recognized that "I cannot make my own freedom my aim unless I make the freedom of others equally my aim"[65]—though this too is an exaggeration.

I do not share the "anguish" of Sartre and Heidegger over the discovery that we are all "contingent." I had supposed that most of us took our dispensability for granted, and felt very little nausea about it. Sartre took over some of Heidegger's *Angst* about inevitable death, but that worry does not long become a philosopher, and I am sure that Jean-Paul has long since ceased to fret about it. Who would want to live forever, and go through an endless series of American presidential campaigns? Man is a "futile passion" only when he has sought unwisely beyond his merit or his means. As to anguish over the "absurdity" of the world, there are few pronouncements so absurd as to call the universe absurd; absurdity, like meaning, is a subjective and prejudiced judgment, and does not belong to things. Doubtless we too seem absurd to an observant dog or a meditative toad.

IV. IN THE RESISTANCE: 1943–44

Published during the German occupation of Paris, *Being and Nothingness* easily passed the German censorship. After all, was not the book admittedly based upon Kant and Hegel, Husserl and Heidegger? And who but a German could understand it?

Despite the conclusion on a note of futility, Jean-Paul and Simone continued to work like rebels *engagés*, committed to turning their skills to the cause of France and freedom. So in 1943 Sartre staged a play, *Les Mouches* (*The Flies*), that spoke allegorically to the moment through another telling of Orestes' famous matricide. Clytemnestra has joined with her paramour Aegisthus in murdering her husband, Agamemnon (the French collaborators had joined with Hitler in cutting down France), and the people of Argos (France) are broken with shame over having permitted these crimes. Orestes returns to Argos resolved to avenge his father (the French Resistance vowed death to collaborators). He interprets the plague of flies which has been darkening Argive skies as the oppression of the mind by absurd doctrines and undue remorse. He refuses to accept the advice of his tutor (as the Paris press advised its readers) to stay aside from public affairs and cultivate prudence and safety; he persuades his sister Electra (the young women of the Resistance?) to join with him in vengeance; he kills his mother and Aegisthus, and then tells the people of Argos that they must feel cleansed of all guilt. Zeus (religion) comes out of the empyrean to reproach Orestes for having violated a divine commandment; Orestes (becoming Sartre) replies that he recognizes no moral values external to his own free judgment.

> ORESTES. Your whole universe is not enough to prove me wrong. You are the king of the gods, of stones and stars, . . . but you are not the king of man. . . . I am a man, and every man must find his way. . . . You are God and I am free; each of us is alone, and our anguish is kin. . . .
> ZEUS. What do you propose to do?
> ORESTES. The folk of Argos are my folk. I must open their eyes.
> ZEUS. Poor people! Your gift to them will be a sad one: of loneliness and shame. You will tear from their eyes the veils I had laid on them, and they will see their lives as they are, foul and futile. . . .
> ORESTES. Life begins on the far side of despair.[66]

When the play was produced, the German censors saw no harm in it, thinking it a mere rehash of Aeschylus; but when the audience cheered the hidden meanings the censors forbade further performances.

Having discovered his talent for the theater, Sartre proceeded to write one after another of the most powerful plays of his time. He had learned that philosophy presented as theory had little influence on the people, but that philosophy presented as literature could move millions. In *Being and Nothingness* he had spoken of other people as one's potential enemies, and of their "look" as one of the tortures of life; now he dramatized those ideas in *Huis clos* (*No Exit*), which was produced at Paris in May, 1944. It is unforgettable.

It was written for a factory manager who wanted some histrionic vehicle for his daughter, but could not afford much scenery or many actors. Sartre met the problem by staging a play entirely in one room —with no window, no mirror, three sofas, and one door—and by confining the action to one theme, one hour, and three characters; the "Aristotelian unities" could not have asked for stricter fidelity. Garcia enters, led by a *valet de place;* the valet departs and locks the door on the outside. Garcia beats upon the door; there is no answer, but a while later the door opens to let in Inez, a proud and angry Lesbian who at once cows Garcia with a look that spurns the whole male sex. The door closes and is locked. Soon it opens again to admit Estelle, a woman still warm in the decline of beauty and passion. The door closes and is locked.

Each of the prisoners gives to the others a false explanation of his or her condemnation. Garcia tells the ladies, "I ran a pacifist newspaper. The war broke out . . . Everyone was watching me, wondering, 'Will he dare?' Well, I dared. . . . They shot me."[67] He later admits that he was cruel to his wife, deserted his post in the Army, was captured and executed. Estelle drowned her baby and drove her lover to suicide. Inez was a vixen bitch. Inez makes love to Estelle, who prefers to offer her body to Garcia; he tries to respond, but Inez glares at them scornfully, and Garcia becomes impotent before this Sartrean look. Each of the three now shrinks from the others, but there is no escape except to shut one's eyes. The room is so brilliantly lit that the light penetrates the closed eyelids, like some persistent truth that pierces every sham. Under that light, controlled only from outside, sleep is impossible. Finally the three realize their damnation and their punishment. Garcia speaks for all of them: "So this is hell. I'd never have believed it. You remember all we were told about the torture chambers, the fire and brimstone, the burning marl. Old wives' tales! There is no need for red-hot pokers. Hell is other people" (l'enfer est l'autre). And Inez adds, "Here we are forever."[68]

Sartre interrupted his gloom when the Germans, faced with the need of manning many endangered fronts, left Paris (August 25, 1944), and the city came back to life as if in some miraculous resurrection. Many years later Simone de Beauvoir described that liberation with all the feeling of one who remembered having lived for two years in an atmosphere of dread and hate. "All that day Sartre and I walked the flag-draped streets of Paris. I saw women in their best clothes clinging round soldiers' necks; the tricolor shone resplendent from the . . . Eiffel Tower. . . . These moments . . . shine out from my past with perennial and untarnished splendor."[69]

V. LITERATURE AS WAR: 1945–47

On January 4, 1945, Sartre was sent to the United States as correspondent for Camus' journal Combat. His income as writer and dramatist had enabled him to give up teaching, and he shared some of it with Simone. In New York he took the absolution of distance to flirt with "a young woman half separated from her husband"; he was so smitten that after returning to Paris he made another trip to America (December, 1945) "to see her again."[70]

Meanwhile (October, 1945) he joined with Simone, Raymond Aron, Jean Paulham, Maurice Merleau-Ponty, and Albert Ollivier in establishing a literary and political monthly, *Les Temps modernes*, which soon became a force in the intellectual life of France. The editors attacked the colonial policy of the French government in Algeria, and for several years they carried on, against the rule of France in Indochina, a campaign analogous in almost all points to the later struggle of American liberals against the military involvement of the United States in Vietnam. They condemned the bourgeois orientation and domination of life in France and America as a cloak for class oppression and a soporific for the public mind. They sympathized with socialism, but criticized Marxism and the French Communist Party as being too doctrinaire and dogmatic for their tastes. When Sartre and Merleau-Ponty declared that in a third world war they would side with Russia, Aron and Ollivier withdrew from the magazine (June, 1946).

Their departure left Sartre and Merleau-Ponty free to pledge the journal to radical causes. In a series of articles running from February through July, 1947 (and later in that year collected in a book, *Qu'est-ce que la littérature?—What Is Literature?*), Sartre called upon prose literature to be *engagée*—to step out of the ivory tower and join in the fray of contemporary affairs. He laughed at academic publications as exercises in mutual contemplation. He blasphemed by comparing libraries to cemeteries. "The dead are there. . . . All that remains are the little coffins stacked in shelves . . . like urns in a columbarium. . . . Written by a dead man about dead things," a book "has no longer any place on earth; . . . left to itself it falls back and collapses; there remain only ink spots on musty papers."[71]* The greatest writers scorned security, came out into the open, and took sides. The *philosophes* of the Enlightenment—above all, Voltaire—challenged state and church and class, and dared, despite a thousand censors, to speak for humanity. Hence "the eighteenth century was the palmy time, unique in history, and the soon-to-be-lost paradise of French writers."[72] After the Revolution French literature crept back into its attics, or catered to the triumphant bourgeoisie, until Hugo, George Sand, Michelet, and Zola led it back to the battle line; then again it became great. After the defeated Commune of 1871 it fled once more: Flaubert denounced the rebels, laughed at democracy, and polished his style; Renan, after exposing Christianity as a miasma of myths, glorified it as the salvation

---

* Or is it the "engaged literature" that dies soonest, bound to issues that fade away? Great literature survives longer because it most often deals, in some time-consuming form of beauty or power, with timeless rather than timely things—with the perennial problems of love and character, laughter and tears, struggle and defeat, life and death.

of social order; and Taine, "who was only a cheap pedant,"[73] buried himself in literary criticism, and joined the political reaction.* Sartre laughed at the Symbolists, the Parnassians, and the art-for-art's-sake dilettantes; he praised Gide for using his pen to compel reforms in the Congo, but he overwhelmed with one sentence Paul Valéry, "who has for twenty-five years been publishing posthumous books."

He realized the internal contradiction in his plea and his life: he was calling to the proletarian cause writers whose roots were in the bourgeoisie. "We remain bourgeois by our culture, our way of life, and our present public. And at the same time the historical situation drives us to join the proletariat in order to construct a classless society. . . . Pulled by both sides, we are condemned to suffer this double exigence as a Passion. It is our personal problem as well as the drama of our age."[74] He could not believe in any sacred "mission of the proletariat, nor that it is endowed with a state of grace; it is made up of men, just and unjust, who can make mistakes, and who are often mystified. But it must be said without hesitation that the fate of literature is bound up with that of the working class."[75]

Nevertheless, because, like a good bourgeois, he believed in freedom as man's vital mark and gift, he refused to join the Communist Party; on the contrary, he condemned it as conservative, dishonest, and dictatorial, as harassing and haunting its members as "K" had been harried in Kafka's *The Trial*. Furthermore, "the politics of Stalinist Communism is incompatible in France with the honest practice of the literary craft."[76] He complained that by current deformation of language to political ends "the word *fascist* means any European who does not vote for the Communists," while in the United States "the term *communist* designates any American citizen who does not vote for the Republicans," and in France almost all conservative parties call themselves Socialist.[77]

Despite these confusions of birth and language, Sartre urged, it was now the moral obligation of writers to "take sides against all injustices, wherever they may come from," and, above all, to unite in preventing the unprecedented catastrophe of a third world war. He agreed with de Gaulle on one point: a third force, between the U.S.S.R. and the U.S.A., should be organized to offer some escape from a degrading choice. "To choose the U.S.S.R. is to give up civil liberties. . . . But after the victory of the U.S. . . . the Communist Party would be annihilated, . . . and capitalism would be more pitiless since it would be

---

* Impenitent, I shall keep Flaubert and Taine among the lares and penates of my ivory tower. And they took sides, even though not Sartre's.

master of the world. . . . As long as circumstances do not change, the fortunes of literature are tied up with the coming of a socialist Europe, that is, a group of states with a democratic collectivist structure, each of which, while waiting for something better, would be deprived of part of its sovereignty for the sake of the whole."[78]

VI. THE PHILOSOPHER AS NOVELIST

Sartre had already begun to write *littérature engagée*. Despite the subtlety of his thought, he surprised his readers by developing, in fiction and drama, a style pungent and clear, and an artistry, in realistic dialogue and penetrating description, not surpassed by any Frenchman of his generation.

In 1945 he issued *L'Âge de raison* as the first volume of a proposed tetralogy collectively entitled *Les Chemins de la liberté*—the diverse and usually foolish ways in which the men and women of France had, since 1938, sought their intellectual, moral, or political freedom. Then, as now, the consciously rising generation cried out for emancipation from the politicians, the generals, the corporations, and the newspapers, that controlled the life of the nation, and from an economic system that daily increased the gap between the rich and the poor, and periodically plunged helpless peoples into wars of competitive destruction and unparalleled homicide.

The scene of *The Age of Reason* is Paris in 1938, and the man around whom the story revolves is Mathieu Delarue, aged thirty-four, professor of philosophy at the Lycée Buffon. We are at once tempted to identify him with the author, but Sartre protests against the interpretation. Mathieu is a bourgeois liberal; he rejects bourgeois moral norms and such bonds as marriage; he sympathizes with radical causes, but refuses to commit himself to any of them; he admires but does not imitate Gomez, who goes to fight for the Loyalists in Spain; he has several Communist friends, but he values intellectual freedom above party discipline. His pupil Boris says of him: "Delarue has his passions, but that does not prevent him from caring for nothing. He is free," and "his freedom is based on reason."[79] Mathieu's education has made him not merely an atheist but also a cynic, skeptical of every doctrine, and of both revolution and reform. He describes himself as a "listless dreamer immersed in his flaccid life,"[80] loving the classic philosophers, his pedagogical post, and a pension to come.

He avoids marriage as contrary to freedom and reason, but he takes

Marcelle Duffet as a mistress. While she sits "blankly naked on the edge of the bed,"[81] they discuss their notions of liberty. "I recognize no allegiance except to myself," says Mathieu. "Yes," Marcelle replies, "you want to be free. Absolutely free. It's your vice. . . . I don't feel such a need to be free."[82] No wonder: Mathieu has unknowingly made her pregnant; now she discloses the fact, secretly hoping that he will marry her. He recommends abortion instead, and goes out to raise the money.

He appeals to his prosperous brother Jacques, who, bourgeois without apology, adds rebuke to refusal: "I should have thought that freedom consisted in frankly confronting situations into which one has deliberately entered, and accepting all one's responsibilities. . . . You have reached the age of reason, . . . but you try to dodge that fact too; . . . you pretend that you are younger than you are. . . . Perhaps you haven't in fact reached the age of reason; it's really a moral age."[83] Mathieu goes next to Daniel Sereno, a homosexual with money; Daniel offers only advice; but when the abortion is too long delayed he comes to Marcelle's semi-rescue by agreeing to marry her and pass off the child as his own—possibly to silence gossip about his propensities.

Mathieu now feels free to fall in love with Boris' sister Ivich, who announces her maturity in the latest terms: "I don't care a curse for morality. Not one curse."[84] She is pretty but sick, and cannot hold her food. "A faint, sour reek of vomit came from her delicate mouth. Mathieu inhaled it escstatically."[85] (A bit of vomit appears in all the volumes of the series. It is a kind of emblem for the running theme: that the intellectuals of Paris in that age had drunk more of the wine of reason than they could hold, had mistaken irresponsibility for freedom.)

This is no book for a weak stomach or a hurried mind. Page after page of trivial conversation and superfluous detail; unnecessary realism, as in the full page devoted to Marcelle's vomiting;[86] and an unrivaled roster of lost and despicable souls. But amid the debris Sartre's literary skill proudly emerges—in perceptive observations of character, in revealing nuances of analysis, and, overspreading all, a powerful picture of moral and social decay. Here, as in *Being and Nothingness*, man is "a futile passion," and life seems unforgivably meaningless. "A child: another consciousness, a little center-point of light that would flutter round and round, dashing against the walls, and never able to escape."[87]

The second volume is leavened with humor, but deepens the tragedy. *Le Sursis* (1945; *The Reprieve*) begins on September 23, 1938, with the opening of negotiations between Germany's Hitler, Italy's Mussolini, France's Daladier, and England's Neville Chamberlain; it ends with the signing of the Munich Pact (September 29–30), which gave the Western Powers a year's reprieve from war. The 445-page book is divided only by the eight days of the conference. Within each day—sometimes within one hour—the narrative passes, with no word of explanation or transition, from place to place in France, England, Germany, Czechoslovakia, Italy, and Africa, and from person to person, including Mathieu, Boris, Gomez, Daniel, and Ivich from *The Age of Reason*. Often the switch of scene and group occurs within the same paragraph, as if Sartre were deliberately teasing and confusing the reader; so the killing of a native by a Belgian in Morocco is mingled with a conversation in France, a fragment of a concert on board a ship at sea, and the passage of diplomats to No. 10 Downing Street. Sartre appears to have taken this tantalizing device from John Dos Passos' *Manhattan Transfer* (1925); and presumably both authors borrowed from the technique of the cinema.

The early pages seek to convey the somber tension of Europe in those testing days: Chamberlain at Godesberg waiting for Hitler to receive him; Daladier admitting to Hitler the helplessness of France; Beneš ordering mobilization in Czechoslovakia; Jews fleeing from Prague and Paris. The novel shows Brunet hoping that the Socialists of Europe, putting class above nation, will take a united stand against war; Mathieu confessing himself a "washout,"[88] but quietly accepting conscription as a decision made for him; Daniel impatiently leading the heavy-bellied Marcelle in a crowd of refugees, and dreaming of a revolution that will make homosexuals respected; Boris expecting to be drafted, and mourning that now he will never realize his high emprise of sleeping with a duchess . . . Day after day the excitement and the terror rise. Then suddenly the radio blares out the news: the pact has been signed; England and France have agreed to let Hitler take the Sudetenland from Czechoslovakia; "peace in our time" fills a hundred million hearts with joy, a million heads with doubts. Conscripts, demobilized, return to their homes and jobs, their quarrels and adulteries; Mathieu again teaches philosophy in the *lycée*. Everything in France is as before, as safe and dull and meaningless.

The reprieve was short; after a year the war came. In Volume III, *La Mort dans l'âme* (1949; "Death in the Soul," translated as *Troubled Sleep*) the French Army is in chaotic flight before the triumphant Germans, and Paris awaits spoliation by rough Teutons eager for French wines and slender women. In the retreat some French officers desert their troops and ride off in style; the privates curse them and loot the villages for liquor. Mathieu, himself a private, is disgusted with their drunken vomiting, but finally joins their carouse in the hope that they will learn to like him; they do so reluctantly, for they resent his education and his polite vocabulary; as for themselves, they assert their manhood by spattering the pages with all the privy wisdom in their memory. Some of them speak admiringly of the victorious Germans;[89] one (quite out of character) expresses himself as reconciled to the idea of a Europe united under Hitler.[90] In the final scene, when the fugitives resist capture by the Germans, Mathieu learns to shoot and kill with a rapture he has never known before; he frees himself from himself by commitment to his group.

Sartre never completed the tetralogy. In November, 1949, he published in *Les Temps modernes* a fragment entitled "Drôle d'amitié," telling how Brunet's Communist ardor was shaken by the Hitler-Stalin pact of August, 1939; Brunet took to debauchery, and slipped heretically into a "curious friendship" with an apostate from the faith.[91] An additional rough draft told how Mathieu joined the Resistance in Paris, was captured by the German police, and died under torture rather than reveal the identity or hiding place of his comrades. Sartre explained his reason for abandoning the story: "to write a novel whose hero dies in the Resistance, committed to the idea of liberty, would be too easy."[92]

Besides, Volume III had not been so favorably received as its predecessors. Perhaps readers had tired of jumping from place to place, from soul to soul, in pursuit of Sartre's elusive narrative and theme. But by and large Paris was agreed that this strange author, who had seemed irrecoverably lost in a morass of metaphysics, had turned out to be a master craftsman in fiction, with at least one foot on the ground, and with eyes, ears, and nose alert to every sensation that could convey, in print, the shape and sound and smell of life. French readers are tough; they took with a good stomach and a hearty laugh Sartre's report of a locksmith's "muffled fart,"[93] or the anxious calls of hospitalized men for a bedpan,[94] or the moans and cries of women in the delirium of coitus.[95]

Sartre gave sex as much prominence in his stories as it has in life. In the first thirty-six pages of *The Age of Reason* there are two scenes of men embracing naked women, who are adequately described. Scatology also gets due place in these novels. We see, on "the miniature death called Sunday, . . . the first line-up outside the urinals on the Place Clichy."[96] *Merde* turns up again and again,[97] but this popular French word has more letters and less smell than its English equivalent.

All in all it is the less fragrant side of French life that Sartre reveals in his novels: a corrupt, cynical world of wastrels, cowards, deserters, criminals, drunkards, homosexuals, itching virgins (like Ivich), prostitutes, pimps . . . ; was all France like this in 1938–40? It is unlikely. Sartre made no claim to having shown the whole picture of France; only a Balzac could do this, being allowed fifty volumes, only a man who stood both in and above the battle. But Sartre was an angry man who wished to make his pen a sword; his novels were frontal assaults upon the status quo; they were bombs thrown at that venal Nothingness the Chamber of Deputies, which had led France through oceans of oratory to surrender and collapse. They were what he had pledged himself to write: literature as war.

VII. THE PHILOSOPHER AS DRAMATIST

He had already conquered the theater with *No Exit* and *The Flies;* now he used the stage more and more to expound his philosophy to those whom he hated most, but who alone came to his plays—the bourgeoisie.

On November 8, 1946, at the Théâtre Antoine, he presented *La Putain respectueuse. The Respectful Prostitute* pictures "a Southern town of the United States" as Sartre imagined it after his visit to New York in 1945. On the train that brings "Lizzie" to the South she is violently molested by a white man; a Negro tries to protect her; the white man shoots him dead, and is arrested. But he is the son of Senator Clarke; moreover, the white men of the town agree that "you can't punish a fellow of your own"[98] race for killing a black man; they accuse another Negro. The hunted man comes to Lizzie's apartment and asks her to hide him; she can't, for she is entertaining Fred, another of the Senator's sons. The Senator himself appears and offers her several hundred dollars if she will sign a statement naming the Negro as her assailant. She refuses, and brands the whites as "filthy bastards"; they play on her fears and force her to sign. The Negro comes to her again and asks to be hidden; she tries to protect him, but Fred returns and kills him. The white murderer is released, and Lizzie becomes Fred's mistress. — When I saw the play in New York some twenty years ago I thought it gave an exaggerated picture of legal injustice in the South, but I understand that it is still considered unseemly there to convict the white murderers of a Negro.

Incredibly fertile, Sartre produced in that same year 1946 another bitter play, gruesomely entitled *Morts sans sépulture* ("Deaths without Burial," renamed in English *The Victors*). These are the officials of Pétain's Vichy regime in collaboration with the Germans; they have rounded up a group of Resistance fighters, whom they torture (off stage) with a view to learning the names and lairs of more important rebels. One of the captives is a young woman, Lucie; she is raped by her torturers, but she fixes upon them a Sartrean look that makes them feel their degradation. Rejoining the prisoners, she sits through most of the play in somber silence, facing the audience. Each of the accused wonders, secretly, will he be strong enough to resist torture when his turn comes. They fear that the youngest of them, the fifteen-year-old François, will be unable to bear the torments and will reveal the secret; they agree to strangle him; he is Lucie's brother, but she assents to his death; thereafter she shrinks from the touch of her fellow prisoners. Finally one of them, racked beyond bearing, "talks" in return for the promise that all will be spared; they are all taken out and shot. — Sartre's flair for the ghastly offended the audience, which did not enjoy the shrieks of the unseen tortured; critics saw no Aristotelian catharsis in such audible suffering; they protested that in a polite play, as in the Greek drama, violence should be reported but not seen or heard. *The Victors* has seldom been staged again.

In *Les Mains sales* (1948; translated as *Dirty Hands*, produced in New York as *The Red Gloves*) Sartre pictured another Resistance group. Hoederer, its chief, is a proletarian who has discarded moral scruples in the pursuit of party purposes; one must soil, even bloody, his hands if he is to guide a great cause to victory.[99] He has developed those qualities of foresight, concentration, decisiveness, and self-control indispensable to leadership, but he remains good-natured and generous within the compulsions of his place and aims. His followers admire him, but turn against him when he proposes a united front with other anti-German organizations in France; they conclude that he has accepted a bribe, and they decide that he must be killed; "one only leaves the Party feet first."[100] Who should fire the shot? They choose Hugo, a young bourgeois idealist who has become a fervent Communist but displeases his comrades by his clothes, his manners, his speech, his addiction to reasoning, and his vacillations. (He is Sartre Resartus.) He accepts the assignment, if only to prove his courage to himself. He becomes Hoederer's secretary. When an opportunity to fulfill his mission arises he cannot decide to pull the trigger. His wife falls in love with Hoederer, who repulses her; she flings her arms around his reluctant neck; Hugo, entering, shoots Hoederer as presumably a seducer; the Communists, thinking that Hugo has carried out their orders, hail him as a hero. Later they receive orders from Moscow to join the French government in a united front; now, having adopted Hoederer's policy, they honor him as a martyr, and decide to kill Hugo as an assassin. — The Communists condemned the play as a bourgeois satire of Communist orthodoxy; one critic concluded that "Jean-Paul Sartre has sold out what remained of his honor and probity for thirty pieces of silver and a mess of American pottage."[101]

Sartre had advised authors to seek a wider audience for their ideas by writing for the cinema and television. In 1947 he tried his hand by preparing a scenario called *Les Jeux sont faits* (*The Chips Are Down*). He used the new media's freedom with space and time to imagine a world in which the dead move among the living as disembodied spirits, seeing but unseen, and audible only to one another. They envy the living who have bodies that can be felt and loved; two of them remember that in life they had become devoted lovers when death overtook them; they long to be alive and touchable again. A master spirit offers them reincarnation on one condition—that they remain lovers, without weariness or jealousy. They agree, recover their bodies, and are happy. But he is poor and she is rich; their different backgrounds, associations, and memories clash; they become uncomfortable in the prison of their vow; their love fades; they quarrel; love, as in *Being and Nothingness*, has become war. Suddenly they are fleshless souls again, wandering shadowless among the shades.

Restless with ideas, Sartre returned to the problems of morality and leadership with a long drama entitled *Le Diable et le Bon Dieu* (1951; *The Devil and the Good Lord*). Satan and God alternate and then unite in a new interpretation of Goethe's hero Götz von Berlichingen. He appears first as the invincible but merciless commander, whom everyone about him fears and hates, respects and obeys. He has renounced all belief in God, arguing (like the Sartre of *Being and Nothingness*) that if God exists—orthodoxly omnipresent and omnipotent—man cannot be free, and can have no real personality or worth. Having conquered every enemy, Götz tires of war; having done every evil, he wonders might there not be a novel pleasure in doing good. He hears Heinrich the priest say that "the stench of the world rises to the stars"; he asks, "Then everyone is doing evil?" "Everyone," replies Heinrich.[102] So

Götz resolves to do good, just to be different. He is converted to Communism, and gives his lands to the peasants; he becomes a saint, and washes their feet. Soon he rejects every pleasure, tortures himself delectably, and calls the woman who loves him "a bag of excrement."[103] He builds a model community, the "City of the Sun," and exhorts his liberated peasants to love one another. They quarrel, and laugh at his preachments of returning good for evil. When Tetzel comes to Worms to sell indulgences (1517) Götz warns the people that they are being fooled; they denounce him as a blasphemous infidel. But when the peasants revolt against their feudal lords, and suffer defeat after defeat, they beg Götz to be their general. He agrees, on condition that they will obey his every command; he may have to sacrifice thousands of them in battle; he will have to do evil ruthlessly in order to achieve the end they hold good. He tells his captains, "I shall take this command against my will. I shall be ruthless. . . . Proclaim immediately that any soldier attempting to desert will be hanged. . . . We shall be sure of victory when your men are more afraid of me than of the enemy. . . . On this earth, at present, good and evil are inseparable. I agree to be bad in order to become good."[104] There the play ends. We perceive that Sartre was struggling to forge a new ethic, and that he was still under the influence of Nietzsche; or was he defending Stalin? "For me," he wrote in 1962, "the essential problem is to reject the theory according to which the Left ought not to answer violence with violence."[105] (He was answering Camus.)

His last play, Les Séquestrés d'Altona (1960; The Condemned of Altona) is a confused echo of World War II. The action takes place in a suburb of Hamburg in 1959. A shipping magnate, about to die of cancer, bequeaths his firm to his second son, who wonders why the bequest has not gone to his brother Franz. But Franz, since 1945, has locked himself in an upper room of the paternal mansion, for a maze of reasons. As a German officer at Smolensk in 1943 he ordered some partisans of the Russian Resistance to be tortured to death because they would not "talk." When the Anglo-American forces took Hamburg they sought him as a war criminal. In his gloomy hiding place Franz went mad with fear, remorse, and shame: fear that the Allies would reduce Germany to slavery and that he himself would be hanged; remorse for his misdeeds and for the horrors of the Hitler regime; shame for the guilt of his father as chief shipbuilder for that regime. At last he comes out of his hiding, and persuades his father to join him in suicide. — Simone de Beauvoir tells us that "almost all the critics agreed with me in placing *The Condemned of Altona* above all Sartre's other plays."[106] I have seen it and read it, and think it clumsy, obscure, and absurd.

In general, Sartre's plays draw overmuch on the playgoer's will to believe. Almost all the plots are incredible, and almost always the action is macabre. Death is the playwright's favorite decree—which, I must admit, is *de rigueur* in the tragic theater. Nearly all the plays bring in the "look" and "the Other" from *Being and Nothingness*; and *The Condemned of Altona* shows Franz pursued by the same crabs that haunted Sartre in Le Havre. The dialogue is usually terse and brilliant, and the characters are distinctly portrayed. However, Sartre offered his dramas not as characters creating situations, but as situations creating ✓ characters. Bracketing his plays with those of Anouilh and Camus, he wrote:

> What is universal to their way of thinking is not nature but the situation in which a man finds himself; that is, not the sum of his ✓ psychological traits but the limits which enclose him on all sides. . . . As a successor to the theater of character we want a theater of situation. . . . The people in our plays will be distinct from one another not as a coward from a miser, but rather as actors are divergent or clashing, as right may conflict with right.[107]

(And yet *Hamlet* is a drama of situation creating character, and *Dirty Hands* is a drama of character—Hoederer versus Hugo—creating situation. It is the believable combination of conflicting characters in a revealing situation that makes the drama live, and lifts it into literature.)

Sartre noted significant similarities between these postwar French plays and the classic theater of ancient Greece. In both cases the dramatist plunges at once into the heart of a critical situation, "at the very point where it is about to reach its climax."[108] In both cases the language is serious and severe, with no alloy of Shakespearean comedy; the action is simple, violent, and concentrated in place and time; the play, by its nature, observes the "three unities." The new dramas ignore the romantic sentiment of Racine and go back to the heroic austerity of Corneille; they ignore Euripides and return to Aeschylus and Sophocles. It is a high claim, and in form it is just; there is lacking, however, the religious feeling that permeates the classic drama, and the situations in the Sartrean theater are too transient in pertinence to hold enduring power.

VIII. THE WAR WITH THE MARXIANS

All this while Sartre himself was caught in a conflict that well exemplified the interplay of situation and character. Compelled as editor of *Les Temps modernes* to take definite stands on moral and political ✓ problems, he felt with rising unease the difficulty of reconciling the psychological and ethical individualism of *Being and Nothingness* with the cooperation required for active involvement in the issues of the day. If conflict is the natural and inevitable relation of man to man, how can cooperation be sincere and real?—how can there ever be a communistic society, or a warless world?

At this point (1946) Simone de Beauvoir came to his aid with a series of articles which were later (1948) published as *Pour une Morale de l'ambiguité.* "Of all my books," she wrote fifteen years later, "it is the one that irritates me the most today. . . . I was wasting time rebutting absurd objections; but at the time Existentialism was being treated as a nihilist philosophy, willfully pessimistic, frivolous, licentious, despairing, and ignoble; some defense had to be made."[109]

By ambiguity she meant that each of us is in almost constant tension between oneself and "the Other"; between the immorality and yet the frequent necessity of using others as means to our ends; between our interests as individuals and our obligations to our group; between our love of privacy and our fear of solitude; between our sense of our worth as thinking persons and our discovery of our cosmic insignificance.[110] How can we find a consistent and acceptable ethic to reconcile these opposites in a society at once orderly and free?

Simone's answer remained essentially individualistic, and infuriated Catholics and Communists alike. She bluntly repudiated "the totalitarian doctrines which raise up beyond men the mirage of mankind";[111] this mankind or humanity to which it is proposed to sacrifice the individual is an abstraction; only individuals exist, and it is to their basic freedom that we must adjust our moral codes and our laws.[112] She admitted that "no existence can be validly fulfilled if it is limited to itself";[113] man "exists only by transcending himself, and his freedom can be achieved only through the freedom of others";[114] but she felt that this principle was being carried too far. There is "a point at which the fascist ideology and the Marxian ideology converge: a doctrine . . . which can propose to man no other salvation than his subordination to the collectivity."[115] She scorned as a conformist anyone who gave up his liberty by being "a member of the Christian Church or the Communist Party."[116] She was willing to accept democracy as the best way yet found of reconciling individual freedom with communal order;[117] nevertheless her heart belonged to Russia; the ambiguity remained. Meanwhile, Simone tells us, Sartre filled "notebook after notebook with minuscule handwriting in his attempt to work out his system of morality."[118]

Attacks upon him came from Right and Left. Catholic critics denounced him for exaggerating the evil in human nature and conduct, and for an atheism that seemed to leave no support for morality except fear of the police.[119] Communist critics charged him with "having ignored human solidarity, with considering man as an isolated being."[120] In 1946 Jean Kanapa, formerly a pupil of Sartre and now an active Communist, issued a pamphlet—*L'Existentialisme n'est pas un humanisme*—which "in the crudest language" accused Sartre and Simone of being fascists and "enemies of mankind."[121] Sartre replied in the same year with a small book, *L'Existentialisme est un humanisme.* He defended existentialism as humanistic because it denied all divine commandments and placed upon man himself the responsibility for working out a moral code, and, above all, because it asserted man's freedom of choice, and reclaimed him from the mechanistic determinism by which Marxism had reduced man to a helpless automaton. But he admitted, "I am obliged to will the liberty of others at the same time as my own," and he adopted one form of Kant's categorical imperative by advising every man to ask himself, before any important choice, "What if everyone acted that way?"[122]

In another booklet of 1946, *Materialism and Revolution,* Sartre took the offensive and questioned the Marxian assumption that consciousness is a material product of a completely material world. He granted that the materialistic "myth" had served as a useful tool in freeing men from supernatural myths and terrors, but he preferred to build a progressive movement upon the conception of man not as a robot but as a free consciousness. Moreover, he urged, the Socialist movement should abandon class struggle as its fundamental theme and strategy, and should invite the middle class to join it in building a society under a freely chosen government.[123]

The bourgeoisie did not respond to this invitation from the man who had called them *salauds.* Their intellectual leaders berated Sartre, like Gide, as a corrupter of youth, and as in part responsible for the spread of family disintegration, sexual license, and anarchic music among the youth of Paris.[124] One of them rechristened existentialism as "excrementalism";[125] another called Sartre "a blockhead and an ass"; one wrote to him that "if the crematory ovens of Germany still existed they would serve well to rid us of people like you."[126] Some former radicals, like Malraux and Koestler, resented Sartre's attacks upon de Gaulle, and withdrew their support of *Les Temps modernes*.[127]

Many liberals had been longing for a halfway house between capitalism and Communism, between the United States and the Soviets. In 1948 David Rousset and Gérard Rosenthal proposed a "Rassemblement Démocratique et Révolutionnaire." Sartre, Camus, and Simone de Beauvoir joined the movement and became its literary protagonists. They explained, in joint *Conversations on Politics* (1949), that they wished to offer a rallying point to progressives and Socialists unwilling to submit to doctrinal direction by the Communist Party of France.[128] The Communists assailed Rousset and Sartre as agents of Wall Street.[129]

The Rassemblement held some enthusiastic meetings. In 1950 it won popular support for its campaign against the war in Indochina; "the people of France," it proclaimed, "are against this dirty war"; and it called for peace negotiations with Ho Chih Minh.[130] The French government (like the American in 1966) defended the war as part of a necessary "anti-Communist crusade."[131] Soon the principle and practice of intellectual freedom raised divisions among the leaders of the Rassemblement. Rousset and others supported the United States in the "Cold War" against Soviet Russia; Sartre declared that Western Europe should keep itself neutral between the rival powers. In October, 1949, he resigned from the Rassemblement.

Thereafter he moved increasingly to the Left. He condemned American foreign policy in nearly all its phases, and at times he defended Stalin's methods on the ground that "a more or less lengthy and critical period of terrorism is unavoidable in the efforts of a revolutionary government to maintain itself against counterrevolutionary plots."[132] In 1952 he joined French Communists as delegate to the Moscow World Congress for Peace. He was given a standing ovation there, and when he returned to Paris his association with the Communist Party was complete except that he still held back from membership.[133]

Amid this turbulence of body and mind he found time to write a strange book of seven hundred pages, *Saint Genet, Comédien et Martyr* (1952). It is to Sartre's credit that he could see much that was attractive in so unprepossessing a personality. Before Sartre met him, Genet (b. 1910) had lived half his life in jails; he exalted crime as a legitimate protest against bourgeois civilization; he proclaimed himself the defender and embodiment of evil; he flaunted his homosexuality in the face of a world mad about women. He expressed his views in prose shockful with candor and obscenities, and in dramas that were stark indictments of modern morality and law. In 1948 Sartre and Jean Cocteau succeeded in getting for Genet a pardon that released him from jail and left him free to write. Now Sartre made him the subject of a meandering essay in existentialist psychoanalysis. He analyzed the career of Genet as exemplifying the theory propounded in *Being and Nothingness*, that a man's life is determined by his basic choice: Genet had chosen to be a thief and a practicing pervert because others had called him so; he would take them at their word. Sartre surveyed him from many sides in a windy discourse on the psychology of masturbation, the art of flatulence, and the theological aspects of sodomy. "The homosexual," says our philosopher, "does not know, in the griping ache of his pain, whether he is expelling excrement or opening himself to a foreign body. . . . And yet, in this abject and ridiculous posture, amidst his suffering and his muck, it is nevertheless his God that he is receiving."[134] (I am reminded of Genet's remark: "Poetry is the art of using *merde* and making you eat it.")[135]

Sartre's *apertura a sinistra* was jarred in 1956 by the uprising of Hungary against Soviet domination, and the suppression of the revolt by Russian troops. When the French Communists refused to condemn this action Sartre ended his entente with the party: "One cannot have any friendship with the leading faction of the Soviet bureaucracy; it is horror that dominates [our reaction]. . . . As for the men who at this time lead the French Communist Party, it is not, it will never be, possible to re-establish relations. Every one of their statements, every one of their actions, is the fulfillment of thirty years of lying and sclerosis" (hardening of the intellectual arteries).[136] But he did not abandon his faith in Communism. In 1960 he and Simone visited Cuba, and soon proclaimed their total agreement with Castro's regime. "In Cuba," he wrote later, "I realized that . . . it is only in violence that the oppressed can attain human status."[137]

While in Brazil he received word that his friend Francis Jeanson had been arrested for conspiring with Algerian rebels. He sent to the French tribunal that was to try Jeanson a letter affirming "my total solidarity with the accused."[138] His friends begged him to stay out of France for a while, but he returned, and no action was taken against him. The radical youth of France now looked upon him as the ablest and bravest champion of rebel causes, but the French Algerians denounced him as a traitor to France. Sartre had gone to live with his mother at 42 Rue Bonaparte; in 1961 a bomb was thrown into this dwelling; it did much damage, but not to persons; Sartre was not there at the time.

Through all this travel and travail he had been preparing the second major effort of his intellectual career. He worked himself into such fever over it that (Simone tells us) he deliberately drank himself into intoxication as a distraction and relief.[139] He published it in 1960 as a *Critique de la raison dialectique*, a critical analysis of dialectical reason—i.e., of reason using the forms of Hegelian logic. Of its 755 pages the first hundred reprinted, as *Question de méthode*, articles written in 1957 for a Polish Communist review.

In this *Search for a Method* he struggled to reconcile his existentialism of consciousness and liberty with Marxian conceptions of history, class war, and proletarian dictatorship. A modest prelude described Marxism as the controlling philosophy of our time, and presented existentialism as merely a modification. But Sartre asked for some concessions before being swallowed by the new leviathan. Existentialism could not accept history as a mechanical operation of purely material bodies; it could not reconcile itself to determinism, or to the depreciation of the individual in history, or to a "proletarian" dictatorship, or to the regimentation of thought; the individual as a free consciousness must be the source of philosophy and the ideal of development.[140] Sartre protested against "the prejudices which sterilize Marxist intellectuals in the French Communist Party. . . . The goal of Marxism is no longer to increase what it knows, but to be itself constituted a priori as an absolute knowledge."[141] He admitted that the freedom of choice which he had expounded in *Being and Nothingness* was considerably limited by lack of economic opportunity and political liberty; it would increase as production expanded and met more of our needs. Marx had said as much in predicting the "withering of the state."[142] But then Sartre adds: "As soon as there will exist *for everyone* a margin of real freedom beyond the production of [the needs for] life, Marxism will have lived out its span; a philosophy of freedom will take its place."[143]

The remaining 655 pages[144] of the *Critique* restate the ideas of the *Question de méthode* in a larger frame of logic and web of terminology. We meet our old friends of the older opus: "Being-for-itself," "Being-in-itself," "the Other," the "look," even, occasionally, "Nothing." There is the same love of word-play and paradox. Sartre adds a magic of dialectics—logical formulas into which the facts and processes of history and sociology are squeezed with a prestidigitation that would have made Hegel proud of the imitation and jealous of the finesse. Even the faithful Simone, reading the manuscript, felt as if she were groping through long tunnels[145] littered with "ambiguities."

As Sartre had followed Heidegger's *Being and Time* with *Being and*

Nothingness, so in this new immensity he paralleled Kant's famous title—*Critique of Pure Reason*—with his own *Critique of Dialectical Reason;* and as Kant had sought to find and chart the a priori forms of thought, Sartre would now try to formulate the a priori foundations of social life; to find in the nature of the human mind the logical forms embracing organized activities and historical events; to explain the patterns of relation and influence between man and man, the citizen and the group, the soul and the world. He undertook to show that the Marxian dialectic of economic and political evolution by internal contradictions and class war could be restated a priori as ever-expanding desires generating efforts and conflicts resolved in compromises and syntheses generating new desires. He hoped to fuse Marxism and existentialism by reconciling the bleak individualism of *Being and Nothingness* with the cooperative socialism of Marx, and the Sartrean insistence upon personal freedom with the Communist demand for party discipline.

Only individuals exist; groups are not entities added to their component individuals, they are relations conceived and felt by individuals. Progress is reducible to the influence of initiative minds upon the environment and the group. Why do individuals form groups? Because to each of us the Other, though a rival and a potential foe, can be also a helper, a protector, or a tool; and the Other finds in us a like possibility of security or aid. This reciprocity of need and use generates and sustains the group. And need is elastic and endless; nearly every individual desires more than he has. There is never enough to satisfy all; and this scarcity (*rareté*), this Nothing between desire and satisfaction, is the impetus to struggle among individuals, groups, classes, and states. Conflict is built in the nature of man, and will continue as long as desire outruns content.

Strange to say, instead of condemning material production, Sartre asks for its increase, and a wider and juster distribution of wealth, in the hope that this will reduce the urgency of need and the violence of competition. In an economy of abundance there could be less regimentation of movement and thought, more freedom for individual variation and experiment. Meanwhile Marxism should abandon its materialist metaphysics, its determinist psychology, and its political tyranny; it should open its arms to those Socialists who value the individual rights and liberties developed by democracy; it should soften the rigor of its dogmas and make room for difference, criticism, and doctrinal growth. Then existentialism will be willingly absorbed into Marxism, and the Marxian philosophy will move from one triumph to another, in one nation after another, raising men to new levels of prosperity and security, and perhaps at last to the wisdom of content.

The *Critique* made few friends. The Right attacked it because it professed to accept Marxism, the Left because it presumed to improve upon the established faith. Sartre promised a second volume that would clear up all difficulties and meet all plaints, but that promise has not yet been kept. We can sympathize with his hesitation. The problem that he faced is the problem that confronts our children: how to reconcile socialism with democracy, to organize a happier distribution of wealth without dictating elections, regimenting labor, and controlling the mind. Another century may be needed before a rational synthesis of those old opposites, liberty and order, will be achieved.

IX. SIMONE AND SEX

The romance of Sartre and Mademoiselle (or Madame?) de Beauvoir had meanwhile suffered some fluctuations. After his return from the United States in 1946 Sartre resumed a liaison with "Mademoiselle M."; and "they envisaged spending two or three months together every year." Simone asked him, "Frankly, who means the more to you, M. or me?" He answered, "M. means an enormous amount to me, but I am with you."[146] When he went to live with his mother "I wondered," she recalls, "if he wasn't going to lose the liberty so dear to our youth."[147]

She herself was using and losing some of her liberty. In 1947, in or near Chicago, "I had lived with Nelson Algren [a Middle West novelist] for only three weeks."[148] In 1948 she went to America to spend a month with him; together they traveled through the United States and Mexico, occasionally visiting "the sleaziest joints."[149] In June, 1949, Algren came to Paris, won Sartre's friendship, and went with him and Simone to Rome, Fez, Marrakesh, and Marseille; now, she tells us, she was deeply in love with him,[150] apparently with a feeling she had not known since her first years with Sartre. In July Sartre left Paris for a month with M. in the south of France; that over, he went with Simone to Algeria. It was a marriage of multiple convenience.

Partly to answer critics of her freedom, partly to offset such misogynist tirades as Henri de Montherlant's *Sur les femmes* and Philip Wylie's chapter on women in *A Generation of Vipers*, Simone issued in 1949 a two-volume treatise entitled *The Second Sex*. I began its seven hundred pages expecting to find a popular discussion of the "modern woman." I was surprised and impressed by the scholarly thoroughness with which

the book covered the biological, physiological, psychological, pathological, psychoanalytic, historical, social, moral, religious, economic, and
political aspects of woman's life, and by the author's wide acquaintance
with the technical literature of these subjects, with the history of
philosophy, and with French, English, and American fiction and poetry
as offering illustrations of her themes.

The evolution of sex, says Simone, was fostered by the fact that
sexual reproduction brought two pools of hereditary qualities into the
offspring, disturbing its equilibrium but enriching its possibilities. Both
sexes were largely sacrificed to continuing the species: one sex to bearing and rearing the new life, the other to getting food. Some especially
brilliant pages (16 ff.) pointed out how in the lower species the parents
begin to decline soon after reproduction, whereas in higher species they
may long survive to develop individual qualities and aims. Biologically
the female is the mainstream of life; the male is incidental, often weak
and transitory, sometimes superfluous. The male's diverse forays for
food developed in him a greater variety of skills, and gave him, in the
more advanced species, economic and mental superiority; the female's
disabilities of periodicity, pregnancy, delivery, urogenital ailments, and
domestic care handicapped her in self-protection, narrowed the range
of her interests, and limited the development of her mind. But the
psychological differences of the sexes are largely due to history and law
rather than to inherent qualities; when given the same opportunities for
varied experiences, "women display intellectual qualities perfectly
identical with those of men";[151] note George Eliot and George Sand.
Woman's character is a social rather than a biological product; her
values, her wisdom, her morality, her tastes, her behavior are to be
explained by her situation and her history; they are not innate.[152]

So Mademoiselle de Beauvoir surveys the record of woman's status
and conduct in Oriental cultures, in classic Greece and Rome, in the
Middle Ages, in modern Europe and America: the hetairas and the
empresses (the author took too little advantage here of the mental power
and governing ability shown by Elizabeth I of England, Maria Theresa
of Austria, Catherine the Great of Russia), the Christian derogation of
woman as Satan's agent in the repeated seduction of men, the Christian
idealization of both virginity and motherhood in the worship of Mary,
and the role of woman in modern literature. Simone applauds "the
freedom of behavior that is enjoyed by young American women and
that French girls are beginning to win for themselves; they go almost
imperceptibly from 'necking' and 'petting' to complete sexual rela-

tions."[153] She studies every stage in the psychosexual development of women today. She believes that "the excessive sentimentality, homosexual fervors, and platonic crushes of adolescent girls, with all their train of silliness and frivolity, are much more injurious than a little childish sex play and a few definite sex experiences."[154] She does not think highly of romantic love. She suspects that moral propaganda has exaggerated the nobility of marriage and the joys of motherhood. "Marriage kills love. Scorned too much, rejected too much, too much an everyday matter, the wife ceases to have erotic attraction." Consequently "adultery can disappear only with marriage itself."[155]

Simone protests against the surviving legal and social disabilities of women. "Their normal destiny is marriage, which still means, practically, subordination to men."[156] To man a woman is "the Other," the potential tool or enemy; she is something to be overcome and possessed. "His domination is expressed in the very posture of copulation,"[157] and coitus is the violation of her body. If she becomes pregnant, man-made laws forbid abortion. If she frees herself by divorce, she receives in French law a ridiculously small pension, and finds it hardly possible to support herself except by prostitution. "For a woman freedom begins in the womb";[158] she should have the right to determine whether or not to have a child.

Simone envies the relatively free status of the wife in the United States. She defends free unions like her own; only so can the woman remain "a complete person."[159] She inclines to Colette's view that erotic pleasure is a dangerously frail basis upon which to build a marriage, but she seconds Léon Blum's advocacy of trial marriages to permit ready divorce for sexual incompatibility. She suggests that within marriage each partner should allow the other a few escapades. "A wife often accepts with good grace the fact that her husband possesses other women."[160] She concludes that "the quarrel" of the sexes "will go on as long as men and women fail to recognize each other as peers."[161]

The Second Sex, its author tells us, caused a scandal in French society. Many readers were shocked by the freedom with which a woman publicly and plainly dealt with the details of male and female genitals, and women were alarmed by Simone's candid admission of feminine devices and faults. Anti-Sartreans smiled at her frequent use of the terminology developed in Being and Nothingness, and at her adoption of the "phenomenological psychoanalysis" with which Sartre had attempted to improve upon Freud. Wits dubbed her "La Grande Sartreuse" and "Notre Dame de Sartres." Communists frowned upon her defense of abortion, which Soviet Russia had frowned upon. Nevertheless *The Second Sex* sold 22,000 copies in the first week after its publication.[162]

In 1950 Simone and Sartre visited the Sahara and studied the exploitation of native labor by French colonials. Later in that year she flew to Chicago to rejoin Algren. "He had bought a house on Lake Michigan; we were to spend two months there together. For me the idea of having a real life with him was a great happiness."[163] (Do we catch here a confession that her semisolitary relation with Sartre had brought her only transient moments of happiness—that she secretly longed for a permanent husband and home, perhaps even for motherhood and children?) When she reached Chicago Algren informed her that "he didn't love me any more," but he invited her to spend the summer with him anyway. She lived with him for a while, until he told her that he was planning to marry his former wife. "By that time despair had drained me of all feeling."[164] After she left him she mourned: "I'll never sleep again warmed by another body."[165] Sartre now "seemed farther away from me than ever before,"[166] and most of his ardor was going into the Marxian war.

In 1952, aged forty-four, she took another lover, Claude Lanzmann, a passionate Zionist, aged twenty-five. "We decided to live together," and Sartre gave them his blessing. The affair continued for seven years. She traveled with him in Switzerland and Sicily; "then I stayed in Rome with Sartre for over a month," and went with him to Capri; Lanzmann joined them in Milan. In 1958 "Lanzmann and I drifted apart. . . . The initiative has been his."[167] Now, turning fifty, she felt old, and wondered whether she would die before Sartre, who was fifty-three.

Her writing had become her spiritual as well as her financial support. She had considerable success with her novels *She Came to Stay* and *All Men Are Mortal;* and in 1954 she won the prestigious Prix Goncourt with *The Mandarins.* In 1958–63 she crowned her career with a leisurely autobiography. The self-portrait is bravely candid. Here is a person in her own right, no mere appendage to Sartre; she accepted many of his theories and terms, but she went her own way, tramped the roads, climbed mountains, ventured everywhere in lust for a full and hearty life. She was a professor of philosophy, highly respected as a teacher, but she did not let this interfere with her taste for café soirees, for late hours at a bar with burly proletaires. "We drank hard in those days" after the liberation,[168] especially after discovering that the politicians who had led France to ruin were still flourishing and quarreling in the Chamber of Deputies. "I wasn't bothered by the coarseness of the language" of the truck drivers she drank with in a Sahara inn after Sartre had gone to bed; "I am perfectly able to use their vocabulary myself when the need arises."[169] She wrote a preface for a new edition of Sade's pornographic novel *Justine*, and later edited a selection of the Marquis' works. Yet we find her deeply moved by hearing the laughter of a child at play.[170] She never experienced what she had sought—the fullness of life. She reached the pinnacle among the women writers of her time in France, but the last pages of her autobiography are a dirge about old age and the terror of death.[171]

X. THE AGING WARRIORS

Sartre remained suspect with French Communist leaders, but the Soviets greeted him as a friend on his repeated visits to Moscow. He spent a month in the U. S. S. R. in 1962 as guest of the Union of Soviet Writers; on his return to France he reported a great improvement in the freedom of literature in Russia. He went again in 1963, with Simone de Beauvoir; they were received by Khrushchev, and rejoiced in the "de-Stalinization" of Russian rule. In 1964 they lectured in Czechoslovakia, and once more sampled the land of their remodeled dreams. This is the normal evolution of liberalism in modern history and in ourselves: we begin by clamoring for individual freedom, and end by appealing to the expanding state.

In 1964 Sartre was offered, and rejected, the Nobel Prize for Literature. "My sympathies," he explained, "go undeniably toward socialism, that is, toward that which one calls the Eastern bloc, but I was born and raised in a bourgeois family. Therefore I cannot accept any distinction from the high cultural authorities, neither of the East nor of the West. . . . I would be just as unable to accept the Lenin Prize if someone should wish to award it to me."[172]

His favorite enemy was now the United States. He called upon France never again to ally herself with America. "Beware!" he cried; "America has the rabies";[173] it was a mad dog consuming the Philippines, Taiwan, Okinawa, Vietnam, and Thailand. For a time he served as chairman of the "jury" of European intellectuals who tried President Lyndon Johnson as a war criminal for intervening in Vietnam. He appealed to Russia to oppose American imperialism even at the risk of World War III.[174]

In May, 1968, he applauded the students' revolt at the Sorbonne, but we are told that he was "merely tolerated when he came to address them during their occupation of the school."[175] He told their leader, Daniel Cohn-Bendit: "What is interesting about your activities is that they put the imagination in power. . . . The working class has often invented new methods of struggle, but they revolted from specific situations. . . . Your imagination is far richer. The slogans on the walls of the Sorbonne prove it. You students have done something astonishing, something subversive, something that challenges everything that has made our society what it is today. . . . Don't retreat!"[176]

He was still a revolutionist, willing to see violence used to overthrow the bourgeois-dominated democracies of Europe and America. But when the armies of the Eastern bloc marched into Czechoslovakia to annul the democratic movement there, he joined the liberals (and the Communists) of Western Europe in condemning the intervention: "I consider it pure aggression of the sort that is defined in terms of international law as a war crime."[177] The sixty-three-year-old warrior continued the conflict, without and within himself, between revolutionary action and freedom of judgment and dissent.

Every year brings him more fame and new enemies. A hundred professors expound him, a hundred critics assail him. He does not make friends easily; he defends his privacy (as writers must), and makes no claim or approach to sociability. He is rich through the spread of his books and plays, but he lives with almost ascetic simplicity[178] in a two-room bachelor suite on the tenth floor of a Paris apartment house. After some divagations he and Simone de Beauvoir are still attached to each other while still cherishing separate citadels. Despite this intellectual romance Sartre does not impress me as ever having loved a woman deeply. He writes with admirable sympathy of homosexuals, but rarely with tenderness of women. He makes the invert Daniel remark that "howevermuch women washed, they always smelt."[179] (È contra the natural fragrance of a clean woman's skin and hair is more pleasant to a man than any perfume.) He makes Johanna say, in The Condemned of Altona, that "no woman is beautiful; there are only ugly women in disguise"; but she counters this absurdity with another: "Any woman is still good enough for any man."[180]

Such suggestions of cynicism in Sartre, and his use of epithets like salauds (filthy ones) for the uninspired and unrepentant bourgeoisie, are balanced by his moral fervor in berating injustice, and by his generosity in sharing his wealth. "Sartre had never taken money seriously; he loathed counting . . . He gave away most of what he earned."[181] He is—or was—capable of sentiment; he "used to cry unashamedly in the cinema."[182] His tastes are spontaneous rather than "cultured"; he likes "Westerns" on the screen, "loves jazz," and favors the music of Schoenberg, Bartók, Webern, and Berg.[183] He is fond of his pipe, and has enjoyed a little inebriation now and then.[184]

He found it forgivable, for he suffered high tension from an excess of ideas and a pathological addiction to logic. In 1929, Simone tells us, "the moment we met [on the platform at Tours] he would grasp my hand and explain, 'I've got a new theory'"; and, some years later, "generally Sartre would propose a theory, which I would criticize. . . . I accepted with some amusement his comparison of English cooking with Locke's empiricism, both of which, he explained to me, were founded on the analytical principle of juxtaposition."[185]

His pessimism may have come not from contemplating the persistent gap between our conduct and our ideals, but from lacking that grain of doubt, that healing humor, which can keep even an epistemologist sane. He has wit (too sharp and caustic), but we miss in him the kindly humor and tolerant philosophy that come together in seeing the part in the light of the whole, and the present in the perspective of history. "Sartre has periods of gloom," says Simone, and some spasms of "fury."[186] He makes Franz predict in *The Condemned of Altona*, "In the thirtieth century, if there is a man left, he'll be preserved in a museum."[187] His despair of man as a "futile passion" has hardly abated with age. "For a long time," he wrote in 1964, "I treated my pen as a sword. Now I realize how helpless we are. It does not matter: I am writing, I shall write, books; they are needed."[188] Perhaps they would have had more effect (and less sales) if they had more often praised the good than denounced the bad; for the good in us expands under praise, and the bad in us swells in anger under a hostile word. No reformer gets to the root of evil until he realizes that the root is also in himself. Consequently saints have been more influential than revolutionaries.

Even so, Sartre's works have been stimulating contributions. They reminded us that mind is not so easily reduced to matter and mechanism as a rebellious positivism supposed in its reaction against religion and in its intoxication with the triumphs of physical science. They reaffirmed our obstinate consciousness of some degree of freedom even within the double prison of heredity and environment. They rescued existentialism from the surrender of Kierkegaard and Marcel to supernatural faiths, and challenged it to face the consequences of the epochal decline in religious belief; they realized that the major task of thought today is to devise an effective moral code based upon social necessity and obligation rather than upon shifting theologies. And they called upon the rising socialism of our times to preserve the conquests that democracy has made in the four freedoms of speech, assemblage, worship, and the press.

The message of Sartre has been weakened by cumbersome terminology, intricate logic, and extravagant paradox, but it has been strengthened, illustrated, disseminated by unique novels and powerful plays. Altogether his "diverse and undulating" genius has made him the living leader of our literary tribe.

CHAPTER XIII

Albert Camus

I CONFESS to a personal prejudice in preferring, for these studies, those authors who have dressed in fiction, drama, or poetry the problems of philosophy, rather than those who sought, by sensitivity, imagination, and artistry, to give some passing beauty a form that could be caressed by generations yet unborn. So I found Schopenhauer in O'Neill, Burke in Eliot, Lucretius in Maugham, Freud in Joyce, Plato in Proust, Hegel in Sartre, and Nietzsche everywhere. In Albert Camus the problems of metaphysics, morals, and politics became the substance of essays, novels, and plays; and he phrased his answers with such subtlety, ambivalence, and art that a million readers were confused and charmed. When an accident killed him at the age of forty-six he was already challenging Sartre for the leadership of the French mind.

He was born of peasant stock in a suburb of Bône in Algeria, on November 7, 1913. His father was of Alsatian origin, his mother was of Spanish descent; their son was ever mindful of his Spanish tincture and his Mediterranean background, and the sun of the south always remained as one focus of his philosophy. The father died in the first battle of the Marne (1914), leaving his family penniless; the widow, silent and somber, supported herself and her children by serving as charwoman in Algiers. Albert lived his childhood there in a two-room apartment with four relatives, and kept to the end a memory of cockroaches and rickety stairs.

He never complained about his early poverty.

> My family lacked almost everything and envied practically nothing. Merely by their silence, their reserve, their natural sober pride, my people, who did not even know how to read, taught me the most valuable lessons. . . . The lovely warmth that reigned over my childhood freed me from all resentment. I lived on almost nothing, but also in a kind of rapture. I felt infinite strengths within me; all I had to do was find a way to use them.[1]

A kindly teacher helped him to win a scholarship at the Lycée d'Alger. The ambitious youth paved his way by taking almost any available job, menial or mental: "I sold spare parts for automobiles, worked in a meteorological office, in a shipping firm, and in a *préfecture.* . . . Finally I worked as a journalist, which gave me a chance to travel."[2]

> I spent two months in Central Europe, from Austria to Germany, wondering where that strange discomfort, . . . the muffled anxiety I felt in my bones, came from. A little while ago, I understood. These people were always buttoned right up to the neck. They did not know how to relax. They did not know what joy was like.[3]

When he came down into Italy—to Vicenza and Venice—his eyes and heart opened up as Goethe's had done 150 years before. "I spend the whole day walking about. . . . Every person I meet, every scent on this street, is a pretext for my measureless love."[4] How different this from Sartre's presentiment that every "other" is a potential foe. These two men were bound to quarrel.

Camus loved books too, and read literature and philosophy from Plato and Plotinus to Pascal, Nietzsche, Spengler, Gide, and Sartre. Offended more by the poverty of others than by his own, he joined the Communist Party (1934); he left it when he discovered how thoroughly Stalin agreed with Machiavelli and most rulers on the right of governments to ignore the Ten Commandments; this conflict between ethics and politics remained to the end a haunting concern in Camus' thought. His philosophic disease of seeing at least two sides to a dispute prevented him from taking sides in the Algerian revolt against France;[5] he admired the stoic fatalism and simple joys of the indigenous population, but he relished the way in which his fellow colonials had adopted the Mediterranean spirit of open-air life.

In 1935 he led a group of students and proletaires in establishing the Théâtre du Travail in Algiers. As producer and actor he learned the technique of the drama and the stage. At the age of twenty-three he wrote and successfully produced a play, *Caligula*, which presented one aspect of government versus morality. The Emperor discovers, in the demise of his sister and mistress Drusilla, that death laughs at status, that Nature is neutral, that the universe has neither morals nor manners nor meaning. He reacts by abandoning all moral restraint, and committing cruelties that mount to obscure madness. He justifies himself by arguing that since everyone must die, the date of a man's death is a trivial detail; moreover, the "only way of being equal with the gods . . . is to be as cruel as they are." In the end he reluctantly admits that "murder is no solution."[6]

An attack of tuberculosis acquainted Camus with the indifference of the gods. His struggle back to health shared in shaping his first significant book, *L'Envers et l'endroit* (1937). The title (*The Wrong Side and the Right Side*) referred symbolically to the inside and the outside of a garment or a cloth; here it meant the horror of death and the love of life. What sort of a world, or a god, was it that flung the fatality of death into the very face of birth? The youth tried to lose that question in the glare and warmth of the sun, or in the expanding population of the night sky "choked with stars."[7] There was some florid writing in that young volume, some sensitive sentimentality, but Camus had struck some initial and lingering chords.

In *Noces* (1939; *Nuptials*) he showed the other side of his brooding —his love of sun and sea. Lying on the sand, watching one wave after another of the Mediterranean obstinately attack and sullenly retreat, or reading some inhibition-releasing book like Gide's *Les Nourritures terrestres* (which we know he read[8]), Camus found more health in paganism than in Christianity—more in welcoming the joys of life and stoically facing its tragedies than in fretting about sin and death. "If there is a sin against life it lies perhaps less in despairing of it than in hoping for another life and evading the inexorable grandeur of the one we have."[9]

But Catholicism cannot easily be shaken off. That disagreeable *memento, homo quod pulvis es, et in pulverem redieris* (remember, man, that thou art dust, and unto dust thou shalt return), pressed upon his childhood every Ash Wednesday, rang in his recollection and his fears. Could he really find a substitute for Christianity in deifying a nature that seemed rather devilish than divine—clouding joy with suffering, beauty with brevity, and everything with death? "Why this eagerness to live in limbs that are destined to rot?"[10]

In this mood he penned an essay darker than any Christian creed. *Le Mythe de Sysyphe* (1942) symbolized "the human condition" by the legend of Sisyphus, King of Corinth, who, for his disrespect of Zeus, was condemned in Tartarus to push a heavy stone up a high hill repeatedly in vain; whenever he neared the top, the rock would slip from his fingers and roll to the bottom. Such, said twenty-nine-year-old Camus, is man's fate. Life is toilsome and tragic, coarsened with competition, bruised with battle, incarnadined with massacre; even as Camus wrote, war was killing fifty million men, and the Hitler regime was murdering millions of Jews—which Camus called "one of the greatest crimes in history."[11] Why should anyone wish to live in such a world? Suicide seemed to be the logical conclusion of truth.

Our philosopher, when he interrupted his deification of nature, knew that we must not call the universe absurd—that absurdity, like beauty, order, chaos, is a subjective opinion, not an objective fact. But the universe may seem *to us* to be absurd because it has no sense, and is beyond our reason. It brings suffering to the "good" as well as the "bad," and it defies our attempts to understand it. Theology has failed to make reality reasonable. We hoped for some centuries that science would do this, but it too has failed. "The world that the eighteenth-century individualist thought he could conquer and transform by reason and science has in fact taken shape, but it is a monstrous one."[12] So far as the human mind can see, the world remains a cosmic surd. The "thinking reed," as Pascal pictured man, finds himself baffled and lost between the unintelligible immensity of the whole and the endless divisibility of the small. At times it seems that this universe, which can destroy a thousand men with one seismic shrug, is man's sardonic foe, laughing at his littleness, his blind persistence, his futile, plaintive brevity. Existence is an anguish which thought makes keener; it is a sickness which only death can cure.

Sisyphus probably reflected Heidegger's *Being and Time* (1927) and Sartre's *La Nausée*. Camus had reviewed the latter rather critically in the *Alger Républicain* (October, 1938). "A novel," he wrote, "is never anything but a philosophy expressed in images. And in a good novel the philosophy has disappeared into the images. But the philosophy need only spill over into the characters and action for it to stick out like a sore thumb, the plot to lose its authenticity, and the novel its life." He felt that *La Nausée* had sinned in this way. He added: "The realization that life is absurd cannot be an end, but only a beginning." Life can be "magnificent and overwhelming."[13] Despite these excellent amendments to *Sisyphus*, that story's emphasis on absurdity led many of the French reading public to label Camus as an existentialist. In 1945 he protested against the appellation:

No, I am not an existentialist. Sartre and I are always surprised to see our names linked. We have even thought of publishing a short statement in which the undersigned declare that they have nothing in common with each other, and refuse to be held responsible for the debts they might respectively incur. It is a joke, actually. Sartre and I published all our books, without exception, before we ever met. . . . Sartre is an existentialist, and the only book of ideas I have published, *The Myth of Sisyphus,* was directed against the so-called existentialist philosophers.[14]

Nevertheless Camus agreed with Sartre that the structure of modern society adds to the general absurdity. Things are so arranged, or have so developed, that superior practical ability—"moral" or "immoral"—receives such superior reward that the wealth of a nation is concentrated in a small minority; the masses are left to wallow in a disease-breeding poverty. If anyone protests against the system he is so frustrated by minority-made laws, courts, and moral codes that he is driven either to brooding hostility or to violent revolt. Many men of good mind withdraw from civilization as from a mortal malady.

Camus illustrated one kind of such alienation in *L'Étranger* (1942; *The Stranger*). The scene is Algiers. The narrator is a clerk named Meursault (*meur* means die, *sault* means leap), whose daily routine has dulled him into a colorless and heartless unconcern. He lacks the will or energy to say either Yes or No to the questions that confront him. He puts his old mother into a house for the aged, fifty miles from where he lives; when she dies he goes to the funeral, but he sheds no tears, and soon forgets her. He takes a girl to bed, but he tells her that he does not love her and that he would as lief have any other girl. He consents to marry her, but repeatedly puts it off. Then suddenly he stumbles into action. He agrees to help an acquaintance defend himself against an injured and vengeful Arab. He meets the Arab, who has a knife in his hand; the sun flashes its light upon the blade; Meursault, thinking that the knife is about to be thrown at him, shoots the Arab down; then, standing over the prostrate man, he fires four more bullets into him. In Meursault's trial for murder he is asked why he fired those extra cartridges; "I found nothing to reply."[15] The judge inquires does he believe in God; he answers, "No." Condemned to death, he writes a detailed account of what led him to the crime, but still cannot explain those supernumerary shots. He does not complain of the verdict; he resents only the denial of cigarettes. He repels all religious ministrations. He remains to the end a "stranger" to modern civilization, and is as confused as the world which he is content to leave.*

Perhaps the imperfections of the tale—the sudden decisive action of an indecisive man, the long autobiographical defense by one supposedly indifferent—were due in part to Camus' rejection of any noncommittal

---

* It is one of the consoling absurdities of contemporary life that this story, written during Camus' lean years, brought his widow $100,000 for the right to make it into a motion picture.

alienation from the problems of mankind. He had ended *The Myth of Sisyphus* by arguing that we must continue to push up our stone; better to struggle than to yield; perhaps on the way up or down the hill there are incidental beauties to be seen, sufferings to be relieved, nobilities to be attained or praised. Man has meaning despite his apparent futility, for while recognizing his ultimate defeat he can welcome the challenges and responsibilities of life.

So in 1942 we find Camus in France, bravely active in the Resistance against the German occupation. The barbarous descent of Hitler's regime from self-idolatry to racial massacre aroused the young philosopher; now he daily risked his life in full commitment to revolt. After the liberation of Paris he became co-editor of a Resistance daily, *Combat*. In his editorials he called for an independent journalism to replace the bought press that had almost persuaded France to surrender to Germany. During the occupation he had begun to write—in 1947 he published—his finest book, which, through the symbol of a plague, presented Hitlerism as a disease and delirium that had nearly destroyed civilization.

La Peste is a remarkably convincing picture of a fictional pestilence which, in the 1940s, took some 200,000 lives in the North African city of Oran. The story symbolizes not only the German conquest of France, but in general the assaults of infectious evil upon mankind, and the diverse responses made to the challenge by different types of men. The narrative is offered as a chronicle written by a protagonist, Dr. Rieux. Perhaps Camus, in describing the social effects of the contagion, was helped by reading Defoe's *Journal of the Plague Year* (1722), which realistically recalled the epidemic that had ravaged London in 1665.

Here the tragedy begins with an irruption of disease-stricken rats from the buildings of Oran; soon there are hundreds of them dying in the streets and poisoning the air. Shortly thereafter the physicians find their waiting rooms unusually crowded with patients suffering from ominously similar fevers and sores. Slowly and reluctantly the authorities admit that an infection has entered the port. A quarantine is declared: no one is to enter or leave the city; relatives are stranded outside, visitors are caught within; cries of protest add to the confusion. All import or export is forbidden; the people rush to the stores to buy and hoard goods; merchants raise prices; smugglers profiteer. As casualties mount, the overworked doctors are denounced for their failure to cure the sick or to stop the plague. A priest, Father Paneloux, in a terrifying sermon, explains the calamity as God's punishment of men's sins; Dr. Rieux wonders, then, why infants too young to sin are among the first to succumb to the pest; later the priest humbly joins the doctor's aides in caring for the victims, and dies in the course of his ministrations. Rieux's wife is infected; with silent courage he continues his labors of medication, public sanitation, and hospital management. Tarrou, a skeptic, asks him, "Why do you show such devotion, considering that you don't believe in God?" Rieux gives Camus' answer: We must continue to struggle against evil, even after repeated defeats. Tarrou interprets the plague as a symbol of the evil in men's hearts— impulses of greed, hostility, and violence, which break down the dikes of moral discipline. How can these unsocial impulses be checked and kept under control without the religious inculcation of divine commands, threats, and rewards? Or, as Tarrou puts it, "Can one be a saint without God?" "That," he adds, "is the problem, in fact the only problem."[16]

As deaths multiply, the reactions of the inhabitants change surprisingly. "In the early days, when they thought the epidemic was much like other epidemics, religion held its ground. But once these people realized their instant peril, they gave their thoughts to pleasure. . . . Luxury and the lavish life, frenzied orgies, . . . were now the quest of the whole populace."[17] In their terror men thought only of themselves; "blind endurance had ousted love from their hearts."[18] Yet Dr. Rieux finds many heroes too, like the sanitation workers who labor almost to exhaustion; and he concludes that "there are more things to admire in men than to deplore."[19] The pestilence itself seems to die of exhaustion; after a terrifying crisis, when all seem doomed, the number of victims declines from day to day, until at long last the authorities end the quarantine. Surviving stranded relatives come back to rejoicing or desolated homes; separated lovers are united; the church bells ring; God is praised. So ends the greatest of French novels since *Remembrance of Things Past.*

The Plague raised Camus' reputation to a height which made him suspect that it must soon begin to fall. The major critics were well disposed, but below that responsible level, he felt, a myriad of small fry waited for an opportunity to attack him. "Paris," he wrote,

> begins by serving a work of art and pushes it. But once it is established, the fun begins. It is essential to destroy it. Thus there are, in Paris, as in certain streams in Brazil, thousands of little fish whose job this is. They are tiny, but innumerable. Their whole head, if I may say so, is in their teeth. And they completely remove the

flesh from a man in five minutes, leaving nothing but the bare bones.[20]

The little fish were delighted when some big fish joined them in attacking Camus' next book. In *L'Homme révolté* (1951; *The Rebel*) he faced the difficult divisive issues of individual conscience versus political expediency, of intellectual freedom versus party loyalty, of the necessity and the moral limits of revolt. Communist Russia had rejected Christianity, Nazi Germany had interpreted Nietzsche as sanctioning not only war but genocide; one state had redefined morality as service to the revolution, the other as service to the state. Whatever helped these new sanctities was good and virtuous; whatever injured or hampered them was bad and vicious, and must be suppressed. Sin was no longer an offense against God and a God-given moral code; it was an act, publication, speech, or thought considered by the existing authorities to be opposed to the revolution, the party, or the government.

Camus had retained enough of his Christian education to be alarmed by these new concepts of morality. He reduced them all to the principle, practiced by nearly every ruling body, that the end justifies the means. He rejected that principle, but he hardly knew by what other standard the means could be judged; if by service to the good of humanity, who was to determine that good? In any case he was convinced that humanity had not been served, but had been deeply injured, by wholesale murders and the idolatry of force and war under Hitler, and by forced labor, regimentation of the press, purge trials, and political assassinations under Stalin. Those authoritarian governments had almost annihilated liberty in the name of liberating mankind, and had destroyed democracy in the name of the people.

But, said Camus, a democrat is "one who allows his opponent to express his views, and agrees to think about them," and he claimed it as a distinction that he had never defamed those who differed from him.[21] He was a humanist in every sense of the word: he directed thought from divine to human affairs; he labored to preserve the cultural heritage of mankind; and he was too humane to accept any ideology that commanded men to kill men. Perhaps for that reason he withdrew from all political parties. "I have no place in the world of today," he made Tarrou say in *The Plague*. "Once I definitely refused to kill I doomed myself to an exile that can never end."[22]

However, he did not require such refusal, such self-exile, from the readers of *L'Homme révolté*. He admitted that when oppression becomes insufferable, violent rebellion may be justified if no other means of reform remains open; but he pleaded for *la mesure*, a sense of measure, a spirit of moderation, in politics as in thought. Let the rebel avoid dogmatic ideologies, absolute "truths"; let him at every step ask himself, Would mankind be more hurt than helped by the violence which he contemplates? To sacrifice others to your ideal is no heroism; if sacrifice is necessary, sacrifice yourself. Gandhi was greater than those who voted for Louis XVI's death.

L'Homme révolté met with mild applause from the French Right, with cries of apostasy from the European Left. The Catholics of France welcomed it as an implicit return to Christian morality; the Communist Party scorned it as a cowardly flight from the necessities and dangers of revolution. Francis Jeanson led the attack with a long article in the June, 1952, number of *Les Temps modernes*. He ridiculed Camus as

> a Mediterranean spirit, infatuated with intellectual transparence, faithful to solar constancy and the pure light of noonday; but, confronted in the real world with contradictions and human suffering, Camus rationalizes the scandal of his reason by representing humanity as unjustly subjugated to the forces of anti-Reason, as condemned to Absurdity and Evil.[23]

And Jeanson suggested that Camus hardly deserved the high reputation accorded him. He implied that Camus' experiences in the Resistance had left him tired and ready to take down his flag. He called upon him to return from his moralistic retreat to active participation in the conflict between the oppressed and the status quo.[24]

Camus replied in the August issue of the magazine with a sixteen-page letter addressed not to Jeanson (whom he noticeably did not name) but to "Monsieur le Directeur"—i.e., to Jean-Paul Sartre as editor in chief. He complained that "the reviewer" had apparently assumed that any other than the Marxist interpretation of history and class conflict was reactionary; and he accused *Les Temps modernes* of "defending Marxism as an implicit dogma without being able to affirm it as an open political policy."[25] Yet many elements in Marx's theories—especially his prophecies—had been proved false by actual developments; obviously some criticism of Marx was justified, even indispensable. Likewise, Soviet policy should not be sacrosanct; every honest voice should speak out against the concentration camps for political heretics in Russia.[26] "The truth is that your reviewer would have us revolt against everything but the Communist Party and the Communist State."[27] Camus added that he was tired of hearing armchair theoreticians lecture those who had faced all the dangers of the Resistance.

Sartre had faced these dangers, and had himself criticized Communists and party leaders as dogmatists unteachable by events. But he resented the challenge to the repute and courage of his magazine, and he felt that his former friend was covering with academic finery his flight from battle. In the same issue that printed Camus' letter Sartre replied with an acerbity that burned all bridges between the two men.

> Your combination of dreary conceit and vulnerability always discouraged people from telling you unvarnished truths. . . . You call me *Monsieur le Directeur* when everyone knows we have been friends for ten years. I agree it is only a joke. You speak to me when your apparent subject is to refute Jeanson. That is a dirty device . . . But I ask you, Camus, just who are you to stand off at such a distance? And what gives you the right to assume apropos of Jeanson, a superiority which nobody accords you?[28]

He accused Camus of misunderstanding the nature of freedom, and he recommended *Being and Nothingness* to him as clearing up that concept. He recalled their years of association in the Resistance; "how we loved you then!" Now, however, "only half of you lives among us, and you are tempted to withdraw altogether. Your morality first changed into moralism. Today it is only literature. Tomorrow, perhaps, it will be immorality."[29] He deplored the retreat of Camus to moral standards that protected reactionary regimes, and to an ineffective sentimentality that wished the end but was too weak to will the means. If, said Sartre, a revolutionary government judged that some control of the press, some forced-labor camps, even some summary executions, were necessary to preserve or advance the revolution, then all followers of the revolution should yield their personal moral judgment to the decision of the leaders; after all, as every conservative would agree, no state could long survive if every individual in it were free to obey or disobey its laws according to his own judgment. But, Camus objected, if only the government is to judge between right and wrong, what would be the difference between a capitalist and a Communist tyranny? — So ended a friendship as famous in the France of the 1950s as that of Burke and Fox in the time of the French Revolution.

Camus dramatized the problems of violence and morality, of "man versus the state," in four plays presented in Paris theaters. *Le Malentendu*

(1944; *The Misunderstood Man*) failed, but in 1945 his old tragedy *Caligula* enjoyed at least a *succès de choc*. In his most powerful play, *Les Justes* (1949), Camus, taking his mood from Dostoevski's *The Possessed*, recounted the assassination of Grand Duke Serge (uncle of the Czar) by Ivan Kaliaev, an idealist-terrorist. In Act II Kaliaev, bomb in hand, sees his appointed victim approaching in a carriage; here is the chance he has waited for—but two children are seated near the Grand Duke; Kaliaev refuses to throw his bomb. A fellow rebel condemns his pity as cowardice; Kaliaev replies that when the revolution is divorced from a sense of humanity he will leave the organization. At the end of Act III he has another opportunity; this time he kills the Grand Duke. He is arrested. The head of the police promises him mercy if he will name his associates; he refuses. The widow of the Grand Duke offers him Christian forgiveness; he rejects it. He welcomes death as an atonement for his action, but he does not regret his resort to violence. In Act IV he is hanged, impenitent to the end. Paris applauded.

For his last major work Camus returned to his favorite device of narrative by autobiographical monologue. *La Chute* (1956; *The Fall*) is a series of talks by Jean-Baptiste Clamence to—hardly with—a chance acquaintance in Amsterdam. Jean had been a prosperous Parisian lawyer, proud of his virtues, respected for his defense of moneyless clients. One day, crossing a bridge over the Seine, he saw a woman leaning over the rail. As he left the bridge he heard a splash, then a cry; the woman had jumped—or fallen—into the river. Should he turn back and try to rescue her? He walked slowly away. Thereafter the memory of that cry haunted him; the thought that he should have tried to save her destroyed his peace of mind. He began to think of himself as a coward. He wondered had not his virtues been a device for popularity and success. Having no religious belief, he could not seek relief by confession to a priest. He looked skeptically, then cynically, at all virtues as stratagems; every "good" man, he concluded, was as calculating and secretly self-centered as himself. He began to despise civilization as a tissue of competing hypocrisies. But if all virtues are pretense, why sacrifice so many pleasures to maintain a public image? He tried some of the sensual delights that Paris provided. As each level of debauchery lost its novelty and tang he sank to even lower depths, until he had ruined his social standing and his professional reputation. He fled from France to Africa, where he was unjustly arrested as a spy. During a severe shortage of water he secretly drank the quota allotted to another prisoner. Released, he came to lose himself in Amsterdam and alcohol. He learned to observe human conduct in a double role—as a rambling penitent and a sardonic judge: he recounted, to all who would listen, his descent from decency and status, and subtly tried to make others see themselves as guilty like himself. Sometimes he longed for his childhood faith; "we have lost track of the light, the moorings, the holy innocence of those who forgive themselves."[30] The final page is written in the expectation of imminent, destitute death.

It is hard—and not necessary—to believe that *The Fall* was Camus' own testament, that his disillusionment with "bourgeois" virtues and Communist ideology had turned all his youthful *joie de vivre*, all his enthusiasm for social reform, into such complete cynicism and unheroic despair. Personally he had much to be grateful for; bourgeois civilization had given him education, travel, freedom of speech, and a spreading fame. By 1952, despite Sartre's slashing indictment, he had come close to top rank in French letters. Young readers relished his lyrical flights; older ones admired his vivid way of making past events live by self-revealing monologues; and Christian conservatives watched his philosophical wanderings attentively, hoping that in due course he would come to Canossa and kneel at the foot of the cross. In 1957 he received the Nobel Prize for Literature, though he was only forty-four. Then, on January 4, 1960, while driving near Marseille, he lost control of his car, crashed, and was killed.

CHAPTER XIV

Thomas Mann

I. THE YOUNG PESSIMIST (1875–1905)

HERE is an author whose career is more interesting than his books—which fascinate us chiefly because they record, under diverse aliases, his own mental and political development. Like Plato deriding democracy and risking his life with a dictator, Thomas Mann emerged from his study to reject democracy, and then stood up, through exile and contumely, to defend democracy and lead a twelve-year war against the most powerful dictator of his age. No wonder more has been written about him than about any other author in the twentieth century except George Bernard Shaw. Here is a full-sized man, whose books were battles, and whose chef-d'oeuvre was his life.

"I grew up on the Baltic, a provincial body of water. And the traditions of my blood are those of the small and old-established city" of Lübeck, "civilized and humane."[1] In that center of the Hanseatic League the wholesale merchants were the ruling patriciate, which had acquired through three centuries almost the aura and stability of an aristocracy of birth. Thomas Mann was born there on June 6, 1875. His father, Johann Heinrich Mann, was a dealer in grain and a senator in Lübeck's governing council. His mother, born in Brazil, was part German, part Portuguese, with a passion for music and literature. The tension in Thomas' heritage, between the Teuton and the Latin, the bourgeois and the artist, stretched his strings from realism and irony to sensitivity and grace. He had an older brother, Heinrich, who for a time rivaled him in fame, and for twenty years fought him in politics.

"School I loathed."[2] He was shy, irritable, and proud; he wanted to choose for himself what books to read, what career to prepare for. Sent to a *Realgymnasium* for training in business, he shocked his teachers and amused his fellow students by writing poetry and plays; he was himself the Tonio Kröger whom he was to describe in one of his most revealing tales. At the age of twelve he quit school, having "never gotten beyond senior high."

In 1891 his father died, leaving the firm, a century old, in such dis-array that it had to be liquidated. With the modest fortune that re-mained the mother and her five children moved to Munich (1893), for she, with the sun of the south in her memory, had always shivered in the cold and mists of the Baltic port. Thomas liked Munich so much that he lived there, with some interruptions, till he went into exile in 1933. Without being formally a student at the University of Munich he took courses in history, political economy, literature, and art. For a time he worked in an insurance office, but after a year he left to accept Heinrich's invitation to join him in Italy. "Almost in the first year of our literary activity my brother and I shared the same secret thought. We wanted to write a book together."[3] They never collaborated there, but while summering with Heinrich in the town of Palestrina (1896), Thomas began to write *Buddenbrooks*. "I carried back to Munich a fearsomely swollen bundle of manuscript."[4]

A medley of authors shared with the events and environment of his youth in forming his adolescent mood. He read French poetry and fiction, and for a time he modeled his writing upon the naturalism of Zola and the Goncourts. He brooded over Dostoevski, and envied the scope and power of Tolstoi. At an unduly early age he was excited by Nietzsche's *Thus Spake Zarathustra*, which had just announced the death of God, the collapse of European civilization, and the coming of Superman. "The contact with Nietzsche was to a high degree de-cisive for an intellect still in its formative stage."[5] He followed the saintly atheist in scorning democracy, exalting instinct, and condemn-ing the bohemian irresponsibility of contemporary art. From Nietzsche he passed to Nietzsche's source, and buried himself, aged twenty, in Schopenhauer's *The World as Will and Idea*. He quite agreed that ours was the worst of all possible worlds, and he explored in dark reveries the least painful ways of leaving it. He resented the tyranny of the will over reason, and especially its blind and hectic drive toward wholesale reproduction; he experienced "a metaphysical intoxication closely re-lated to a late violent outbreak of sensuality. . . . In those days I was emotionally close to suicide."[6] He derived from Schopenhauer a sym-pathy with death as a release from the striving of the will, and he found inspiration in Schopenhauer's notion that artistic creation, by a resolute attempt at objectivity, might, at least in appearance and for a moment, free the intellect from the will. "I will not quite pass over the great decisive impressions that came to me from reading Schopenhauer and Nietzsche."[7]

He followed Nietzche into sensing artistic decay in the mythopoesy and theatricality of Richard Wagner. But his love of music was too strong for a total rejection of *Parsival, Die Meistersinger*, and *Der Ring*. At first he responded warmly to Wagner's nationalism, and entered happily into Wagner's idealization of death. "I recalled the enormous influence which the equivocal magic of this art had upon my youth—an influence which might even be called determining. The sinister side of this art had [not yet] been revealed by the role it played in the Nazi state."[8]

Mann's spiritual history was a long and complex struggle of his natural vigor and humor to free himself from the hypnotism of Wagner, the nihilism of Nietzsche, and the pessimism of Schopenhauer. The sense of irrationality in the ways of nature, and of futility in the ambitions of life, gave a somber tone to many of his compositions before 1905. His first published story, *Disappointment* (1896), told of a clergyman's son who lost his father's faith in the ultimate triumph of good under God, and concluded that death is the only peace. *Der kleine Herr Friedmann* (1898), Mann's first published book, contained five pieces, of which one was entitled "Death." The title story told of a hunchback who, obsessed by sexual desire, wondered why God or nature had infused such passions into so ungainly a body. Finding himself alone with a beautiful woman who had been kind to him, he tried to embrace her; she repulsed him with such horror on her face that he crept to a nearby stream and drowned himself. Already, in these tales, Mann dissociated himself from his subjects by an emotional control and narrative objectivity that saved his sanity and later became distinctive elements in his style.

By some remarkable quickening of development he passed from these somber tentatives to one of the masterpieces of German fiction. "In its first draft," according to brother Heinrich, "*Buddenbrooks* was simply our story, the life of our parents and grandparents."[9] The Fischer Verlag of Berlin, which through all vicissitudes was to publish nearly all of Mann's works, protested the length of the novel (743 pages in the English translation), but issued it nevertheless (1900). It ran through a thousand printings in fifty years,[10] and remains to this day the most successful of Mann's books. Literate Germany rejoiced to have found in the youth of twenty-six a skilled craftsman worthy of comparison with those English novelists—Dickens, Thackeray, Trollope —who had in their day spun the history of a family through generations and reams. Mann, however, traced his inspiration not to the British but to the French: to Zola's *Rougon-Macquart* series, and to the *Renée Mauperin* of the brothers Goncourt; these also had traced the rise and fall of a family. (Galsworthy latter took a similar theme in the many novels of his *Forsyte Saga* [1922].)

The unnamed scene of *Buddenbrooks* is Lübeck; the period is 1835–75; the principal characters belong to old commercial families proud of their time-hallowed wealth and their Hanseatic lineage; the subject is the growth and decay of one of those families. The story opens with a dinner celebrating the purchase, by the Buddenbrooks, of "the most beautiful house in the town" from the Ratenkamps, who, formerly so prosperous, had built this mansion, but were now compelled by their impoverishment to sell it; and the book ends four generations later when the Buddenbrooks, facing bankruptcy, sell the property to their *nouveaux-riches* rivals, the Hagenströms. During this ebb and flow of the Buddenbrook tide we hear on the side the spite and jealousy of relatives and rivals, but we also feel the mutual loyalty that holds a family together till death. Consul Johann Buddenbrook II writes to his troublesome daughter: "My child, we are not born for . . . our small personal happiness. We are not free, separate, independent entities, but like links in a chain."[11]

The founder of the firm is Johann Buddenbrook I, strong, kindly, ambitious, and devoted to his business, but honoring some moral restraints in his deals. "My son," he counsels his successor, "attend with zeal to thy business by day, but do none that hinders thee from thy sleep at night."[12] Johann II accepts not only a moral code but the entire Protestant theology and ethic; Mann anticipates Max Weber by twenty years in finding an easy compatibility between the economic gospel of enterprise and industry and the Protestant benediction of work, thrift, and wealth.

Johann II's children carry the burden of the tale. Christian Buddenbrook rejects the bourgeois-patrician code of discipline, duty, tradition, and family cohesion; "at bottom," he says, "every businessman is a rascal";[13] he takes to literature and wit, samples women, contracts a disease, and threatens to infect the Buddenbrook clan with his decadence of body, morals, and will. His pretty sister Tony (Antonia) goes through a frolicsome youth to a romantic love for a rural worker, and is suddenly reined in by her father's decision that, for the good of the firm, she must marry Herr Grümlich, merchant of Hamburg. She resists, weeps, storms, yields, and rides off to live in self-indulgent extravagance as a neglected wife. When her husband goes bankrupt she divorces him and marries Herr Permaneder of Munich. She finds him too much in love with ease and beer to meet her needs for sex and finery; she leaves him and returns to the parental home, mildly chastened but lastingly immature.

She is the liveliest portrait in the book, and the most interesting except for her brother Thomas, who succeeds Johann II as head of the family and the firm. He seems to have inherited all the business zeal and skill of his forebears, all their firm character and civic spirit. He rises from consul to senator, and dominates the municipal senate; in 1848 he quiets with a commanding word the local form of that year's revolutionary agitation. He gives generously to public charities, and helps hard-pressed associates. He marries the music-loving Gerda of Amsterdam; she gives him a son, Hanno; he hopes to train this boy to succeed him in business and politics when his own hand grows slack. But he makes some mistakes. He has had a flower-girl mistress; he reads philosophy; and he sells the ancestral mansion to build a new home, costly and traditionless; the family, its roots cut, scatters to divers residences and ideas. Thomas himself wearies under the strain of family troubles, business losses, unmannerly competitors. "For the first time in his career he had fully and personally experienced the ruthless brutality of business life, and had seen how all better, gentler, and kindlier sentiments creep away and hide themselves before the new, naked, dominating instinct of self-preservation."[14] He himself lets his sister Tony persuade him into a secret shady transaction; when this fails, and his rivals displace him in wealth and power, he takes comfort in Schopenhauer's eloquence on the blessedness of death as a release from the treadmill of desire, realization, and desire. He sees his son absorbed in music and poetry, and quite without interest in business, grain, and thalers. He loses the will to live. A careless dentist helps him to peace by surgical tortures that end the beating of his heart.

As the book nears its close the pages are darkened by a sense of decay—in individuals, the family, and civic life. Hanno, brooding over his piano, confesses that he has neither the ability nor the wish to take over the leadership of the firm; "I can't will anything," he says; and like his father he opens his arms to death. He succumbs not merely to typhoid fever but to exhaustion of the will to live. The sole surviving male in the family is Christian, who is dying half insane in a distant sanitarium. Only the women remain, old, dependent, and despondent. The hustling, ruthless Hagenströms buy the new Buddenbrook mansion, move into it, and lead the city's senate. The individuals come and go; the names change; the events are as before.

One function of the novel is to present with more memorable and effective intensity a proposition which, simply and abstractly stated, might have left no active impression upon mind or character or history. *Buddenbrooks* fulfills that function. But how could so young a man have felt the sweep of time, the succession of generations, the kaleidoscope of superficial change on a background of persistent reality? Partly because he had experienced this process in his own home, on his own flesh. Thomas Buddenbrook was his father, Gerda was his mother, Hanno was Thomas Mann. The book was an indictment of a father so dedicated to business that he could not bear with his son's addiction to art.[15]

The success of the book must have moderated the author's pessimism. "Money flowed in streams," he tells us. Now he could decorate his bachelor apartment in a style befitting one who never forgot that he was of patrician stock. He mingled for a time with the writers, artists, and musicians who wandered through the studios and cafés of the *gemütlich* Bavarian capital, but he did not feel at home among them, and he wondered whether these proud paupers were not maggots in the decaying body of Western civilization. He was not sure that he himself was not part of the general decadence. In December, 1900, he wrote to Heinrich: "There is still something left in me which is not mere irony, something which is straightforward, warm, and good. No, not everything in me has been distorted, corroded, laid waste by cursed literature [Nietzsche and Schopenhauer?]. Literature is death, and I shall never understand how one can be enslaved by it without hating it."[16]

Among the brilliant short stories which he produced with uncontrollable fertility throughout his literary life, two in particular, at this stage of his development, reveal his concern with the unhealthy aspects of art. In "Tristan" (1902) a neurotic author falls in love with a beautiful but consumptive pianist; at his importunate urging she plays a piano transcription of the "Liebestod"—with such growing abandon that at the end she expires of tuberculosis and ecstasy. Here both literature and music are presented as possible forms of decadence. Wagner's music, Mann would later say,[17] was in some aspects a "reactionary narcotic" poisoning the soul of man with fantasies of love and death, and the soil of Germany with chauvinistic myths. Later he was alarmed to find that Hitler enthusiastically admired the *Ring*.

In *Tonio Kröger* (1903), which Mann in 1930 described as "dearest to my heart of all that I have written,"[18] the problem is the divorce between art and life. Tonio—one more self-analysis by the author—gets his name from Antonio, brother to his mother, Consuelo, who (like Mann's mother) comes from the south and has transmitted to her son a love of music and poetry. His father (like Mann's) is a grain merchant and city counsel in Lübeck. Tonio plays the violin (Mann played the piano), and writes verse, to the consternation of the business community. He is deeply attached to Hans Hansen, who laughs at his rhymes. Both youths fall in love with Ingeborg Holm; she chooses Hans, whose father owns "the big wood-yards down the river." Tonio withdraws into authorship and music, feeling that "one must die to life in order to be utterly a creator."[19] His own creator, intoxicated by his own *Prospero*us magic, adds: "Tonio surrendered completely to the power that to him seemed the highest on earth, to whose service he felt called, which promised him elevation and honors—the power of intellect, the power of the word, which lords it with a smile over the unconscious and the inarticulate."[20] Tonio moves to Munich. After years of struggle he achieves excellence and wins fame, but at the cost of such seclusive concentration that he loses all sense of community with the people around him. Sometimes he envies their life, especially the steady and steadying work, the family joys and care, the gay social activities, of the middle class; what if this, and not the hectic world of arts and letters, is the better way? Yes, he admits, "it is the normal, respectable, and admirable that is the kingdom of our longing—life in all its seductive banality!"[21] By contrast he has come to suspect, even to despise, the bohemian artist, as living in a world of narcissistic fantasies, sexual chaos, stomach troubles, and monetary dearth. "I cherish at the bottom of my soul," says Tonio (Mann), "all the scorn and suspicion of the artistic gentry—translated into terms of the intellectual— that my upright old forebears there on the Baltic would have felt for any juggler or mountebank that entered their houses."[22] He sadly concludes: "I stand between two worlds, I am at home in neither, and I suffer in consequence."[23] Surrendering to nostalgia, he returns, aged thirty-two, to his native Lübeck. No one there recognizes him; he is distrusted as an alien; he is arrested as a spy. Released, he takes a boat to Copenhagen. On it, himself shyly unseen, he watches with envy a successful burgher—yes, it is Hans Hansen—walking happily arm in arm with the wife who Tonio had hoped would be his own.

Mann looked at another side of the debate between art and life by picturing the contest between Savonarola and Lorenzo de' Medici for the leadership of Renaissance Florence. This time he took drama as his medium. *Fiorenza* (1905) contained too much talk and too little action to win acclaim when it was produced (1907), but it is a sensitive portrayal of the artists, writers, and sycophants—and the art treasures— that surrounded "the Magnificent"; and it conveys in passionate language the fervor of the ambitious preacher who denounced the loose morals of Florence as a decadence that could be arrested only by making Christ the invisible king of the republic, with Savonarola as his only authorized voice. Between the two men flits the imperiously seductive Fiore, who turned Savonarola into a saint by rejecting his love, and gave herself to Lorenzo as the lord of all Florentine beauty and splendor. Lorenzo dies, Savonarola is burned, and the problem of reconciling art and life remains unsolved.

II LOVE AND WAR: 1905–18

Mann solved it for himself by two drastic measures: he married (1905), and he plunged as literary combatant into the First World War. Katja Pringsheim was the only daughter of a rich Jew who taught mathematics, collected art, made piano transcriptions of Wagner's operas; his palace was a gathering place of Munich artists and intellectuals; he was a living denial of the dichotomy between art and life. Katja brought Mann not only an easeful dowry but faithful and sedulous love, and several children: Erika (born 1905); Klaus Heinrich (1906–49), Gottfried (1908), and Monica (1910).

Erika may have taken her name from Tony's daughter in *Buddenbrooks;* Klaus Heinrich shared his name with the prince who, in Mann's next book, *Königliche Hoheit* (1909; *Royal Highness*), showed the author in a rare euphoria born of a happy marriage and bright children. The prince, who suffered from a crippled hand (Kaiser Wilhelm II, then ruling Germany, had a withered arm), was an artist, and aspired to spread comfort and beauty among his people. He mourned his lack of means: taking a hint from his creator, he married a rich heiress, and proceeded with his reforms.

This merry mood did not last in Mann's writings—though he himself was much more cheerful than his books. During the month that he spent on the Lido in the spring of 1911 Venice must have served him some of her rainy or cloudy days, when all her architectural pearls are shrouded in mist, and all her gaiety is muted or deferred. In any case Mann conceived there and then one of his saddest and most perfect *novelle—Der Tod in Venedig* (1913; *Death in Venice*). Much of the story was provided by his experiences: a beautiful Polish youth, an epidemic of cholera, a departure postponed because of lost baggage; "everything was given."[24] Even the central character was given, for he was Mann himself, in one more disguise, meditating on the decadence potential in every art that evades order and moral restraint.

Gustav von Aschenbach is pictured as an aristocrat who has made himself the most honored German author of his time. He has overcome the nihilistic temptations of his thought, and the defects of his style, by applying to himself a discipline as severe as that of a Prussian soldier; moreover, he has put his art at the service of the state by taking, as theme of his major work, the life and genius of Frederick the Great. Now, fifty years old, he feels himself entitled to a stay on the Lido. But the Lido is outside the Prussian range; it is a center of luxury and beauty, dangerous to morals and relaxing to the will. There on the beach, day after day, running or bathing or stretching himself on the sand, is Tadzio, a Polish youth whose nearly naked body, bronzed and firmed by sun and sport, arouses every aesthetic feeling in Gustav's flesh and spirit, and something more. While that fever heats him a cholera epidemic enters Venice and its environs. It reaches the Lido, where the hotel keepers strive to keep its presence from their guests. Aschenbach learns of it and departs, but his baggage does not follow him to the station; he returns to recover it; he sees Tadzio again, and decides to stay. The plague spreads; the odors of pestilence and death mingle symbolically with the seductiveness of Venetian life. Tadzio proves immune, but Gustav is infected; yet he remains day after day, bundled and shivering in a beach chair, indulging homosexual fancies as his eyes follow every movement of the handsome boy. Tadzio perceives his interest, and gives him an alluring smile. The weakened author rises to go to him, falls back into his chair, and dies.

Is there a moral here? Perhaps Mann implied that the sense of beauty can be a lure and a snare as well as a creative stimulus; that art is always tempted to wander into extravagance, to relax into impulse and disorder; that discipline is the staff of art as well as of character. But all this was surely secondary to telling a story well, checking loquacity, making every part, every person and incident, a necessary element in a united whole. Here especially Mann refrained from judgment, pathos, or sentiment; he wrote objectively and impartially; he let the facts and their inherent irony speak for themselves. And here he deployed all the resources of his style: visualized details, characteristic mannerisms, recurrent leitmotivs, prognostic nuances preparing for future developments; sentences composed like music or hypnotically accumulated or prolonged; symbolic moods of weather in the sky or on the sea suggesting the progress of the tale from spring loveliness to summer heat and autumn darkness and decay. Artistically this *novella* is Thomas Mann at his best.

In 1914, seizing an opportunity to bridge the chasm between the writer and the people, and as if practicing the theory he had ascribed to Gustav von Aschenbach, Mann turned his pen to the service of his ambitious and imperiled fatherland. Like Gustav he sought to inspire his fellow Germans by writing of their most brilliant hero; in an essay, "Friedrich und die grosse Koalition," he pictured his country as again standing bravely and almost alone, as in 1756, against an apparently overwhelming alliance of encompassing foes. Heinrich Mann, taking a directly opposite stand, in an essay on Zola (November, 1915), condemned the Germans as slavish robots of an authoritarian state, and assailed its intellectual defenders as reactionary dupes of imperialistic sentiment and propaganda. So began, between the brothers, an ideological conflict that continued till 1922. Thomas knew that he himself was attacked; he was deeply moved; and he spent three years (1915–17) in writing his 677-page defense. He published it in 1918, shortly before the end of the war, as *Betrachtungen eines Unpolitischen* ("Reflections of a Nonpolitical Man").

To understand this remarkable outburst we must see it in the perspective of the place, the time, and the man. Some of us who are now sufficiently near death to risk mingling impartiality with patriotism can understand how a fortunate and prosperous German who had inherited Bach, Handel, Mozart, Beethoven, Wagner, Brahms, Kant, Goethe, Schopenhauer, and Nietzsche—a German who could reasonably be proud of German universities, science, and scholarship, and of beautiful and well-governed cities—could rise to the defense of his native land as hemmed in and besieged by Russia, Italy, and France, and as struggling to evade British control of the seas by building a railroad from "Berlin to Baghdad," thereby opening an avenue to Asiatic outlets for the swelling products of German industry. Thomas Mann, like every patriotic American in 1917, felt that his country had a case. Moreover, he had not yet recovered from Nietzsche.

Frankly calling himself a bourgeois despite the stigma that had gathered about that term, he opposed democracy as then practiced in France and England, though he accepted it as an ideal of human brotherhood.[25] He rejected egalitarianism as biologically unreal: we may aspire to be brothers, but we can never escape the inequality of ability that nature, as well as circumstance, has established among men. Since all government is minority rule, an aristocracy of birth is at least as good as an oligarchy of money, and perhaps better, since it transmits a steadying tradition of leadership by a trained class and protects a nation against aberrations of taste and the tyranny of an illiterate populace or an irresponsible mob. Universal suffrage is merely a guarantee of mediocrity in office. "It is stupid to think that life in a republic is more worthy of humanity than life under a monarchy."[26] The German government under Bismarck had proved itself a better instrument of orderly progress and social justice than the chaos of parties and parliaments which, as in France, "affect all of a nation's life like a pestilence."[27]

In his martial enthusiasm Mann advanced to attack almost everything French and to defend almost everything German. He preferred German philosophy to French cynicism, German feeling to French intellect, the German Romantic movement to the French Enlightenment. The worship of reason was stultified by reason's subservience to the will; and the French idolatry of wit, beauty, and art regardless of monogamy and morality had culminated in individualistic anarchy, moral decadence, and national debility. While Spengler (then, like Mann, living in Munich) was writing *Der Untergang des Abendlandes* (1918–22), Mann already (1915–17) formulated the contrast, now associated with Spengler, between a degenerative *Zivilisation* of great industrial cities, infested with intellectuals, and the sustaining *Kultur* of a whole people respecting its traditions, its faith, and its orderly ways. He concluded by counseling the German people to be *unpolitische*—to avoid politics; to cherish their leadership in philosophy and music; and to serve as *das Volk der Mitte*—the people of the middle—in mediating between East and West, feeling and intellect, instinct and reason. In that synthesis he hoped that Europe would find an escape from decadence and repeated war.

Even as he published these "reflections," he realized that he had fought for a losing cause. Germany was defeated, its martial monarchy was overthrown, its leaders were going to do public penance at Versailles. Mann retreated for a time into the peace of his home, and wrote an idyl about his dog—*Herr und Hund* (1919); the intelligence of "Bashan" seemed sounder than the intellect of man. In 1921 Bonn University gave him an honorary degree—*Doctor honoris causa*. In 1922 he returned to politics with an address in Berlin "On the German Republic"—defending the Weimar government in its desperate attempt to check inflation and restore social order. He was accused of turncoat opportunism in supporting the new democracy, but he felt—and predicted—that the alternative to the republic was a fascist dictatorship such as Mussolini was establishing in Italy. He marched up and down Germany pleading for the fragile regime, as if he foresaw the coming of Hitler. Meanwhile, industrious and indefatigable, he labored on the book that was to win the acclaim of the Western world.

III. ON THE MOUNTAIN: 1919–24

Buddenbrooks had appeared under the sign of Schopenhauer chanting the defeat of the will by death; the *Betrachtungen eines Unpolitischen* had followed the mood of Nietzsche deriding democracy as a toboggan to decay. But year by year Mann was freeing himself from these brilliant Cassandras by following the development of Goethe from passion to understanding. The first evidence of his new line was a substantial piece, "Goethe and Tolstoi," which appeared in a volume of musings called *Bemühungen* (1922). Other essays on Goethe were added during the next decade; soon Mann was thinking of himself as Goethe's heir and spokesman, almost his avatar, struggling to reconcile nature and spirit, life and art, order and liberty. He reread *Wilhelm Meisters Lehrjahre* as the classical instance of the *Bildungsroman*—the story of an education in mind and character. Mann himself, like Wilhelm, had been formed by experience rather than by schools; he felt himself in the midst of that painful process; and it occurred to him that he might echo and contemplate his vacillating thoughts in some fictitious personage traveling through sickness, politics, war, love, philosophy, and the shadow of death. He thought of Schopenhauer's remark, "The novel will be a higher and nobler type the more inward and the less outward the life which it presents."[28]

"In 1912," he tells us, "my wife had been attacked by a catarrh of the tip of the lung. . . . Then, and again in 1914, she was obliged to stay for several months in the Swiss Alps. In May and June of 1912 I spent three weeks with her in Davos, and accumulated . . . fantastic impressions."[29] That mountaintop in eastern Switzerland seemed an ideal *mise-en-scène* for a large perspective of human affairs, ideas, and passions, and of man's significance in a godless world. Since every experience suggested a story, he began in that year 1912 to write *The Magic Mountain*. The war and the *Reflections* interrupted the enterprise, but when the war was over he resumed the novel. He planned it as a brief *novella;* it grew to twelve hundred pages. He published it in 1924 as *Der Zauberberg*, for the mountain at Davos was known in legend as the home of wicked spirits who lured souls to death by magic spells.[30] In four years the book went through a hundred printings.

The starting point is Hamburg, a city, like Lübeck, of merchants and the race for wealth. The hero, Hans Castorp, is no hero, for Mann describes him as a sick weakling who takes seven years and a thousand pages to make up his mind. Nevertheless, he too was Thomas Mann— "as if I had ever dealt with any other subject than my own life."[31] Like his creator, Hans is the scion of a senator in a stronghold of the Hanseatic League. He does not do well in business; he ails, and in 1907 he is sent to Davos for a cure. Five thousand feet above the plain is the Berghof, or Mountain House, a sanitarium that treats tuberculosis with drugs, psychoanalysis, and fresh air.

Castorp comes intending to stay for a few weeks; he remains month after month, year after year, as if held by some magic influence, or lulled by the ease of a rich patient's life. (He is heir to 400,000 marks.) Having lost his Protestant creed, he has lost also the ethic of work and thrift; perhaps his withdrawal from business to a mountaintop symbolizes the retreat of sensitive and meditative souls from the materialism and challenges of a commercial career. His interest in science attracts him to the doctors of the sanitarium—who keep on testing his blood and organs until they find a bit of moisture in his lungs. Castorp is not entirely sorry that he has become a patient; he finds that introversion through disease and rest, plus rarefied air and a little sexual exaltation, lifts him to new levels of perception and understanding.

As his stay at the Berghof is prolonged to seven years, he feels the elasticity of time. In this quiet and uneventful life little occurs to hasten or differentiate the days; soon Hans ceases to count them, or the weeks; the subjective unit of time is enlarged to a month, then to the season; hardly anything is noted except the first staying snow and the timid sproutings of a new spring. He relaxes willingly in this almost timelessness. He neglects the daily newspaper and the weekly pabulum of print sent up from the chaos and conflict below; the events they record and inflate lose their urgency and importance on these heights, which seem so near to the apparently timeless stars. Now change becomes maya—appearance, surface, unreality. The present is as the past was, as the future will be; the present is the past in sum and the future in seed. But where there is no change there is no time.

Not all the patients take time in this heedless way. Hans Castorp's cousin, Joachim Ziemssen, is a soldier and patriot; he trembles at the daily crises of his fatherland; he waits impatiently for even a half-cure that may let him rejoin his regiment. He has no taste for philosophical argument; privately he thinks it a cowardly avoidance of decision and action. He plays the part of Martha to Castorp's Mary, and in the end his way wins, even while he loses his life.

Clavdia Chauchat, from the Russian East, is the Venus and siren of Davos. Hans is drawn to her not only because her every curve is an invitation, but because she seems to embody the Orient's discovery of wisdom in silent acceptance of a reality obstinately obscure. Languid and leisurely, she turns up her perfect nose at the bourgeois haste to get up and move, to do and undo, to make a fortune as quickly as possible and then be too spent to spend it wisely and with content. She is sensuous but skeptical, pleased but amused by the eagerness of her male entourage for labial contacts and epidermal explorations. She pays little heed to reason, for its voice seems to her a hesitant whisper beside the confident commands of her instincts. In her semi-Oriental blood and mood are stern traditions and mystic convictions too deeply rooted to be disturbed by windblown arguments or change.

Different is Lodovico Settembrini, who comes from Italy hot with Garibaldi and the French Enlightenment. He is all for reason, progress, and democracy. He is a Freemason and an atheist; he will have nothing to do with mysticism or the Church. He calls upon Castorp to slough off the well-fed unconcern of a German bourgeoisie composed of "beer, tobacco, and music." He looks hopefully for a revolution that will establish a world republic, even if in the process a hundred cities should be destroyed. Hans shudders.

He is not comforted by Naphta. This is not a chemical but a Jesuit; a strange and dangerous compound nonetheless—a Jew converted to Catholicism, a Catholic converted to Communism; his order has taken advantage of his tuberculosis to deposit him in a Davos hostelry amid sterilizing snow. There Settembrini too takes up his residence, and then Castorp hears atheist and Jesuit debate religion versus rationalism, dictatorship versus democracy. (Mussolini came to power in 1922, Hitler made his "Beer Hall Putsch" in Mann's Munich in 1923.) Through Naphta and Settembrini and their arguments, Mann told a U.S. Library of Congress audience, "I made a friendly alter ego [Castorp] pass through the adventures of European intellectual controversies."[32]

Naphta echoes the author of the *Reflections of a Nonpolitical Man*. He scorns the *Zivilisationsliterat* which Settembrini represents; he thinks that the Enlightenment has ceased to be a creative force, that it has degenerated into logic-chopping ridiculously removed from living problems and realities. He exalts medieval theology as far profounder than the *philosophes*. He laughs at democracy as a numbers game and a mathematical surd; no multiplication of mediocrities can constitute wise leadership or beget integrity. We cannot rely upon capitalism to rescue the masses from poverty and ignorance, for capitalism concentrates wealth and knowledge in a proud and selfish minority; we shall have to accept some form of authoritarian Communism, which will end poverty and illiteracy not through a count of noses but through an oligarchy of executive brains—unhampered by any obligation to explain its policies to the populace. To achieve this better, saner world a revolution may be necessary, costly in wealth and blood; but the end will justify the means. However, no society can long survive without a supernatural religion that will meet man's need for meaning, comfort, and peace of mind; no moral code without supernatural sanctions will tame the ape and tiger in the human breast; therefore Communism, sooner or later, must make its peace with the Catholic Church. —Meanwhile the ailing Jesuit urges Castorp not to underrate disease: sickness promotes meditation and mystic understanding; it arouses the nerves to abnormal sensitivity; it is the seed of genius; therefore "all progress, insofar as there is such a thing, is due to illness, and to illness alone."[33] Naphta's own nerves are so tautly strung that he cannot debate Settembrini without rising to violent vituperation. In the end the two fight a duel; Settembrini gallantly aims at the clouds; Naphta fires into his own head, and dies.

Castorp is torn between their pros and cons. (He is Mann oscillating between Lenin and Mussolini, Voltaire and Maritain.) He agrees with Naphta that capitalism is "hard, cold, . . . cruel, and ruthless,"[34] and that atheism leads to pessimism and moral chaos, but he is not ready to abandon reason, persuasion, and orderly reform. Besides, he is in love with Clavdia Chauchat (whose husband is at a safe distance), and philosophy can wait. For a long time he fails to penetrate her reserve; but the Carnival celebration relaxes her stateliness and loosens his tongue. He declares his love in a meticulous exaltation of the body of woman—"its marvelous symmetry, . . . the shoulders, the hips, the blossoming breasts (*les mamelons fleurissants*), . . . and the sex hidden between the thighs, . . . what a feast it would be to caress those delicious" arcana "of the female form!—After such a feast one could die without complaint. . . . Let me perish, my lips to yours!"[35] It sounds silly, but it is an ecstasy that every male man has felt, and that every female woman, smiling at it indulgently like Mona Lisa, loves to hear and see. Perhaps it represented for Thomas Mann a prime example of the Schopenhauerian life force overriding reason, of intellect happily surrendering to will. Clavdia accepts the threnody with the calm of a goddess secure in the imagina-

tiveness of men. Having condemned Germany as a land too fond of
order and too fearful of freedom, she can hardly refuse to hear this
postulant, adoring her on his knees; besides, his anatomical litany is
phrased in a French that forgives a multitude of sins. "Petit bourgeois,"
she coos as she fingers his hair; "nice bourgeois with a little touch of
fluid [in his lungs]. Is it true that you love me so much?" She leaves
him, but her backward last glance seems to invite him to her room. We
are not told what happened there; Mann's French failed him at this
juncture; but he informs us later, in his dilatory way, that Clavdia
gave Hans the memento he had begged for—an X-ray picture of her
body. (Could anything be more disastrous to romance?) Hans's memory and imagination clothed the bones with a charming integument.

Clavdia leaves Davos on the morrow, and years pass before she returns. Hans has time now to brood over the ideas bandied by Naphta
and Settembrini. He labors to unite feeling and intellect, authority and
freedom, mythology and enlightenment in a compromise by which
Germany might mediate between East and West. Unable to resolve
the conflict, he welcomes to the Berghof a hearty Dutchman from
Java, Mynheer Peeperkorn, whose dogmatic activism dismisses arguments as the intellectual pastimes of weaklings who make philosophy a
refuge from life. Beside him both Settembrini and Naphta seem as irrelevant as thought without will, intellect without blood.

Clavdia accompanies Peeperkorn as his complaisant mistress, pleased
to find a man who can dominate her and take her without words.
Castorp is only passingly jealous; he has almost forgotten that integument; the man of intellect yields the prize to the man of action. He
comes to rival Clavdia in admiration for Peeperkorn's decisive ways.
But Peeperkorn has brought in his veins a malignant fever from his
tropical plantations; he has become impotent; his strength is as nothing
before the multiplying microbes. He ends the absurdity with suicide.

Castorp turns for perspective to solitary skiing on the mountain
snows. Defying the sanitarium's rules, he climbs to rarefied heights,
and skis recklessly over uncharted slopes and curves until he loses
all sense of direction and goal. At first he is exhilarated by his danger
and solitude in the white immensity; the trivialities and irrelevancies
of his days and thoughts fall away into chasms of emptiness. He remembers the race for wealth in the towns far below, and rejoices that he
has withdrawn from it; that endless conflict of jealously individual
animalcules seems now a massive pullulating futility. He feels that in
this clear expanse, where he is but a dot in space and an instant in
eternity, he can escape from the prison of self and the treadmill of

time. What if he should never find men again? What if the cold of the air and the snow should freeze his blood and dull his brain to death? Would not that cool release be a boon? But suddenly, in a listless turn, he sees a light, then a hut, in a cleft of the hills. His freezing body is warmed with gratitude, and with a happy affection for mankind. He sees man no longer as a proliferating absurdity but as a miracle of consciousness and feeling, suffering, defeat and resolution. With open arms and heart he hurries down to that light.

Not many days thereafter news comes to Davos that France, England, Russia, Italy, and Japan have declared war against Germany and Austria, and that the Kaiser has called to all Germans to come to the aid of their country. Now Hans Castorp feels that life without time is death, and that the leisurely pampering of ailments is a cowardly escape from the "character-building stream of the world." He decides to take his place and chance with his fellow men. He leaves the mountaintop, joins the German Army, marches with it into the Netherlands, and disappears in battle and mire.

Almost everything in the story is a symbol—*Alles Vergängliche ist nur ein Gleichnis*. Castorp, of course, is first of all Mann himself, remembering his own sins and ailments, his own doubts and wonderment; hesitating between thought and action, art and business, Germany and France, East and West, even between life and death. But also Castorp is man, twentieth-century European man, vacillating between religion and science, feeling and intellect, order and liberty, socialism and capitalism, democracy and dictatorship. The mountain is a symbol of lofty, airy meditation; the sanitarium is a symbol of a sick society coddling its ills and weakening its will. Since everything in *The Magic Mountain* means something besides itself, the clutter of symbols and the clash of opposites becomes confusing; and a hurried reader still avid of life longs at times for a story direct and clear. But Thomas Mann, though he is a storyteller by profession, a master and magician of words, is also a philosopher, a man mad about meaning. "In what does the significance of a significant subject lie? In the fact that it points beyond itself, something universal, a whole world of thought and feeling."[36] So it was not Hans Castorp that interested him, it was modern man, lost in the glare of the Enlightenment, tangled in the maze of his inventions and ideas, weary with the meaninglessness of wealth.

The book is faulty if judged by standards which its author implicitly rejects. Its long disquisitions on scientific topics seem superfluous, even pretentious. We wonder why we must listen to so many digressions on anatomy, physiology, pathology, chemistry, radiology, psychology, meteorology, and theology; we do not feel that these discourses are integrated into the narrative as essential elements in an ordered whole. Mann would reply that he was writing a *Bildungsroman*, whose basic characters are ideas. We acknowledge admiration for the varied erudition displayed, and especially for the knowledge of medicine. But Mann tended to force into his works not only the application but the details of the studies by which he had conscientiously prepared himself for them; the result is almost a *Konversationslexikon*, a "dictionary of debates." Not many of us relish the dallying with disease; the repeated suggestion that disease is a spiritual stimulation, liberation, clarification; the notion that "death is the principle of genius." This, of course, is Schopenhauer again, and again Nietzsche; yet *The Magic Mountain* was Mann's effort to rid himself of these ghosts of his youth. He never forgot that he himself was the subject of his books—the long, fond story of his intellectual, moral, and political development, the meandering epic of the artist blessed and ridden with words, despising and loving mankind.

Whatever its flaws, *The Magic Mountain* remains one of the peaks of contemporary literature. Those details that weary us build up a background and a mood that finally cast a spell over us and make us feel the scene; those debates illuminate our age, even if they leave conclusions as inconclusive as in life. Millions of readers, in a dozen languages, forgave the faults, followed the swollen stream to its end, and acclaimed the book as raising Thomas Mann to the lordship of European letters in his generation.

IV. SORROWS AND GREATNESS OF THE MASTER

Such was the title—"Leiden und Grösse des Meisters"—that Mann gave to his essay on Richard Wagner. We apply it now to himself, for soon after his exaltation came an eventful decade of humiliation and grief. In 1925 Munich celebrated his fiftieth birthday with official ceremonies in the city hall, and *Die Neue Rundschau* dedicated an entire number to the event. In 1929 he received the Nobel Prize for Literature. Everywhere, abroad as well as in Germany, he was in demand. And everywhere he defended the ailing Weimar Republic.

In 1930 he issued a short novel, *Mario und der Zauberer* (*Mario and the Magician*), in which a charlatan hypnotizes an audience to such submission of judgment that it obeys all his commands and rejoices in being rid of freedom; obviously the book was a satire of Fascist propaganda. A similar demagoguery was preparing to enthrall Germany; *Mein Kampf, published in 1925*, was making its way into the German mind. The depression of 1929 in the United States so weakened the economy of Germany that the National Socialist Party of Adolf Hitler received 6,500,000 votes in the election of September, 1930. On October 10 Mann opposed the "new wave" with his "Deutsche Ansprache: Ein Appell an die Vernunft," a "German Address: An Appeal to Reason," delivered in Berlin. He was so heckled and threatened by Nazi followers that after his speech he had to be guided by Bruno Walter and other friends to a secret exit from the hall. In 1932, on the centenary of Goethe's death, Mann tried again: in a lecture on "Goethe as Representative of the Bourgeois Age" he pleaded with the German middle class to free itself from the undertow of reaction and join the intellectual community in working for a humane order under a Socialist government.[37] The bourgeoisie responded rather to nationalist propaganda and the call to revenge against the Treaty of Versailles.

Hitler became chancellor in 1933, and began a regime of thought control and racial agitation. Mann and his wife were then vacationing in Switzerland. On March 11 Klaus Heinrich and Erika Mann telephoned their father from Munich that the weather there was stormy, and advised him to postpone his return home. On the next day they fled from Munich and rejoined their parents, bringing with them the manuscript of *The Young Joseph*.[38] When Thomas Mann (perhaps fearing for the safety of his Jewish wife) refused to return to Germany, the new government confiscated his house, his car, and all his seizable funds.[39] After a summer in France he settled at Küsnacht on the Lake of Zurich. In 1936 the German government rescinded his citizenship; and the University of Bonn withdrew the degree it had conferred upon him in 1921. His reply to the rector of the university was so strong a condemnation of the new regime that it was translated into several languages, and made a stir throughout Europe. "I could not have lived or worked," he wrote, "I should have suffocated, had I not been able now and again to cleanse my heart, to give from time to time free vent to my abysmal disgust at what was happening at home—the contemptible words and the still more contemptible deeds."[40] In 1937 he issued a *Warning to Europe* (*Achtung, Europa*), predicting that the policies of Hitler would lead to Germany's disgrace and defeat. The preface to this tract was written by André Gide, who had visited Mann at Küsnacht. "I was moved," Gide reported, "by the gentle manners and the exquisite consideration with which he conceals a great firmness of character, an inflexible will."[41] Few of Mann's readers imagined, at this time, that from the battle between a dictator and a novelist the latter would emerge victorious and justified.

He strengthened himself by going back to Goethe, and writing a long reverie on him in the form of a novel, *Lotte in Weimar* (translated as *The Beloved Returns*). "I wrote the last chapters . . . during a six months' bout with infectious sciatica. . . . Never have I endured such wild pain."[42] The book was published at Stockholm in 1939, while Hitler was rushing into war; too late it offered to the German people another picture of Goethe as a "good European" who had refused to take part in a nationalistic stampede.

It is amusing to see how Mann by imagination expands to 453 pages one day (in 1816) in the life of Charlotte Kestner, whom Goethe had loved to the verge of suicide some forty-four years before. Now sixty-three, widowed and the mother of eleven children, she comes from Hannover to Weimar with her twenty-nine-year-old daughter and a maid, to visit her sister, and if possible to see her rejected lover, aged sixty-seven, the acknowledged sovereign of European literature. On her arrival she sends Goethe a note, asking may she come with her daughter. When the neighboring folk hear that the virtuous heroine of *Werther* has taken rooms at the Hotel Elephant, so great a crowd gathers before the inn that "the police had their work cut out to keep order." Lotte dresses, and is about to go to her sister when Goethe's secretary, Councilor Riemer, comes and talks (forty-eight pages) about his master's ideas, including the possible unity of God and the Devil.[43] She responds with a quite improbable description of her own youthful loveliness: "He [Kestner] wanted me because I was so splendid. . . . And in the next four years I developed physically and took shape as a woman—quite a pretty shape—but my time was come, poetically speaking, to turn into a blossom from a bud."[44] Then Adele Schopenhauer, mother of a budding philosopher, detains Lotte with gossip (one hundred pages) about Goethe, his wife Christiane, his son August, his daughter-in-law Ottilie, and his admiration for Napoleon. Then August comes, bearing Goethe's invitation to dinner, and relates (seventy pages) his father's recent history. Now at last Lotte goes to her sister (page 280).

Goethe enters the story, and daydreams (eighty pages) about his collection of minerals, and how "nobody can get along with the Germans, be it in triumph or defeat,"[45] and the unconscious roots of conscious thought, and the nature of greatness. "Greatness comes only with the weight, endurance, power, and mental equipment of age. . . . Love, too, comes only then; what is any youthful love beside the spiritual and intellectual strength of love in age?"[46] (This is Mann—now sixty-four —thinking of Katja, rather than Goethe thinking of tipsy Christiane; that old lecher was soon prowling around among virgins.)

Finally (page 394) Lotte—coyly wearing a white dress with a pink sash, such as she wore when Goethe courted her—comes to dinner; but Goethe has invited a court of relatives, who keep the conversation safely trivial. However, he sends her a ticket for the Weimar Theater, and has his coach meet her when the play is over. She is surprised and pleased to find him seated beside her. Now they talk frankly of their old romance. She reproaches him for having ignored her for the past forty years; he tells her it was better so; he discourses on his present life as a harmonious fusion of art, science, and public service. He is much relieved when she departs. All in all the book is an unsuccessful attempt to make the dead poet live, or to express Goethe's philosophy in terms characteristically Goethean. But Stefan Zweig thought it, to its date, Mann's "most perfect masterpiece."[47]

Before its publication the author had moved to the United States. Between 1934 and 1938 he had made several lecture forays into America; in 1938–41 he dwelt in the ivy groves of Princeton, lecturing occasionally at the university; and in 1941 he built a house for himself and his family in Pacific Palisades, California. There he became the center of a distinguished group of fellow exiles: Franz Werfel, Otto Klemperer, Bruno Walter, Alfred Neumann, Lion Feuchtwanger, Lotte Lehmann, Arnold Schoenberg, and Heinrich Mann—reconciled to a brother now reconciled to democracy. Thomas issued pamphlets in support of the Allies; he broadcast fifty-five appeals to the German people to renounce Hitler; he saw his two sons enlist in the United States Army; and in 1944 he became an American citizen.

In that year he joined some lesser scribes at a meeting of the Pen Club in Beverly Hills. There I saw him for the first time, and was struck by his quiet composure, his keen eyes and speech. When I explained to him that I was trying to write a history of medieval civilization with such impartiality that no reader could tell whether I was a Catholic, a Moslem, or a Jew, he commented slyly, "Then you must be an atheist." Despite that chastening thrust he agreed to speak at a dinner of the "Declaration of Interdependence," where his presence and support helped us to finance an apparently futile campaign for mutual understanding and tolerance among races and creeds.

He did not make friends easily. He was too occupied with his work, literary and political, to spare much time for the amenities of social life. A succession of dogs provided him with a faithful and silent companionship not often found in friends. The narrator in *Doctor Faustus* confesses, "Perhaps my own nature has a certain stiffness and dryness that makes me inept";[48] and Felix Krull says, "In early youth an inner voice had warned me that close association, friendship, and companionship were not to be my lot, but that I should instead be inescapably compelled to follow my strange path alone, dependent entirely upon myself."[49] He found some good in his break with Nazi Germany: it gave him that contact between the artist and the world which had been the theme of many stories and the longing of many years. Those who came to know him well found him genial, kindly, generous, modest, and patient.[50] For the rest he protected himself from indiscriminate invasion by a patrician reserve and what his Felix Krull called "a sense for the natural hierarchy" of men.[51]

Among his friends was Franklin Roosevelt, who appreciated the support of Germany's leading author against Hitler's Germany. Mann welcomed the New Deal as promising a peaceful absorption, by American capitalism, of many elements in socialism.[52] He was one of the hundreds of millions who mourned Roosevelt's death (April 12, 1945), and he heard with horror of "people who opened bottles of champagne on hearing the news."[53] A month later, having been chosen a fellow of the Library of Congress, he delivered there an address in which he made new enemies by saying that books printed in Germany between 1933 and 1945 were stained with blood and shame. German writers retaliated by calling him a coward for leaving Germany;[54] they forgot that by remaining he would have subjected his wife and children to Hitler's anti-Semitic rage. When Hitler fell, Mann hailed the defeat of Nazi Germany as a victory for reason. Many German-Americans joined in the attack upon him, and "the insults they hurl at me . . . add their bit to overcoming any joy I might feel."[55] When Russia was transformed from a partner into a foe of the United States, Mann's sympathy for the Soviets led to allegations that he was a Communist; and he learned that sleuths of Senator Joseph McCarthy suspected him as a "fellow traveler." In April, 1947, he abandoned his California home, and on May 11 he sailed for Europe.

V. JOSEPH AND HIS BROTHERS

Amid the crisis of his life with the coming of Hitler to power, and amid the anti-Semitism rising in Germany, Mann undertook the heaviest of his literary tasks—to write an epic of an ancient Jew despised and rejected at home, and becoming, in exile, the savior of his people. "To write a novel of the Jewish spirit was timely just because it seemed untimely," he told his Library of Congress audience, for "Judaism and Hellenism are the two principal pillars upon which our Occidental civilization rests." Always feeling an affiliation with Goethe, he had noted a remark, in *Dichtung und Wahrheit*, about the Joseph saga in the last twenty-four chapters of Genesis: "This natural story is highly amiable, only it seems too short, and one is tempted to carry it out in all its details."[56] It was a splendid gesture of defiance to write this idyl of ancient Jewry amid the massacre of the German Jews. Were these four volumes an offering to Katja, for whose sake he went into exile, like Jacob to the land of Laban, like Joseph to Egypt? Furthermore Mann was inspired by Wagner's music epic, *The Ring*;[57] he longed to produce something on an equally grand scale, something that would not be merely a narrative but a probing into the meaning of life and history.

So he began, about 1928, his fifteen-year labor of love—*Joseph und seine Brüder*. "The whole work . . . through one and a half decades of outer stress was my steady companion."[58]* He prepared himself like a German scholar. He studied the archaeology and history of ancient Palestine and Egypt, and he venturesomely described their peoples, clothing, language, dialects, houses, manners, morals, religion, music, games, medicines, laws, economy and government. He visited the Near East and Egypt in 1930; "I myself went down into the depths [the valley of the Jordan], and looked from the western shores of the evil-tasting Sea of Lot [the Salt or Dead Sea], saw all with my own eyes."[60] Meanwhile he delved more deeply into the works of Freud, Frazer, and Jung, and almost lost himself in the psychological and mythological origins of religion.

Itching to philosophize, he began with a fifty-six-page prelude entitled "Höllenfahrt"—"Trip to Hell," by which he meant the past. "Very deep is the well of the past. Should we not call it bottomless?"[61] Dig as we will, we never reach the beginnings of that mighty stream of

---

* The four volumes were collectively entitled *Joseph und seine Brüder* (*Joseph and His Brothers*). Vol. I, *Die Geschichten Jaakobs* (*The Tales of Jacob*), was published in Berlin in 1933. Vol. II, *Der junge Joseph*, was written in Munich and (as related above) was salvaged in manuscript by the Mann children in their flight from Munich; it was published in Berlin in 1934. Vol. III, *Joseph in Ägypten*, completed in Switzerland, was published in Vienna in 1936. Vol. IV, *Joseph der Ernährer* (*Joseph the Provider*), written in California, was published at Stockholm in 1943. "The California sky, so like the Egyptian, smiled on my work; to it the story undoubtedly owes much of its cheerfulness."[59]

events of which the present is the momentary accumulation and result. Is there any meaning in that engulfing stream? Yes, Mann answers—if we can open our minds to the esoteric wisdom of ancient myths. In a rationalistic and individualistic age we fall into the superficial view that a myth is nonsense if it is not literally true, and we tend to judge the myth in terms of its worth to the individual rather than to the group. (So the expulsion of Adam and Eve from Eden for eating fruit from the Tree of Knowledge presented dramatically what Ecclesiastes said more briefly: "He that increaseth knowledge increaseth sorrow.") In tribal days, Mann suggests, the individual did not so sharply differentiate himself from his fellows as now; he participated more often in communal dangers and tasks; and he readily accepted the traditions, myths, and ceremonies that sustained the unity, courage, and continuance of his group. (Compare the patriotic myths with which school books and holiday festivities glorify a nation's history, cleansing it of corruption, injustice, and defeat, and transforming martial aggression into moral crusades.) So the descendants of Abraham cherished the inspiring story of the covenant that he made to serve Yahveh and multiply Yahveh's worshipers in return for a special and transmissible divine blessing that would ensure the good fortune of its recipients.

The myth that especially consoled and strengthened the tribes of the ancient Near East was that of the dying, resurrected, and redeeming god. Almost every people around the Eastern Mediterranean had some form of it. The Babylonians' told of Tammuz, the lovely young god who had been killed by a boar, and had been snatched into the dark underworld; whereupon the earth lost its fertility until the mother-goddess Ishtar, or Astarte, went down into hell and brought him back to visible life, so restoring the growth of the soil and the vigor of the race. The Greeks' told of the handsome Adonis, who, slain by a boar, disappeared into Hades, but was annually returned to the earth by the pleas of Aphrodite, and brought with him the burgeoning of spring. Similar stories were told of Osiris in Egypt and of Dionysus in Greece. Now, what if the legend of Joseph was ancient Israel's variation of this resurrection myth? He was a godlike youth who was thrown into subterranean darkness, emerged triumphant in three days, worked many miracles, and saved his people from starvation. Did not his figure, fate, and revival prefigure Christ? Joseph himself (his re-creator thought) was conscious that his career followed the form of a life-giving tribal memory or myth; he was an "individual person filling out in present time . . . a mythical frame that was established by the fathers."[62]

The story of the beautiful, dying, resurrected, and saving god is but one of many similarities, in events and persons, that assimilate the present with the past; so Napoleon repeated Caesar, who repeated Alexander, who repeated Cyrus . . . Mann saw history as in some measure an eternal recurrence—not as thorough as Nietzsche visioned it, but as repeating traditional situations, forms, institutions, personalities, or ideas. Everything present or future has its counterpart in the past. "We move in the footsteps of others, and all life is but the pouring of the present into the forms of the myth."[63] In its recurrent embodiments the myth binds the present into the past and offers to the people a strengthening nourishment from ancient roots.

So Mann gave to *Joseph and His Brothers* a double scope and pertinence: it would be the story of one Israelite, but it would symbolize the life and hope of man. "I took the step in my subject matter from the bourgeois and individual to the mythical and typical."[64] The double enterprise stirred the author to "a curious heightening of his artistic temper"[65] and powers. Beginning it, Mann felt both exaltation and fear.[66] In 1936, after completing all but the final volume, he wrote: "I know not how to express the feelings which possess me—something like a joyous sense of divination of the future—when I indulge in this encouragement of the unconscious to play, to make itself fruitful in a serious product, in a narrational meeting of psychology and myth, . . . of poetry and analysis."[67] He rightly judged this book to be his finest, and he dedicated to it all the resources of his mind and art.

Being a compulsive storyteller, he devoted Volume I to the history of Joseph's father, Jacob, with some flashbacks to Jacob's father, Isaac, and to Isaac's father, Abraham—"a brooding and inwardly unquiet man," who left "Ur of the Chaldees" to escape the tyranny of Nimrod, and was the first individual Jew to emerge from the anonymity of the tribe; this, to Mann, was "the birth of the mythical collective."[68] Perhaps the outstanding personality in the four volumes is Jacob, who carried out with dignity the divine blessing transmitted from Abraham, and fulfilled his part of the covenant with piety and fertility. But the pearl of this and all the volumes is the story of Rachel, who loved Jacob when she was thirteen, waited for him seven years, was cheated of him by Laban's substituting her older sister Leah in the marriage bed, became only his second wife, suffered for thirteen years the bitter shame of barrenness, then bore Joseph, and, nine years later, died giving birth to Benjamin. All of Jacob's life from that night of agony was his memory of her tender loveliness, and his devotion to her firstborn son.

He comforted himself with the boy's beauty and imaginative mind, and spoiled him by choosing him, and not any of Leah's much older sons, as prospective heir to the blessing. *The Young Joseph* tells how his brothers, angered by his preferment, his tale-telling, and his ability to write, his half-erotic relationship with his father, and his flaunted dreams of his coming supremacy, took his robe from him, and cast him, bound hand and foot, into a pit.

Mann interprets the pit as a multiple symbol of death, of the under-world or hell, and of the unfathomable past. It is also the pit of peni-tence, where Joseph profits from his leisure to repent his pride and insolence, and resolves thereafter to walk humbly before his God. Jacob, told by the brothers that Joseph has been torn to pieces by a wild animal (the Tammuz-Adonis myth), goes almost insane with grief, thinks of seeking entry into the nether world to bring his son back to life, and reproaches God for lagging behind man in justice and moral sense.[69]

Joseph is rescued from the pit, and is sold as a slave to Peterpe (Potiphar), an Egyptian prince. *Joseph in Egypt* (which Mann con-sidered "the artistic zenith of the work") shows the brilliant youth rising like some dime-novel hero from poverty and degradation to wealth and mastery. His handsome form and face persuade the Egyptian populace that he is a god—probably a reincarnation of Osiris; his poetic and ingratiating speech and his rapid development of executive ability lead Peterpe to appoint him chief steward of his principality. Peterpe is impotent, and his chief wife, Mut-em-enet, pining for a man, be-comes desperately enamored of Joseph. She offers herself to him, he refuses her advances, she accuses him of having tried to seduce her, and begs Peterpe to condemn him to torture and death. Peterpe suspects the truth, and sends Joseph off to genteel imprisonment.

In *Joseph the Provider* the hero so successfully interprets dreams for his jailer that he is sent for to interpret the dreams of the Pharaoh. (By some novel poetic license Mann identifies this ruler with Amenhotep IV, whom we have come to know as Ikhnaton, apostle of the sun, c. 1375 B.C. —some five hundred years after the period to which Jacob is now loosely assigned.) Here the author deploys his Egyptological studies, presenting a detailed reconstruction of a pharaoh's court, and puts into Joseph's mouth a long discourse on Egyptian and Babylonian myths. Amenhotep is so pleased with Joseph's analysis of his dreams that he empowers him to tax the rich as a means of laying up stores of grain in "fat" years to keep the poor from starving in "lean" years of drought. (Mann called Franklin Roosevelt "an American Hermes, a brilliant messenger of shrewdness, whose New Deal is unmistakably reflected in Joseph's administration of national economy.")[70] When drought comes, and spreads through the Near East, Jacob sends his sons to ask help from Egypt's stores. Joseph meets his brothers, forgives them the pit, gives them grain, and invites them and Jacob and Jacob's seventy surviving progeny to settle in Egyptian Goshen—just east of the fertile delta of the Nile. The old patriarch, rejoicing, comes with all his tribe, and Joseph enriches them. Jacob now becomes again the center of the tale, as in Volume I, and the beginning of the saga is artfully united with the end. Dying, Jacob asks to be buried near Hebron; it is granted, but his children remain in Goshen, and multiply there till Moses leads the Exodus.

Through all this classic tale Mann seeks to revive, for the encouragement of a Schopenhauerian-Nietzschean generation, the ancient myth that periodically a new and saving god is born (in this case Franklin Delano Roosevelt). For the comfort of those who fondly recall the old faith, he speaks at times of a supernatural deity who "creates the world of Nature in order to know Himself,"[71] and who punishes the wicked and rewards the good; but in slightly soberer moments Mann agrees with Gide that God is a human conception of ideal power, taking nobler and fuller form with the moral development of mankind.

Such flights into theology, and long deviations into archaeology, anthropology, psychology, architecture . . . mar the artistry of *Joseph and His Brothers*. Here we have Mann's gleanings from *The Golden Bough*'s assortment of savior gods, from Jung's picture of the unconscious as a junkshop of old tribal myths, even from Freud's notion that every son wants to be the husband of his mother (Reuben seduces his father's wife). The author enters every alley, tells every story, and rationalizes his weakness lovingly. The novelist, he says, "does not aim at a mere fragment or episode, he wants the whole of things, the world with its innumerable episodes and details, over which he will forgetfully linger. . . . He is in no hurry, he has infinite time [!], his is the spirit of patience, of playfulness, of perseverance, of a slowness made enjoyable through love, the spirit of bewitching tediousness."[72] So he tarries over every incident, carefully building and carelessly forgetting his plot, forming his phrases and savoring his words.

He later described the style of the Joseph novels as "a stylized and bantering language, . . . very close to persiflage, or at any rate to irony."[73] I did not find it so; I thought it a very pleasant union of classically simple statement with Biblical poetry and rhythm, a gently flowing style that neither excited nor tired. At times it reminded one of *Tristram Shandy*, and indeed Mann confessed that in these volumes his manner of speech was influenced by "Sterne's wealth of humorous expressions and inventions, his genuine comical technique";[74] but "comical" is hardly the word for *Joseph*'s light and graceful strain.

I found that my habit of skipping, formed through years of hurried searching for specific items in scholastic treatises, would not do here; I learned to surrender myself, to move contentedly with the majestic leisurely stream. But I had to smile when, after 525 pages of Volume IV, the author remarked: "With amazement we note that this story nears its end. Who would have thought that it would ever be finished, or the well run dry? At some point the lips of the teller must close." However, he went on for eighty pages more. Nevertheless we may accept his own estimate: "The song of Joseph is good, solid work. . . . A measure of durability is, I think, inherent in it."[75] Our grandchildren will read it, and perhaps theirs too.

VI. THE NEW FAUST

In preparing the Joseph tetralogy Mann had again read Goethe's *Faust*, patiently wading through Part II as "this enormous mixture of magic opera and mankind's tragedy, of puppet show and cosmic poem."[76] He remembered the finale of *Faust* when he made Joseph forget himself and labor for his people. But he remembered, too, the beginning of *Faust*, for he felt that his own country had sold its soul to the Devil, and was sinking into a hell of punishment and despair. "Today," he said, in the spring of 1945, "the Devil is literally bearing away the soul of Germany."[77]

In 1943 he had begun to write not his best but his most powerful book. He called it *Doctor Faustus*, for it would again tell of a learned man surrendering himself to Satan in return for knowledge and power; but it would recount also, in ominous concurrence, the enslavement of Germany by a Hitler who appeared to Mann as the very embodiment of evil. "I knew what I was setting out to do, . . . to write nothing less than the novel of my era, disguised as the story of an artist's life, a terribly imperiled and sinful artist."[78] As he went on with this duplex task, and the news told of millions of Jews being murdered in Germany and Poland, it seemed to him that he was writing the book with his blood. "Like no other of my books, this one consumed and took a heavy toll of my innermost forces. . . . Never before has any work so agitated and moved me."[79] He pressed forward with the narrative as the war reached its end and Hitler's regime collapsed in a Wagnerian conflagration and *Götterdämmerung*. When he had written the final line he hesitated to offer the book to the public; it "contained too much of my life, too many of my secrets"; it put salt in too many wounds.[80] Of course no publisher in Germany would take it; it appeared in Stockholm in 1947 as *Doktor Faustus: Das Leben des deutschen Tonsetzers.* It recorded "the life of the German composer" and the death of an age.

The narrator is Serenus Zeitblom, Ph.D., university professor, Catholic liberal, and humane humanist; through him Mann sympathetically presents the virtues and weakness, the good intentions and political timidity, of the German middle class. Zeitblom begins on May 23, 1943 (the day on which Mann began the book), a biography of his tragic friend Adrian Leverkühn. As Zeitblom proceeds he is more and more disturbed, in his life and his writing, by the historic events crowding around him. In 1932 he welcomed the rise of Hitler as signifying the revival of German pride after the humiliating Treaty of Versailles; by 1943 he is disillusioned, and watches with consternation the evolution of National Socialism into a reactionary and militaristic dictatorship. Almost unwittingly he intersperses the political history of Germany from 1932 to 1945 wth his account of Leverkühn's career from 1885 to 1941. The two narratives develop side by side, like counterpoint in a massive and somber fugue. Gradually it dawns upon the reader that the two stories are one: the rise and fall of the half-mad composer symbolizes the rise and fall of National Socialist Germany. The double story doubles the power and effect of the tale.

Adrian Leverkühn resembles his biographer only in the place of their birth and in their schooling. He is almost all intellect, so that even his musical compositions become exercises in tonal mathematics. He keeps all his power for his art, leaving little for women or friends. His brilliant and ironic mind rejects all traditions, moorings, and social restraints. An old, stuttering organist teaches the youth the arcana of composition; his admiration shares in setting Adrian on a course of ever more complex contrapuntal experiments. At the University of Halle he takes courses in theology, and sheds his orthodox faith; Nietzsche is in the air, and infects Adrian's philosophy. But he sympathizes with some students who argue that though "the scientific superiority of liberal theology . . . is incontestable, . . . its theological position is weak, for its moralism and humanism lack insight into the demonic character of human existence. Cultured indeed it is, but shallow; of the true understanding of human nature, and the tragic nature of life, the conservative tradition has at bottom preserved much more."[81] We are prepared for the demonic elements in Leverkühn's music and Hitler's Germany.

The next step in Adrian's education is his encounter with prostitution and syphilis. A streetwalker accosts him; he repulses her; but the next night, moved by impulses of sex and curiosity stronger than his reason, he visits a brothel, is awarded a secretly coveted certificate of virility, and comes away with a spirochete in his blood. Year by year he moves toward mental and musical disturbance, while his sense of sin and infection intensifies his love of isolation. He sees men as all engaged in a desperate struggle between innate evil and moral good, between the Devil and God. Sometimes, he thinks, "God" and "the Devil" are two aspects of one demonic cosmic force.

He develops in his compositions a music abstract and formalistic, based on a twelve-tone scale, and so similar to that of Arnold Schoenberg that the author of the *Gurrelieder* insisted on being credited with originating the system. Mann had known Schoenberg in California, and admitted that he had "pumped him a great deal on music and the life of a composer"; in later editions of his novel he added to Chapter XXII a note "spelling out the intellectual property rights for the uninformed."[82] Mann had prepared himself for *Dr. Faustus* with as zealous a study of musical history and theory as he had prepared for *The Magic Mountain* with studies of medicine and psychology, and for *Joseph and His Brothers* with researches in anthropology, archaeology, and religion. His chief California mentor in music was Dr. Theodor Adorno, who lent Mann his manuscript *On the Philosophy of Modern Music*—which argued that Schoenberg's system would lead to chaos. (Was Leverkühn's music a satire of Schoenberg's?)

Mann seems to have felt that what Spengler called the "Faustian" element in European music since Mozart—its fascinated search for the formless infinite, its rejection of tradition, rules, and forms—reflected the modern individual's longing to escape from the restraints and obligations of communal life.[83] We note that even while Leverkühn experiments with a new scale of tones he aspires to return from the "harmonic subjectivity" of nineteenth-century music to "polyphonic objectivity" —from the individualistic music of the absorbed self to the choral music of a disciplined group. He longs for objectivity as the secret of health in art, but he feels himself condemned to failure by the sickness in his body and soul. Mann never forgets Goethe's admonition, "Classicism is health, romanticism is disease."[84]

At this point our author, inheriting the full German tradition in literature, goes back from Goethe's Faust, who sells his soul for youth, beauty, and power, to Johann Spiess's form of the legend (1587), wherein Faust surrenders himself to the Devil in return for twenty-four years of unhindered pursuit of knowledge.[85] In a secret manuscript, which Zeitblom inherits, Leverkühn tells how he saw the Devil in a fitful vision, and argued with him; it was, let us suppose, the diverse elements in his nature fighting for control of his life. Despite his somber subjectivity, he begs for the power to rise above the chaos in his soul, and to achieve objectivity, order, and truth in his work. The Devil laughs at him as a petty bourgeois scared of the law; objectivity, he assures Adrian, is impossible, and truth is an ever-receding mirage. On the contrary, he urges, your uncured syphilis is the source and nourishment of your genius; it spurs you to insights far profounder than reason, and to achievements forbidden to sobriety; yield to these inspirations, scorn limits and laws; yield to me—the magnificent, daring, lawless one—and I will give you supernatural powers of musical artistry. But, adds the Devil (or Adrian's ingrown spirit), you must surrender also the right to love any human being. Leverkühn binds himself to these terms, isolates himself with his piano and a peasant family, and composes *The Lamentation of Doctor Faustus*.

He suffers from the Devil's prohibition of love. He thinks to evade it by a homosexual liaison with Rudi Schwerdtfeger. However, a bevy of cultured and charming women appears in the nearest town; Adrian gets a passing sight of them, some scent of their fragrance, some melody of their form and grace. He resolves to defy the Devil, and sends Rudi to propose for him to Inez Rodde; he loses both, for Inez prefers Rudi. Leverkühn consoles himself with a handsome nephew who comes to live with him; he becomes inordinately fond of the young Adonis; the boy dies. The desolate composer buries himself in his work. Having completed the *Lamentation*, he invites Zeitblom and others to hear him play a piano transcription of the piece. He prefaces his performance with a rambling address evidencing insanity. Beginning to play, he falls unconscious to the floor. He is taken away, lingers for a time in a Nietzsche-like alternation of awareness and delusion, and dies.

Meanwhile, at every stage of the story, narrator Zeitblom has noted developments in the history of the Third Reich. More and more, as the novel progresses, the reader perceives that the ambitions, hubris, and collapse of Hitler's Germany are symbolized in the pride of the young composer, in his self-abandonment to evil, in his insanity and death. Leverkühn is for Mann the German people in the creative ecstasy of its music and in the derangement of its ethics by Nietzsche and of its politics by Hitler—a nation in a demonic secession from its humanist heritage and its European environment. Perhaps also he is the modern soul, which, having lost God and forgotten Christ, reverts to its animal past "beyond good and evil," and goes mad by cutting the moral roots of its social order and growth. Leverkühn himself speaks of "an age of destroyed conventions and the relaxing of all objective obligations—in search of a freedom that begins to lie like a mildew upon talent, and to betray traces of sterility."[86]

This strange book, like its predecessors, has many flaws, but it stands head and shoulders over most of the novels of our time. It is overdone: prolix in speech, spreading out the author's musical erudition, filling pages with experiments in early German, ruining the Devil's reputation for brilliance by assigning to him tedious harangues, and making Zeitblom—i.e., Mann—comment with immoderate pessimism on the situation of Germany in 1944 as if it were a lasting and irremediable insanity. "It is all up with Germany. . . . She is marked down for collapse economic, political, moral, spiritual, . . . unparalleled final collapse. . . . I wish for it [that collapse] today, and will welcome it, out of hatred for the outrageous contempt of reason, the vicious violation of the truth, the cheap, filthy, backstairs mythology, the criminal degradation and confusion of standards, the abuse, corruption, and blackmail of all that was good, genuine, trusting and trustworthy in our old Germany."[87] The Germans, struggling a year later to rise out of shame and ruin, found it hard to forgive these despairing words of a man who had forgotten the perspectives of history in the depths of his suffering.

VII. THE AUTHOR

It was by exception that Mann made his novels deal with so ordinary and transitory a phenomenon as an administration or a war. In his *Reflections*, in *Mario*, and in *Faustus* he left his study for the battlefield, but by preference he dealt leisurely with the more lasting issues of psychology, religion, and philosophy. He was most happy when, secluded in his study, he could absorb himself in what he called "the beautiful feast of narration and re-creation."[88]

He had a high opinion of his trade—"Great is the writer's art"[89]—but as a technician rather than as a preacher. "The writer," he said whimsically, "is a man who finds writing more difficult than other people";[90] but he enjoyed the difficulty, and regularly begot leviathans. He always meant to be brief, but the minuteness of his perceptions, the retentiveness of his logical mind, multiplied each experience into thought, and each event into a problem in philosophy. "The glance which one casts as an artist on external and internal things is different from the one with which one regards them as a human being: it is colder and at the same time more passionate; . . . your demon forces you to 'observe,' to perceive in a flash, with painful malice, every detail which is characteristic in a literary sense, has typical significance, opens perspective, marks distinctively the racial, social, or psychological element."[91] Partly through these keen observations of personalities and situations, he was able to visualize localities (like the family, flowers, and pigs of Adrian's childhood home), and to project himself into characters so diverse as Tonio Kröger, Mario, Zeitblom, and Felix Krull.

He was proud and careful of his style. "Here [in *Tonio Kröger*], perhaps for the first time, I learned to use music to mold my style and form,"[92] to give nuances to his words, cadence to his sentences, thematic unity to his paragraphs, structure to his plots. He followed Wagner in using leitmotivs—some characteristic habit, garment, or word—to signalize and identify the persons of his tale; so Madame Chauchat always let the door slam behind her, and Settembrini's checked trousers proclaimed his coming. And Mann, as we have noted, liked to make an event or a character serve as a symbol of some larger significance. Such adornments sometimes shared with the length of his sentences and the profusion of his ideas in confusing his style. He tells us that he read *Salaambô* again before beginning *Joseph and His Brothers*,[93] but it is hard for a German to achieve the clarity of a Frenchman; he knows and says too much.

Mann's style was made still more complex by its recurrent irony. Since he usually saw many sides to a situation or a character, he often added a surprising tag to his descriptions—as when he remarked how Tony Buddenbrook's burst of tears over her brother's corpse "refreshed" her.[94] "Irony," he said, "is the pathos of the middle";[95] it is the refusal to see only one side. Originally it may have grown out of his patrician background, which viewed human affairs with a condescending smile; it may have taken occasionally a bitter or satiric tang from his early addiction to Schopenhauer and Nietzsche; but more basically it was the philosopher's resolve to seek impartiality, objectivity, and perspective; to check sentiment with intellect and yet to distrust intellect as too ready to remain on the surface of things. He accepted Nietzsche's advice to take life as a dramatic or aesthetic spectacle, and he responded with a grim smile to "life's little ironies." "Lightness, . . . the artful jest—that is God's very best gift to man. . . . God gave it to humanity that life's terribly serious face might be forced to wear a smile."[96] As he grew older he softened his irony with sympathy, and disarmed it with humor. His children assure us that he was ever ready to join in their laughter.

He began as an artist and he ended as a philosopher. He was at first a Tony Kröger feeling the isolation of art from the problems of political or economic life; in his maturity he accepted a passionate involvement in national and international affairs. He gave his youth to Nietzsche and Schopenhauer, and his declining years to the re-creation of God. In his *Reflections* he rejected the French Enlightenment as a dangerous idolatry of a reason too ready to sell its services to the will (i.e., to the algebraic sum of desires); see what this had come to in the France of 1792! But when he saw what the triumph of the "will to power" had come to in the Germany of 1939 he moved away from Schopenhauer's voluntarism, and longed for an enlightenment of the nations by a reasonable humanism checking collective egos with conscience and intelligence. When he saw his country recklessly adopting a new ethic "beyond good and evil," of "a good war [that] halloweth any cause," he repudiated the Nietzschean philosophy of power as "degenerating into a maenadic rage against truth, morality, religion, humaneness, and everything that might serve to tame the savage in us."[97]

Man, as Mann saw him, was a compound of savage and saint, of nature and spirit (*Natur und Geist*). All reality, he thought, has these two faces, both of them expressing soul—the principle of life. The goal of religion is to subdue nature by spirit; the goal of philosophy is to reconcile and unite nature and spirit; the goal of art is to spiritualize nature through aesthetic representation. Mann hesitated between a Goethean acceptance and enjoyment of nature and the senses and a Dostoevskian struggle to overcome sensuality by a religious defiance of the animal in man. In his later years he inclined to Dostoevski, acknowledged the reality and power of evil and sin, and wandered in a maze of myths seeking God.

In the Joseph novels he talked so long and ambiguously about God, sin, grace, redemption, and death that an unsympathetic reader might apply to him Madame Chauchat's description of Castorp as *"un joli bourgeois à la petite tache humide"*[98]—"a pretty bourgeois with a little touch of moisture" in his brain. But he was reluctant to abandon the idea of divinity. At times he thought of God in vaguely pantheistic terms: God is the being (or reality) of all beings, the final union of all elemental opposites—of nature and spirit, body and mind, evil and good, darkness and light. Or he presented God as the totality of spirit, or as the leader or goal of man's struggle to transform nature into spirit and sin into unselfishness. Finally, he saw God as a human conception of a cosmic power and law being slowly transformed by man's spiritual and moral growth into the picture of a just judge, then of a loving and forgiving father. "God too is subject to development. He too changes and advances from the desert-like and demoniacal to the spiritual and holy; and He can no more do so without the help of the human spirit than the human spirit can do without Him."[99] Mann teases us on this as on every other question. "I dare not say that I believe in God. And even if I did it would be a long time, I think, before I would say so."[100] At last he followed Schweitzer's lead, and defined religion as "reverence —primarily for the mystery that man is, . . . for the difficulty and nobility of being a man"[101]—which does not sound convincing in these bloody days.

Despite his Protestant heritage, Mann by 1945 had come to look upon the Catholic Church as a bulwark of social order, moral discipline, and mental stability, and upon the Reformation as a gigantic mistake. "Its results for Germany," he wrote, "were the Thirty Years' War, which depopulated the country, caused a cultural retrogression, and probably, through its immorality and pestilences, made something different and worse of German blood than it was, perhaps, in the Middle Ages."[102] Like so many non-Catholic scholars, he preferred Erasmus to Luther; he kept a picture of Erasmus over his desk.[103] He agreed with Max Weber in affiliating capitalism with Protestantism.[104] He chose a Catholic, Zeitblom, as the narrator in *Doctor Faustus*, and made him say:

> I see in the Church, even as she is today, secularized and reduced to the bourgeois, a citadel of order, an institution for objective disciplining, canalizing, banking up of the religious life, which, without her, would fall victim to subjectivism and demoralization, to a chaos of divine and demonic powers, to a world of fantastic uncanniness, an ocean of demonry. To separate Church and religion means to give up separating religions from madness.[105]

We might have expected an author with such respect for religion to have little sympathy with a Communist Russia which was condemning religion as an antirevolutionary sedative for the poor. In *Reflections* and the essay on "Goethe and Tolstoi" (1922) he opposed the Russian Revolution as a relapse from Western civilization to Asiatic Slavophil policies, and he deplored the Bolshevik suppression of the individual by a totalitarian government.[106] Yet in *The Magic Mountain* (1924) he made both Settembrini and Naphta—the rival tutors in this "story of an education"—advocate some form of Communism; and Naphta approved the terror methods of the Soviets as the only means of preserving the Revolution. In the essay on Schopenhauer (1938) Mann returned to hostility: "We know the inhuman horrors of a doctrine by which it would be the destiny of a man to be consumed in the state; know it from its consequences, for fascism as well as communism came from Hegel."[107] When Hitler's army invaded Russia (1941) Mann hoped for a Russian victory, and renewed his sympathy for Communism as a possible answer to poverty. In 1945 he refused to condemn Russia's occupation of eastern Germany.[108] A radical critic, Georg Lukácz, appealed to him to throw in his lot with the Communist movement; Mann refused to commit himself; but in *Doctor Faustus* he made the Catholic narrator say, "The dictatorship of the proletariat begins to seem to me, a German burgher, an ideal situation compared with the now possible one of a dictatorship by the scum of the earth."[109] In 1952 some American conservatives expressed their suspicion of Mann as a secret Communist; he retorted that the suspicion "would wrong me—or, if you like, do me too much honor."[110] The land of his adoption became almost as uncomfortable as the land of his birth.

VIII. GOING HOME

Toward the end of *Doctor Faustus* Mann, through Zeitblom, wondered whether he would ever be allowed to reenter Germany; whether the Germans would ever forgive "my having fled in horror from my country's guilt."[111] A dozen critics in Germany had called him a deserter, a Communist, a nihilist, or an atheist. He was consoled by the general agreement, outside of Germany, that he had fought a good fight, that he had risked much grief and calumny to stand up against Hitler, and that he was the greatest living author. On June 25, 1945, hundreds of Americans prominent in literature or public affairs gathered in Chicago to celebrate his completion of seventy years (on June 6), and to present him a substantial purse for any use he chose. On May 11, 1947, he sailed with his family on the *Queen Elizabeth*.

Knowing that he would be unsafe in Germany, he took up residence at Kilchberg, near Zurich. His daughter Erika was now famous as actress and author. His son Klaus Heinrich, soldier and author, darkened his father's last years by dying in 1949 at the age of forty-three. In that year Mann further offended the West Germans by going to Weimar, in East Germany, to receive an award from the Communist powers. He lectured in both sections of his divided fatherland, insisting that everything should be done to reunite the severed halves. Accusations of Communism were multiplied.

His pen was his constant refuge. In 1947 he assembled *Essays of Three Decades*. In 1951 he published a minor novel, *Der Erwählte* ("The Chosen"), which in English became *The Holy Sinner;* it was a study of sin as a road to insight and genius; it echoed Freud, and Luther's *pecca fortiter*—"sin powerfully." Then, leaving no topic unturned, he took up a fragment which he had written in 1911, and expanded it into a book which alarmed some of his readers: *Bekenntnisse des Hochstaplers* [*Confessions of the Swindler*] *Felix Krull* (1954). Here Mann imagined himself into the character of a confidence man, expounded such a man's tricks and views, and gave him not a hanging but a suspended sentence. He had some sympathy for Felix as one of those "men who feel not so much with pride but with acquiescence, that fate has something special for them. This feeling creates around them an atmosphere or emanation of coolness, which, almost to their own regret, foils and repels all honest efforts of friendliness and companionship."[112] He may have been thinking of himself when he made Krull speak of "my natural inclination to taciturnity and reserve, my insistence upon privacy and separateness, . . . which I consider one of the basic elements of my character."[113] Or again: "I am a conservative by nature," says Krull, "and have always had an unforced affection for traditional procedures in preference to the vulgarities of progress."[114] Felix turns out to be quite likable, even lovable, as Madame Houpflé found. Mann's pages about that nymphomaniac, and about Lord Strathbogie, reveal his humor still rich after eighty years of reality, and his sexual interest as keen as ever (e.g., page 176). He must have had pleasure in writing this book, but death surprised him at page 384— when he was just getting into his stride.

In his final year, as lovingly described by his daughter,[115] he had many consolations. In May, 1955, Lübeck honored its native son with ceremonies that brought together the leading dignitaries of the seven-hundred-year-old city. On June 6 his family and friends celebrated his eightieth birthday. In July he and Katja, after their golden-wedding festivities, went to the Netherlands for a seaside vacation, but Thomas' phlebitis became so painful that they returned to Zurich. There, on August 12, 1955, he died of a heart attack.

I have found more meat in him than in any other writer of my time (i.e., those whose peak came near or after 1920). Joyce was a brilliant satirist, a clever alienist studying the inanities of Dublin's nonentities, but he shrugged his shoulders at the philosophical and political problems that surrounded him. Proust was subtle, but he could never get out of his ingrown ego long enough to see humanity. Gide wrote beautifully, but he too was immured in himself, always fretting about his sexual inversion or the public reception of his books. Beside these men our American novelists, I believe, must take a lower rank; O'Neill, however, dug as deeply as Mann in our frantic search for a lost God. None of all these searchers pretended to have solved the puzzles about deity, or the meaning of life, or the elimination of war, injustice, or poverty. Mann suffered nights of the "honorable sleeplessness" that Chekhov had described in *A Doctor's Visit*—the insomnia of a restless mind seeking answers to unanswerable questions. He had to comfort himself with another story by Chekhov, *A Tedious Tale*, in which Katya, an actress stranded on the shores of time, asks an old sage, "What shall I do? Just one word, Nikolai Stepanich; I implore you, what shall I do?" To which Nikolai answers, "I don't know. Upon my honor and conscience, Katya, I don't know."[116] And Thomas Mann, perhaps speaking to his own Katja, begged forgiveness for not knowing, for having begun with so many answers and ending with none. "Nevertheless one goes on working, telling stories, giving form to truth, hoping darkly, sometimes almost confidently, that truth and serene form will avail to set free the human spirit, and prepare mankind for a better, lovelier, and worthier life."[117]

CHAPTER XV

Franz Kafka

I. CHAMBER OF HORRORS

FIRST, let us suffer Kafka's principal writings, taking them at their face value as stories. Second, we look at his life, character, ailments, and loves. Third, we try to interpret the stories in the light of the life. Fourth, obituary. It is unpleasant to end so many of these essays with a funeral, but death is so unavoidable a conclusion! ✓

Kafka's stories are quite intelligible as stories; they are simple and clear in plot and style; a child can follow them; but through that apparently transparent front the author has expressed or concealed his philosophy. "The Judgment" (1913) is an eighteen-page account of how Georg, cursed by his father for trying to replace him as head of the family firm, drowns himself after crying out, "Dear parents, I have always loved you."[1] *The Penal Colony* (written in 1914, published in 1920) is a tale of horror recalling Poe's "The Pit and the Pendulum." An insane commandant carefully and proudly sets up a complicated mechanism whose swinging blade cuts deeper and deeper slices from a pinioned convict according to the enormity of his crime. The operation of this machine is so morbidly fascinating that "it was impossible to grant all the requests to be allowed to watch it from nearby. The commandant in his wisdom ordained that children should have the preference."[2]

The Metamorphosis (1915)—seventy-two pages—is the macabre tale of Gregor Samsa, commercial traveler, who is turned overnight into a gigantic insect. Gregor has been a hard worker, the chief support of his parents and sister, but he has secretly aspired to replace his father as the head and lawgiver of the family. His suffering is multiplied by his retention of his human mind, feelings, and memories. Lying on his hard carapace back, convulsively wiggling his many legs, he recalls the monotony of his former life, and broods over the disgrace of his present state. His parents are horrified by hearing this insect talk like their son; disgusted and fearful, they lock him in his room, and seldom look in upon him. His sister Greta pities him, daily brings him food, cleans his waste, and pushes Gregor's old armchair up to the window so that her transmigrated brother may climb upon it and look at the passers-by—as Gregor was wont to do. But she cannot bear the sight or odor of him, and he, perceiving this, crawls under a sofa when she comes in. To support the family the mother takes in boarders, and the father, formerly retired, goes unwillingly back to work. Greta too takes a job, and comes home so tired that she becomes negligent in feeding Gregor or cleaning his room. He grows thin and weak. One day the door is carelessly left open, and he creeps out, to the dismay of the boarders; they leave; the father throws some apples at Gregor; one hits and cripples him. Worse yet is the pain he feels when he hears his sister say, "We must get rid of him." He loses all will to live; he refuses food and drink, grows thin and weak. "Soon he made the discovery that he was now unable to stir a limb. . . . His head sank to the floor of its own accord, and from his nostrils came the last flicker of his breath." He dies, and a charwoman throws his corpse into the garbage can. "Thanks be to God," says his father.

The Trial tells of a bank official named "Joseph K," who is suddenly summoned before a tribunal on an unstated charge. He asks what crime he has committed; he is not told, but is advised to confess as the best way of clearing the case and paying the penalty. He is allowed to return to his apartment. Soon he is called again, makes the same plea, receives the same answer and advice, and is freed under custody. His acquaintances, then his friends, look upon him with suspicion, and convict him in their minds. He himself begins to feel a general sense of guilt, though he is not clear as to the nature of his offense. Called back to the court, he is pronounced guilty, with still no specification of his crime; he is led away, and is stabbed to death by the officials. — It reads like the report of a "purge" trial under Stalin, but it was written in 1914, three years before the Russian Revolution, and was published in 1925, only a year after Stalin's accession to power.

The Castle (written in 1921–22, published in 1930) is the story of "K," who is sent to survey the property of an unnamed lord living in a hillside citadel which dominates the village in view and in law. K proposes to call upon the seigneur and to present his credentials, but he is denied entry for reasons not intelligibly stated. He tries to make friends of the villagers, but they distrust him as an alien, and make life unpleasant for him. To the end of the story he keeps on seeking access to the castle and its lord; to the end he fails. That is all.

The unique quality of these books is the clear, precise, matter-of-fact style in which the most improbable events are reported, with minutely observed details that give apparent reality to bizarre imaginations. Kafka told Milena Jesenská that "in bed one gets, instead of sleep, the best ideas";[3] but many of his visions are like nightmares experienced with open eyes. He notes in his diary: "My talent for portraying my dream-like inner life has thrust all other matters into the background."[4] Not since Swift has any European writer achieved such verisimilitude in describing the unreal; seldom has the subjective been presented with such deceptive objectivity. Sometimes, as we read, we fear that the author is nearing insanity; yet he speaks with a calm restraint hardly characteristic of madmen. Kafka is just the opposite of Proust: he expresses no feelings, and relates without comment the strange incidents that he has dreamed or seen. We suspect in that calm an almost malicious irony, which presents the macabre as the common quality of human life. Perhaps these stories were self-mutilations or self-purgations, a catharsis through expression. Hence, it may be, their tantalizing inconclusiveness. Despite all urgings by his publishers, Kafka never completed any of his three novels; once he had washed himself with words he had no further interest in the tale. Besides, life was so often like that, leaving everything unfinished, except life.

II. THE KAFKA CHRONICLE

Obviously these stories meant something more than they told. It was as if the author laid them before us with a proviso and an invitation: "If you wish to understand these books you must understand me; you must enter into my life, character, sufferings, and dreams." So we knock at his door.

We find him difficult of access, reticent in speech, absorbed in his interior life as if in solitary confinement. Yet he lived his first thirty-two years (1883–1915) with his parents and three sisters, in a house in the Jewish quarter of Prague. "In Hebrew my name is Amschel."[5] There were many pious scholars in his ancestry, some of them given to eccentric dreams. His father was a wholesale clothing merchant, with a warehouse and shop in Old Town Square; a tall, strong, stern, practical man, just the person to frighten and alienate his timid, brooding son. Franz was a weak and delicate child; a precocious and willful boy, who resented school and synagogue as a punishment and a bore. In school the language of instruction was not Czech but German, for Prague was

the capital of the Kingdom of Bohemia, which, till 1918, was part of
the Austro-Hungarian Empire. Hence Kafka wrote his books in
German.

Later he reproached his parents and teachers as having "done me
great harm; . . . [they] tried to make another person out of me than
the one I became."⁶ In 1919 he wrote a "Letter to My Father," which
he did not send, but turned over to Max Brod; it accused the father of
trying to break the will of the boy. "In your presence . . . I began to
stammer and stutter, . . . I could neither think nor speak in front of
you."⁷ His dislike of his father was hardly an "Oedipus complex," for
he resented his mother too, since she sided with her husband in disputes
with the son. They expected him to go to work in the warehouse, and
to prepare himself to take over the business on his father's retirement;
he refused, and they charged him with unwillingness to work.

Reluctantly he studied law. In 1906 he received a degree. After two
years of indecision he took a post as clerk in a Workmen's Accident
Insurance Association. He performed his duties there reasonably well;
his superiors liked him and allowed him frequent absences; he worked
only till 2 P.M. daily, and was thereafter free for his favorite occupa-
tions—reading and writing. His parents objected to this apparent idleness; they urged him to spend part of each weekday in the warehouse;
and when the father fell ill (1912) Franz consented to serve, in the
afternoons, as assistant superintendent. But he was unhappy there; he
had no love for business, nor any competence in management; and he
could not bear the sight of the "dirty, untidy, disheveled" and underpaid girls who operated the machines.⁸ His ambition to be a writer
seemed doomed by his double task. In 1915 he rebelled, left the warehouse and the paternal home, and took a room where he could enjoy,
despite the noise of the city, the privacy that for so many years he had
longed for. Now, after his morning's work, he could write.

He did not think of writing as a means of livelihood; rather, he called
it "a form of prayer,"⁹ for it gave him precious interludes of exaltation
amid his normal moods of melancholy diffidence. He recorded "the
feeling of happiness which . . . I have within me from time to time, . . .
and that persuades me of the existence of abilities of whose nonexistence
I can convince myself with complete certainty at any moment."¹⁰ Sometimes, borne on the afflatus of his words, he wrote till long after midnight; so "I wrote 'The Judgment' at one sitting during the night of
the 22nd–23rd [of September, 1912] from 10 P.M. to 6 A.M. I was
hardly able to pull my legs out from under the desk, they had got so

stiff from sitting. The fearful strain and joy."[11] It was his writing, more than his office work, that exhausted him.

He was not quite a recluse. He had several acquaintances who became as famous as himself: Martin Buber, Rainer Maria Rilke, Franz Werfel, Hugo von Hofmannsthal; and so soon as 1902 he began a lifelong friendship with the novelist and poet Max Brod. One or more of these stimulating men met with Kafka in cafés; and though they described him as often silent and brooding, they persuaded him to take an interest in sports, in social movements, in the Yiddish theater, finally in Zionism. He took several trips abroad, usually with Brod. But he had no genius for friendship, or too much genius to leave room for friendship. "A friendship without disruption of one's daily life is unthinkable."[12] On December 18, 1911, he wrote in his diary: "I hate Werfel. . . . He is healthy, young, and rich, everything that I am not. Besides [he is] gifted with a sense of music . . . I am entirely shut off from music."[13] Even "dear Max" palled on him at times; on November 24, 1913, he confided to his diary: "Max is becoming more and more a stranger; he has often been one to me; now I am becoming one to him too."[14]

Brod was patient with him. He described Kafka as "extremely gentle and tolerant, rarely angry"; he recorded also his black hair, sharp features, intent and penetrating eyes. Gustav Janouch, a youthful devotee of Kafka, assures us that his "voice was . . . wonderfully melodious . . . Gesture, look, all radiated the peace of understanding and goodness."[15] When circumstances permitted, Franz lived on a vegetarian diet,[16] avoided alcoholic drinks,[17] and was "a fresh-air and nature enthusiast."[18] Brod adds that he was "a good horseman, swimmer, and oarsman."[19] However, he was weak in heart, stomach, and lungs; in 1917 he developed tuberculosis.

His ailments, his alienation from his parents and sisters, and his daily encounter with proletarian misery at the Workmen's Accident Insurance Association, shared in turning him more and more into a recluse brooding over the shortcomings of the world and his own. He felt a sense of guilt in relation to his father,[20] and saw much truth in his father's scorn of his weakness and vacillation. "I am a quite impossible bird," he told Janouch; "I am a jackdaw—a kavka, . . . a thief." When Janouch asked him, "Are you lonely?" he answered, "As lonely as Franz Kafka."[21] Now and then, in his diary, he bade himself, "Don't despair . . . Just when everything seems over with, new forces come marching up, and precisely that means that you are alive."[22] However, under the same date is a more characteristic entry: "Miserable creature that I am! . . . Nothing, nothing, nothing. Weakness, self-destruction, tip of a flame of hell piercing the floor."[23] "Thus I waver, continually fly to the summit of the mountain, but then fall back in a moment. . . . It is not death, alas, but the eternal torments of dying."[24] He submitted himself to psychoanalysis, with no perceivable benefit.[25] He read much of Strindberg, Dostoevski, and Pascal, eagerly adding to his gloom.

He longed for and feared the other sex. He assured himself that "though I am . . . rather short and a little stout, I still please many, even girls. . . . Only recently one of them said something very intelligent: 'Ah, if I could only see you naked once, then you ought to be really pretty and kissable.' "[26] "I intentionally walk through the streets where there are whores . . . One woman probably knows me by now. I met her this afternoon . . . We looked at each other fleetingly. . . . Then I really ran away."[27] He did not trust himself with women; it was easier to imagine them than to manage them. "Women are snares, which lie in wait for men on all sides in order to drag them into the merely finite."[28] Then, in brief bravado: "They lose their danger if one voluntarily falls into one of their snares."[29] He longed for the solicitous companionship of a woman. "It seems so dreadful to be a bachelor, . . . never being able to run upstairs beside one's wife; to lie ill and have only the solace of the view from one's window."[30] In the "Letter to My Father" he confessed his secret ideal: "To get married, to found a family, to accept all the children that arrive, to maintain them in this uncertain world, and even to lead them a little on their way, is, in my opinion, the utmost that a man can ever succeed in doing."[31]

So, in 1912, began his five years of courting and fleeing from "Felice." She lived in Berlin, but Kafka met her at Max Brod's home when she was visiting Prague. He was moved not so much by her beauty as by her essential femininity, a softness of contours in body and mind; here was a girl who might be a good wife and a good mother, and give him manhood and a home. After her return to Berlin he began a long correspondence with her. In the years of his love for her his creative imagination and literary power reached their height. But even then his imagination was abnormal, and his fear wilted his will. He drew up in his diary (July 20, 1913) a "summary of the arguments for and against marriage." He hesitated to abandon his privacy. "I must be alone a great deal. All that I have accomplished is the result of being alone. . . . Single, I might perhaps one day really give up my job. Married, it would never be possible."[32] Brod detected in him "a certain temporary mistrust of his sexual capacity."[33] Kafka's diary for August

14, 1913, described "coitus as punishment for the happiness of being together," and he counseled himself: "Live as ascetically as possible, more ascetically than a bachelor—that is the only possible way for me to endure marriage." On August 15: "Agonies in bed toward morning. Saw only solution in jumping out of the window."[34]

His mother urged him to marry. "I said she didn't understand me. . . . 'Well, then, nobody understands you,' said Mother; 'I suppose I also am a stranger to you, and so is your father.' 'Certainly, you are all strangers to me; it is only blood that connects us.' "[35] Kafka withdrew into himself. "I shall shut myself up from everything until I have lost all recollections. I shall set myself at enmity with everybody, speak to nobody."[36] On August 17, 1913, he proposed marriage to Felice. A month later he confided to Brod, "The very idea of a honeymoon fills me with horror." Nevertheless he went to Berlin, and allowed the engagement to be made official; "I was bound like a criminal."[37] From Prague he wrote to Felice's father (September 21, 1913) that he was too near to collapse to enter upon marriage. "Nervous states of the worst sort control me without pause. . . . Everything that is not literature bores me and I hate it. . . . I lack all aptitude for family life."

But the longing for Felice, for woman, remained, and so revived in the warmth of spring that Kafka renewed the engagement. He dreamed of going to live in Berlin and to support his prospective marriage by his pen.[38] His parents must have kept some love for him, for they found "a beautiful apartment for F. and me" in Prague. During this revived betrothal Felice took long train trips to spend a day with him at various resorts; after being alone for two hours with him in a room at Bodenbach she remarked, "How well-behaved we've been!" Another break followed, then another renewal; he engaged a flat and bought some furniture (1917). But in August he began to cough up blood. "He heralded his tuberculosis," Brod tells us, ". . . as a way out . . . from the marriage he had been planning."[39] In December he went to a sanitarium at Zürau; when he returned to Prague he told Felice that he was in no condition to marry. She found another suitor.

In 1919 Kafka courted a Prague girl known to us only as "J. W." Twice he was engaged to her, twice he withdrew, despite her pleas and the threats of her relatives. While still engaged he began (1920) a liaison, chiefly epistolary, with Milena Jesenská, who lived in Vienna in an unhappy marriage. She was Gentile and twenty-four, Kafka was Jewish and thirty-eight. He was first drawn to her by articles that she had published in a Prague newspaper. She undertook to translate some of his stories into Czech. In 1920 he visited her at Merano in Italy.

When he returned to his bachelor quarters he could hardly think of anything but her; in his imagination he knelt before her and caressed her feet; he pictured her as "a woman whom one carries in one's arms out of the world, out of the fire, . . . and she presses herself willingly and trustingly into your arms . . ."[40] In June he braved several laws by going to Vienna and spending four days in secret love with Milena. Back in Prague, he wrote to her of his sweet memories: "You are lying on the wretched bed in a deep slumber for an excellent reason, and you're slowly and unconsciously turning over from right to left toward my mouth."[41] A week later his Prague fiancée begged him to make up his mind about marrying her. He put her off, and went again to Vienna to spend some hurried hours with Milena. He dreamed "what an easy life it will be when we are together." She shattered this vision by saying that her husband had become spiritually dependent upon her, and that she loved him too much to leave him; meanwhile she asked Kafka had he been faithful to her.[42] Money tarnished their idyl: Milena entrusted him with a transaction concerning some property that she owned in Prague; he did his diffident best, but she accused him of bungling and sent him such "lashing" letters[43] that he begged Brod to prevent Milena from ever seeing him again.[44] She died in a German concentration camp in 1944.[45]

III. INTERPRETATION

The letters to Milena reveal a mind scattered, fear-ridden, and sometimes childish: recounting dreams, fussing about trivialities, arguing, complaining, too distrustful to greet the world with open arms and heart; a man born to write books, commanded to sell clothing, and breaking in two between the hostile drives.

Max Brod had hailed him as a brilliant author as early as 1907, six years before Kafka had published anything; finally he equated him with Thomas Mann. It was Brod who ushered him into print by persuading a Leipzig firm to publish a slim volume, *Contemplations* (1913), which celebrated the absurdity of human life. Later in that year Kafka issued "The Stoker," which won him a prize named after the German author Theodor Fontane. He used this story as the first chapter in an unfinished novel, *Amerika*, which he described as "nothing but an imitation of Dickens."[46] It told of a German youth who, resenting Europe, emigrated to America, picked up jobs and mistresses on his way, and settled in Oklahoma; perhaps it represented Kafka's longing to escape a feudal monarchy, a domineering father, and an unsympathetic family. I have not read the book, but I gather that it is uncharacteristically cheerful.

Most of the Kafka stories are so simple that they invite inquiry into their hidden significance. Kafka led the way by identifying the Georg of "The Judgment" with himself, and Georg's fianceé with Felice; obviously the irate father is Kafka *père*. Georg goes to pieces because he worries over marriage, and feels guilt for having thought of killing his father; when, oppressed by the parental curse, he commits suicide, he is acting on an idea that must more than once have entered the author's head. So Kafka remembered Mitya Karamazov, and tried to exorcise his devil with a bowl of ink.

"The Country Doctor" describes in nine pages the maltreatment of a conscientious physician by his superstitious, intolerant, malicious village patients; here Kafka seems to reject democracy as persistently stultified by the fertility of ignorance. *The Burrow* pictures a frightened animal digging a long and tortuous tunnel in which to hide itself from the noises and dangers of the world. "The most beautiful thing about my burrow is the stillness";[47] we can see Kafka fleeing from marriage and wincing under the turmoil of a metropolis. After seventy pages the story suddenly breaks off, as if some gigantic superterranean beast had stepped upon the tunnel and illustrated the diverse ingenuity of death. In the "Letter to My Father" Kafka reported his parent as calling him "vermin";[48] in his diary he mourned, "I can only crawl on, no better than some sort of vermin," and complained that he was leading "a dog's life";[49] in *The Investigations of a Dog* he tried, not quite convincingly, to imagine himself a dog.

In *The Metamorphosis*, with painstaking verisimilitude, he portrayed himself as transformed into an insect, dowered, however, with human understanding and sensitivity. His term for this creature was *Ungeziefer*, which my German dictionary describes as "a monstrous oversized vermin, with a hard back and many little legs." Obviously the word "vermin" had burned Kafka's memory. He seems to have felt some justice in his father's rejection of him for refusing to carry on the family's economic enterprise; in his debased form he mourns that he can no longer support the family and let his father retire. But the curses of his father are too bitter to bear; they are the missile that breaks his back. Nor can he forget how his sister's tenderness has turned into revulsion and condemnation. When the insect dies it is Gregor and Kafka longing for the balm and absolution of death. We are told that sometimes, immersed in writing, the author experienced a liberating ecstasy;[50] was it a sense of having exorcised his devil into paper and ink, or a revengeful indictment of his family, or the consciousness that he had achieved a cameo of almost perfect art?

The neurotic contemplation of punishment continued in *The Penal Colony.* The accused man is caught in a baffling maze of bureaucratic red tape, in a world that has lost divine justice and moral significance. He is not told the nature of his offense, and he can judge its enormity only by the degree of torture to which he is subjected. Here Kafka unknowingly forecast the Nazi concentration camps—in one of which (Auschwitz) his three sisters were fated to die.

The same obscurity as to the nature of the crime, the same vague sense of guilt, befog *The Trial.* In the year (1914) in which Kafka began this major work he wrote in his diary: "There is no doubt I am hemmed in all around."[51] He suffered the isolation of a Jew in a Christian community. Society in general weighed upon him with its dogmas, taboos, prejudices, and laws; the mass of humanity pressed upon him like an impersonal, merciless enemy; for him, in Sartre's words, hell was "other people." He shrank in revulsion from the scene of Europe in 1914: official tyranny, blind obedience, venal journalism, imminent all-embracing war. In *The Trial* Joseph K, described as "an important functionary in a bank," is summoned to appear before a court manned by poor people in a city slum. He is a symbol of man as the anxious, wandering victim of some unintelligible and unappeasable power holding the sword of judgment over him for committed or contemplated crimes. Kafka himself felt guilty: of secret sexual actions, of disappointing his parents, of keeping fiancées in an agonizing suspense of engagements and withdrawals, of escaping into isolation from the problems and responsibilities of life. In the "Letter to My Father" (composed in 1916, shortly after beginning *The Trial*) he said: "My writings were about you; in them I poured out the lamentations I could not pour out upon your breast." In any case this book is the most powerful of Kafka's productions. "The anguish that it gives off," said Gide, "is at moments almost unbearable, for how can one fail to repeat to oneself constantly: 'That haunted creature is I'?"[52] This brooding anxiety over a conscious but indefinable guilt has led the existentialists to claim Kafka as one of their own.

And now what is the castle that gave its name to Kafka's final fantasy? Who is the man who comes to the castle to survey the seigneur's lands? The Joseph K of *The Trial* has here become merely K; the survival of the initial suggests that the author had himself in mind, as well as man in general. According to Brod, the novel "seems to have been

begun as a story in the first person," but Kafka later changed the "I" to
"K."[53] One of K's assistants tells him, "You have no sense of humor";[54]
this seems true of Kafka himself, whose humor was rather a bitter and
ironic perception of life's absurdities than a sympathetic amusement
over life's incongruities.

K is to survey the land: is this a symbol of the quest for truth? The
villagers refuse to accept him: was Kafka thinking of the Jew as
"despised and rejected, a man of sorrows and acquainted with grief"—
or is the seeker after truth always suspected by the people? The castle
is manned by secretive officials, and is barricaded with formalities: is it
a memory of Austrian feudal rule, recently ended? Or is the castle a
symbol of paternal and social acceptance, longed for and long denied?
Does the seigneur represent an elusive God? But his officials are
riotous rascals with no trace of justice, mercy, charity, majesty, or love;
if their master is God he is a deity without morals, the embodiment of a
somber cosmic mystery. Did Kafka have all his frustrated quests in mind
when he thought of that unattained castle—his parents' love, a happy
marriage, Jewish and Christian equality, a solution to the puzzles of
philosophy and theology?

In his solitude he drove himself almost insane over questions that
theologians had formerly answered with such homicidal certainty. He
had lost religion,[55] and now the godless universe seemed a cold confusion
of irrationality and absurdity; here Kafka joined mood with the existentialists, felt all their spiritual homelessness and insecurity, their
anxiety and guilt. Why was there so much injustice and cruelty in the
world, and no visible lessening of them in history?

He was a skeptic of history as well as of theology. He doubted progress.[56] He pitied the hardships of peasants and proletaires, but he put
little trust in solving such problems by political revolution or reform.[57]
Janouch asked: "You don't believe in a wide expansion of the Russian
Revolution?" Kafka answered: "As a flow spreads wider and wider
the water becomes shallower and dirtier. The Revolution evaporates,
and leaves behind it only the slime of a new bureaucracy. The chains
of tormented mankind are made of red tape."[58] Sometimes he thought
of man as inherently evil, and then he out-Calvined Knox:

> At a certain period in self-knowledge . . . you find yourself
> execrable. . . . You will see that you are nothing but a rat's nest of
> miserable dissimulations. . . . The filth you will find exists for its own
> sake. You will recognize that you came dripping into the world with
> this burden, and will depart unrecognizable again—or only too

recognizable—because of it. This filth is the nethermost depth you will find.[59]

His diary in 1915 contained a prayer addressed to God, revealing the echoes of his lost faith, and the humility of a broken spirit:

> Have mercy on me. I am sinful in every nook and cranny of my being. But my gifts were not entirely contemptible. I had some talents, squandered them, . . . am now near my end. . . . If I am condemned, then I am condemned not only to die but to struggle till I die. . . . Let me only have rest at night.[60]

IV. OBIT

He had often thought of death, he had sometimes wished for it. "Things melt away; only my gray, hopeless prison wall remains."[61] "There will certainly be no one to blame if I should kill myself."[62] After his first coughing of blood (August, 1916) he felt that he had only a few years left to live. He accepted treatment impatiently, without hope. "This whole monstrous dust, which thirty-eight years have kicked up, has settled in my lungs."[63] In 1921 he went to a sanitarium in Slovakia, and returned to Prague improved; but soon he was coughing blood again. In the summer of 1923 his sister took him for a vacation to Müritz, a Baltic resort favored by Berlin Jews. There he fell in love with Dora Dymont, aged twenty; Kafka was now forty. He followed her to Berlin, and lived with her in brief happiness, harassed by inflation. In March, 1924, the coughing grew worse. Brod came and took him back to Prague. His parents received him with love and care. As his condition became more critical, they sent him to a sanitarium in Vienna, then to another at Kierling; there Dora Dymont stayed with him to the end. He died on June 3, 1924, and was buried in the Jewish cemetery in Prague. His parents survived him, and were later buried by his side.

Before his death he asked Max Brod to destroy all his remaining manuscripts. Brod held them for a time, then decided to give them to the world as part of the most significant literature of our age; by this chance *The Trial* and *The Castle* were preserved. Kafka's books were among those burned by the Nazis as decadent.[64] They had described with magic clairvoyance and feverish power the despotism and terror that were to come.

CHAPTER XVI

Nikos Kazantzakis

I. THE ATHEIST

HERE, looming out of the Greek Renaissance, is another soul without answers, seeking them in a dozen countries, religions, and philosophies, rowing his Odyssean bark from "truth" to "truth," surrendering them all, discarding even hope, but concluding with passionate commands: "Go forth nevertheless; seek; what if the hunt is better than the prey?"

I wish I had years enough, and enough knowledge of modern Greek, to study the devoted men and women who, till recently, filled the cities of Greece with a sparkling literary life. I know most of these authors by hearsay only: George Seferis (who received the Nobel Prize in 1963), Costis Palamas, Anghelos Sikelianos, Photos Politis, Evanghelos Papanoutos, Constantine Cavafis, Petros Vlastos, Pandelis Prevelakis . . . I name them as abounding evidence of a lusty life in twentieth-century Greece. I choose Nikos Kazantzakis as their representative (though he was not quite typical) because he has been translated into some thirty languages, and has been to me a major and exciting revelation.

I begin with his novel *Freedom or Death* (or *Kapetan Michalis*, Athens, 1950), for it is in part the story of his father, and, for the rest, a moving picture of his native Crete in one of her many revolutions. "Crete," he says, "is a red rock in an indigo sea";[1] hot enough in summer to make passions flame, cold enough in winter to toughen women and men. "The face of Crete is stern and weathered"; she is "hard of approach, rebellious, harsh. . . . One could not tell whether she loved her children or hated them. One thing was certain: she scourged them till the blood flowed."[2] And yet, with her rough mountains and her mad seas she enthralled them into wonder and devotion. "Ah!" cried Michalis, "if only I were an eagle, to admire the whole of Crete from an airy height!"[3] Harsh, too, was the Cretan heritage—proud memories of a Minoan civilization two thousand years older than Homer, and bitter memories of conquest by the Dorians, the Romans, the Arabs, the Venetians, and the Turks (1669).

Time after time the Cretans revolted against their Turkish masters—in 1821, 1866, 1878, and 1889; in this last rebellion Kazantzakis' father fought, and Nikos himself, then a boy of six, began to learn the facts of life. (The Turks departed in 1898, and in 1908 Crete joined the King- ✓ dom of Greece.) That long subjugation and resistance forged the Cretan temper: pious and somber in the women, violent and morose in the men; all lusty and passionate, all waiting for a chance to strike out for freedom, and readying themselves to kill any available Turk. Captain Mandakas, ninety years old, carried with him, as a kind of auricular confession, a jar of pickled ears—one for every Turk he had slain.[4]

Half the action of *Freedom or Death* occurs in Megalokastros (now Herakleion), where nearly every Christian home had sacred pictures of the Cretans who had led the great revolt of 1821, with their weapons, their cartridge belts, their bristling mustaches. The book's protagonists are Captain Michalis and the local Turkish ruler Nuri Bey. Even so they admire each other; they become sworn brothers by each cutting the other's arm and drinking their mingled blood. But when Michalis sees the Bey's voluptuous Circassian mistress Eminé he forgets his pledge of peace in his desire to be lost in her curves and drowned in her eyes. For to a Cretan male the meaning of life is to love women and beget upon them "yardfuls" of sons to fight Turks; and to a Cretan female it is to capture men and warm them into begetting such sons. The married women mourn that they must take so much time to bring their tired mates to ardor at night. "Curse my fate," mutters the wife of tepid Demetros; "I ought to have taken for a husband a guzzler, a swiller and wencher, who'd have begotten a dozen children on me before I was tamed."[5]

Two Cretans bursting with hatred for the Turks ignite the revolt of 1889: Captain Michalis by riding his horse into a Turkish café and clearing the place of Turks; and his brother Manusakas by carrying his ass on his back into a mosque "to join in the prayers."[6] A concatenation of assassinations follows, leading to a massacre of Christians by Turks. Michalis escapes to a monastery in the mountains; he recruits an armed band, and gives it a battle cry: "Freedom or death!" Fevered by visions of the wanton Eminé, Michalis leaves his troupe during the night, rides into the city and to Nuri Bey's villa, captures the mistress, secludes her under guard, and gallops back to the monastery, to find that in his absence his ragged volunteers, surprised and poorly armed, have been almost wiped out by a company of Turks. He leads the survivors in a forlorn attack, in which he and nearly all his men die.

Kazantzakis' father, Bernardone, was not quite another Michalis; he was a rebel, of course, but also he plowed a farm, and managed a store in Herakleion. He was imperious and stern; he hardly spoke except to command. Nikos (born February 18, 1883) disliked him, and worshiped his gentle and saintly mother; he described his own nature as an unstable inheritance of his mother's piety and his father's intensity. When Bernardone expected the Turks to renew their raids, he made Nikos swear that if they crossed the Kazantzakis threshold he, still a child, would join his father in killing his mother and sisters to prevent their violation and enslavement; Nikos swore, though he "didn't know how to kill a fly."[7] In 1897 another insurrection so endangered the family that it moved to the island of Naxos. There Nikos studied for two years at the French School of the Holy Cross, which was directed by Franciscan monks; now he learned French and Italian, the technique of spiritual exercises, and the love of Christ. But he was shocked to find from his private reading that man was a "great-grandson of the ape," and that the earth was a modest satellite of the sun. He repudiated the earth as a submissive slave, but he honored the sea for never relenting its attack upon the shore.[8]

He returned to Herakleion in 1899 to spend three years in the *gymnasium*, or secondary school; then for four years he studied law in Athens. On a holiday he journeyed to Sounion. "As I emerged from the pine forest, I saw the white columns of the temple of Poseidon, and between them the hallowed sea, a deep scintillating blue. . . . This is beauty, . . . the summit of joy; man can reach no higher. This is Greece."[9] (Seen on its high promontory from the Mediterranean below, that classic shrine is one of the most inspiring sights on our planet, attesting an aesthetic sense never quite regained.) Law seemed dull after that transcendent vision, and could be borne only with the help of whiskey and wenches. The father promised his son a year of travel if he should pass the final examinations with honors; Nikos emerged triumphant, and began a lifetime of wandering among countries and ideas. "I viewed, smelled, and touched Greece, proceeding all alone on foot, an olivewood staff in my hand and a carpetbag over my shoulder."[10] Then to Italy with a girl student, Galatea Alexiou, who in 1911 became his wife. Then he went on alone to Paris, the center of the white man's intellectual world.

If we may believe him he spent his three years there in studious seclusion, "without student love affairs or student inebriation, without political or intellectual conspiracies."[11] His landlady suspected him of being a conspirator because "you come home early every evening, you never receive visitors, either men or women, you keep your light on past midnight";[12] no decent student in Paris would behave like that. Nikos took romance via literature: he read all he could of Rousseau, Chateaubriand, Musset, Hugo, Lamartine.[13] He attended the lectures of Henri Bergson, rejected materialism, rated intuition above intellect, poetry above science or philosophy, and accepted the *élan vital* because he was bursting with it.

Almost at the same time he discovered Nietzsche; he devoured him and never escaped from his influence; his final ideal, Odysseus, was Nietzsche without syphilis and without hope. He thrilled to Zarathustra's cry that "God is dead," and took the news as mankind's liberation rather than a cosmic bereavement; as late as three years before his own end he wrote: "Three cheers for Nietzsche, the murderer of God."[14] For a time he accepted the Superman as a fair exchange for the Deity; "God is not man's ancestor but his descendant."[15] In 1909 he earned a doctoral degree from the University of Athens by writing a dissertation, *Friedrich Nietzsche and His Philosophy of Right.* Later, in his travels, he piously followed Nietzsche's trail from Röcken to Naumburg to Basel to the Engadine, the Riviera, Turin, Nice. He adopted Nietzsche's answer to Schopenhauer's pessimism: the "tragic optimism" that gladly accepts life's struggles without delusion or reward. He scorned "the Church of Christ in the state to which the clergy had brought it," as "an enclosure where thousands of panic-stricken sheep bleat away night and day, . . . stretching out their necks to lick the hand and knife that are slaughtering them."[16] However, he continued to love Notre Dame de Paris, as one loves a woman loved and lost.

II. THE SOCIALIST

In 1912, the spirit of nationalism still strong in him, he volunteered for service in the First Balkan War, in which Greece joined other Balkan states in expelling the Turks from nearly all of Europe. For a time he was assistant to the secretary of Prime Minister Venizelos. For some years thereafter he supported himself by translating works of Nietzsche, Darwin, Bergson, Plato, Eckermann, Maeterlinck, and William James. Suddenly caught by a return of interest in religion, he set out with the poet Anghelos Sikelianos to visit Greek Christian shrines (1914–15). He was so strongly moved by the monks of Mount Athos that he remained there for forty days, trying by ascetic practices to reach spiritual contact with Christ. Failing, he determined to make the world his monastery: he would apply the technique of ascetic meditation to forming souls for dedication to mankind. From that high resolve he descended to mining lignite in the Peloponnesus (1917) with a dynamic entrepreneur, Alexis Zorba; this part of his odyssey Kanzantzakis described with fictional garnishment in *Zorba the Greek*. When the mine collapsed he tried Zurich. Soon he was called to Athens (1919) to become director general of public welfare in the Venizelos government. He went on a special mission to the Caucasus and south Russia to bring back to Thrace and Macedonia 150,000 Greeks who were suffering persecution by the Armenian Kurds. Having accomplished this, he resigned with the fall of Venizelos (1921), and went for a year to Crete.

He was now thirty-seven years old, and felt that he had achieved nothing. His marriage with Galatea had lapsed into a friendly separation. A dozen religions and philosophies danced in his brain, and he oscillated dizzily between Nietzsche and Christ. Restless, he took to travel in the hope that the objective world might check his brooding. In Vienna he fell sick almost to the point of death (May, 1922) and had his first attack of a virulent eczema which repeatedly returned to him in later life. He dictated some of his fancies to a nurse; e.g., "A worm sleeps in God's heart and dreams that God does not exist."[17] During his convalescence he read about Buddha, and felt the fascination of Nirvana: the release from individuality, the escape from rebirth, and meanwhile the obligation to universal sympathy. "I had submerged myself in Buddha. My mind was a yellow heliotrope and Buddha the sun . . ."[18]

That febrile ecstasy did not endure. The European and American spirit is too eager for action to make a religion out of heat and fatigue. Kazantzakis hungered for a gospel that would give a more active form to the zealot in his soul. He found it among the Socialists of Berlin (1922–24). There he read Spengler's *Decline of the West* (Volume II had just appeared), and at once agreed that Western civilization was dying; "that strange, perfumed, wormeaten apple called civilization"[19] was rotting away. Germany, defeated in war and ruined by inflation, was ripe for a dirge of despair and yet hungry for a gospel of hope. Kazantzakis joined a discussion group composed chiefly of Jews suffering from poverty and anti-Semitism, and finding solace in the works of

Karl Marx. Nikos was too much of a poet to bear *Das Kapital* patiently, or to accept materialism as either a metaphysic or a philosophy of history.[20] But he was at the nadir of his physical and economic resources, and the invitation to socialism offered an outlet from despondency. He joined a radical group, inspired it by his enthusiasm, and became its intellectual leader. Eleni Samios described him:

> In that delicate, slender, disciplined body of his, in those burning eyes, in that dialectical talent which could bring order out of chaos, these young people put their trust; it was from him, so they thought, that salvation was to come. . . . Certainly he thought so himself for a brief period of time. He would abandon art, . . . deny his most recent love, Buddha. He would learn a manual trade to earn his living. Then he would expand his field of action, and go to the U.S.S.R.[21]

Among his new associates he became especially fond of five Jewish girls—Rahel, Elsa, Leah, Itka, Dina—all of them passionately Communist and darkly beautiful. When Rahel recited to him the Song of Songs in Hebrew he was so moved that he thought of marrying her; arm in arm they would remake the world. "Her eyes filled with tears," his notebooks tell us; "how I was waiting for you!" she said. On November 19, 1922, he writes: "If her mother were to learn that she [Rahel] was living with me, she would die of it."[22] A year later it was Elsa's turn to stir his blood and prose. "Your hands in my hand, I walk upon this earth, . . . and I sing very softly, so that God will not hear me, a joyous song of love."[23] He did not marry either of them (he was still legally bound to Galatea Alexiou), but continued to write love letters to them till the end of his life. Through them he learned to sympathize with the problems of the Jewish people, even to the point of declaring himself a Zionist. So, on March 10, 1925, he wrote to

> Leah, Leah, dear herring-comrade: beautiful, marvelous Jewess. . . . How often and how deeply I think of you. I hope to see you this year. I'm going to Palestine this summer—I've become a Zionist. Ah, why am I not a Jew? I feel no affinity at all with my own people. I find myself at home, in my own climate, when I talk with Jews, when I laugh and am silent with them.[24]

For these devoted youngsters he composed the mystical rhapsodies which he published in 1927 as *The Saviors of God*. He told them that by their devotion to the Communist cause they would join the sacred succession of men and women—Moses, Homer, Mohammed, Dante,

Cervantes, Shakespeare, Nietzsche, Lenin—who had labored to "spiritualize matter," to give form to mankind's inspiring ideal. This ideal he called God; these heroes of man's development had shared in creating this ideal; they were the saviors of God. For his disciples the new prophet suggested "spiritual exercises" by which the mind and heart could be trained, could be lifted up, step by step, to fitness for advancing the growth of God. "Formerly kings, priests, noblemen, and burghers created civilization, liberated the divinity. Today God is a worker, made savage by toil, wrath, and hunger. . . . The wind of destruction is blowing; that is now the breath of our God."[25] So the Nietzschean atheist strove to recapture the inspiring force of the religious ecstasy. And the influence of Nietzsche (scorner of socialism) was so strong in him that he adopted the style of *Thus Spake Zarathustra* in applying the methods of Ignatius Loyola to form a new army for his new God.

Meanwhile his restless spirit moved from place to place, from creed to creed. In January, 1924, he left Germany, wandered through north Italy, stopped at Assisi for eleven weeks, fell in love with Saint Francis, and laid up memories which, a generation later, filled *The Poor Man of God* (1953). Then to Crete, where he was indicted for his minor part in a Communist plot.[26] He prepared an astonishingly candid "Apology." Some part of it:

> I believe the bourgeois system is no longer capable of regulating the present-day needs and anxieties of the social entity.
>
> Economically, it is based on the predatory individualistic organization of production and the unequal distribution of wealth.
>
> Socially, there is no longer any morality to support human relations.
>
> Politically, the ruling class manages the political authority for its own benefit, to the detriment of the great majority of the people; and every change of persons or institutions proves futile. . . .
>
> We are confronting a spectacle, the likes of which can be observed at the end of every civilization. A single class—in the very beginning it was the priests and the magicians, then the kings, then the feudal lords, then the bourgeois—assumes power, after shattering the preceding class. Then, . . . when it too has passed all the phases of the high point and the decline, another class comes (fated to follow the same curve) and takes its place. Such is the undulating pattern of history. . . .
>
> What class is going to succeed the bourgeois system? I have the adamantine conviction that it will be the working class—workers, farmers, people productive in the spirit. . . .

The new class, said Kazantzakis, is rising on all continents; Asia and Africa are joining in the revolution. And this movement has a leader— "an enormous state, one sixth of the earth, possessing a very strong army, inexhaustible raw materials, great scientists, implacable political leaders and, above all, . . . a new faith—Russia." He confessed to having written, for Greek periodicals, articles aimed to promote an impartial study of the new movement; they "did not please either the Communists or the bourgeois."

> I am not so naïve as to believe that once an idea has been formulated, it can be transformed immediately into reality. My aim has been to make as many people as possible contemplate more profoundly the historical moment we are experiencing and prepare themselves for a rebirth of their individual and social life: a psychological rebirth first of all, of course; and then a spiritual and social one; and finally (in time) an economic and political one. . . .
>
> Whatever you do and however much time passes, Your Honors, I am convinced that the few will always multiply; the victims of injustice will always come out stronger; and the class perpetrating the injustice will always fall.
>
> This is what I believe. I considered it my duty to state it with absolute sincerity—and your duty, if you find my thought worthy of punishment, to punish me.[27]

We do not know if this declaration was transmitted to Kazantzakis' accusers. Apparently he decided on hiding until the affair lapsed. He isolated himself in a cottage at Tripiti on the Cretan coast, and began to write his *Odyssey*.[28]

He was now definitely separated from his wife Galatea Alexiou, though he did not obtain a divorce till 1926. They had been married fifteen years, but he had spent ten of these in travels that left her husbandless in their Herakleion home. How could so flighty, passionate, self-willed a man be a good husband? He was made for enterprises of great pith and brief moment, and for long sessions of wild thought and painful art that called for solitude and peace. Nevertheless he liked Eleni Samios, whom he met in 1924; she shared his enthusiasm for socialism and Soviet Russia; she became his lover and (so far as her chronic illness allowed) his companion from 1926; finally, in 1945, he married her. In 1957 he wrote that to her "I owe all the daily happiness of my life; without her I would have died many years ago."[29]

In the fall of 1925 he realized some part of his dream: he saw the Russian Revolution at first hand. His first impression was sad: "The women here in Moscow are all extremely ugly"[30] (he had not seen Pavlova). He talked with some "leaders" (Lenin was dead), and reported: "Their worthiness consists in their action and in their holy impulse with all its flame and smoke; their thinking seems to me too simple-minded."[31] He returned to Athens slightly sobered.

Between April, 1926, and January, 1927, he traveled in Palestine, Cyprus, Egypt, Italy, and Spain as paid correspondent for Greek journals. Eleni accompanied him to Palestine; there they found two of his Jewish sweethearts: Elsa in Jerusalem, Leah in Tel Aviv. In Toledo Kazantzakis was delighted with the home and relics of El Greco; "this meeting of the two Cretans was so violent," he wrote to Eleni, that his heart began pounding.[32] Henceforth he thought of himself as a spiritual descendant of "the Greek" who had conquered Spain. He received at Toledo five letters: one from Eleni, one from Elsa, one from Leah, three from Rahel. He told this to Eleni, who seems to have shown no jealousy. It was a wonderful relationship, when four women allowed one man to love each of them.

From Spain he went to Pisa, Florence, and Rome. Renaissance art now seemed to him cold, formal, and standardized, compared to the spiritual elongations of El Greco. After his interview with Mussolini, Eleni, who had joined him in Rome, asked, "What strikes you most about Fascism?" He answered, "That it has several points in common with Communism." "How so?" "The same suppression of individual liberty, the same faith in a better future."[33] While Eleni went to Paris as a newspaper correspondent Kazantzakis returned to Athens and published articles on Russia, Spain, and Italy. "The Communists call me a heretic and a mystic." He expected that his essay on "Metacommunism" would bring "a big rupture with Communism—not in a backward direction, of course, but terrifyingly forward." However, he planned to go to Crete in 1929 and present himself as a Communist candidate for parliament.[34] He was happy to receive, in 1927, an invitation from the Soviet government to come and join in celebrating the tenth anniversary of the October Revolution.

In Moscow he developed a friendship for Panaït Istrati, a wildly enthusiastic Communist; with him he toured south Russia and the Caucasus. His own fervor was cooling, because (he wrote to Eleni) the Revolution "has passed beyond the heroic phase, . . . and because I am not a man of action. . . . I'm not interested in man but in the being I so imperfectly designate as God."[35] Nevertheless, having a free pass for all Russian rail and water transportation, he sailed down the Volga (1928), crossed the Caspian Sea, and rode on through Azerbaijan,

Georgia, Armenia, Turkestan, Siberia, and Manchuria to Vladivostok (1929); then back to Moscow and Berlin.

Isolating himself in Gottesgab, a village in the Erzegebirge of Czechoslovakia, he wrote in French, "during a single writing stretch," *Toda Raba*, a novelized account of his Russian trip; he saw it published in Paris in 1931. I took up the book with intent to glance through it hurriedly as probably the payment of a propaganda debt to the Soviets, and it began that way, describing the diverse celebrations of the October Revolution by Communists in a dozen lands. But not all was propaganda. Almost at the outset an old skeptic interrupts a private gathering at Kiev with a gloomy prophecy: "As soon as the attackers [the revolutionists] get the power . . . they too will start to get fat and paralyzed. And other hungry, suffering masses will rise on earth again. So will waves of human beings rise and fall in an increasing rhythm until the end of time."[36] Kazantzakis himself attacks Marxism, and Russia's fever of industrialization; he shudders at the thought of Russia becoming another America; and he forecasts rival imperialisms clashing in war. "Every youthful idea," says Geranos (i.e., Kazantzakis), "is imperialistic. It hopes to save the world, as its own apologists claim, or, as its enemies claim, to conquer it. Naturally the world resists."[37] However, Geranos keeps the faith: "Today in the U.S.S.R. the human heart is beating more forcefully than anywhere else in the world. Once it was Athens or Benares or Mecca or Jerusalem. Today it is Moscow."[38] Kazantzakis remained a socialist to the end.

III. THE PAGAN

Since he was still in thrall to Nietzsche, he extended his revolt against Christianity to a rejection of its ethics. He did not admit that wine, women, and song are enemies of virtue. Like a good Greek he drank moderately, and he interrupted his ascetic moods with cautious forays into feminine charms. He liked everything about women except marriage. He was especially fond of their smell, which aroused him to enervating heat; their armpits, he thought, exuded ambrosia. He suspected that women were similarly excited by the odor of a man; the Circassian dancer in *Freedom or Death* "could not have enough of the stench of men."[39] He celebrated the "wide loins" of women, "containing whole yards of noisy children";[40] and he seldom mentioned young women without speaking of their "firm breasts" and shining thighs. He believed that the breasts of healthy women hurt when desirable men appeared; and he was sure that babies lay hidden in every mature womb, itching to get out.[41] He praised men for having many children, but he himself acknowledged none. He had many intimacies, but he resented their permanence. He felt that women checked his grand designs. "They're a pest. 'Forward!' you say, and they say, 'Stop!'"[42] (Some pundits have thought the opposite.) "The age-old heart inside me . . . repulses women and refuses to trust them or permit them to penetrate deeply within me and take possession. Women are simply ornaments for men, and more often a sickness and a necessity."[43] In healthier moments he listed four gifts as basic to a man's life: earth, water, bread, and woman;[44] or, again, "food, drink, woman, and the dance."[45]

He liked to dance, but (like most Orientals) alone, or in union with others of the same sex; the dance was to be a stylized expression of many emotions, of which sex should be but one. Who can forget the dance of Zorba when his great enterprise had collapsed? Probably every city in the world has now seen that dance, for a remarkable motion picture has made *Zorba the Greek* Kazantzakis' most widely known book. It was his memory of the Alexis Zorba who had been associated with him in a mining enterprise in 1916. Hear the tribute that Kazantzakis in old age paid to his strange partner.

> If . . . I wished to designate which people left their traces embedded most deeply in my soul, I would perhaps designate Homer, Buddha, Nietzsche, Bergson, and Zorba. . . . Zorba taught me to love life and have no fear of death. If it had been a question in my lifetime of choosing a spiritual guide, . . . surely I would have chosen Zorba. For he had just what a quill-driver needs for deliverance: the . . . creative artlessness, renewed each morning, which enabled him to see all things constantly as though for the first time . . . ; the sureness of hand, freshness of heart, the gallant daring to tease his own soul, as though inside him he had a force superior to the soul; finally, the savage bubbling laugh from a deep, deep wellspring deeper than the bowels of man; a laugh which . . . was able to demolish (did demolish) all the barriers—morality, religion, homeland—which that wretched poltroon, man, has erected around him in order to hobble with full security through his miserable smidgen of life.[46]

The book is an uneven dialogue between Buddha and Rabelais, between the trustful idealism of the unnamed narrator and the sensual realism of his aide. The narrator seeks peace through understanding and

acceptance; Zorba seeks life through liberated instincts, sensual enjoyment, a ready passage from thought to action, and a will to absorb the
meat or juice of every offered experience. He has rejected God as "the
old skinflint"[47] who through so many years deceived him into denying
his instincts and kept him from relishing his sensations. He has rejected
nationalism as the "mad bitch" that mothered insane wars;[48] he scorns
the Greeks of his time as "lousy . . . tavern loafers" whose "backbiting . . . politics are ruining Greece."[49] What, then, does Zorba believe? He believes in his own body and soul: in his arms and legs and
head, in his natural impulses, in his lusty senses and clear perception.
"I have been consumed with one desire: to touch and see as much as
possible of the earth and the sea before I die."[50] "Earth" included
women—not one but as many as possible. "You keep teasing me and
saying I'm too fond of the women. Why shouldn't I be fond of them,
when they're all weak creatures who . . . surrender on the spot if you
just catch hold of their breasts?"[51] In these matters Zorba takes Zeus as
his model, and gives a new explanation of the divine adulterer:

> ". . . He loved women, of course, but not the way you think, you
> pen-pushers! Not at all! He was sorry for them! He understood
> what they all suffered, and he sacrificed himself for their sakes!
> When, in some godforsaken country hole, he saw an old maid
> wasting away with desire and regret, or a young wife—or even if
> she wasn't at all pretty, even if she was a monster—and her husband
> was away and she couldn't get to sleep, he used to cross himself,
> this good fellow, change his clothes, take on whatever shape the
> woman had in mind, and go to her room. . . . Often enough
> even he was dead-beat . . . How could anyone satisfy all these she-
> goats? . . . At dawn he'd come home, saying: 'Ah, my God! when
> shall I be able to have a good night's rest? . . .' But suddenly he'd
> hear a sigh: down there on earth some woman had thrown off her
> bedclothes, gone out onto the balcony almost stark naked, and was
> sighing enough to turn the sails of a windmill! And my old Zeus
> would be quite overcome. 'Oh, hell! I'll have to go down again!' . . .
> And it went on like that to such an extent that the women emptied
> him completely. He couldn't move his back, . . . became paralyzed,
> and died. . . ."[52]

Well, there is a pretty widow in town, who, the narrator reports,
"passes by me like a wild animal in heat, distilling musk."[53] Zorba too
has a nose for musk. He sees his employer-friend eying her but
avoiding her; he urges him to go to her and be relieved. "I did not dare,"

the narrator confesses; ". . . I had fallen so low that if I had had to choose between falling in love with a woman and reading a book about love, I should have chosen the book."[54] Zorba rebukes him: "He who can sleep with a woman, and does not, commits a great sin. . . . If you're looking for any other paradise than that, . . . there is none!"[55] And in general he is disgusted with his master's habit of reading a book in the evening. "I'm going to tell you an idea of mine, boss, but you mustn't be angry. Make a heap of all your books, and set fire to them! After that, who knows, you're no fool, you're the right sort, we might make something of you!"[56] Follow your instincts, Zorba urges; stop thinking so much; stop trying to understand; "if you didn't [try to] understand you'd be happy!"[57] It is an effervescent mixture of Casanova and Bergson.

It does not always work. A villager, in a burst of instinct and zeal, cuts off the widow's lovely head. Zorba's expensive contraption of pylons and cables, built without benefit of mathematics, collapses, exhausting his master's funds. However, he spends no time in grief; he takes up his samisen (banjo), and strums an old song; or, better, he dances. "Whenever I feel I'm choking with some emotion, the devil in me says, 'Dance!' and I dance. . . . I feel better for that, as if I had been bled."[58]

In his autobiography Kazantzakis tells us that Zorba went to Serbia, struck a rich vein of magnesite, "married a pretty, fun-loving widow . . . , and had a child by her."[59] Some years later a letter came from a village schoolmaster in Serbia:

> I am writing to inform you of the sad news that Alexis Zorba . . . passed away last Sunday . . . He called for me during his death agony and said, "Come here, teacher. I have a certain friend in Greece. When I die, write him that I'm dead, and that I was in my right mind to the very last, . . . and was thinking of him. And that no matter what I did, I don't regret it. Tell him I hope he stays well, and that it's high time he put some sense into his head. . . . And if any priest comes to confess me and give me communion, tell him to make himself scarce, and may he give me his curse! I did this, that, and the other thing in my life, yet I did very little. Men like me should live a thousand years. Good night!"[60]

IV. THE POET

In 1935, financed by the newspaper *Akropolis*, Kazantzakis traveled in Japan and China. Like Keyserling some twenty years before him, he was charmed by Japanese art, manners, dress, the tea-service ritual, the grace of the women, the quick intelligence of the men, the loving care of gardens and patient sculpture of trees. Humbled, he presented himself to Nippon as a "Western barbarian."[61] He did not resent the minuteness of Japanese etiquette; he understood when a Japanese scholar told him: "Etiquette is order, the august mother of social life. I feel free in her talons";[62] i.e., he was secure in counting upon the proper behavior of others; and even the criminals were courteous. The poet in Kazantzakis appreciated the delicacy and finesse of the haiku—a touch of nature, a warmth of feeling, a subtlety of symbolism, a depth of understanding, all conveyed in a poetic cameo of four or five lines, "piercing little poems that fly swift as an arrow and lodge deep in the heart."[63] Above all, he recovered the Buddhist mood of escape from the self into the whole. "Buddha! The world fell dim and sweet as a drop of honey. Never in my life had I enjoyed happiness so calm and so intense."[64] A few squares away from the temple a factory filled the air with noise; the manager caressed his gleaming dynamos as if acting a play by Eugene O'Neill. "Made in Japan! Made in Japan!" he cried as he fondled his products. But his girl employees, Kazantzakis noted, were pale and thin, obviously overworked and underpaid, yet not daring to complain since there were so many others competing to take their place. However, Nara and Nikko and Kyoto were so beautiful that the Greek barbarian "realized one day that I loved Japan."[65]

On his return to Europe he wrote, in French, a novelized account of his trip—*Le Jardin des rochers* (1936; translated as *The Rock Garden*); and a more factual record, *Japan/China*, in which I find a priceless lesson from Buddha: "Alms, in money, can nourish [a man] for seven years, but a good word can nourish him for seventy-seven years."[66]

Then this paragon of all forms and fancies set himself to prepare for the press the enormous epic which he hoped would be his lasting monument. He had already translated Homer's *Iliad* and *Odyssey* into modern Greek. He was especially fascinated by the story and character of Odysseus-Ulysses, the man beyond good and evil, the warrior, wanderer, and seducer, the master of crafts and craft, the challenger of men and gods; here was a superman, in action and philosophy, three thousand years before Nietzsche. The message of Zorba, that action is its own reward—had not Odysseus lived that axiom on an almost cosmic scale? Now, having walked for a time with Nietzsche, then Buddha, then Lenin, Kazantzakis turned to follow Odysseus to the ends of the earth, resolved to face life without hope and death without fear. *Sans peur et sans espoir!*

My youth had been nothing but anxieties, nightmares, and ques-
tionings; my maturity nothing but lame answers. . . . What agony
to hunt out God . . . ! I took one road, reached its end—an abyss.
Frightened, I turned back and took another road; at its end the abyss
once more. Retreat again, a new journey, and suddenly the same
abyss . . . My youth and maturity had revolved in the air around the
two poles of panic and hope, but now in my old age I stood before
the abyss tranquilly, fearlessly. . . . I created him [Odysseus] to
face the abyss calmly, and in creating him I strove to resemble him.
. . . I entrusted all my own yearning to this Odysseus . . . Whatever I
yearned for and was unable to attain, he would attain. . . . He was
the Archetype.[67]

And so in 1925, three years after Joyce had published *Ulysses*,
Kazantzakis began to write *The Odyssey: A Modern Sequel*. He prepared himself with many hours of research; so, for example, he was able
to describe the ancient Minoan games and festivals. To *Liebe Genossin*
(Beloved Comrade) Eleni he wrote from Herakleion in 1925: "I write
all day long, sleep all night long, live all alone . . . I'm striving to
resurrect the primeval souls of our ancestors at Knossos. I live the entire
vision, gaze at the faces, weep, laugh, die and love along with all these
painted women showing their bare breasts—and all these slender-
waisted, proud men."[68] He composed Books I–VI in Crete; in 1927 he
moved to a simple cottage on the island of Aegina, off the southeast
coast of Greece; there, in a torrent and fury of poetry, in four months,
he formed Books VII–XXIV. During the next eleven years, chiefly at
Antibes, he rewrote the poem seven times, pouring into it the full
wealth of his imagination, and all that remained of his religions and
philosophies. Finally, in 1938, still unsatisfied, he surrendered it to
publication at Athens in an expensive edition of three thousand copies.
Twenty years later, in one of their many brave ventures in creative
publishing, Simon and Schuster, in New York, issued a remarkable
translation by Kimon Friar, who had spent four years on the exacting
task, some of them with Kazantzakis at his side. The poet declared the
translation to be as good as the original—of which he had said: "This
is the book that I'll carry with me in the grave."[69]

The new epic consists of twenty-four "rhapsodies," totaling 33,333
lines—three times the size of Homer's *Odyssey*. I have not read all
those lines; after all, I am nearly dead, and have passed the age of
heroism; however, I am the last man who should complain of an eight-
hundred page book of crowded lines. Those who have time for the
enterprise should read this "sequel"—not more than a canto ("book") at

a time—as a picaresque novel in verse, a succession of adventures by a man seeking the meaning of life after the death of the gods.

The poet addressed his Prologue to his one remaining deity:

> O Sun, great Oriental, my proud mind's golden cup, . . . sniff out all quarries that I love, give them swift chase; tell me all that you've seen on earth, all that you've heard, and I shall pass them through my entrails' secret forge, till slowly, with profound caresses, play and laughter, stones, water, fire, and earth shall be transformed to spirit, and the mud-winged and heavy soul, freed of its flesh, shall like a flame serene ascend and fade in sun. . . .

And then, calling to you and me:

> *Ahoy! cast wretched sorrow out, prick up your ears—*
> *I sing the sufferings and the torments of renowned Odysseus.*

Book I: Returning as king to Ithaca after the siege of Troy and years of wandering, Odysseus is greeted by a crowd of his retainers, and cows them with his challenge:

> *Who runs, drinks, fights, or makes love better than I?*
> *What other mind can think up truths or lies like mine?*[70]

He is a man toughened and brutalized by hardship and war, with "cutting glance" and ever ready sword. He fondly smears with blood the breasts and thighs of a statue that represents his favorite goddess, Athena.[71] He demands of his slaves how many slaves they have begotten or borne in his absence. He shocks old and young by a novel toast: "I drink not to the gods but to man's dauntless mind!"[72] His wife Penelope is frightened by his violence; his son Telemachus, gentled by education, avoids him.

Book II: Odysseus scorns them, and suspects them of hoping for his early death; his royal palace now seems to him a tomb. He longs to reject the chores of government and resume his life of battle and adventure on land and sea. He gathers a miscellaneous band of sailors, drunkards, artisans, mountaineers, and the poet Orpheus, bids them build a sturdy vessel, and at night, after filling the ship with food, drink, and loot from his palace, he sets sail without a goal and for whatever fate. "Let your soul fly with freedom, and let come what may!"[73]

Book III: Odysseus dreams that Helen of Sparta is so weary of Menelaus that blood oozes from her once fragrant armpits. He resolves to rescue her. He leads his band to Sparta, notes the invasion of the Peloponnesus by northern "barbarians" armed with iron weapons, and heralds the replacement of bronze by the Iron Age. *Book IV:* He predicts the failure of Menelaus as a ruler because he has "a mind that has not learned as yet how the world's governed, and what a cruel and crafty heart a leader must have."[74] As for himself, "I freely mold my fate as though it were my will."[75] He laughs at Zeus as an "unhappy creature of our hearts, . . . born of our fear," and predicts that this old fantasy will soon "fade in air."[76] He abducts Helen and leads her to his boat.

Book V: As he and his men row or sail toward Crete they feast their eyes on Helen, who wisely husbands her charms, offering good advice:

> *It's best that women keep their breasts well hidden, clothed,*
> *to veil them like wild flames, and so preserve their strength;*
> *that which you wish to give, keep hidden and unspent.*[77]

They find the land of Crete parched by a long drought, which the people ascribe to the sexual impotence of their King Idomeneus. The aging monarch begs the Bull God to restore potency to himself and fertility to the soil. He agrees to hold a public festival in which he will mate with a woman-calf, and the people will copulate freely, as hints to the sky to fertilize the barren earth. Odysseus arranges to have Helen play the part of the calf. *Book VI:* In the ritual games (brilliantly described) Helen lies naked in the center of the arena, and receives the King, while the people frolic lawlessly, and Odysseus mates with the Sacred Harlot Diktena. He notes the wealth of the court and the aristocracy in contrast to the poverty of the people; he joins in a conspiracy of the poor to overthrow the King. *Book VII:* He reflects that the poor have the same instincts as the rich, the same greed and cruelty, but he hopes that the revolution will nevertheless advance the growth of the god in man. *VIII:* The revolution succeeds, Odysseus condones the slaughter, and entones a glorification of war.[78] (Here the poet mates Lenin with Nietzsche.) Idomeneus is killed, and Odysseus sets one of his crew, Hardihood, upon the Cretan throne. Helen, having found no comfort on a throne, becomes (like Lady Chatterley) the contented spouse of a lusty gardener. Odysseus and his crew set off for Egypt.

IX: They move up the Nile. One of the men, tired of roaming and rowing, suggests that they dismantle their boat, build cabins, till the soil, take wives, and bring up families: his mates ridicule him as a conformist weakling, and they all go on, living by plunder. (The story seems to suggest that the pursuit is better than the goal, but) Odysseus inspires them with resolve to find the sources of the Nile. *X:* En route they join a group of revolutionaries led by Rala, a pretty Jewess who pleases Odysseus by acknowledging only one divinity, man's free mind. *XI:* The revolution fails, Rala is killed; Odysseus and his men are imprisoned; they escape, and trudge through African jungle. He appeases their weariness and rebelliousness by promising that when they reach the headwaters of the Nile he will lead them in building an ideal city-state. *XII:* He explains to them his new theology: God is the product of the human mind, and is slowly evolving into an ever higher form through the mental and moral development of mankind. An old Egyptian admonishes Odysseus:

> *You gab too much of God, and pass him through too fine*
> *a sieve until there's nothing left of him to eat.*
> *I hear but one cry only, more than enough for me:*
> *"Never ask why, but follow a soul greater than yours!"*[79]

XIII: The band arrives at the source of the Nile. Odysseus climbs a mountain to meditate on a code of laws for his proposed city-state. *XIV:* Stage by stage, as he mounts, his self and mind are enlarged: he feels himself a part of the Greek nation, then a part of mankind, then a part of the earth. Reaching the top, he stands proud and happy in the clear air; "his chest laughed, his heart danced."[80] He sees in a moving vision the long evolutionary line from matter to conscious mind. He feels both sexes within him: the female calling from the heart with love and tenderness, the male speaking from the intellect with cautious thought. He sees hundreds of animals of different species crowding about him; he welcomes them as his ancestors and brothers. He senses a force in himself that is struggling to liberate itself from the coarseness and limitations of matter and become free spirit; this force and process he calls God; and in this conception he trusts that he has found a faith that can take the place of a dying myth and give fresh meaning, courage, and direction to human life. He goes down from the mountain resolved to build a city fit to serve as a temple and tribute to his new God.

XV: His men obstruct the enterprise by their jealous quarrels. Nevertheless the city grows, and attracts an expanding population. Odysseus gives it a socialist economy and government, and full freedom of sex. The young are encouraged to breed lustily, without marriage; the mates will part after coupling; children will be brought up and educated in common. Aged persons will be allowed to die without antibiotic procrastination.

XVI: A volcanic eruption destroys the new city, killing most of its inhabitants; Odysseus' hair turns white with grief. He becomes skeptical of his theology; this new god is a figment of man's mind; let us rejoice in our freedom, and face our destinies with our own strength. ✓

> And when God fell to earth the mind of man leapt up
> within his head like a broad-breasted cock, and crowed;
> it seemed day broke, sweet light flowed down the mountain
>   slopes,
> and the god-slayer's heart grew warm, his black chest opened,
> till like a bridegroom with curled locks, smelling of thyme,
> he drew the bolts and let the world stroll in his heart.
> The nightingale appeared once more, perched on his head
> as though the heart were an unruffled bird that sang
> with no unsolved enigmas now on green earth's highest bough.[81]

A mermaid, hearing this hymn to atheism, cries, "Cursed be the heart that knows no reverence"; but Odysseus answers with a magnificat to life:

> O trees, get drunk and burst in bloom; girls, swell your
>   breasts;
> and you, brave youths, hatch in your minds all your desires—
> life's but a lightning flash, my lads, and death is endless!
> I gaze on earth and love her, I don't want to die!
> I gaze on a man's and a maid's body, and I shout. . . .
> I love to stroll and watch maids at their window sills,
> to see the fragrant smoke arise at dusk from roofs,
> to hear beds creak and crack at midnight in the dark.
> I pass by towns and lands, bless them and shout in air:
> "O mankind, joys and tears, warm bodies, O my children!"[82]

XVII: Odysseus, still in ecstasy, chants a paean to man's mind. *XVIII:* He tells the story of Buddha, and, in a Nirvana mood, glorifies death. *XIX:* As he makes his painful way through an African jungle he feels death touching him, but he persuades death to let him reach his favorite element, the sea. *XX:* He sees the cruel rites of an African tribe, and grieves to think how long is the road from savagery to understanding. *XXI:* He reaches an African port, and is amused to learn that some

Cretan sailors, shipwrecked there, worship a god whom they variously name Slayer, Savior, or Odysseus. He meets a young Negro who preaches Christian love and turns the other cheek when Odysseus slaps him; he warns the convert that life is war as well as love. The old rover builds a boat in the shape of a coffin, puts into it some food and tools, and shoves off.

XXII: Nearing the South Pole, he encounters an iceberg, is thrown into the sea, swims to land, sees igloos, joins in the life of the ice-dwellers, builds himself a kayak, and again dares the ocean. *XXIII:* His kayak is smashed by an iceberg. He clings to the iceberg, and sings the praise of woman. He rejoices in having lived a hundred years, so that death will win from him no spoils but skin and bones. *XXIV:* In delirium he fancies that his former mates are coming to his aid, and he sees Helen dying on a riverbank in Crete, surrounded by her children and grandchildren. His visions fade; darkness settles upon him; and the poet ends sadly: "Today I've seen my loved one vanish like a dwindling thought."

What does it mean? Apparently it gave enthusiastic assent to Ivan Karamazov's conclusion: "If there is no God, everything is permitted" —which is generally the answer of our "permissive" time. Those young Greeks who had the stamina to traverse these eight hundred pages must have been thrilled to hear that the Ten Commandments had been repealed, and that every desire of the soul or the flesh was the divine itching of an imprisoned deity. The hero lies, steals, wenches, and kills, but he remains the poet's hero, profusely proclaimed. Odysseus deserts his wife, who had waited and wilted, weaving and grieving, for twenty years. He scorns his son for loving justice more than power. He has no sense of social order or obligation; he suggests a bedlam of supermen, each brandishing his muscles and seeking omnipotence. There is no memory here of Buddha's gentleness, and the Negro neophyte's echo of Christ is dulled by Odysseus' second blow on the cheek. That Kazantzakis should have taken for his model a life of action loosed from all moral restraint is a puzzle to which the probable solution is that he was overcome with Zorba, and solaced his years of literary hermitage by dreaming of desperate deeds and odorous women.

Women play only incidental roles in the epic—Penelope, Helen, Krino, Phida, Rala; it is in the main a story of marauding men and slaughtered gods. And yet the poet leaves no canto complete without extolling the magic perfume of a woman's armpits[83] and the fragrant smoothness of her breasts.[84] Furthermore,

> *Between her supple thighs a heavy whirlpool swirls,*
> *Two rivers crash, and woe to him who slips and falls!*[85]

The men who carry the tale are nearly all homeless tramps of land or sea, living by robbery, killing with relish, and knowing hardly any virtue except loyalty to their chief. Such rough and ready marauders must have laughed, off stage, at Odysseus' talk of a new god evolving through their bloody climb to excellence. Probably they anticipated his final doctrine—that his new god was just another soporific against the pains of struggle, and that man must fight on with no hope of more than transitory victories.

What makes the poem great despite the nihilism of its philosophy is its animal vigor, its sensuous warmth, its torrent of action, its richness of imagery, its bubbling current of style. Of course, it is too long; each scene or sentiment is elongated to thinness; attention lags after repeated circuits of the same idea; even excellence palls if it never ends, Nevertheless, when I compare this feast of words and deeds with the devitalized trifles, pretentiously obscure, of so many poets since Whitman and Swinburne, I am inclined to rate this second *Odyssey* as the outstanding poem of our century.

V. THE CHRISTIAN

In this epic, as in Homer's, there is a heap of braggadocio; the hero strikes his hairy chest too often, and does not convince us when he proclaims the splendor of hopelessness. Nor was Kazantzakis convinced. After so many revolutions in philosophy, religion, and government, where did he arrive? At Golgotha.

He continued to the end to denounce churches and theologies, and to renounce the idea of an external deity; but he longed to keep the word "God" as "a heavy name loaded with all the hopes and tears of the world."[86] He still rejected all notions of a life after death, but he was not sure that moral and social order could survive without the support of supernatural beliefs. "What does *There is no God* mean? It means there is no bridle on our instincts, no reward for good or punishment for evil, no virtue, shame, or justice—that we are wolves and she-wolves in heat."[87] So Kazantzakis remained, despite his *Odyssey*, a battleground between Nietzsche and Christ: he wanted to rejoice in his instincts, and to "sin bravely," but he echoed a famous psalm about the fool who said in his heart "There is no God."[88]

Sometimes he thought in pantheistic poetry. "I said to the almond tree, / 'Sister, speak to me of God.' / And the almond tree blossomed."[89] Or he expressed his interpretation of Spinoza: "This world is not God's vestment, as I once believed; it is God himself; form and essence are identical." But on the same page he described a more mystical vision: "I felt a command . . . to become one with the fearful, enticing Lover who lies in wait in the darkness and whom we call God. . . . I felt that love, death, and God were one and the same. [The process of life, love, reproduction, death, new life, love . . . is itself God, as a continuous creative force and flow.] As the years went by, I became ever more deeply aware of this terrifying Trinity . . ."[90] Sometimes he united God and Satan in a "new synthesis" expressing the moral ambivalence of a world fluctuating between good and evil.[91] Or he identified God with the Heracleitian flux, almost with revolution: "God is not the power that has found eternal equilibrium, but the power that is forever breaking every equilibrium, forever searching for a higher one."[92] Or again, like Thomas Mann, he offered God as the progressive "spiritualization of matter" by the heroes of man's mental and moral growth; these nobles of the soul gave developing form and substance to man's ideal; they were the "creators of God." So the word "God," which had expressed the highest ideal of men through groping centuries of myth and hope, must not be allowed to die because one of its forms has faded from the minds of educated men. At the age of sixty-seven Kazantzakis was still "longing for God."[93]

Even more powerfully the figure and story of Christ revived in his memory as he emerged from utopian hopes and hopeless deeds. One man, more by his joyful saintliness than by his theology, had been lifted up as an inspiration embracing all lovers of the developing God. No one who had once known that man could ever forget him—even if he should be a composite of reality and legend. In 1953, says Pandelis Prevelakis, he "turned his back upon everything he had achieved up to 1948, retaining nothing but *Zorba the Greek*,"[94]—and so discarding even Odysseus. Retiring in 1948 to solitude in Antibes, he composed in the next five years three books which constituted a palinode celebrating Christ.

The English-reading world knows *The Recrucifixion of Christ* (1948) as *The Greek Passion*, and chiefly as an unforgettable motion picture called *The Man Who Must Die*. Manolios, a Cretan shepherd, turns away from worldly things, tries to live the ethics of Christ, and suffers all tribulations without retaliation or reproach. A group of friends gathers about him, feeling a divine power in his prayers. Panayotaros, the rich saddler, hates him as a silent indictment of lust and greed. The ruling priests, living in luxury and swollen with food and drink, denounce Manolios as a heretic, and teach the folk to fear and shun him. Panayotaros betrays him; the mob puts Manolios to death. Kazant-zakis aims his sharpest barbs at the common people, brutalized by poverty and ignorance; "what a wild beast the heart of man is!"[95] Albert Schweitzer thought this book to be Kazantzakis' best; he said that he had never read anything more moving.[96] But it raised a tempest among the clergy and populace of Crete, and brought the author close to excommunication.

Kazantzakis offered no amends in what impressed me as his greatest novel. In a letter to a friend he described the pains of literary pregnancy. "The new novel is working in my vitals, and, like the embryo, con-suming my flesh, drinking my blood, wanting to grow and emerge free into the sun. I hope that soon the great pangs and great joys of birth will begin."[97] As *The Last Temptation of Christ* (1950) begins, Jesus is a carpenter, who, in the routine of his work, makes some of the crosses used by the Roman authorities in crucifying Jewish rebels; therefore he is hated by the people, who long for a savior from foreign rule. He is an epileptic, subject to convulsions and falling fits. He has erotic dreams of the village harlot, Mary Magdalen; but also he dreams that God calls him to be the Messiah, to lead men not so much to politi-cal liberty as to a new morality and a new faith in the Kingdom of Heaven. At first he refuses this call. "I can't. I'm illiterate, an idler, afraid of everything. I love good food, wine, laughter. I want to marry, to have children. . . . Leave me alone . . . I don't care about the King-dom of Heaven; I like the earth. . . . I want Magdalen, even if she is a prostitute."[98]

God persists, and prevails. The carpenter leaves his shop, without a word of farewell to his bewildered parents, and walks many miles, night and day, to reach a monastery and become a monk. The abbot thinks he sees a halo of light around the novice's head; dying, he nomi-nates Jesus as a divinely chosen successor to his abbacy. The monks demur; Jesus leaves them, and proclaims the Kingdom of Heaven to roadside gatherings. He recommends persistent, unresisting love as the secret of happiness and as the best revolution; for "if the soul within us does not change, the world outside us will never change."[99] But he accepts hospitality, "likes festivities,"[100] and is no foe to joy. He counsels lenience to sinners, protects Magdalen from a threatening crowd, and spends a virtuous night in her home as the only available refuge from a violent storm. He finds that his faith and the touch of his hand can heal the sick and accomplish apparent miracles; he believes that he has supernatural insight and powers; gradually he comes to think of himself as the son of God, as God himself in an earthly form and visitation. His mother, after a long search, finds him preaching ecstatically, thinks him sick and deluded, begs him to come home with her. He refuses, and she is about to curse him as an ungrateful child when a neighbor quiets her.[101]

Apostles follow him, hoping that he will be the Messiah to deliver Israel from Rome, and trusting that they will find cozy berths in his future ministry. Judas begs him to lead a revolution; Jesus rebukes him, but, as his disciples multiply, he inclines to Judas' view.[102] He desires and expects arrest, and is resigned even to crucifixion, if this will arouse the people to revolt. Disciple Andrew asks, "Rabbi, why don't you laugh any more, why aren't you joyful, as you were before? Why have you grown continually more ferocious?" Jesus does not answer.[103] He asks Judas to betray him to the authorities;[104] Judas does, hoping that the arrest of the beloved preacher will inflame the masses. Jesus forbids Peter to resist the soldiers; he is arrested and crucified. The apostles lose faith in him, and disband.

At this point the pagan in Kazantzakis unleashes his imagination. On the Cross Christ faints, and his early vision of a happy married life returns in a dream. He roams a pleasant field, meets Magdalen, lies with her, satisfies her, and then weeps in her arms. "Beloved wife," he tells her, "I never knew the world was so beautiful, or the flesh so holy. It too is a daughter of God, a graceful sister of the soul. I never knew that the joys of the body are not sinful. . . . I went astray because I sought a route outside the flesh."[105] While he sleeps peacefully, Magdalen walks about, is captured by the soldiers of Caiaphas, and is killed. An angel of dubious origin tells Jesus of her death, tries to comfort his grief, and leads him to Mary and Martha, daughters of the Lazarus who had come back to life at Jesus' call. The angel expresses envy of normal earthly pleasures. "Paradise," he tells Jesus, consists of "thousands of small joys. To knock at a door, to have a woman open it for you, to sit down in front of the fire, to watch her lay the table for you; and, when it is completely dark, to feel her take you in her arms"— even the angels (who have no sex) envy this. "I understand," says Jesus.[106] He marries Mary, and is happy as never before. But Martha also loves him, and night after night she sleeps devotedly at his feet. He takes pity on her, and makes her too his wife, in full conformity with Jewish law. "An infant sits mute and numb in the womb of every woman. Open the door and let him out!" "I'll send a message to have my tools brought from Nazareth. I'll have my embittered mother come, too, so that she can bring up her grandchildren and feel some sweetness on her lips at last."[107]

Children come. Jesus works as a carpenter and a farmer. He feeds his brood, is respected by his neighbors, is proud and content. But Judas rises up before him, and upbraids him for having failed to free his people from Rome. Then Paul of Tarsus appears, spreading the glad tidings that the crucified Christ has risen from the dead, has mounted to heaven, and waits there to reward all those who have believed in him as God-made-man. Jesus reveals himself and rebukes Paul: "Don't go around the world to publish lies." Paul begs him not to declare the truth; would it not be better to let the story of his divinity, of his atonement for the sins of men, and of his triumphant resurrection, be a lasting consolation to mankind? "Now," says Paul, "I will create Christianity." The last temptation of Christ is to reject Paul's appeal, to repudiate the task of redeeming sinful humanity, and to enjoy the earthly paradise of life with his wives, his children, and his daily work. Then the bucolic vision vanishes, and Jesus wakes to find himself dying in agony on the Cross.

The usual interpretation of this remarkable book is that Kazantzakis presented the dream as a device used by Satan to corrupt Jesus' soul in those final hours; and that the burden of the message is, Reject even the lawful joys of this world if they hinder your pursuit of a noble humanitarian goal. Yet the author described the dream at such length, in such loving and enthusiastic detail, that one is tempted to see in it his oft-repeated view that it is a great sin to repudiate the flesh and the pleasures of common life, and certainly a mistake to renounce them in the hope of some posthumous reward. He himself, however, while preaching the pagan gospel of Zorba and Odysseus, avoided the joys and tribulations of marriage as long as he could, and dedicated himself to the quest for "truth" and the transmutation of "matter" into "spirit."

It was just as well that he left his meaning obscure, for the leaders of the Greek Orthodox Church discovered many heresies in this Fifth Gospel, and thought again of excommunicating the author. Perhaps he mollified them by the piety with which he told the story of Saint Francis in The Poor Man of God (1943). I have not gone beyond the Prologue, which sufficiently reveals a rising mystical mood:

While writing this legend, . . . truer than truth itself, I was overwhelmed by love, reverence, and admiration for Francis, the hero
and martyr. Often large teardrops smeared the manuscript; often a
hand hovered before me in the air, a hand with an eternally renewed
wound [the "stigmata" resembling the wounds in the hands of the
crucified Christ]: someone seemed to have driven a nail through it.
. . . Everywhere about me, as I write, I sensed the Saint's invisible
presence. For me Saint Francis is the model of the dutiful man, the
man who by means of ceaseless, supremely cruel struggle, succeeds
in fulfilling our highest obligation, something higher even than
morality or truth or beauty: the obligation to transubstantiate the
matter which God entrusted to us, and turn it into spirit.[108]

VI. THE MORTAL

Kazantzakis went through so many adventures, countries, creeds, and
moods that it is hard to say what his final conclusions were. He surrendered himself in turn to one philosophy after another, and found
none fit to sum up his experience or satisfy his "undulant and diverse"
soul. Yet he could not quiet his quest. "I have one longing only: to
grasp what is hidden behind appearance; to ferret out that mystery
which brings me to birth and then kills me; to discover if, behind the
visible and unceasing stream of the world, there is hidden an invisible
and immutable presence."[109] He wanted to know what made the plant
grow; what made men struggle not only for food but for beauty. "I
pitied man's soul, and marveled at its achievements. How was this lowly
silkworm able to extract such divine silk from its entrails?"[110]

Since he was a poet, seared with sensations, he moved more and more
toward pessimism. He was saddened to find nature so indifferent, so
hostile to man, snuffing him out as carelessly as a man steps upon an ant.
Even the fossils that man leaves in the rocks will disappear and "a great
silence . . . will one day cover the world like piles of ashes."[111] "Only
the spontaneous, purest laughter can neutralize—not, of course, overcome—the horror of life,"[112] or "this funeral procession that we call
life."[113]

His enthusiasm for Nietzsche faded with the years. When Hitler
came, Kazantzakis asked the shades of his youthful idol: "The Superman
has come; is this what you wanted?" And in this vision Nietzsche answered, "Yes!"[114] Sick of politicians,[115] grasping merchants,[116] and industrial lords,[117] Kazantzakis clung to a fading faith in Communism—but
"I believe unshakably in the inequality of man."[118] He had long since

ceased to be active in the Communist movement. As far back as 1931 he had made his mouthpiece Geranos say:

> To limit myself and become a militant fanatic, to renounce all the delights of pure speculation and beauty . . . —I am incapable of doing it. I have chewed and rechewed too many books . . . What intensely interests me is not man, nor the earth, nor the heavens. It isn't Russia that interests me, but the flame consuming Russia. Amelioration of the fate of the masses or of the elite, happiness, justice, virtue—these things, which lure so many people, do not catch me. Only one thing thrills me; I look for it everywhere, and my eyes follow it with joy and fear. The red line . . . ; all I love is this red line. . . . Everything else seems to me ephemeral, smugly philanthropic and vegetarian, unworthy of a soul now emancipated from all hope.[119]

He did not define this "red line" except as the perpetual struggle of man for self-development. "My own guide is neither Faust nor Hamlet nor Don Quixote, but Don Odysseus,"[120] who did not need the mirage of hope to beckon him to ever fresh adventure, enterprise, and search.

Kazantzakis' last novel, *The Fratricides*, written a year before his death, made a priest its idealistic hero, but showed him a helpless victim of rival tyrannies—royalist and Communist. The scene is Castello, a town in northern Greece, where centuries of monarchy, theology, and poverty have left the people ignorant, superstitious, hard, and laughterless. The time is 1946–47, during the attempt of the royal government (helped by the United States under President Truman) to suppress a Communist insurrection. In this civil war, towns and families are torn by the hostile factions into hatred and violence. Father Yanaros asks a youth with bleeding head, "Who wounded you?" The youth replies "Some Communist because I am a Christian—some Christian because I am a Communist: I couldn't tell who."[121] A monk whispers to the priest that Christ has returned to earth in the form of Nikolai Lenin. The son of Father Yanaros leaves him, and, as Captain Drakos, leads a Communist band in besieging Castello. The priest, risking suspicion at home and murder en route, goes out to negotiate a peaceful surrender of the town to the Communists on condition of their promise to refrain from revenge. They enter, establish their power, and insist on executing the local royalist leaders. Yanaros protests; they kill him.

In the conflicts of its ideals and the disorder of its structure *The Fratricides* reflects the chaos and contradictions in Kazantzakis' character. "My principal anguish," he wrote, "and the source of all my joys and sorrows . . . has been the incessant, merciless battle between the spirit and the flesh. Within me the dark, immemorial forces of the Evil One, human and pre-human; within me too are the luminous forces, human and pre-human, of God—and my soul is the arena where the two armies have clashed and met";[122] in short, he was a Zoroastrian. Or, in Nietzschean terms, he was a Dionysiac spirit, dancing with joy and fury, with imagination and art, and yet longing for the Apollonian ideal of moderation and discipline: "Discipline is the highest of all virtues."[123]

He divided men and women not into good or bad, nor into beautiful or ugly, but into warm or cold; and only the warm could enter his paradise.[124] He praised love, gentleness, and justice, but he exalted the violent, tricky, and adulterous Odysseus as representing indefatigable energy and will. Age may have quieted Nikos down, for his second wife described him as "a man who preached violence though he had no violence in himself; who was indulgent with others, but remorselessly severe with himself."[125] He called upon all men to love one another, as the only way to happiness and peace, but he confessed: "I did not love many men, either because I failed to understand them or because I looked upon them with contempt . . ."[126] He traveled from Gibraltar to Vladivostok, but he cultivated solitude. He admired a Zorba who preached sensual pleasure and an active life, but he himself ate and loved sparingly and lived like an ascetic, brooding about God and writing many books.

He savored words, was a master of them, and scattered them abroad like windblown leaves from a dying tree. His double secret was that he turned his words into feelings deeply felt and pictures intimately seen. "Night like a panther prowled the royal graves." "The dream clung to him like a woman."[127] He described a hundred characters, and made each of them so distinctly and consistently individual that we see and know the leaders of Megalokastro and Castello more clearly than we do our neighbors. What to us would be a sunrise was to him a love affair:

> The sun had waked the birds and fitted their little throats with tunes. Having climbed over the peaks of the mountain, he spread over its slopes and the plain, opened the doors in the village and went in. He found the widow still in bed; . . . he slid furtively over her hair. He found Maiori [the priest's daughter] in her yard watering her flowers, and hung himself around her neck. He went to look for the women of the village in the same way, and caressed them like a master.[128]

And this was the way spring came to Palestine:

> All day long, . . . even during the night, . . . spring had been gradu-
> ally pushing aside rocks and soil . . . In one night the plains of
> Sharon in Samaria and Esdrelon in Galilee filled with yellow daisies
> and wild lilies; and shortlived anemones—large drops of blood—
> sprouted among the sullen rocks of Judea. Protruding crablike eyes
> appeared on the vines . . . A guardian angel stood by each tiny leaf
> and helped it grow. You thought the first days of creation were re-
> turning, when each word of God which fell upon the freshly turned
> soil was full of trees, wild flowers, and greenery.[129]

A Japanese spy, assigned to watch Kazantzakis, pronounced him quite
safe, for he was a poet in love with words.[130]

Not content with filling eight hundred pages with his *Odyssey*, he
planned, late in life, to write *Faust: Part Three*—as if Part II was not
already long enough; even so, he would compose "a tragedy of the fate
of contemporary man, who, after having reached the peak of his intellectual perception, has now arrived face to face with the abyss."[131]
Then, hearing the swish of the Reaper, he began at Antibes in 1956 his
Report to Greco. This, he warned the reader, "is not an autobiography";
it would be an account of his mental and spiritual development, whimsically submitted to "my grandfather" El Greco, who, like himself, had
been born in Crete. He summed up the steps in his growth by four
names: Christ, Buddha, Lenin, Odysseus.[132] He made no apology for
having repudiated the civilization of his time; "Sometimes it seems to
me that this world is another Sodom and Gomorrah," deserving divine
wrath and destruction.[133] He had come to sense a certain jejune arrogance in Nietzsche's excoriation of Christianity,[134] but he still resented
the Christian rejection of the flesh; the new religion he hoped for "will
embrace and sanctify the body as well as the soul."[135] "If you wish to
conquer temptation, there is only one way: embrace it, taste it, learn
to despise it. Then it will not tempt you again."[136]

He never finished his *Report*, for in 1957, though suffering from
lymphoid leukemia, he accepted an invitation from the government of
Mao Tse-tung to visit Communist China. Aged seventy-four, he set out
(June 5) with Eleni and a friend on his final peregrination. They
traveled by train to Bern, Zurich, and Prague, by plane to Moscow and
Peking. They went down to Hankow, then up the Yangtze to Chung-
king, then to Canton. There Kazantzakis was vaccinated against small-
pox and cholera. Of this arduous trip he left notes for another book,

Twenty Years After; he did not live to write this, but the surviving fragments attest his wonder at the progress that China had made since his visit in 1935 (after the Japanese invasion):

> Then, filth, epidemics, open sewers, stinking streets, many beggars in rags, annoying and dangerous. Political anarchy, civil wars. Corruption in government. Illiteracy, poverty, feudalism.
>
> Now: clean streets, railroads, clothes. No epidemics, flies, or mice. No beggars. Sanitation and literacy spread. . . . Government strong and disciplined. Rulers apostles of economy; no waste, no luxury. Ascetic. . . .
>
> Liberation of the Chinese woman. . . .
>
> Politeness: they welcomed me with smiles.[137]

After thirty-three days in China Kazantzakis and his wife went to Japan, where they admired the women and the flowers but resented the skyscrapers and the revived industrial monopolies. They flew to Alaska, and over the North Pole to Copenhagen. On this trip his vaccination developed a serious infection, which became Asian influenza. He was taken to Freiburg, where he received the most loving care from his favorite physician. But he had run his course, had exhausted all adventures and all theories; and though "a heap of books will be left inside me,"[138] it must have been a relief to die (October 26, 1957).

"My work," he had written, "is the purification of unspeakable struggles and joys. . . . I have tried for many years to save what I could of my soul, so that when I die men [may] know how much I too have loved and felt life, and how I have gazed upon and touched the sea, the soil, woman; and so that they [may] learn that I was not a beast or a stone, but a man with warm flesh and an insatiable soul."[139] I feel closer to him than to any other hero of these pages.

CHAPTER XVII

Literature Under the Soviets

THE Russians frighten me. I feel their ability, stamina, courage, and power in their literature and their armies, their scientists and their composers, their ballet and cinema, their maintenance of their complex government and heterodox economy through fifty years of internal hardship and disorder, external hostility and attack. In the second half of the nineteenth century the Russians produced the two greatest novels of all time—*War and Peace* and *The Brothers Karamazov*—and an outburst of music that challenged the German supremacy in symphony and the Italian supremacy in opera. It was a title in Turgenev—*Fathers and Sons*—that revealed the "generation gap"; and a line in Dostoevski —"If there is no God everything is permitted"—that inaugurated the moral decline of Christendom while Russia toughened itself with poverty and discipline. It was the Russian rollback of Hitler's armies from Stalingrad to Berlin that won the war against Nazi Germany. Today the Russia that was in chaos and desolation in 1917 is in control of half of Asia, and of Europe from the Urals to the Elbe. A map of the world frightens me.

I cannot speak with any authority about Russia or its literature. I cannot read the language, so that its poetry is lost upon me—though I have read its novelists and dramatists with rising astonishment and admiration. I visited Russia in 1912, and traveled from St. Petersburg to Yalta, but I was a novice of twenty-seven then, too young to ask the right questions or to understand the answers. I returned to Russia twenty years after, crossing from Harbin to Omsk to Moscow to Warsaw; but I remained only a month under the Soviets, and then reported with immature haste in *The Tragedy of Russia* (1933). I suspect that the Soviets will survive me. However, long before Khrushchev, I detected the smell of Ivan the Terrible in Joseph Stalin.

Of Russian authors since Chekhov (d. 1904) I have read only Sholokhov, Pasternak, Solzhenitsyn, and Yevtushenko. Behind them is a host of other writers, mostly untranslated into English. I have chosen for discussion Sholokhov as friendly to the Soviets, Pasternak as remembering prerevolutionary graces, Solzhenitsyn as blasting Stalin, and Yevtushenko as reconciling criticism with loyalty.

I. MIKHAIL ALEKSANDROVICH SHOLOKHOV

From these limited studies I came to the unexpected conclusion that the greatest single work of literature known to me and produced under the Soviets is Sholokhov's *The Silent Don*. I began its 1,289 pages prepared to be bored; I caught fire, read nearly every page, and finished the book with the conviction that my distaste for Sholokhov's political orthodoxy had unwisely kept me from the finest Russian novel of this century.

He was born in the town of Veshenskaya, in the region of the Don Cossacks. His father passed through farming and cattle breeding to serving as salesman in a store; his mother was half Cossack and half peasant. At the age of fifteen Mikhail joined the Communist Party. He went to Moscow, but soon returned to his native surroundings; he has always disliked and deplored city life, and has remained faithful to the Don. He learned to know the Cossacks well, in all their half-martial, half-rural ways, their courage and brutality, their love of horses and the land, their family solidarity and adulterous diversions. After experimenting with short stories, he found his place and forte by taking the Don Cossacks as the subject of a four-volume novel which he fondly entitled *Tikhil* [quiet, peaceful] *Don*.* He sent it out in installments in 1928, 1929, 1933, and 1940. When the final volume was published, some readers stood in line for hours waiting for the Moscow bookshops to open.[1] Half of literate Russia wanted to know the fate of Gregor Melekhov.

Gregor is the second—Piotr the first—son of lame and cranky Pantaleimon Melekhov, who owns and tills a plot of land along the Don. The river is the quiet undercurrent of the four volumes, loved by the Cossacks as the nourishing mother of their soil, the patient carrier of their products and themselves. Usually it remains in the background of the narrative, as something daily seen and unnoticed; but now and then it plays a part in the story, as when the Red Guard army of the Soviets faces the rebellious Cossacks across the peaceful stream.

---

* The English translation, under the general title *The Silent Don*, appeared in two volumes: *And Quiet Flows the Don* and *The Don Flows Home to the Sea*. Honor to Alfred Knopf for bringing so many foreign masterpieces to America.

The theme of the work is the life of the Don Cossacks during the First World War and the early years (1917–21) of the Revolution. The structure of the book is frankly modeled upon *War and Peace:* Part I of Volume I is entitled "Peace"; Part II, "War"; Part III, "Revolution." The scene oscillates between love and death, between the orderly and creative routine of the farm and the confused and destructive riot of war. History is a pendulum and alternation between the bed and the battlefield; and every victory becomes a defeat.

Gregor is a brave soldier who can never find what he is fighting for, whether against the Germans or the Bolsheviks. He loves Russia, but hates the Czar; he desires a socialist state, but only if it leaves the Cossacks their family ownership of land. He might have made a good husband, but his father compels him to marry the virtuous and gentle Natalia when Gregor is dreaming night and day of his friend Stepan's luscious and adventuresome wife Aksinia.

Piotr's wife, Daria, is "at heart a rake"; while he marches off to war she cools her heat with any partner. Her father-in-law thinks to chasten her with a blow, and "for some days Daria went about quieter than water, lower than grass."[2] Then, burning again, she invites limping Pantaleimon to love her in the hay; when he refuses she taunts him with impotence. "I haven't seen my husband for a year!" she cries. "What am I to do—lie with a dog? A fig for you, one leg! . . . I can't do without it. I need a Cossack, and if you don't want to . . . I'll find one for myself." And the paterfamilias hobbles off "chewing his beard" and muttering, "Maybe I should have sinned with her?"[3]

Gregor and Piotr learn the art of war as leaders of Cossack regiments in the Russian Army fighting Germans and Poles. An old Cossack instructs Gregor in using a saber:

> "This is the way! Cut a man down boldly! Man is as soft as butter! Don't think about the why and wherefore. You're a Cossack, and it's your business to cut down without asking questions. To kill your enemy in battle is a holy work. For every man you kill God will wipe out one of your sins."[4]

But one young Cossack whispers to a fellow sentinel:

> "What do you think, Alexei? I'm only a lad, but I'm hungry for life. When I remember how many beautiful women there are in the world my heart begins to pinch. . . . I've grown so tender to women that I could lie with them all, tall or short, lean or fat, so long as they

were pretty. And life lets you have only one at a time, and you've got to keep with her till death, until you're fed up with her."[5]

So they kill and get killed until the czarist government is overthrown by the Kerensky Revolution of February–March, 1917. Gregor, wounded, hears from another patient in a Moscow hospital the gospel of the Bolsheviks:

> "War has gone on since the beginning of time, and will go on so long as we don't sweep away the evil government. But when every government is a workers' government they won't fight any more..., When the Germans and the French and all the others have got a workers' and peasants' government, what shall we have to fight about then? Away with frontiers, away with anger! One beautiful life all over the world." . . . Gregor's mind awoke.[6]

Soon the Russian soldiers get the secret message. An officer in the trenches reads to his companions an article by Lenin. Russian troops begin to fraternize with their German enemies. A Russian, capturing a trench, finds a solitary German there, and bids him go in peace. "Give me your hand. We're brothers, you know."[7]

The Bolshevik Revolution comes (October–November, 1917), and men have to find new reasons for new wars. The "Whites" under Kaledin, Kornilov, etc., attack the "Reds." Trotsky, organizer of victory, gets only a line of mention, as Bronstein. Gregor joins the Bolshevik forces, but is disgusted when he sees Reds kill White prisoners, and Whites kill Red prisoners, with equal zest. He cannot make up his mind on which side to fight; "behind him everything was tangled, contradictory."[8] Only one thing was clear to him: that he longed for his home, his family, their piece of land.

> When he thought that soon it would be time to get the harrows ready for spring, . . . that he would be driving out into the steppe, his labor-yearning hands gripping the plow handles; when he remembered that soon he would be breathing in the sweet scent of the young grass and the damp-smelling earth turned over by the plowshare, his heart warmed within him. He longed to collect the cattle, to toss the hay, to catch the . . . scent of the cloves, the twitch, the pungent smell of dung. He wanted peace.[9]

In Volumes III and IV (known in England and America as *The Don Flows Home to the Sea*) the major theme is still war—the rebellion of the Cossacks against the Soviet government; while the minor theme is the growth of the soil and the family as a foil to war. Here and there the story stops to contemplate the river, the forest, the fields, the sky. "Fructified by the spring, an invisible, almighty, and palpitant life was unfolding in the steppe. The grass was growing luxuriantly; in their secret lairs birds and animals were mating; the plowed lands wore a fine brush of innumerable young shoots."[10]

The protagonists are principally Cossacks. Sholokhov loves them, but does not spare them. He describes their lustful young women, their tough and tearful old women, their gossiping elders and blustering youths. Nearly every one of them has lice in his hair and violence in his heart; the villagers enjoy beating to death the Reds captured by the Cossack soldiery;[11] they steal, fornicate, adulterize, and kill. Says one Cossack to another, "It is easier for a man to kill another man than to crush a louse. Men have grown cheap during the Revolution."[12] Gregor's father, Pantaleimon, steals everything he can lay his hands on in a neighboring cottage whose residents have fled from the advancing Reds; he calls his daughter "You daughter of a bitch!"[13]—though his hard-working wife has put up with him for thirty years despite his infidelities.

Gregor himself has been brutalized by the war. "In the teeth bared beneath his mustache, in his narrowed eyes, the innate Melekhov animal traits emerged still more clearly."[14] He gets drunk more often. When his wife complains of his drinking and whoring, he answers, "How can you [i.e., anyone] feel shame when all your life's messed up? There you are killing people. You don't know what all the mess is about. . . . Something here is sucking and sucking at me. I've dabbled so much in men's blood that I've got no pity left for anyone. The war's dried it all out of me. I've grown hard. . . . Look into my soul and you'll find a blackness like an empty well."[15] Leading his beaten Cossacks in retreat from the Reds, he bids his wife stay at home with the children, but he takes his mistress Aksinia with him. Aksinia is shot by Red sentries; Gregor buries her in a grave dug by his fingers, and rides on. Natalia, finding herself again pregnant by her faithless husband, tries abortion, and dies of a hemorrhage. Daria, rotting with syphilis, kills herself. Old Pantaleimon dies of typhus.

Gregor, coming upon the corpse of his father, "shuddered with horror and disgust. Over the gray, waxen face, filling the sockets of the eyes and the furrows of the cheeks, lice were crawling. They covered the face with a living, moving film; they swarmed in the beard, stirred in the eyebrows."[16] At the end Gregor, his sister Dunia, and his son Mishatka are the sole survivors of the once vigorous family. He returns to his village and comes upon the boy, who gazes "in terror" at "this bearded and terrible-looking man."[17] We merely guess that Gregor will try to restore the farm, that Mishatka will marry and raise a family with love and blows, and that life will stumble on. "The wind carried the chaff dust through the village; a sweet scent of threshed, rusty straw hung everywhere,"[18] and the Don, nourishing the earth as if nothing had happened, flowed calmly home to the sea.

It is a powerful book, pouring out the evil and good of life, mingling the brutalities and tenderness of men and women, in an immense procession and alternation of war destroying and love rebuilding in a land and age of revolution. It is a realistic picture. A thousand items attest the author's wide experience and keen observation: he knows the details of army life in barracks, trenches, and hospitals, the strategy of commanders and the tactics of battle; he is familiar with agricultural processes, feminine logic, rural speech, and barn morality. He colors no facts, stresses no sentiments, sheds no tears; the death of Natalia is described in simple narrative, sparing of words. The events are briefly recorded, the characters are swiftly sketched—not by description but by their words and deeds. Like Dostoevski and Tolstoi, Sholokhov paints masses rather than individuals: we see a village stirring, a province in turmoil, a nation suffering and giving birth.

Judging from Sholokhov's unpopularity in America, I had expected *The Silent Don* to be unfairly weighted in favor of the Soviets. I did not find it so; the author's sympathies are obviously with the Cossacks, merciless though he is with their faults. Official censors objected to some passages that showed the Communists in unprepossessing array. Other orthodox critics condemned the conclusion of the story; they had confidently expected Gregor to end up as a good Bolshevik, and they were much put out by his remaining hostile to the last page.[19] Nevertheless the novel received the Stalin Prize in 1941, and the final section was broadcast on the government radio.[20] In 1953 Sholokhov issued a new edition, in which he improved the conduct of his Communists, and "toned down the exuberance of his style."[21]

In 1932 he interrupted his masterpiece to issue another leviathan, *Virgin Soil Upturned*, describing, in the form of a novel, the collectivization of agriculture in the Don region. (I have not read this.) Two million copies were sold in fifteen months. Stalin, then supreme, was not satisfied, for Sholokhov, though always a loyal Communist, had not concealed his sympathy for the resisting Cossacks.[22] When, in 1936, the author sent Part II to the monthly magazine *Novy Mir* (*The New World*) the editors returned the manuscript as needing revision. Instead of complying, Sholokhov went back to work on *The Silent Don*. In World War II he came out of his semirural seclusion to serve as a war correspondent. Meanwhile his house in Veshenskaya was destroyed, and his mother was killed by a German bomb.[23]

Part II of *Virgin Soil Upturned* was serialized in *Novy Mir* and *Pravda* in 1955–60. Again the ending displeased the orthodox, for the hero, Davidov, dies in a Stalin purge. Khrushchev, who was now in power, might have accepted this, if only as conforming to Aristotle's view of tragedy as a cathartic, but he arranged a compromise: on a visit to Veshenskaya he apparently persuaded Sholokhov to give Davidov a different death.[24] In 1960 Khrushchev took the author with him to the United States as Russia's leading man of letters. In that year Sholokhov received the Stalin Prize for *Virgin Soil Upturned*, and in 1965 the Nobel Prize capped his awards. From that height he descended (1966) to defend the Soviet government's condemnation of Sinyavski and Daniel (1965) to years of hard labor for having, in material transmitted to the West, criticized the invasion of Czechoslovakia by the armies of the Warsaw Pact. Sholokhov seems to have decided that the preservation of Communism was more important than the freedom of the mind. The orthodox in every country would uphold that sentiment with the change of only one word.

II. BORIS PASTERNAK

I. The Poet

Few Americans would agree with me in ranking *The Silent Don* as the supreme production of literature under the Soviets. Pasternak's defense of intellectual freedom, and of the individual against the state, has won him far more friends in Europe and the United States than Sholokhov can ever expect to have. American readers of *The Silent Don* are probably but a tenth of the number who have read *Doctor Zhivago*, and even a smaller fraction of those who have seen the excellent transfer of the events (hardly of the intellectual content) of that book to the screen. Not *Doctor Zhivago* alone, but remarkable poems and a tragic life, made Pasternak the outstanding figure in Russian literature since Chekhov.

In 1931 he wrote an eighty-page account of his youth, under the cryptic title *Safe Conduct*. It is chaotic and fanciful, jolted now and then by literally farfetched metaphors and dizzy turns of phrase or thought. The author was a poet, not an historian; and a poet is not committed to logic. He warned us: "I am not writing an autobiography. . . . The history of a poet is not to be presented in such a form."[25] The book is a strange succession of moods, only occasionally coinciding with chronology.

We learn elsewhere* that Boris was born in Moscow on February 10 (New Style), 1890. His father, Leonid Pasternak, was a Sephardic Jew from Odessa, who accepted conversion to Christianity, but later became a fervent Zionist.[26] In 1887 Leonid married Rosalin Kaufman, of mixed German and Jewish descent. She studied piano with Theodor Leschetizky and Anton Rubenstein, gave recitals with diminishing returns, and contributed to the family income by taking pupils. Leonid took up and then abandoned medicine, turned to painting, and achieved considerable excellence; note his strong portrait of Rainer Maria Rilke.[27] In 1898 Tolstoi chose him to illustrate *Resurrection*, and in 1892 *War and Peace*. The aging giant became a friend of the family; "our whole house was permeated by his spirit";[28] we shall see this reflected in Zhivago's gospel of love and in the intensified and mystic Christianity of the poems appended to the novel. For a time the Pasternak household moved to Yasnaya Polyana so that the artist might be in frequent touch with his employer. In 1910 Tolstoi's widow summoned Leonid to Astapovo to paint her husband on his deathbed. Boris, then twenty, went along; the sight of Tolstoi dead never faded from his memory; and to the end of his life he ranked him as the greatest of all Russians.

In 1893 Leonid was made director of the Moscow School of Painting, Sculpture, and Architecture. The family received a comfortable apartment in the school, in a fashionable quarter of the city. Boris grew up in an atmosphere of art, music, and literature; this was the cultured air that Zhivago would miss after the Revolution. Leonid prospered sufficiently to rent a small *dacha*, or country house, in Obolenskoyo, some seventy-five miles from Moscow. There Boris was thrown from a horse and broke a leg; the bone was reset too short; he limped sufficiently thereafter to be exempted from military service.

Aleksander Scriabin was a neighbor at Obolenskoyo. Boris, already advancing in music under his mother's instruction, fell in love, or at least in awe, with the ecstatic composer. When Scriabin left for Italy he came to say goodbye to the Pasternaks; "into the general heap of parting benedictions mine fell like a clot of blood."[29] Scriabin's return

---

* The biographical data in this essay are largely filched from Robert Payne's scholarly but eloquent *The Three Worlds of Boris Pasternak*.

was celebrated with a ringing of church bells; Pasternak, continuing his bizarre images, recalled that "along the somnolent streets the hanging tongues of the belfries sank into the mist. In each a solitary bell clanged once; the rest remained in friendly silence together, with the full restraint of fasting metal."[30] Boris played some of his own piano compositions before Scriabin; their noncommittal reception discouraged the youth, and after a few more years of effort he turned to poetry.

He had his first taste of revolution when, as a boy of fifteen, he watched the slaughter of protesting Russians before the Winter Palace in St. Petersburg (January 20, 1905); he was struck down by a Cossack sword; he commemorated the day in his poem "The Year Nineteen-Five." He went through a course of studies at the University of Moscow, where he was intoxicated alternately with the music of Wagner and the philosophy of Nietzsche. In 1912 his mother gave him two hundred rubles which "she had saved from her earnings" as a piano teacher and had "economized from the household expenses, . . . with the advice that I should go abroad a bit."[31] He went to Marburg, eager to study Neo-Kantianism under Hermann Cohen. It disappointed him, and he wrote poems instead of dissertations.

He was relieved when his parents invited him to join them in Italy. In Milan he saw the ornate cathedral as "a melting glacier";[32] it is still there. Venice enthralled him with its architecture, its women, its music rising from churches and gondolas. "Venice is a town inhabited by buildings—by the Campanile, the Cathedral, the Doge's Palace . . . The word the architects spoke in stone is so lofty that no rhetoric can stretch to its heights,"[33]—and indeed Venice has had no great literature. How could a man who had felt the graces of a dying culture be happy, a few years later, amid the coarse and unmannerly ways in which a new civilization gets born? Here, perhaps, the mournful mood of Dr. Zhivago began to form. *Nessun maggior dolore che ricordarsi del tempo felice nella miseria.*[34]

Returning to Moscow, Pasternak took his degree at the university and earned his living by tutoring. During World War I he spent two years in the Urals, unwittingly laying the locale for much of his novel. He was back in Moscow shortly after the Revolution of February–March, 1917; he welcomed the attempt of the Duma to provide an orderly transition, and he found a place as librarian in the Ministry of Education.

Meanwhile he had published several books. *The Last Summer* (1916), a short story, is the dreamy recollections of a tired man about his first love affair in "the last summer when life appeared to pay heed to individuals, and when it was easier and more natural to love than to hate."[35] Here so soon Pasternak reached out for recondite similes: "The abruptly interrupted crowing of a raucous cockerel quivered like a tiny splinter on a thread."[36] *The Adolescence of Zhenya Luvers* (1918) tried to trace the mental development of a girl through her reactions to the long absences of her father, the scoldings and caresses of her mother, the frowns and blows of her governess ("the image of concentrated pedagogy"[37]), the awesome discovery that babies come from the bodies of women, and her first flow of menstrual blood—which she interpreted as punishment for her sins. There, suddenly and strangely, the story ends: "One day Zhenya went out and vanished, leaving no trace, dying somewhere as a nameless number in the concentration camps in the north."[38]

Pasternak's first book of poetry (1914) made no stir, but in 1922 he startled the elite with a volume entitled *My Sister, Life*. We catch the mystic afflatus of the poet in the author's remembrance of its composition: "When *My Sister, Life* appeared, and was found to contain expressions not in the least contemporary as regards poetry, which were revealed to me during the summer of the Revolution, I became entirely indifferent to the identity of the power which had brought the book into being, because it was immeasurably greater than myself and than the poetical conceptions surrounding me."[39] Some of the poems pleased the new government, as when Lenin was described addressing a Congress of Soviets:

> *He was like the thrust of a rapier . . .*
> *He was the face which spoke to them;*
> *When he appealed to the facts*
> *He knew that when he rinsed their mouths*
> *With the momentum of his voice,*
> *History was passing through them. . . .*
> *He became the country.*[40]

But a later poem, written in 1920, suggests a growing skepticism. Pasternak pictures himself as sitting in a snowbound cottage, reading and writing poetry, and smiling at utopias:

> *With a muffler rounding my throat,*
> *Shielding myself with the palm of my hand,*
> *I'll shout across the courtyard: "Dear ones,*
> *What millennium are you celebrating out there?"*

However, he is thankful for some restoration of social order:

> *Who cleaned that pathway to my door,*
> *That hole all choked with sleet and snow,*
> *While I was smoking with Lord Byron*
> *And drinking wine with Edgar Allan Poe?*[41]

He has retired into himself, and is more interested in the mysteries of the soul than in the crass events of political history. He forgets the transmigrations of power and writes a cycle of lyrics about some unnamed lady whom he loved in 1917.

I have read all of *My Sister, Life,* and confess myself baffled by the language barrier. An excellent scholar and translator admits that Pasternak "defies translation," and that "no one has yet succeeded in conveying in English the richness of his vocabulary, the leaping brilliance of his rhythms."[42] He is as full of rhymes as his tintinnabulating Poe; he adds alliteration and assonance, and flashes short circuits of grammar and syntax that have mystified even his fellow practitioners. "Pasternak," writes Yevtushenko, "was as yet unintelligible to me [at age sixteen]. He seemed too complicated, and I lost the thread of his thought in the chaos of his imagery." But the younger poet wisely adds: "I have never had the arrogance of those who, when they fail to understand an artist, blame the artist, not themselves. [*Caveam ipse.*] . . . One day Pasternak became crystal clear, and ever since then he has been to me . . . as simple as the sky and the earth."[43] You must know the Russian sky and earth well to say that.

Clearer than Pasternak's sexual ecstasy is his passionate love affair with nature. Perhaps reflecting the rough course of his romance, he celebrates not only her proud trees and ever varied and reborn flowers, but her terrors, storms, quakes, and floods, and, above all, the rain that responds to his darkening mood. He spends hours and strophes noting the play and relics of the rain: "the rain will clobber the roof with buckshot," and will leave "slugs crawling over the eyes of garden statues."[44]

He is a madman with images, and makes forced marriages of the incongruous: "the rye, inflamed, was fiery red, a hairy erysipelas," and "he washed the sun away like blood from a knife."[45] In *Safe Conduct* Pasternak defended metaphor as something inherent in nature but perceptible only by the artist. "Art . . . is realistic, since it has not itself invented metaphor but has discovered it in nature and reproduced it faithfully."[46] "The direct speech of feeling is allegorical, and cannot be replaced by anything."[47] In this sense poetry is truer than prose to the subtle similitudes of the world.

If many Russians worked their way through Pasternak's obscurities it may have been because they loved the earth that he described, the trees and flowers that he celebrated by name, and even the stern climate that made men strong. "A whole generation of Russians grew up learning his poems by heart, so that on the rare occasions when he recited his poems in public and forgot his lines, the whole audience would thunder them back to him."[48] When, in 1926, he issued a small volume of verse honoring Lieutenant Schmidt, one of the heroes of 1905, the Communists almost forgave him his introversion and solitude. By 1940 he was recognized as the leading poet in the Soviet Union.

In 1923 he married Eugenia Muratova, who bore him two sons. The union was ended by divorce; he took a mistress, went with her to the Caucasus, married her, and received a third son. The Union of Soviet Writers leased him a country house at Peredelkino, a suburb of Moscow. He supported the Communist regime till 1932, when the rising brutality of Stalin's rule made the poet shrink into political silence. Orthodox critics noticed this withdrawal, and accused him of disloyalty. In a remarkable address at the First Congress of Soviet Writers (1934) Nikolai Bukharin analyzed Pasternak's silence brilliantly:

> Boris Pasternak is one of those poets who stand remote from the problems of the present time. . . . He has departed from this world and entered the pearly shell of his own personal emotions, where, with infinite delicacy and tenderness, he continues to work on the problems of his wounded heart. . . .
>
> We see that Pasternak is completely original, and that is his strength and his weakness. His strength because it removes him at an infinite distance from the banal, from clichés, from rhymed prose. His weakness, because originality is transformed into egocentricity, when the images are no longer comprehensible, when the trembling of his breathless rhythms and the meanderings of his linguistic armory, though contrived with exquisite precision, become showers of erratic images which no longer possess any recognizable meaning, for they arise out of the most intimate recesses of subjectivity.[49]

Despite the friendliness of this critique, Pasternak felt increasingly insecure as Stalin's purges eliminated one after another of the Revolution's heroes, even Bukharin himself. In 1935 the poet was allowed to go to Paris to attend the First Congress of Writers in Defense of Culture. There he met Malraux and Gide, and enjoyed the surviving graces of the old civilization; he read a paper on the poet's task, but said nothing about Communism. Back in Peredelkino, he supported himself by translations, especially from Shakespeare and Goethe. When Hitler invaded Russia (1941) Pasternak wrote some patriotic poems, served as a fire warden, and was knocked unconscious by the explosion of a German bomb. In 1942 and 1945 he published new volumes of poetry. Critics attacked him as an individualist who had lost all touch and union with Communism. Aleksander Fadeyev, secretary of the Union of Soviet Writers, publicly demanded: "Why do we fawn on a man who in the course of so many years has refused to accept our ideology? . . . Anyone who translates Shakespeare in wartime . . . is attempting to disarm us by inoculating us with the poison of an alien ideology."[50] At this time Fadeyev was a neighbor of Pasternak at Peredelkino.

2. Doctor Zhivago

Discouraged by hostility, Pasternak retired still further into himself, and, on and off through nine years (1945–54), poured his secret feelings into a book which he hoped to leave as his last intellectual testament. He would have approved the guiding principle of these our studies—that an author's interpretation of life is the kernel of his work. "You can call it an idea, a statement about life, so all-embracing that it can't be split up into separate words; and if there is so much as a particle of it in any work that includes other things as well, it outweighs all the other ingredients in significance, and turns out to be the essence, the heart and soul of the work."[51]

He chose the novel as his medium, for the poetic forms in which he was skilled were too narrow, compact, and inflexible to allow the full expression of his thought. On March 5, 1953, Stalin died; in September Nikita Khrushchev came to power as first secretary of the Communist Party, and in 1956 he opened his attack upon Stalinism; a period of relaxed censorship and more humane rule seemed to have begun. In the summer of 1956 Pasternak sent a copy of Doctor Zhivago to Novy Mir, and about the same time he sent a copy to Giangiacomo Feltrinelli, a publisher in Milan. In September the editors of the magazine returned the manuscript with a long explanation of their unwillingness to publish it.

Your heroes, and particularly Doctor Zhivago, spend the years of the Revolution and the Civil War in search of relative well-being

... and the enjoyment of spiritual life. And what is the spiritual life they are always seeking? It is the life they lived in the past . . . Because the Revolution steadfastly requires them to take sides, they turn . . . from a feeling of alienation to a feeling of active hostility toward it . . . We find your novel profoundly unjust, and lacking in historical objectivity in its portrayal of the Revolution. . . . We regard it as a profoundly undemocratic work, and without benefit to the people.[52]

Another Russian publishing house, Goslitizdat, offered to issue the book if Pasternak would allow the omission of passages that might offend the Soviet government. He agreed, and signed a copy to this effect; meanwhile he sent Feltrinelli a request to postpone the Italian publication for six months. Feltrinelli did so. Soon thereafter Pasternak fell ill, and spent most of the winter in a hospital; six months passed, and Feltrinelli permitted extracts—mostly unfavorable to the Revolution —to appear in the periodical *Espresso* in the summer of 1957. Friends of the author persuaded him to send Feltrinelli a telegram recalling the manuscript; but an Italian writer passing through Moscow received a letter from Pasternak to Feltrinelli advising him to use his own judgment.[53] In buying the manuscript, Feltrinelli had acquired the copyright; and as the Soviet Union had not signed the Bern Convention giving international protection to copyrights, he considered himself free to proceed with the enterprise, on which he had already spent a considerable sum. In November, 1957, the Italian edition appeared as *Il dottor Zivago;* the edition of six thousand copies was sold out in a few days; two further editions appeared in the next two weeks; and translations were soon published in France, Germany, England, and the United States. Publication in Russia was now out of the question; *Pravda* denounced *Zhivago* as a slander on the Revolution. Pasternak complained that critics on both sides had judged the work by the same few excerpts—"three pages, perhaps, out of a book of seven hundred pages."[54] But to a German journalist he said, "You have the right to ask me whether I believe what I have written. My answer is yes."[55]

Like all of Pasternak's publications, *Doctor Zhivago* is a strange book. It begins as a group study, introducing some thirty characters before the doctor himself definitely enters the story; then for a time it is a family chronicle; in the second half it is the intimate history of two individuals. The word *zhivago* means alive; some readers[56] have seen in the choice of this name a mystic suggestion of resurrection and immortality; *caveat emptor.* He is not described physically, except for his outstanding nose; but enough is said of his background and character to make the sequel credible. Son of a rich industrialist, he enjoys not only the luxuries of upper-class life in czarist Russia, but also the stimulus—perhaps the enervating influence—of an intellectual and artistic entourage. His Uncle Nikolai is a rich liberal, bubbling with ideas, and inclined to utopian hopes for the future of mankind; for good measure he anticipates the new theology by deposing God and worshiping Christ. "It is possible to be an atheist; it is possible not to know whether God exists, or why, and yet believe that man does not live in a state of nature but in history, and that history as we know it now began with Christ, and that Christ's Gospel is its foundation."[57] (So Pasternak, three-quarters Jewish by birth, came to believe in Christ —not quite in Christianity—as the only salvation for a mankind repeatedly verging upon barbarism.) Young Zhivago adopts this view, "striving through his life . . . to love everyone, not only his family and his friends, but everyone."[58] In one of the poems that Pasternak ascribes to him, Zhivago embraces Whitmanic inclusiveness:

> *I feel for all these people*
> *As if I'd been within their hides . . .*
>
> *The nameless ones are part of me.*
> *Children also, the trees, and stay-at-homes.*
> *All these are victors over me—*
> *And therein lies my sole victory.*[59]

He loves his wife, Antonia, especially. But when the First World War sends him as a physician to the front, and his virtue silences the male hunger for a woman's warmth and tenderness, he cannot help following with his eyes the charming Lara (Larisa) Guishar, the most devoted nurse in the military hospital. Of French and Russian descent, she has been seduced by a prominent lawyer, Victor Komarovsky; she has tried to kill him, but her shot wounds another; now she is trying to steady herself with service. She has a husband, Pavel (Pasha) Antipov, who has been reported missing in action. She, like Zhivago, has inherited a middle-class culture, and has been refined with the literature, music, and art of two countries. When the Russian Army breaks up in defeat and revolution she disappears, but the doctor cannot forget her.

He returns to his prewar work in the Hospital of the Holy Cross in

Moscow, and wins a local reputation for selfless service. He welcomes the Revolution, seeing in it a step toward the realization of universal brotherhood. His ardor slackens when the Bolsheviks seize power; he does not like their crude directness of action and thought, their confiscation of property, their nationalization of the land; but he bears patiently their appropriation of every extra room and bed from the well-to-do for the poor. He, "Tonia," and their child suffer with the rest during the terrible years of the civil war, when the Revolution had to fight for its life on a dozen fronts: the disruption of agriculture, industry, transportation, trade, and finance; the shortage or absence of the simplest necessaries of life; the spread of every kind of crime; the inflation annulling all savings and reducing the middle class to the common destitution. It was no time for poets, for sheltered spirits recalling chamber concerts and literary soirees. "In these five or ten years," says Zhivago, "we have experienced more than other people do in a century."[60] At last he, his wife and child and Uncle Nikolai join the hundreds of desperate families huddled in stations waiting for tardy, limping trains to take them elsewhere, anywhere; they fight like the rest for a foot or two of space in passenger cars, freight cars, cattle cars; they go through days and nights of anxiety, hunger, and cold, and at last reach Yuriatin in the Urals. They go thence to the village of Varykino, hoping to evade there the eyes of the Revolution; they find a cottage, plant a garden, and survive.

Some time later, by one of those coincidences which seem indispensable to fiction, Zhivago finds Lara working in Yuriatin. She has an eight-year-old daughter, Katenka; her husband, renamed Strelnikov, has survived, but has left her to devote himself wholly to the Revolution. Zhivago falls in love with Lara; he struggles against the passion, and resolves to renounce her; but on his way back from what was to be his last visit to her he is captured by Red "partisans" and is made to serve as their physician in their campaign against Kolchak.

After more than a year of this employment he escapes, makes his way on foot through miles of wilderness and ruined villages, and is appalled by the almost universal destitution. "There were isolated cases of cannibalism. . . . The jungle law was in force."[61] Exhausted, disheveled, and in rags, he reaches Yuriatin and finds that wife and children have returned to Moscow and have fled thence to Paris. He rejoins Lara, who tells him how nearly everything that Yuriatin and its environs produce is seized for shipment to Moscow; "nothing is left to us," and "the Cheka is savagely putting down the slightest sign of discontent."[62] Stalin is filling Siberia with prison camps. A survivor of one camp says:

"I think that collectivization [of agriculture] was an erroneous and unsuccessful measure, and it was impossible to admit the error. To conceal the failure people had to be cured, by every means of terrorism, of the habit of thinking and judging for themselves, and forced . . . to assert the very opposite of what their eyes told them. This accounts for the unexampled cruelty of the Yezhov period,* the promulgation of a constitution that was never meant to be applied, and the introduction of elections that violated the very principle of free choice. . . ."[63]

Lara, her daughter, and Zhivago find a hiding place in Varykino, and there, fighting starvation, cold, and howling wolves, they dream of an idealized past. Lara protests that the Revolution has destroyed not only the comforts and graces of the old regime, but the very elements of civilization.

". . . All customs and traditions, all our way of life, everything to do with home and order, have crumbled into dust in the general up-heaval and reorganization of society. . . . All that's left is the naked human soul stripped to the last shred . . . And you and I are the last remembrance of all that immeasurable greatness which has been created in the world in all the thousands of years . . . , and it is in memory of all those vanished marvels that we live and love and weep and cling to one another."[64]

This sounds like Pasternak, son of a prosperous artist, but his other mood speaks through another voice. Zhivago reproves Lara's exaggerations. He recognizes the injustices and barbarities of the czarist regime; he admits the need of revolution, but he attributes its excesses to sham "proletarians" who cover their incompetence by silencing their critics with a bullet in the neck. He regrets the fall of Kerensky; if the Revolution had continued under middle-class leadership, there would have been less derangement of the economy, less suffering and degradation. All attempts to reform society are hampered by the nature of man, which is disposed to greed and violence; the only real revolution would be one which moderates that nature. "Nothing can be gained by brute force. People must be drawn to good by goodness";[65] Zhivago returns

* Nikolai Yezhov was head of the secret police, 1936–38.

to love as the final wisdom and resort. He does not despair of Russia; he has seen countless deeds of goodness among the people; and even amid the wreckage that surrounds him his heart goes out to "this vast expanse . . . Russia, his incomparable mother; famed far and wide, martyred, stubborn, extravagant, crazy, irresponsible, adored; Russia with her eternally splendid and disastrous and unpredictable adventures."[66]

To Lara and Zhivago, almost snowbound in their cottage, their food and fuel running out, comes the man who inaugurated Lara's tragedy. Komarovsky has been commissioned by the Soviets to establish a Communist stronghold in Vladivostok. He offers to take Lara and her daughter on his sled to Yuriatin, and thence by train to the Far East, where, he promises, he will arrange her escape from Russia. Zhivago persuades her to go. He himself, by every transport and device, finds his way to Moscow; he marries again, lives by writing textbooks, and sinks again into poverty. Riding in a tram, he suffers a heart attack; he stumbles from the car, and falls dead at the curb.

Lara, who has returned from Siberia, comes upon her dead lover as his corpse is being prepared for burial. "She . . . made three sweeping signs of the cross over the body, and pressed her lips to the cold forehead and hands. . . . It was as if she had lived twenty lives, and had lost Yuri [Zhivago] countless times . . ."[67] As for her own (and the story's) end, one day she "went out and did not come back. She must have been arrested in the street at that time. She vanished without a trace, and probably died somewhere, forgotten as a nameless number on a list that afterwards got mislaid, in one of the innumerable mixed or women's concentration camps in the north."[68]

Pasternak appended to his masterpiece a sheaf of poems which he ascribed to Dr. Zhivago, but which obviously reflect his own final longing for a faith that could overcome suffering and death. They are his final verses, and his last testament. "Scattered over the years of my life," he said, "and collected in this book, the poems were, in effect, preparatory steps to the novel. . . . The plan of the novel is outlined by the poems accompanying it."[69] They correspond loosely to Zhivago's passage through love to nature to vitalism to Christ.

Of the twenty-four poems seven celebrate love, sometimes uncharacteristically physical.

> For my part, all my life long
> I have stood like a devoted slave

In reverence and awe before the miracle
Of woman's hands, her back, her shoulders, and her sculptured throat.[70]

In another poem he explores these glories, but with a touch of remorse for ignoring the call of the Revolution and the grim saying that "whosoever looketh on a woman to lust after her hath committed adultery with her already in his heart."[71] He pictures himself (like Lady Chatterley's lover)

here with you in the forester's hut. . . .
We are the only ones now
For the walls of logs to regard in melancholy.
We made no promises to storm barricades;
We shall go down to perdition openly. . . .
You shed your coverings in much the same fashion
As this grove sheds its leaves,
Whenever you fall into my embraces
In your dressing gown with its silken tassels.
You are the blessing in a stride toward perdition . . .[72]

Perhaps his sensitivity to woman intensified his adoration of nature. Like so many poets, he thought that he found in the forms and voices of fields, trees, forests, and a mercurial sky sympathetic correlations of mood with his own vacillations between love and fear; nature seemed to be a feeling entity, or a multitude of entities, knowing joy and sorrow, growth and death, like man. "Never, never, even in their moments of richest and wildest happiness, were they [Zhivago and Lara] unaware of a sublime joy in the total design of the universe, a feeling that they themselves were a part of that whole, an element in the beauty of the cosmos. This unity with the whole was the breath of life to them."[73] They could not think of nature as a mechanism and determinism of physics and chemistry; it was a living organism, endowed with will, perhaps with purpose and intelligence. Life, said Zhivago, "is never a material, a substance to be molded. . . . Life is the principle of self-renewal; it is constantly renewing and remaking and changing and transfiguring itself . . ."[74] Pasternak told Stephen Spender that he believed "reality itself had freedom and choice, and was building itself out of numberless variants and versions."[75]

He himself rarely attended church services, and gave no adherence to Christian theology, but he felt the philosophy behind the mythology, and was moved beyond expression by church art and ritual. More and more, as he grew older, he returned to the story of Christ that had inspired his youth; if this was not history it was the greatest poem ever composed. He felt that Marx's gospel was not working; it had raised a new breed of masters as cruel as the old, and far more crude; what was left, then, to man's hope but the "good tidings" of Christ—that happiness and peace can come only through an ever-widening love, in which the individual is content to be absorbed in the whole?

> For life, too, is only an instant,
> Only the dissolving of ourselves
> In the selves of all others,
> As if bestowing a gift . . .[76]

Seven of these Zhivago poems are intimations of Christ. Six of them recall aspects of Christian creed or ritual: "Holy Week," "Star of the Nativity," "Miracle," "Evil Days," "Magdalene," and "The Garden of Gethsemane." The initial poem, though entitled "Hamlet," is phrased in the words of Christ's prayer while the Apostles slept: "If Thou be willing, Abba, Father,/Remove this cup from me"; in that invocation the Jew and the Christian are combined. In "Holy Week" the poet, "hearing spring," wonders whether "Death itself can be overcome/ Through the power of the Resurrection."[77] And in the final poem Christ says:

> I shall descend into my grave. And on the third day rise again.
> And even as rafts float down a river,
> So shall the centuries drift, trailing like a caravan,
> Coming for judgment, out of the dark, to me.[78]

With those words the strange volume ends, as if summoning the nations and the Revolution to the judgment seat of Christ.

3. Man Versus the State

Doctor Zhivago is astonishing and yet natural: an idealistic novel amid the wash of "socialist realism" bound to an ideology; and yet an expectable reaction against a doctrine that left too little room for poetry and sentiment, tenderness and imagination, and the dreams of a solitary, meditative soul. The book holds us because it is about a man ✓ and a woman, about life and death, not about a nation or an idea. Zhivago is obviously the author himself, fleeing from the coarseness and turmoil of events; and for that matter, Pasternak too went to the Urals and fell in love with a woman not his wife. The Soviet editors and orthodox critics felt that for a writer to absorb himself in his own individual feelings and romance was treason to the Revolution.

They had many reasons for rejecting the book. They argued that the Revolution had been relatively peaceful until half a dozen nations had sent armies against it; that the economic dislocation, the summary executions, the brutality and suffering, that had so shocked Zhivago and Lara had been caused by the civil war rather than by the Revolution; that it was childish to think that the czarist autocracy could be overthrown, and its defenders repulsed, without widespread hardship, poverty, and death. The Soviet leaders, and their literary voices, could be forgiven for finding something grand and heroic, however bloody, in the victory of the Revolution; and they had just seen the historic triumph of the Soviet troops over the apparently invincible German invaders during the terrible years of 1941 to 1945. It seemed to Pasternak's enemies absurd to imply that the whole Revolution had been a mistake because a poet and his women, despite their cultured heritage, had had to suffer like the soldiers and the commonalty. What were the tribulations of Zhivago, Antonia, and Lara compared with the daily ordeal of the millions besieged for years in Leningrad, or of the soldiers and civilians who gave their lives to drive Hitler's troops, mile by mile, back from Stalingrad to Berlin? Some angry patriots, including Sholokhov, branded Pasternak as "an internal *emigré*"[79]—a man who had in spirit fled from his country to the West. And the resentment of Soviet leaders was inflamed when they found that the organs of opinion in the West were using *Doctor Zhivago* as part of the Cold War, as evidence that the finest writers in Russia were disowning the Revolution.

Pasternak felt that he had not really rejected the Revolution; he had affirmed its necessity; he had revolted only against the unchaining of the worst instincts of the worst men. The Revolution meant to him not only the heroic defeat of the Wrangels, Denikins, and Kolchaks, and the sharp suppression of internal conspiracies externally financed; it meant also the reigns of terror under Stalin, the "purge" after "purge" of the very men who had made the Revolution, the banishment of countless men and women to forced labor in concentration camps, the deceptive "democracy" of one-party elections, the control of literature and the press by the government, the suicides of ardent but disillusioned souls. It seemed, in 1956, that the time had come to speak out, to call the nation back from Stalin to civilization.

Probably it was one of the many services that Khrushchev performed for Russia that no physical harm came to the author of *Doctor Zhivago*. The book was denied publication, but Pasternak himself was not touched; he continued to live in the *dacha* leased to him by the Union of Soviet Writers, and his mail was delivered to him—including foreign encomiums—with no apparent interference. No royalties came to him from the publication of his book in the West. Gradually the furor subsided, and Pasternak, as still the premier poet of Russia, was invited to official functions in Moscow.[80]

The truce suddenly ended when, on October 23, 1958, the Swedish Academy offered Pasternak the Nobel Prize for Literature, and asked him to come to Stockholm on December 10 to receive the award. He wired back: "Infinitely grateful—touched and proud—astonished—confused." His rivals and foes leaped upon him with fury. They had hoped that Sholokhov would win the prize for *The Silent Don*, as a book expressing the scope and spirit of the new Russia; for so unsympathetic a work as *Doctor Zhivago* to be chosen instead seemed to them both an insult and an injury. The Soviet press denounced Pasternak as "a black sheep," "a pig," "the running dog of the bourgeois slaves." The editor of *Komsomol* bade him leave Russia before an aroused populace took the matter into its own hands. On October 28 the Union of Soviet Writers expelled Pasternak from its leadership. Its secretary suggested to the Swedish Academy that Pasternak would be allowed to receive the prize if it were given equally to Sholokhov; the Academy could not accept such outside influence. On October 31 Pasternak wrote to Khrushchev, Chairman of the Council of Ministers: "It has been made known to me . . . that the government will raise no objection if I leave the U.S.S.R. For me this is impossible. I am tied to Russia by my birth, my life, and my work. . . . To be exiled would be a sentence of death. I beg you not to take these extreme measures against me." He wired the Swedish Academy that he could not accept the award "because of the significance attached to it in the society I am living in." He wrote to *Pravda* accusing himself of errors, and affirming his loyalty to the Soviets. Attacks upon him continued in the press, but he was not further disturbed.[81]

He had two more years of life. A portrait made about this time shows him still erect and apparently strong, with white hair casually brushed back, a stern, serious face, whose dark and deepset eyes recalled many griefs. He now renounced as artificial and "impure" all that he had written before 1940, and wished to be remembered only for *Doctor Zhivago*. He never recanted its message—that the individual is the ultimate value, and must not be enslaved by the state. Shortly before his death, having been asked to leave his final testament to posterity, he spoke into a tape recorder—in Russian, German, and French—his proud demand: *"Il faut être libre souverainement, en roi.* One must be sovereignly free, like a king."[82]

But earthly affairs dimmed in his eyes as he aged. He seemed to be searching desperately for the God he had lost in his youth. Not quite finding him, he clung to a vaguely vitalistic philosophy. "During our short space of life," he said in 1958, "we must find our own insight into our relationship with the existence in which we participate so briefly. Otherwise we cannot live. This means, as I see it, a departure from the materialistic view of the nineteenth century. It means a reawakening of the spiritual world, of our inner life—of religion. I don't mean religion as a dogma or a church, but as a vital feeling."[83]

In 1958 he began to cough with painful frequency. He told a few intimates that he suspected cancer of the lungs, but he begged them not to reveal this to his (second) wife. Perhaps for this reason he refused to summon doctors; they came nevertheless, and diagnosed his case as heart disease. In the end he proved right. He died May 30, 1960. No priest, no state official, no representative of the Union of Soviet Writers attended his funeral, but a few students carried the coffin from his home to his grave.

III. ALEKSANDER SOLZHENITSYN

The Western world, obsessed with Khrushchev's shoe, hardly noticed that, while seeking to arm Cuba against the United States, he was resolutely leading a movement for the liberalization of Soviet life and thought. Except for him Pasternak might have suffered Siberian exile; it was he who protected Yevtushenko against "Stalin's heirs"; it was he whom the editor of *Novy Mir* named as his authorization for publishing, in the issue of November, 1962, a story by a new and venturesome author, describing life in a Russian prison camp. "It is our duty," Khrushchev had said to the Twenty-second Congress of Soviets, "to go carefully into all aspects connected with the abuse of power. . . . We must tell the truth to the Party and the people. . . . This must be done to prevent such things from happening in the future."[84] Yevtushenko has testified that *One Day in the Life of Ivan Denisovich* "was published through the direct help of Khrushchev."[85]

Its author was born in 1918, into a Cossack family of some cultural attainments. From his studies and degree at the University of Rostovon-Don his specialty and destiny seemed to be in science; and his books impress us by their knowledge of mathematics, physics, and medicine; but he longed to be a writer. World War II snatched him into a life of action; he earned two decorations, and rose to the rank of an artillery captain. However, in one of his letters from the front he allowed himself the luxury of criticizing the military errors of "the man with the mustache"—Stalin. He was sentenced to eight years in a prison camp, and then he was condemned to three years more. Under Khrushchev's rule he was released (1956), and he settled down as a teacher of mathematics in Ryazan (120 miles southeast of Moscow). He resumed his writing, and found his forte in a new kind of realism—one that neither darkened nor polished the facts but tried to be just to the evil and the good that have come down in our blood from a million years of hungry, bloody hunting and a brief dozen millenniums of family love in settled life.

He wrote of a prison camp in Siberia in the year 1951. The story is told as if by one of the prisoners, and in language customary to men driven down to elemental life and common speech; the reader must prepare himself for most of the four-letter words now sprinkled over much American fiction.[86] The convicts are hardened by time and cold; their terms are seldom less than twenty years; they work in the open air even in temperatures sixteen degrees below zero Fahrenheit; their clothing is "rags tied with bits of string."[87] They risk their lives to smuggle into their barracks a bit of wood to keep alive the one stove that gives them a little heat; the food allowed them is stale and scanty; and at any deviation from routine or command they may be shot. However, they have a rare privilege: they are allowed to write to their families once a year. Some of the guards can be bribed to yield a cigarette; some of the work managers are occasionally humane. Strange to say, it is the work they must do that comforts these condemned men; when they are building walls they fall into an exciting rivalry, and rejoice in the skill and product of their hands. Ivan Denisovich gets so accustomed to the prison and its routine—free from all necessity of thought—that he is not sure he wishes to be freed;[88] besides, he hears no inspiring news about any freedoms left in the outside world.

All this is put down without resentment or prejudice. Even so it startled its millions of readers, for there was hardly a family in Russia that had not had a member in a concentration camp; stories about them had come secretly and fearfully from the survivors, and now it was a relief that someone could dare to speak the truth, and that it had been published with the explicit "approval of the Central Committee of the

Communist Party of the Soviet Union."[89] "This stark tale," said the editor of *Novy Mir*, "shows once again that there is no aspect of our life that cannot be dealt with and faithfully described."[90]

The fate of Solzhenitsyn's *The First Circle* darkened this dream. It is dated on its last page "1955–1964"; the work had been in progress for ten years. No Russian publisher would print it, but the author allowed some friends to make copies of the manuscript; these were handed from one reader to another; a copy reached New York, and Harper and Row shocked the Soviets by issuing it in an excellent translation in 1968. Solzhenitsyn claimed that this copy had been sent out of Russia over his protest. So far as we know, no harm has come to him.

The title refers to the first circle in Dante's *Inferno* (Canto IV) as the limbo (or vestibule to hell) to which the poet assigned Virgil, Aristotle, and other presentable pagans who could no longer be allowed to suffer the tortures of those who had had the advantages of a Christian rearing. In like manner some victims of Stalin were confined not in prison labor camps, but in *sharashka*s or special barracks, where they would be more mercifully treated in return for placing their scientific or other skills at the service of the state. The scene of the book, then, is a *sharashka* at Mavrino, a suburb of Moscow. The time is toward the end of 1949. The prisoners, though educated, have been toughened and coarsened in revolution and war; Russia, we are told, is "a land where every second person had gone through [concentration] camp or front-line schools of cursing, where foul oaths are commonly used not only by drunks in the presence of children (and by children in children's games), . . . but sometimes even in heart-to-heart conversation."[91] "Ruska and his whole generation had been taught to believe that 'pity' was a shameful feeling, that 'goodness' was to be laughed at, that 'conscience' was priestly jargon. At the same time they were taught that informing was a patriotic duty."[92]

The 280 prisoners are assigned various tasks severely limited in permitted time, and culminating in an order from Stalin to design electronic devices both to disguise telephone messages by transforming words into noises and to decode noises into words. If they remain on good behavior they are allowed decent food and bedding, and periods of amusement or conversation. However, they are under constant watch by armed guards and unidentifiable spies; their reading is restricted; they have no privacy, and no access to women; they may meet their wives and relatives only a half hour in each year, in a public room with a guard at their elbow listening to every word. This lack of sexual companionship becomes a major misery. The imprisoned men worry about their wives' fidelity and their children's development; it is part of their genteel torture to feel that during their ten or twenty years' confinement they will be forgotten, in face and soul, almost in name, by those they loved. Gleb Nerzhin, who carries the thread of the labyrinthine tale, has been separated from his wife first by the war and then by imprisonment; he fears that by the time he is freed she will be too old to bear healthy offspring; Stalin, he feels, "has robbed him and Nadya of children." Now, facing a long term, he writes to her:

> My darling! You waited for me through four years of war—don't be angry at having waited in vain. Now it will be ten years more. All my life I will remember, like a sun, our short happiness. But now be free from this day on. There is no need for your life to be ruined. Marry![93]

Nearly all the prisoners are victims of Stalin's purges, suspicions, or dislikes. The guards and spies obey his orders literally, fearing him even more than the convicts do. Some of these forgive him, saying that though he has erred in their cases he has provided the steel discipline needed to bring order out of revolution, and victory out of war. But Nerzhin (Solzhenitsyn) hates and despises him as a monster of vanity, treachery, cruelty, and lust for omnipotence, and can never forget the murderous "purges."

> Then the same Old Bolsheviks who had made the entire Revolution, and whose life it had been, began by the dozens and the hundreds to drift into nonexistence. Some, not waiting to be arrested, swallowed poison in their apartments; others hanged themselves . . . But most let themselves be arrested, and appeared in court and unaccountably confessed, loudly condemned themselves with the worst vilifications, and admitted serving in all the foreign intelligence agencies in the world. It was so overdone, so crude, so excessive, that only a stone ear could fail to hear the lie.[94]

"Stalin," Nerzhin concludes, "enjoyed killing."[95]

Solzhenitsyn's occasional pictures of life under Stalin leave the impression that all Russia was a concentration camp. The peasant, barring an acre or two, had to abandon his century-long dream of owning the land he tilled; technology compelled large-scale agriculture in Russia as in America; farming became an industry controlled by private capitalists in America, and in Russia by one inescapable, omnipresent, omnipotent capitalist called the state. Technology, in both countries, turned the craftsman, with some exceptions, into an industrial machine. One *sharashka* inmate asks of another:

> "Do you remember how, long ago, we used to read that the Ford assembly line turned the worker into a machine—that the assembly line is the most inhuman aspect of capitalist exploitation? But fifteen years have passed, and now we acclaim that assembly line, renamed the 'flow line,' as the best and newest form of production."[96]

In Russia, as elsewhere, the man with the lesser ability, or adaptability, sinks to the bottom, and the man with skill, aggressiveness, or conformability rises toward the top, like diverse particles finding different levels in a moving load. A new upper class is forming after the victory of the "class war," and it is not the proletariat, it is the technicians, the managers, the bureaucrats, the successful politicians.[97] There are three classes not only on the railroads but in every town in Russia; privilege is restored, and gets its way; there are special cars, stores, clinics, vacation resorts, for the successful and their wives; "you can't go a step without pull, you can't get anywhere without greasing a palm; we grow crafty and clever";[98] a "chasm" exists "between starving poverty and the insolence of fattening wealth."[99] To prisoner Ruska it seems unbearable hypocrisy to call all this the workers' paradise. What shameful dishonesty the intellectuals of Russia committed in lauding this state capitalism under Stalin![100] "Russian writers who dared trace their spiritual inheritance from Pushkin and Tolstoi wrote sickly-sweet eulogies of the tyrant. Russian composers . . . laid their servile hymns at his pedestal."[101]

Worst of all, in that Russia as Solzhenitsyn saw it, was the constant fear of arrest—not for crime but for the slightest criticism of the regime, the slightest doubt that the ogre in the Kremlin was the greatest blessing that Russia had ever had. Take Innokenty Volodin, who by faithful work and speech has brought his family to some modest comfort; he has won a place in the diplomatic service; his wife and children are proud of him. But he has to watch every word he utters, even in the privacy of his home. He is as innocent as his name, but he has been for some time a friend of a man who has just been arrested; how long will it be before he is taken away on a charge of guilt, if only by association? Too late he reads in a book of philosophy that "Epicurus influenced his pupils against participating in public affairs."[102] He dares not accept invitations for fear of speaking a friendly word with someone who may have been marked as suspect by the secret police. He creeps into a shell of humility and silence. He is arrested nevertheless. In the Lubyanka Prison he learns the ways whereby a prisoner's will and pride are broken till he will sign any statement placed before him.[103] At times he is left naked and shivering in a damp, unheated cell. He must urinate on schedule or not at all. Soon he disappears from the world.

The First Circle is a powerful book. Doubtless, like all books, it is one-sided and prejudiced; even Stalin must have had some good points; and only a private citizen like Edison or Ford can make a revolution without cracking skulls. Solzhenitsyn, born a year after the Revolution, had no personal memories of the czarist regime. In describing the *sharashka*, as we have noted, he tried to be fair; and he laid some stress on the fact that several of the prisoners still kept their belief in Communism as a bright hope if not yet an amiable reality. Apparently all the inmates of this intellectual jail were freed soon after Stalin's fall.

I came to his third book, *The Cancer Ward*, deceived by the general opinion that it fell short of its predecessor in excellence. Now, after having read it almost verbatim, I should rank it as Solzhenitsyn's best.

Again he wrote—not so bitterly as before—from his own experience. While a prisoner in a Siberian labor camp he developed a cancerous tumor; he was operated upon, apparently with success; but the evil recurred, and he was sent to a clinic in Tashkent (capital of the Uzbek Soviet Republic). There he received better treatment, and was released to both health and freedom. In his short story "The Right Hand" (published in Prague but not yet in Russia) Solzhenitsyn described Tashkent as seen by a former prisoner in a labor camp but now a patient in a hospital. It is another picture of life under Stalin: starving veterans and pretty girls—history marching on through misery and desire.

The last page of *The Cancer Ward* dates its composition "1963–67." The story is timed to some eight weeks early in 1955; the place is a hospital in a large city resembling Tashkent; the theme is men approaching death. Cancer Ward No. 13, for men, has nine patients, nearly all of them in exile. The hospital is reasonably well equipped with instruments and medicines, but is short of personnel; altogether it seems a credit to the Soviet government that even to its exiles it offered such careful treatment. Solzhenitsyn's method, as in *The First Circle*, is to go from person to person among the inmates and the officials, revealing each one's history and character, until, by adding bit to bit, he offers us a crowded living picture, and the reader becomes concerned with each body and soul.

The first figure is the portly pompous Rusanov, who, as manager of a local industrial plant, has risen to a good income and a "spotless apartment unstintingly furnished";[104] he worries whether his son will marry below his class, or will smash the new car.[105] As a very important person, he expects special attention to the swelling tumor on his neck; but he gets no favors, and slowly adjusts himself to the leveling that comes to unequal men before a common fate. As he lies on his cot he thinks, with more fear than remorse, of the men who were condemned to demotion or imprisonment because of his bearing false witness against them to please his superior and gain his own advancement.[106]

His nearest bed neighbor is Oleg Kostoglotov, from a distant Uzbek village; tough in body, tender in heart, sensitive to every touch of a woman's hand. Rusanov tries to take a superior tone with him, but Kostoglotov soon brings him down to reality. He has no delusions about his condition, or about Communism, or about medicine. Oleg wonders why the doctors or nurses daily puncture him with injections. "Must every medicine be administered through an injection? Where do you see such a thing in nature? . . . In a hundred years this will be laughed at as savage."[107] He learns, too late, that the female hormones shot into him will weaken or destroy his sexual potency, and he wonders, is not the cure worse than the disease? Dr. Leonidovich tries to console him: "Women are not the only attraction in life"; Kostoglotov rises in protest: "There is nothing else serious left in my life."[108] All the more so since he is daily falling more deeply in love with the kind and lovely woman physician Vera Gangart.

The hidden grief of the younger victims is that even if they are discharged as "cured" the fear of recurrence will almost bar them from marriage. Demka, a handsome youth, devoted to scientific studies, has had his cancerous leg amputated; amid the pains that he feels in his absent toes he mourns that he will be doubly handicapped in the pursuit of love. However, one night when the lights are dimmed, there comes to him from the women's cancer ward his boyhood girl friend Asya, seventeen, to tell him that the doctors have decided to remove her right breast. She wets his cot with her tears. "Who," she whispers, "wants a woman with one breast?" Equating a missing breast with a missing leg, Demka asks her to marry him. She bends over him, opens her hospital robe, lowers her condemned breast to his face, and begs him to kiss it. "Demka, you're the last one who can still see it and kiss it. No one, nobody else, will ever kiss it! . . . Kiss it, at least you!" He kisses it again and again, and takes the nipple between his lips. "She did not remove it . . . His lips quietly did what her future baby would never be able to do at this breast. . . . He went on kissing the marvel that hung above him. Today a marvel, tomorrow in the basket."[109]

Three of the women doctors, still subject to sexual tremors, give the grim story, now and then, a romantic glow. Zoya brings life into the ward with her pretty face, her youthful confidence, her cheerful talk. Vera Kornilyevna Gangart stirs some of the sick men with her slender legs and shapely ankles, but her heart is not as light as her tread. Her betrothed was sent to the front in 1941, and soon killed; Vera felt so bound to his image that she offered no lure to marriageable men; now she is fourteen years older. She is part of a larger tragedy:

> There were so many single women in the country [Russia] that one was almost tempted to count one's friends to see if there were more single women than married ones. These single women were all of an age, . . . contemporaries of the men who died in the war. The war had been merciful to the men, it had taken them. The women were left to live out their agony.[110]

To add to her grief, she knows that Kostoglotov is in love with her, while her duty requires her to give him, as cure for his cancer, injections that are destroying his sexual power.

Head of the women physicians is Lyudmila Afanasyevna Dontsova. She is devoted to her patients, and works overtime day after day, while her superiors warn her that she is approaching exhaustion. She too attracts Kostoglotov; of course she knows it, and as the years mount over her she wonders should she go with him to his Uzbek village, when he is provisionally cured, and surrender all the attractions of a city for the consolations, however spiritual, of a husband and a child. But she feels a constant pain in her left side. Can it be that she, the specialist in cancer, has cancer?

She goes to the oldest and most trusted doctor in the hospital, Dormitont Tikhonovich Oreshchenkov. Since the death of his wife he has lived in semi-monastic poverty, except that he accumulates more books every year. Lyudmila asks him to examine her and tell her the truth. After putting her through all the tests, he can only tell her that a cure is still possible. She makes the bitter transition from doctor to patient. She bids herself forget marriage and motherhood.

Solzhenitsyn feels that these secret concerns of the individual soul

touch life more deeply and constantly than the replacement of capital- ✓
ism with Communism in the relations of masters and men. He observes
how, day after day, the mores of the people in the Soviet Union (even
in the larger cities of Central Asia) come closer and closer to those of
Western Europe and the United States. In Siberia, as in America, corruption and bribery are common; plumbers will not do good work unless a private bonus is added to their state-regulated pay; the plumber
might put a dead rat in your drainpipe if you don't "come across."[111]
The radio is becoming a nuisance through its uninvited emergence from
almost every public wall.[112] Young men, in Tashkent as in New York,
laugh at marriage as bondage, use a girl and pass on;[113] and many lasses
fall in with the new fashion of free fornication. "The earlier, the more
fun," says Atya; "why put it off? It's the atomic age!"[114] Solzhenitsyn
can forgive all this, since he knows that morals and manners change
with the economic structure and technical equipment of a society. But
he still hates, as in *The First Circle*, the governmental censorship of
literature, the hypocritical press,[115] the sudden arrests, the incom-
municado imprisonment, the forced confessions,[116] the political assassinations, the attack on the Jewish doctors (1952) and their deportation
to Siberia in freight cars;[117] and he remembers with pleasure how the
prisoners in a labor camp, commanded to remove their caps at the an-
nouncement of Stalin's death, not only removed them but threw them
in the air.[118] He lets Shulubin, usually a silent patient, break out in a
slashing rejection of the whole Communist regime under Stalin;[119]
Shulubin sums it up in four lines from Pushkin:

> *In this, our age of infamy,*
> *Man's choice is but to be*
> *A tyrant, traitor, prisoner;*
> *No other choice has he.*

   Despite all, Solzhenitsyn holds fast to socialism. The same irate Shulubin says, "Don't conclude just because of your sufferings and those hard
years, that socialism was to blame . . . No matter how you feel, history
has nevertheless rejected capitalism forever."[120] But the mistake was,
"we thought it would be enough to change the mode of production, and
people would change [not only their mores but their nature] immediately. Not a bit of it! They didn't change at all. Man is a biological
species; it takes thousands of years to change him."[121] Well, then, what
else is needed besides socialism? Shulubin answers, "For Russia, . . .

with Dostoevski, Tolstoi, and Kropotkin, there is only one true socialism: moral socialism."[122] We must cease to hate and learn to love.[123]

This sounds like an echo of Christianity—which, in Soviet Russia, would be one of the seven deadly sins. Yet Solzhenitsyn, like Pasternak, dares to sympathize with religion. He notes the patience it taught many women and some men with the burdens and griefs of life, the nobility some reached through the spiritualization of their flesh, the comfort they derived from its myths and rituals,[124] the consolations they received in the hour of death. What could science give to the dying, or to those fated to be beaten in the struggle for existence—inevitable under any economic or political system? "Ah, sacred science," cries Kostoglotov, "if it were all so unquestionable it wouldn't have to be revised every ten years."[125] The religion of Communism had upheld a generation, but Stalin had damaged that faith as Torquemada had damaged Christianity. And what if the bright vision of Communism should fade into a monster of a state spreading its claws into its neighbors, and censoring every book, every thought?

Dr. Oreshchenkov concludes that "modern man is helpless in the face of death; . . . he seems utterly unarmed to meet it."[126] As for himself, he falls back upon philosophy, and speaks almost in Spinoza's terms.

> At such moments the whole meaning of existence—of his own life, . . . and his late wife's, . . . and everybody's in general—seemed to be not in their chief activity, in which they were constantly engrossed . . . It was in the degree by which they were able to keep unmuddled, unfrozen and undistorted the image of eternity that sits within each person.
>   Like a silver moon in a calm pond.[127]

We do not know if Kostoglotov reaches such peace, but he achieves in his own way an honorable end. When he is discharged as cured *pro tem*, he wonders where he should spend the night before his train leaves, early the next morning, for his Uzbek village. Zoya whispers to him that he would be welcome to stay overnight in her apartment. Vera secretly makes him a like offer; so hungry are these women for the touch of an honest man, potent or not. For hours he wanders about the city, unable to decide which invitation to accept, if any; finally he judges that it would be a hurt, rather than a blessing, for either of these women to attach herself to his crippled life. He goes to the depot, and waits there through the night for his train; when it comes he climbs into an upper berth of wooden slats, and returns to the place of his youth.

So simply ends this remarkable book. I know it has faults: a style too breathlessly staccato to reach the heights, a satire sometimes too severe and unforgiving, a tendency to make simple men talk like specialists or philosophers.[128] But what tireless observation of human frailties and generosities, what insights into the secrets of our souls and the problems that haunt our times! No wonder Yevtushenko calls Solzhenitsyn "our only living Russian classic."[129]

He has reached this position despite the fact that only his short stories and *One Day in the Life of Ivan Denisovich* have been published in Russia. His major novels are known to his countrymen only in manuscripts or in furtive reading of foreign editions. By some underground route a manuscript copy reaches an emigré publishing house in Frankfurt am Main, which sells rights of translation into West European languages. Solzhenitsyn has protected himself by publicly opposing the unlicensed export of his works; and he still remains a member of the Union of Soviet Writers. He lives now in relative comfort in a cottage some fifty miles from Moscow; "I am a country man, a villager," he told Victor Louis; "I live and breathe real air."[130] He has grown a beard, and looks like a cheerful chimpanzee.

He is not finished. He is now (1969) only fifty-one, which is the prime of life for a villager. He has gone through more than the first circle of hell; he remembers, too, the deeper hell of the prison labor camp; and this, we are told, is the scene of his new novel, *Arkhipelag Gulag;* this "Archipelago of Prison Camps" is circulating in manuscript, and will soon find a Western publisher. But I hope that before he dies Solzhenitsyn will write also of his hopes for mankind; that he will tell us more of the good that lies in us amid our hates and crimes. The circle will be complete when this new Dante finds some Beatrice to lead him out of his bitter memories into the peace that comes when selfishness has burned itself out.

After this last paragraph was sent to the publishers the news came that Solzhenitsyn had been expelled from the Union of Soviet Writers on November 6, 1969, for reasons described in the Moscow *Literary Gazette* of November 12: "antisocial behavior," and failure to move against the publication of his works abroad. "Through some of his actions and declarations he has in essence helped the spreading of an anti-Soviet hullabaloo around his name." When this expulsion was first voted by the branch of the Writers' Union in Solzhenitsyn's home town, Ryazan, it has been reported, he responded defiantly:

"Yes, I am ready to die, not only to be expelled from the Writers' Union. Vote; you are the majority. But do not forget that the history of literature will be interested in today's meeting. One cannot succeed indefinitely in keeping quiet about Stalin's crimes, for they were crimes committed against millions of human beings. To pretend that they did not exist is to pervert millions of other human beings."

And to the head organization of the union he wrote an open letter which is being secretly circulated in Russia by his friends:

It is time to remember that we belong first of all to mankind. Mankind has separated itself from the animal world by thought and speech. They naturally have to be free, but if they are suppressed we become again animals. Free speech—honest and complete free speech—that is the first condition of health in any society. . . . He who does not want free speech for the motherland does not wish to cleanse it of sicknesses, but to drive them inside, so that they rot there.*

I am not sure that freedom should ever be complete, nor do I know just where its limit should be set; but I am certain that any man who dares defy the Russian state today deserves to be remembered among the heroes of history.

IV. YEVGENI YEVTUSHENKO

The revolution first inspired Russian poets, then conscripted them to propaganda, and then drove some to disillusionment as they saw the nature of man overriding his aspirations.† The new rulers, like the watchdogs of the czars, thought it necessary to control literature in order to maintain their power; and in the compulsion to orthodoxy some potential Miltons may have remained inglorious or mute. Nevertheless hundreds of poets have strummed the Russian lyre since 1917. I know them only scantily and superficially, since their language and literary art are closed to me; and my little knowledge has been made more dangerous by the natural tendency of the West to pay more attention to the disillusioned singers than to the rest. We shall pay our

---

* Los Angeles *Times*, Nov. 13 and 15, 1969.
† I too (for I was once a poet!) wrote an ecstatic alleluia—"Holy Russia"— in 1919.[131]

respects to the memory of two who killed themselves in youth, and then surrender ourselves to the still exuberant Yevtushenko.

Sergei Yesenin began as a peasant in love with horses, green fields, and waving wheat. He went to Moscow at eighteen (1913), and worked with his father in a butcher shop; there is hope for all of us. He moved to St. Petersburg, and published poems full of cows and harvests and religious piety. He welcomed the overthrow of Czar and Duma, and joined joyously in the overthrow of God.[132] He read his poems to enthusiastic revolutionary gatherings. Isadora Duncan, coming to Russia, was fascinated by his verses, he by her legs. They were married in 1922, he aged twenty-seven, she forty-four. She took him with her to the United States, where he denounced capitalism and challenged the Americans to join in the march to Communism. Singer and dancer were soon divorced. Returning to Russia, Yesenin began an epic on Pugachev, who had led a peasant revolt against Catherine the Great; he never finished the poem, and never quite adjusted his rural heritage to the dictatorship of the proletariat. He laughed at the claim of the Revolution that it would bring equality to all men, and concluded that power had merely changed its personnel. He began to long for his adolescent days of farming and religious faith:

> I am ashamed that I believed in God;
> I bitterly regret that I don't believe today.[133]

He took to drink and tarts, wrote "Verses of a Brawler" and "Songs of a Drunk"; and in 1925, age thirty, physically and spiritually exhausted, probably insane, alone in a hotel room, he hanged himself.

Vladimir Mayakovski had a different origin (1893) and followed another route to the same end. Son of a minor nobleman, he demanded, even before the Revolution, a revolution in both politics and art. He studied Karl Marx at twelve, but preferred the colorful and romantic Ferdinand Lassalle. He relished Poe, Whitman, Jack London, Villon, Verlaine, and Rimbaud. At Moscow he enrolled in that same School of Painting, Sculpture, and Architecture where Pasternak's father was teaching. He welcomed Cubism and Futurism, dressed his lusty torso in a bright-yellow blazer, insulted opponents readily, and knocked them down with pleasure; he was as proud of his fists as of his verses. He hailed the Revolution ecstatically, and took up with delight the vocabulary of the proletariat. Those same well-to-do graces of word and life that Pasternak wished to preserve, those rustic simplicities and pieties that Yesenin longingly recalled, were condemned by Mayakovski as cultural treason and political immaturity; he celebrated the cities, the industries, and the battles that were sickening uprooted souls. He rejected all classic literary forms and rules, and thought that Pushkin had deserved a firing squad.[134] All literature, he thought, should be judged by its service to the new state; his own verses, he vowed, should be bullets shot for the Revolution.[135] He joined the propaganda agencies of the government, and gladly helped to prepare posters, slogans, and appeals for support of the Soviet armies. He visited the factories and stirred the workers with his readings. In an epic-satiric poem called *150 Millions* (1920) he pictured so many Ivans invading America and winning it to Communism. Leaders and masses acclaimed him as the poet of the Revolution. Soon his excesses of fervor and speech wore him out; he became weary of versifying propaganda; he dared to criticize the rising bureaucracy and secret police; he offended the Communists by not joining the party. He traveled abroad, relaxed in Paris, was "entranced" by New York, and returned with some dents in his ideology.[136] Worse yet, he allowed a love affair to dominate him, to make him forget, in his longing for a woman, that the Revolution and the Soviets claimed his supreme devotion. The lady rejected him; he sank into despondency; one day all Moscow was shocked to hear that Mayakovski had shot himself (1930) at the age of thirty-six. He left behind him an appeal to the tax collector:

> *Comrade government,*
> *Have pity on my mother,*
> *Take care of my lily sister.*
> *In the desk there are two thousand;*
> *Let the tax collector take his due.*
> *And I shall quietly die.*[137]

In 1963 Yevgeni Yevtushenko published in a Paris weekly *A Precocious Autobiography;* he was only thirty, but the amiable little book showed that he could write prose as well as poetry. At fifteen, he recalls, he quarreled with his mother, and "traveled on the roof of a train all the way" from his birthplace at Winter Station (in the Irkutsk Region) to Kazakhstan in Central Asia. There he worked as a day laborer; but he found time to read Pushkin, Dostoevski, Tolstoi, Chekhov, Hemingway, Faulkner, Joyce, Freud, Proust, Thomas Mann . . . He returned to his mother, worked hard; with his savings and hers he bought a typewriter. So armed, he made his way to Moscow, bubbling with poetry. His first published verses appeared in the magazine

Soviet Sport (1949); its subject was soccer, in which he was a "star." "Well," sighed his mother, "there's no hope for you now."[138] In 1952 he found a publisher for his "collected poems." "I went home, reread my book, and suddenly realized with the utmost clarity that it was of no use to anyone."[139] His mother took hope.

But he persisted, and now he resolved to describe things as he saw them, instead of hugging the party line. The death of Stalin (1953) freed the youth's pen; the rise of Khrushchev gave him courage; and though he was expelled from the Literary Institute and then from the Komsomol, he rose to the defense of Pasternak, and visited him at Peredelkino when it was dangerous to be Pasternak's friend.[140] He recognized that a new class was forming. "It was with the vigilance of a revolutionary that I watched the erection in Moscow of blocks of tall apartment houses destined for the bureaucratic elite, while thousands of Muscovites lived in tiny, wretched, overcrowded rooms";[141] he had still to learn that inequality is as natural as greed. "It was strange and unaccountable to me that even people with party cards in their pockets would love money so much."[142]

He denounced not only the brutal decrees that had sullied Stalin's decaying years but also, in "Stalin's Heirs," the men who were trying to maintain the rigor of that rule. He mourned "the many poets who died in Stalin's camps," and recalled with revulsion Stalin's dying attack upon the Jewish doctors. Later he wrote: "Now that ten years have gone by, I realize that Stalin's greatest crime was not the arrests and the shootings he ordered. His greatest crime was the corruption of the human spirit. . . . He did not in theory preach careerism, servility, spying, cruelty, bigotry, and hypocrisy, but these were implicit in his practice."[143] He admitted the achievements of Stalin in peace and war, but he begged that the guard over the ogre's tomb be doubled and trebled "so that Stalin should not rise, and with Stalin, the past."[144] Magazine editors did not dare publish "Stalin's Heirs," but *Pravda* printed it at Khrushchev's command.

Probably under Khrushchev's protection Yevtushenko was allowed to visit Western Europe and the United States in the summer of 1961. The poet, still but twenty-eight yet already famous in and beyond Russia, proved to be a welcome emissary of the new Soviet regime. Returning to Moscow, he raised fresh commotion by publishing (September 19, 1961) an outstanding poem entitled "Babi Yar." This was the name of a ravine, on the outskirts of Kiev, where Hitler's invading army, in two days of September, 1941, massacred and buried 34,000 Jews. Yevtushenko wanted to know why the Soviet authorities had not raised some monument to keep this crime in human memory, and he implied that this neglect was one of many signs that the Russian state— and perhaps the Russian people—secretly preserved the anti-Semitism that had flourished under the czar.

I am indebted to Herbert Marshall and his publishers for permission to quote here his magnificent translation of this remarkable poem.

*Babi Yar**

There are no memorials over Babi Yar.
Only an abrupt bank like a crude epitaph rears.
I stand terror-stricken.

          Today I'm as ancient in years
as the Jewish people themselves are.
It seems to me at this moment—

          I am an Israelite.
Now I'm wandering over Ancient Egypt in captivity.
And now on the cross I perish, crucified,
and to this day the marks of the nails are on me.
I am Dreyfus now,

          inside my mind.
My informer and judge

          the Philistines.
I am behind bars.

          I was trapped in the roundup.
Persecuted,

        reviled,

          hounded.
And ladies with flounces of Brussels' lace
shriekingly poke parasol points in my face.
It seems to me—

          I'm a boy in Bialystok.
Blood flows over the floor, red-running.
Outrages are committed by bullies of vodka shops,
stinking of drink and raw onions.
I lie helpless, by jackboots kicked about.
I plead to the pogromites in vain.
"Beat the Yids! Save Russia!"

          they shout:
My mother by shopkeeper is beaten and flayed.
Oh, my Russian people!

         By nature

* From *Yevtushenko Poems* by Yevgeni Yevtushenko, translated by Herbert Marshall. Copyright © 1966 by E. P. Dutton & Co., Inc.

you are international
                       I know.
But often with unclean hands, such creatures
besmirch your own clean name.
The goodness of my native land I know.
How foul it is, that—
                       without turning a hair—
anti-Semites a title self-pompously bestowed:
"We're 'The Union of the Russian People,' " they declared.
I am Anna Frank
                       it seems to me,
as frail as a twig
                       in April weather.
And I love.
                       And for empty phrases have no need.
I want
            just that we should see each other.
Yet how little one can see
                                 and smell!
We're forbidden the leaves,
                                 forbidden the sky as well.
But we can still do so much—
                                 tenderly
embrace each other in the darkness of the room.
They're coming?
                       Don't be afraid—that is the din
of oncoming Spring itself—
                                 quickening.
Come to me.
                 Give me your lips quickly.
They're breaking down the door?
                                      No, that's Spring—ice-breaking in. . . .
Over Babi Yar only rustling wild grasses move.
The trees watch sternly,
                              like judges arrayed.
Here silence itself cries aloud—
                                      my hat I remove,
and feel
            I am gradually going gray.
And I myself
                 am like an endless soundless cry,
over these thousands and thousands of buried ones.
Each one

of these murdered old men
                    am I.
I
  am each of their murdered
                    sons.
Nothing will ever forget this
                    within me.
Let the "International"
                    thunder its might
when will be buried for eternity
the earth's last anti-Semite.
No Jewish blood my veins runs through,
but I am hated with an encrusted passion,
by all anti-Semites, as if I
                    were a Jew,
and because of that
                    I'm a genuine Russian![145]

When Yevtushenko read this poem at the Polytechnical Institute, the audience applauded for twenty minutes. When the *Literary Gazette*, after much hesitation, printed it, twenty thousand letters came to the magazine—thirty or forty hostile, the rest acclaiming "Babi Yar" as one of the finest Russian poems of the century.[146] Shostakovich chose it as one of four poems to accompany his Thirteenth Symphony.[147]*

I like this young Lochinvar rising in the East, singing of love and justice and the zest of life. A healthy body and a warm heart have tuned this lyre.

I like to laugh
    into the faces of my foes
and carrying a woman over a stream.
To gnaw into books,
    carry logs for stoves . . .
I can sing and drink,
    no thought of death at all;
throwing out my hands,
    onto the grass I fall,

* Anatoli Kuznetsov expanded the grim tale of Babi Yar in a documentary novel (1966). Discouraged by the censorship that distorted this and others of his works, Kuznetsov, age thirty-nine, defected to Great Britain in 1969. He has repudiated all Russian editions of his books, and has changed his name to A. Anatol.

and if in this wide world I die,
then I'll die through joy that I am alive.[148]

He can write the usual love poems,[149] but he can write even better about "Uncle Vassya"—an old man who finds his greatest happiness in helping others. "For me," he tells us, "the aristocrats of the spirit are not those who can quote from books for hours on end, starting with Plato and ending with Kafka and Joyce. For me the aristocrats of the spirit are those whose hearts are open to others."[150] He praises his fellow poets, and especially celebrates Mayakovski, though finding him so different in mood and manner from himself. He names "the three greatest Russians": Pushkin, Tolstoi, and Lenin.[151] He forgives the faults of his countrymen because "throughout the many centuries of their history the Russians have suffered perhaps more than any other people on earth." He loves them because "they have never become cynical, they have never lost their faith in the original purity of the revolutionary idea, in spite of all the filth that has since desecrated it."[152]

In his most ambitious poem, *Bratski G.E.S.*, he renewed his attack upon the "filthy," and reaffirmed his faith. G.E.S. is the State Hydroelectric Station—a symbol of the industrialization which he accepted as indispensable to Russia's self-preservation. The poem is epic in length but popular in form, even conversational in tone. It begins with the usual prayer for inspiration—not to celestial gods but to Pushkin, Lermontov, Yesenin, and Mayakovski. He apologizes for having written so much trivial poetry, and assures his critics that their censures were "really kind compared to my own self-condemnation."[153] Then, in rollicking cantos, he commemorates the Cossack revolt (1670) under Stenka Razin, the "Decembrist" conspiracy of 1825, and the Winter Palace holocaust of 1905. Part IX supplies the "ABC of Revolution," and Part XVIII mourns Mayakovski's suicide. Part XI, "The Bolshevik," describes one of the engineers who built the dams that feed electric power to Russia's industries; how this sturdy worker was shocked by the "purge" trials under Stalin, but remained firm in his Bolshevism; how he was arrested and tortured by the secret police to make him sign false confessions:

When those swine tortured and abused me,
my face they beat, my arms they broke—
and did such things and so misused me—
to explain I can't force this tongue of mine!—
they tried to bribe me: "How about a drink?"

and thrust lying statements for me to sign;
but one thing I cried hoarsely: "I'm a Bolshevik!"

They replied with a grin: "All right!"
pushed me on a chair: in my eyes they flashed a lamp,
yes, they flayed me and beat me with electric light.
That you must never forget, my lad:
changing shifts, in front of Lenin's portrait,
those bastards tortured me with electric light
which I had produced for the happiness of men!

To that portrait I whispered in a frenzy:
"Do forgive us, forgive us, Comrade Lenin,
that such scoundrels your name involve.
Let it be bad for us, let worse be on the way—
but we'll never betray, Comrade Lenin, our souls,
and Communism we'll never betray![154]

This is Yevtushenko today, critical of the Soviet state, but loving his people and their dream. He assures us that

the first mistake made by Western students of the Russian Revolution is to judge the revolutionary idea not by those who are genuinely loyal to it, but by those who betray it. Their other mistake is that they still regard the idea of Communism as something imposed by force upon the Russian people, without realizing that by now it is a part of the Russian people's flesh and blood.[155]

We cannot say how much of this is protective coloration, and how much is sincerity. But it may be wise for us of the West to assume that the spirit of Russia today is voiced not by the tender longings of Pasternak, nor by the bitter memories of Solzhenitsyn, but by the ardor and courage of Yevtushenko. "I want to believe," he writes, "that everything is still ahead of me, as it is for my people."[156] Let us heartily wish them well in their internal affairs despite their sins and ours. Perhaps their experiments and their sufferings will bring some costly but precious increment to the frail intelligence of mankind.

Appendage

OUR voyage is not complete, for there are many figures—like Carl Sandburg, Sherwood Anderson, Vladimir Nabokov, Jules Romains, Isak Dinesen, Pirandello, Alberto Moravia—who might well have charmed us on the way. Nor is the literature of the United States and Europe all the literature of "our time"; a wider learning could have found illuminating "interpretations of life" in South America, Islam, Israel, China, Australia, and Japan; our knowledge is a fragile fringe on our ignorance. And perhaps my choice of authors and their themes has been distorted by preoccupation with the influence of the "death of God" upon the thought and morals of our century.

I felt that crisis intimately in 1905, when I was a sophomore in a Jesuit college, and the clandestine reading of Darwin, Thomas Huxley, Herbert Spencer, and Ernst Haekel left me naked of theology and drunk with intellectual pride. My hubris challenged all surviving gods when, in 1909, still without religious faith, I entered the seminary and prepared for the priesthood, with the high resolve of working from within to convert the Catholic Church in America to socialism. I attended Mass daily and took Communion weekly. The peace I felt in the old ritual was disturbed by the secret reading of Spinoza's *Ethics;* gradually I realized the depth of my foolishness and hypocrisy. I left the seminary in 1911, at the cost of much suffering to those I loved most. Soon I plunged into the radical movement in New York, hoping to find a faith that might fill the atheistic void.

In the chapter called "Nadir" in *Transition* (1927) I described the secret anguish that had come to many youngsters through the replacement of the Christian drama—of creation, sin, redemption, and divine and human resurrection—by a picture of man's career as a struggle for existence in which nothing was certain except suffering and death. What meaning or nobility remained in such a denuded existence on a planet shorn of moral grandeur or significance? I asked this question of various notables in a letter of July 15, 1931, and presented and considered their replies in a small volume *On the Meaning of Life* (1931). Quite unwittingly I was caught—contemporaneously with Heidegger's *Sein und Zeit* (1927) and a few years before Sartre (*Nausea*, 1938)— in the "existentialist" quest for the meaning and worth of human life after the disappearance of God. Because that quest has held my interest for sixty-four years, it may have too darkly colored my inquiry into the philosophies underlying the literature of our age.

So the general impression left by my report is one of predominant pessimism—from Faulkner's somber annals of evil days, and Hemingway's shotgun summary, to Pasternak's mourning for the departed amenities of a cultured bourgeois life, and Solzhenitsyn's description of prison camps under the Communist czar. O'Neill's picture of life was as gloomy as his or Maugham's face; Ezra Pound reflected the chaos of the world in that of his mind; T. S. Eliot had no other prescription than a return to a mummified deity perfumed with Anglican-Catholic ritual; Proust preferred the odor of a dying aristocracy; Joyce drowned the obscenities and prejudices of Dublin life (as he remembered one day of it) with humor, word play and alcohol. I like Mann, as a man, best of all these men, because, amid the moral and political collapse of his native land, he never lost hope, and fought to the end. Kafka saw all life as an insect's dream, or as an unintelligible trial always ending in unexplained conviction and sudden death. I found much to relish in Kazantzakis, but he placed over the portals of life the terrible warning that Dante had visioned over the gates of Hell: "All hope abandon, ye who enter here."

In 1770 Edmund Burke issued a pamphlet entitled *Thoughts on the Cause of the Present Discontents*. Obviously, discontent is a perennial, if only because there is a sly satisfaction in being superior to the world. The sources of pessimism vary from century to century, but they derive from two persistent facts: (1) desire always outruns fulfillment; and (2) we are, or have to be, more keenly aware of our hurts and woes than of our health and blessings. Health and good fortune are not crises that demand immediate attention; ailments and mishaps, however, send urgent and useful warnings to consciousness through pangs of pain or grief. In like manner the pessimists who call our attention to actual or impending evils are a beneficent nuisance, and their harsh strictures rightfully carry more sound and weight than the diffident reminders, from gayer spirits, that amid the flowers of evil many roses bloom.

So we have ended this book with Yevtushenko on a hopeful and fraternal note, conscious of the evils that enmesh us, but remembering too the many hopeful things that men have done in creating that soul of history which is civilization. The twentieth century is the age of Nietzsche, as he predicted it would be: the age of dictators unmoved by any moral tradition, of wars made more deadly and devastating by the progress of science; the age of the "death of God" for those who lead the parade in thought and power. Sensitive spirits will long suffer a desolating emptiness where our kindest visions and fairest myths once chastened our conduct and warmed our hearts. But the poets and artists and dreamers are not dead; they will tell new stories, paint new pictures, of our heroes, our achievements, and our possibilities; we shall be inspired and strengthened again; and we shall go on to add to our heritage.

Bibliographical Guide*

to the Notes

ALEXANDER, DORIS, *The Tempering of Eugene O'Neill*. New York: Harcourt, 1962.

ALEXANDROVA, VERA, *A History of Soviet Literature, 1917–64*, New York: Doubleday, 1963.

BAKER, CARLOS, *Ernest Hemingway: A Life Story*. New York: Scribner, 1969.

——, *Hemingway: The Writer as Artist*. Princeton, N.J.: Princeton University, 1963.

BARKER, RICHARD H., *Marcel Proust*. New York: Criterion, 1958.

BEAUVOIR, SIMONE DE, *The Ethics of Ambiguity*, in NOVACK, GEORGE, *Existentialism versus Marxism*. New York: Dell, 1966.

——, *Force of Circumstance*. New York: Putnam, 1965.

——, *Memoirs of a Dutiful Daughter*. Cleveland: World, 1959.

——, *The Prime of Life (La Force de l'âge)*. Cleveland: World, 1966.

——,*The Second Sex*. New York: Knopf, 1957.

BOWEN, CROSWELL, *The Curse of the Misbegotten: A Tale of the House of O'Neill*. New York: McGraw-Hill, 1959.

BRÉE, GERMAINE, *Gide*. New Brunswick, N.J.: Rutgers University, 1963.

BRENNAN, JOSEPH G., *Three Philosophical Novelists*. New York; Macmillan, 1964.

BRETALL, ROBERT, ed., *A Kierkegaard Anthology*. New York: Modern Library, 1959.

BROD, MAX, *Franz Kafka*. New York: Schocken, 1947.

BURNIER, MICHEL-ANTOINE, *Choice of Action: The French Existentialists on the Political Front Line*. New York: Random House, 1965.

CAMUS, ALBERT, *The Fall*. New York, Knopf, 1956.

——, *Lyrical and Critical Essays*. Knopf, 1968.

——, *The Plague (La Peste)*. Knopf, 1964.

——, *The Rebel*. Knopf, 1954.

——, *The Stranger*. Knopf, 1946.

CARGILL, OSCAR, *et al.*, *O'Neill and His Plays*. New York: New York University, 1966.

COCTEAU, JEAN, *The Difficulty of Being*. London: Owen, 1966.

---

* We are deeply indebted to many of the publishers here named, for the privilege of quoting from their publications.

COHN, RUBY, and DUKORE, BERNARD, *Twentieth Century Drama*. New York, Random House, 1966.
COLLINS, JAMES, *The Mind of Kierkegaard*. Chicago: Regnery, 1965.
CORRIGAN, ROBERT W., *The Modern Drama*. New York: Macmillan, 1967.
CRANSTON, MAURICE, *Sartre*. Edinburgh: Oliver, 1965.
CRUIKSHANK, JOHN, *Albert Camus and the Literature of Revolt*. New York: Oxford, 1959.

DESAN, WILFRID, *The Tragic Finale: An Essay on the Philosophy of Jean-Paul Sartre*. Cambridge, Mass.: Harvard, 1954.
DURANT, WILL, *The Mansions of Philosophy*. New York: Simon and Schuster, 1931.
———, *Transition*. New York: Simon and Schuster, 1927.
———, WILL and ARIEL, *The Age of Louis XIV*. New York: Simon and Schuster, 1963.

ELIOT, T. S., *After Strange Gods*. New York: Harcourt, 1934.
———, *The Cocktail Party*. New York: Harcourt, 1950.
———, *Collected Poems*. New York: Harcourt, 1936.
———, *Essays, Ancient and Modern*. London: Faber and Faber, 1928.
———, *Essays on Elizabethan Drama*. New York: Faber and Faber, 1956.
———, *Four Quartets*. New York: Harcourt, 1943.
———, *The Idea of a Christian Society*. New York: Harcourt, 1940.
———, *Milton*. London: Cumberlege, 1948.
———, *Notes towards the Definition of Culture*. London: Faber and Faber, 1948.
———, *Selected Essays*. London: Faber and Faber, 1932.
ELLMANN, RICHARD, *James Joyce*. New York: Oxford, 1959.

FAULKNER, JOHN, *My Brother Bill: An Affectionate Reminiscence*. New York: Trident, 1963.
FAULKNER, WILLIAM, *Absalom, Absalom!* New York, Random House, 1936.
———, *As I Lay Dying*. New York, Random House, 1964.
———, *Essays, Speeches, and Public Letters*. New York: Random House, 1965.
———, *The Hamlet*. New York: Random House, n.d.
———, *Intruder in the Dust*. New York: Random House, 1948.
———, *Light in August*. New York: Modern Library, 1950.
———, *The Mansion*. New York: Random House, n.d.
———, *Requiem for a Nun*. Penguin Books, 1965.
———, *Sanctuary*. Penguin Books, 1965.
———, *Sartoris*. New York: Harcourt, Brace, 1951.
———, *The Sound and the Fury* and *As I Lay Dying*. New York: Modern Library, 1929.
———, *The Town*. New York: Random House, 1957.
FLORES, ANGEL, *The Kafka Problem*. New York: New Directions, 1956.
FRASER, G. S., *Ezra Pound*, Edinburgh: Oliver, 1960.
FROST, ROBERT, *Selected Poems*. New York: Holt, 1928.

GIDE, ANDRÉ, *The Counterfeiters*. New York, 1957.

———, *The Immoralist*. New York: Knopf, 1921.

———, *Journals*, 2v. New York: Knopf, 1956.

———, *Lafcadio's Adventures (The Caves of the Vatican)*. New York: Knopf, 1928.

———, *The Living Thoughts of Montaigne*. New York: Longmans, Green, 1939.

———, *Pretexts: Reflections on Literature and Morality*. New York: Meridian, 1959.

———, *Strait Is the Gate*. New York: Knopf, 1948.

———, *Two Symphonies: Isabelle and The Pastoral Symphony*. New York, 1962.

GREENE, NORMAN: *Jean-Paul Sartre: The Existentialist Ethic*. Ann Arbor, Mich.: University of Michigan, 1966.

GRENE, MARJORIE, *Dreadful Freedom: A Critique of Existentialism*. Chicago: University of Chicago, 1948.

HATFIELD, HENRY, ed., *Thomas Mann: A Collection of Critical Essays*. Englewood Cliffs, N.J.: Prentice-Hall, 1964.

HEIDEGGER, MARTIN, *Being and Time*. London: SCM Press. Translation by J. M. and E. Robinson of *Sein und Zeit* (Halle: Saale, 1927).

———, *German Existentialism*, New York: Wisdom Library, 1965.

———, *Introduction to Metaphysics*. New Haven, Conn.: Yale University, 1959.

HELLER, ERICH, *The Ironic German: A Study of Thomas Mann*. Boston: Little, Brown, 1958.

HEMINGWAY, ERNEST, *Death in the Afternoon*, New York: Scribner, 1932.

———, *The Essential Hemingway*, Penguin Books, 1964.

———, *A Farewell to Arms*. New York: Scribner, 1929.

———, *For Whom the Bell Tolls*. New York: Scribner, 1940.

———, *A Moveable Feast*. Penguin Books, 1966.

———, *The Old Man and the Sea*. New York: Scribner, 1952.

———, *The Sun Also Rises*, in *The Essential Hemingway*.

HOFFMAN, FREDERICK J., *William Faulkner*. East Lansing Mich.: Michigan State University, 1961.

HOLDER, ALAN, *Three Voyagers in Search of Europe*. Philadelphia: University of Pennsylvania, 1966.

HUBBEN, WILLIAM, *Four Prophets of Our Destiny*. New York: Macmillan, 1952.

JANOUCH, GUSTAV, *Conversations with Kafka*. London: Verschoyle, 1953.

JEFFERS, ROBINSON, *Selected Poetry*. New York: Random House, 1937.

JOLIVET, RÉGIS, *Sartre: The Theology of the Absurd*. New York: Newman, 1967.

JOYCE, JAMES, *Finnegans Wake*. New York: Viking, 1939.

———, *Letters*, 3v., ed. Richard Ellmann. New York: Viking, 1966.

———, *Portrait of the Artist as a Young Man*. New York: Viking, 1956.

———, *A Shorter Finnegans Wake*, ed. Anthony Burgess. New York: Norton, 1967.

————, *Ulysses.* Paris: Shakespeare Bookshop, 1926.

KAFKA, FRANZ, *The Castle.* Penguin Books, 1957.
————, *Diaries,* 2v. New York: Schocken, 1948.
————, *The Great Wall of China.* New York: Schocken, 1948.
————, *Letters to Milena.* New York: Schocken, 1953.
————, *The Penal Colony.* New York: Schocken, 1963.
————, *Selected Short Stories.* London: Schocken, 1952.
————, *The Trial.* Penguin Books, 1953.
KAZANTZAKIS, HELEN, *Nikos Kazantzakis.* New York: Simon and Schuster,
    1968.
KAZANTZAKIS, NIKOS, *The Fratricides.* Simon and Schuster, 1964.
————, *Freedom or Death.* Simon and Schuster, 1956.
————, *The Greek Passion.* Simon and Schuster, 1954.
————, *Japan/China: A Journal of Two Voyages to the Far East,* Simon
    and Schuster. 1963.
————, *The Last Temptation of Christ.* Simon and Schuster, 1960.
————, *The Odyssey: A Modern Sequel,* tr. by Kimon Friar. Simon and
    Schuster, 1958.
————, *Report to Greco.* Simon and Schuster, 1965.
————, *The Rock Garden.* Simon and Schuster, 1963.
————, *Toda Raba.* Simon and Schuster, 1964.
————, *Zorba the Greek,* Ballantyne Books, 1964.
KENNER, HUGH, ed., *T. S. Eliot.* Englewood Cliffs, N.J.: Prentice-Hall, 1962.
KIERKEGAARD, SØREN, *Repetition.* Princeton, N.J.: Princeton University,
    1941.

LÖWITH, KARL, *Nature, History, and Existentialism.* Evanston, Ill.: North-
    western University, 1966.
LOWRIE, WALTER, *Kierkegaard.* New York: Harper, 1962.
LUKÁCS, GEORG, *Essays on Thomas Mann.* New York: Grosset, 1964.

MALLET, ROBERT, ed., *Self-Portraits: The Gide/Valéry Letters.* Chicago:
    University of Chicago, 1966.
MANN, ERIKA, *The Last Year of Thomas Mann.* New York: Farrar, 1958.
MANN, KLAUS, *André Gide and the Crisis of Modern Thought.* New York:
    Creative Age, 1943.
MANN, THOMAS, *The Beloved Returns (Lotte in Weimar).* New York:
    Knopf, 1940.
————, *Buddenbrooks,* 2v in 1. New York: Modern Library.
————, *Confessions of Felix Krull, Confidence Man.* New York: Knopf,
    1955.
————, *Doctor Faustus.* Knopf, 1948.
————, *Essays of Three Decades.* Knopf, 1947.
————, *Joseph and His Brothers,* 5v, Knopf, 1934 ff.:
    I, *The Tales of Jacob.*
    II, *The Young Joseph.*
    III and IV, *Joseph in Egypt,* 2v.
    V, *Joseph the Provider.*

————, *Joseph and His Brothers*, IV. New York, 1934.

————, *Last Essays*. Knopf, 1959.

————, *A Sketch of My Life*. Knopf, 1960.

————, *Stories of Three Decades*. Knopf, 1936.

————, *The Story of a Novel: The Genesis of Doctor Faustus*. Knopf, 1961.

————, *Three Essays*. Knopf, 1932.

————, *Tonio Kröger*, in *Stories of Three Decades*.

MARCEL, GABRIEL, *Being and Having*. London: Dacre, 1949.

MAUGHAM, ROBIN, *Somerset and All the Maughams*. New York: New American Library, 1966.

MAUGHAM, W. SOMERSET, *Cakes and Ale*. New York: Doubleday, 1930.

————, *Complete Short Stories*, 2v. Garden City, N.Y.: Doubleday, n.d.

————, *The Moon and Sixpence*. New York. Modern Library.

————, *Of Human Bondage*. New York: Modern Library.

————, *Points of View*. New York: Bantam, 1961.

————, *Summing Up*. New York: New American Library, 1964.

MAUROIS, ANDRÉ, *Portrait of a Genius: Marcel Proust*. New York: Harper, 1950.

McCAFFERY, JOHN, *Ernest Hemingway*. New York: World, 1950.

NATANSON, MAURICE, *A Critique of Sartre's Ontology*. Lincoln, Neb.: University of Nebraska, n.d.

NEIDER, CHARLES, *The Frozen Sea: A Study of Franz Kafka*. New York: Oxford, 1962.

————, *The Stature of Thomas Mann*. New York: James Laughlin, 1947.

NORMAN, CHARLES, *Ezra Pound*. New York: Macmillan, 1960.

NOVACK, GEORGE., ed., *Existentialism versus Marxism*. New York: Dell, 1966.

O'NEILL, EUGENE, *Complete Works*, 2v. New York: Random House, 1924.

————, *Long Day's Journey into Night*. New Haven, Conn.: Yale University, 1963.

————, *Nine Plays*. New York: Modern Library.

Oxford Book of English Verse, The. Oxford, 1931.

PARKER, EMMETT, *Albert Camus*. Madison, Wis.: University of Wisconsin, 1965.

PASCAL, ROY, *The German Novel*. Manchester, Eng.: Manchester University, 1957.

PASTERNAK, BORIS, *The Adolescence of Zhenya Luvers*. New York, 1961.

————, *Collected Prose Works*. London: Drummond, 1945.

————, *Doctor Zhivago*. New York: Pantheon, 1958.

————, *The Last Summer*. London: Avon, 1959.

————, *Poems*. Yellow Springs, Ohio: Antioch Press, 1964.

————, *Safe Conduct*, in *Collected Prose Works*.

————, *My Sister, Life*. New York: Washington Square Press, 1967.

PAYNE, ROBERT, *The Three Worlds of Boris Pasternak*. New York: Coward-McCann, 1961.

POUND, EZRA, *The Cantos* (I-XCV). New York, New Directions, 1956.

————, *Selected Poems*. New York, New Directions, 1957.

PREVELAKIS, PANDELIS, *Nikos Kazantzakis and His Odyssey*. New York: Simon and Schuster, 1961.

PROUST, MARCEL, *À la Recherche du temps perdu*. Paris: Vol. I, Grasset; Vols. II–XVI, Gallimard, 1913–27. English translation, New York, Knopf, in eleven volumes: 1913–27.
I and II, *Swann's Way*, 2v.
III and IV, *Within a Budding Grove*, 2v.
V and VI, *The Guermantes Way*, 2v.
VII and VIII, *Cities of the Plain*, 2v.
IX, *The Captive*.
X, *The Sweet Cheat Gone*.
XI, *The Past Recaptured*.

RICHARDSON, W. J., *Heidegger: Through Phenomenology to Thought*. The Hague: M. Nijhoff, 1963.

ROBBINS, R. H., *The T. S. Eliot Myth*. New York: Schumann, 1951.

ROWLAND, MARY F. and PAUL, *Pasternak's Doctor Zhivago*. Carbondale, Ill.: Southern Illinois University, 1967.

RUSSELL, BERTRAND, *Autobiography*, Vols. I and II. Boston: Little, Brown, 1967.

———, *Autobiography*, Vol. III. New York: Simon and Schuster, 1969.

RYF, ROBERT S., *A New Approach to Joyce*. Berkeley, Calif.: University of California, 1967.

SALVAN, JACQUES, *The Scandalous Ghost*. Detroit: Wayne University, 1967.

SARTRE, JEAN-PAUL, *Being and Nothingness*, tr. Hazel E. Barnes. New York: Philosophical Library, 1956, cloth ed. unless otherwise stated.

———, *The Chips Are Down (Les Jeux sont faits)*. New York: Knopf, 1948.

———, *The Condemned of Altona*. New York: Knopf, 1961.

———, *The Devil and the Good Lord, and Two Other Plays*. New York: Knopf, 1960.

———, *The Emotions*. New York: Philosophical Library, 1940.

———, *Literary Essays*. New York: Philosophical Library, 1957.

———, *Nausea*. New York: Penguin Books, 1964.

———, *No Exit and Three Other Plays (The Flies, Dirty Hands,* and *The Respectful Prostitute)*. New York: Knopf, 1946.

———, *Of Human Freedom*. New York: Philosophical Library, 1966.

———, *The Philosophy of Existentialism*. New York: Philosophical Library, 1965.

———, *Roads to Freedom (Les Chemins de la liberté)*, 3v.:
I, *The Age of Reason*. New York: Penguin Books, 1947.
II, *The Reprieve*. New York: Modern Library, 1947.
III, *Troubled Sleep*. New York: Bantam Books, 1951.

———, *Saint Genet: Actor and Martyr*. New York: New American Library, 1963.

———, *Search for a Method*. New York: Knopf, 1963.

———, *What Is Literature?* New York: Philosophical Library, 1965.

————, *The Words*. New York: Braziller, 1964.

SHOLOKHOV, MIKHAIL, *The Don Flows Home to the Sea*. New York: Knopf, 1946.

————, *Quiet Flows the Don*. New York: New American Library, 1959.

SLONIM, MARC, *Soviet Russia in Literature*. New York: Oxford, 1967.

SOLZHENITSYN, ALEKSANDER, *The Cancer Ward*. New York: Harper, 1968.

————, *The First Circle*. New York: Harper, 1968.

————, *One Day in the Life of Ivan Denisovich*. New York: Praeger, 1963.

STEINBECK, JOHN, *East of Eden*. New York: Viking, 1952.

————, *Of Mice and Men*. New York: Modern Library, 1937.

————, *Tortilla Flat*, New York: Modern Library, 1935.

STERN, ALFRED, *Sartre: His Philosophy and Existential Psychoanalysis*. New York: Delacorte, 1967.

THOMAS, R. HINTON, *Thomas Mann: The Mediation of Art*. New York: Oxford, 1956.

UNGER, LEONARD, ed., *T. S. Eliot, A Selected Critique*. Minneapolis: University of Minnesota, 1966.

UPDIKE, JOHN, *Couples*. New York: Knopf, 1968.

WAGGONER, HYATT, *William Faulkner*. Lexington, Ky.: University of Kentucky, 1959.

WEIGAND, HERMANN J., *The Magic Mountain: A Study of Thomas Mann's Novel*. Chapel Hill, N.C.: University of North Carolina, 1964.

WHITE, ANDREW, *Thomas Mann*. New York: Grove, 1965.

WILLIAMSON, GEORGE, *A Reader's Guide to T. S. Eliot*. New York: Farrar, 1966.

WITTGENSTEIN, LUDWIG, *Philosophical Investigations*. London: Routledge and Paul, 1966.

————, *Tractatus Logico-Philosophicus*. London: Routledge and Paul, 1961.

YEVTUSHENKO, YEVGENI, *Poems*, tr. Herbert Marshall. New York: Dutton, 1966.

————, *A Precocious Autobiography*. New York: Dutton, 1963.

————, *Selected Poems*. New York: Dutton, 1962.

Notes

PREFACE

1. Durant, *Transition*, 41–43

CHAPTER I: FAULKNER

1. Updike, John, *Couples*, 372.
2. Faulkner, William, *Sartoris*, 172–73.
3. *Ibid.*, 162.
4. 26.
5. 199.
6. 169.
7. 9.
8. 279–82.
9. 35.
10. 29.
11. E.g., 203.
12. *The Sound and the Fury*, 67.
13. *Essays*, 177.
14. Hoffman, Frederick J., *William Faulkner*, 119.
15. Faulkner, William, *Sanctuary*, Introd.
16. Waggoner, H., *William Faulkner*, 110
17. Faulkner, John, *My Brother Bill*, 174
18. *The Sound and the Fury*, 207.
19. *Intruder in the Dust*, 204.
20. *Ibid.*, 153.
21. 151.
22. 154.
23. 155.
24. *Light in August*, 221.
25. *Ibid.*, 218.
26. *Essays*, 86, 93, 96, 99; Faulkner, John, *My Brother Bill*, 268.
27. *Intruder in the Dust*, 204.
28. Shakespeare, *King Lear*, V, ii, line 9.
29. E.g., *Light in August*, 326–38; *Intruder in the Dust*, 205.
30. *As I Lay Dying*, 156.
31. *Sartoris*, 277, 300.
32. *Intruder in the Dust*, 28, 39, 55.
33. *The Town*, 322.
34. *Sartoris*, 6, 7, 32, 162.
35. *Light in August*, 101.
36. *Sartoris*, 19.
37. *Light in August*, 22.
38. *Ibid.*, 6.
39. Faulkner, John, *My Brother Bill*, 273.
40. Hoffman, 21.
41. Faulkner, William, *Essays*, 62, 65.
42. *Intruder in the Dust*, 155.

43. *The Town*, 265.
44. *As I Lay Dying*, 111.
45. *Light in August*, 11.
46. *As I Lay Dying*, 111.
47. *Absalom, Absalom!* 8.
48. *Light in August*, 227.
49. *Ibid.*, 213.
50. *The Town*, 342.
51. *As I Lay Dying*, 15.
52. *The Town*, 88.
53. *Light in August*, 180.
54. *Sanctuary*, 1.
55. Waggoner, 97; Faulkner, Wm., *As I Lay Dying*, 510; *The Sound and the Fury*, 95.
56. *Requiem for a Nun*, 227.
57. *The Town*, 102.
58. Introd. to *Requiem for a Nun*.

CHAPTER II: HEMINGWAY

1. Hemingway, Ernest, *The Essential Hemingway*, 461.
2. Baker, Carlos, *Ernest Hemingway: A Life Story*, 9.
3. McCaffery, John: *Ernest Hemingway*, 52.
4. Baker, 21.
5. *Ibid.*, 34.
6. 58.
7. 75, 78.
8. 120.
9. Baker, Carlos, *Hemingway: The Writer as Artist*, 3.
10. *Oxford Book of English Verse*, 142.
11. Baker, *Ernest Hemingway: A Life Story*, 199.
12. Hemingway, *Death in the Afternoon*, 2.
13. *Ibid.*, 16, 21.
14. 4.
15. 6.
16. In *The New Republic* for June, 1932.
17. Baker, *Life Story*, 228.
18. *Ibid.*, 317.
19. Hemingway, *A Farewell to Arms*, 178.
20. Baker, *Life Story*, 280.
21. *Ibid.*, 271, 277.
22. 332.
23. 346.
24. Cowley, Malcolm, in McCaffery, *Ernest Hemingway*, 37, 41.

25. *Shenandoah* magazine, Autumn, 1952.
26. Hemingway, *The Old Man and the Sea*, 102.
27. *Ibid.*, 33.
28. 114.
29. Baker, *Life Story*, 220.
30. *Ibid.*, 522.
31. 381.
32. 297.
33. 534.
34. 465; *cf.* 344, 452.
35. 435.
36. 132, 465
37. 217.
38. 351.
39. 226.
40. "A Clean, Well-Lighted Place," in *The Essential Hemingway*, 394.
41. *Death in the Afternoon*, 134–39.
42. *A Farewell to Arms*, 185.
43. Baker, *Life Story*, 449.
44. *A Farewell to Arms*, 249.
45. Baker, 271.
46. *Ibid.*, 556.

CHAPTER III: STEINBECK AND SINCLAIR

1. Steinbeck, John, *Tortilla Flat*, 11.
2. *Ibid.*, Preface.
3. Steinbeck, *Of Mice and Men*, 129.
4. *Ibid.*, 28, 180.
5. 71.
6. *Tortilla Flat*, 40, 99.
7. Steinbeck, *East of Eden*, 451.
8. *Cf. ibid.*, 222.
9. 578.
10. 210.
11. 497.
12. 132.
13. 217.
14. 293.

CHAPTER IV: O'NEILL

1. Bowen, Croswell, *The Curse of the Misbegotten*, 314.
2. *Ibid.*, 19.
3. O'Neill, Eugene, *Complete Works*, I, 430.
4. O'Neill, *Long Day's Journey into Night*, 153.
5. *Ibid.*, Act IV.
6. Bowen, 168.
7. *Ibid.*, 164.
8. 96, 144.

9. 152.
10. *Strange Interlude*, Act IX; O'Neill, *Nine Plays*, 681.
11. *Ibid.*, 680.
12. O'Neill, *Lazarus Laughed*, Act II, sc. i.
13. Bowen, 185.
14. *Ibid.*, 184.
15. O'Neill, *Homecoming*, Act I, in *Nine Plays*, 706.
16. O'Neill, *Days without End*, Act I.
17. Bowen, 233.
18. *Ibid.* and 316.
19. New York *Times*, Nov. 4, 1956; Cargill, Oscar, *O'Neill and His Plays*, 95.
20. Bowen, 183.
21. *Ibid.*, 286–88.
22. O'Neill, *The Iceman Cometh*, Act I.
23. *Ibid.*
24. Bowen, 211.
25. *Long Day's Journey into Night*, Act I, p. 33.
26. *Ibid.*, Act IV, p. 129.
27. Pp. 25, 77, 78.
28. O'Neill, *More Stately Mansions*, Act III.
29. *Ibid.*, p. 72.
30. Bowen, 360.
31. New York *Times*, Nov. 4, 1956.
32. O'Neill, *The Great God Brown*, Prologue; *Long Day's Journey into Night*, Act IV, p. 153.
33. Bowen, 174.
34. Alexander, *The Tempering of Eugene O'Neill*, 63.
35. O'Neill, *All God's Chillun Got Wings*, Act II, sc. iii.
36. Letter to Barrett Clark in Cargill, 401.
37. Bowen, 310; Alexander, 214.
38. *The Iceman Cometh*, Act I.
39. *Long Day's Journey*, Act II, sc. iii.
40. *The Great God Brown*, end.
41. *Ibid.*, II, i.
42. Letter to Mary Mullett, in Bowen, 143.

CHAPTER V: JEFFERS and POUND

1. Frost, Robert, *Selected Poems*, 168.
2. *Locus* lost; remembered from my schoolboy youth.
3. Jeffers, Robinson, *Selected Poetry*, xv.
4. *Ibid.*, 29.
5. 65.
6. 171.
7. 168.
8. 258.
9. 168.
10. 41.

11. Norman, Charles, *Ezra Pound*, 23; Holder, Alan, *Three Voyagers in Search of Europe*, 37.
12. Norman, 104.
13. Pound, Ezra, *Selected Poems*, 53.
14. London *Times Literary Supplement*, April 25, 1968, p. 426.
15. *Ibid.*
16. Pound, *Selected Poems*, 184.
17. Norman, 109, 169.
18. Kenner, Hugh, *T. S. Eliot*, 34.
19. Norman, 156.
20. Eliot, T. S., *After Strange Gods*, 45.
21. Pound, "The Plunge," in *Selected Poems*, 82.
22. Baker, *Ernest Hemingway: A Life Story*, 8.
23. Norman, 269.
24. *Ibid.*, 270
25. 98.
26. Pound, *Cantos*, X.
27. In Holder, *Three Voyagers*, 183.
28. Canto VII.
29. Norman, 274.
30. *Ibid.*, 301, 297, 303.
31. 281.
32. Letter to T. E. Lawrence, Nov. 29, 1934, in Holder, 41.
33. Norman, 321.
34. *Ibid.*, 301.
35. 322–23.
36. In Holder, 178.
37. Norman, 287 ff.
38. *Ibid.*, 352.
39. 396.
40. Fraser, G. S., *Ezra Pound*, 21–23.
41. Norman, 459.

CHAPTER VI: JOYCE

1. Joyce, *Portrait of the Artist as a Young Man*, 32–40.
2. *Ibid.*, 247.
3. Ellmann, Richard, *James Joyce*, 228. The biographical elements in this essay are taken chiefly from this masterly work.
4. Ryf, Robert, *A New Approach to Joyce*, 83.
5. Norman, Charles, *Ezra Pound*, 172–73.
6. *Ibid.*, 200.
7. Ellmann, 678.
8. *Ibid.*, 393.
9. Joyce, *Ulysses*, 59.
10. *Ibid.*, 393.
11. 371.
12. 373.
13. 373.

14. Ellmann, 542.
15. *Ibid.*, 388.
16. *Ulysses*, 734.
17. Ellmann, 642.
18. *Ibid.*, 535.
19. 603, 589, 597, 621.
20. *Ibid.*, 597.
21. Brennan, Joseph, *Three Philosophical Novelists*, 53.
22. Ellmann, 706, 716.
23. *Ibid.*, 715, 393.
24. 387.
25. Joyce, *Finnegans Wake*, 620.
26. *Ulysses*, 314 ff.
27. *Ibid.*, 559.
28. 489.
29. 470.
30. 468.
31. 210–15.
32. 407.
33. 198.
34. Ellmann, 755.

CHAPTER VII: ELIOT

1. Kenner, Hugh, *T. S. Eliot*, 17.
2. Norman, Charles, *Ezra Pound*, 251–52.
3. Eliot, T. S., *Selected Essays*, p. 200 ("Dante").
4. Eliot, Introd. to Pound, Ezra, *Selected Poems*.
5. Eliot, *The Waste Land*, lines 19–20, in *Collected Poems*.
6. *Ibid.*, lines 56, 62–63.
7. Dante, *Inferno*, iii, 56.
8. *The Waste Land*, lines 176–82.
9. Eliot, *Selected Essays*, 314.
10. Iris Barry in Norman, 198.
11. F. V. Morley, in Holder, Alan, *Three Voyagers in Search of Europe*, 140.
12. Holder, 136; Unger, Leonard, ed., *T. S. Eliot*, 21; Robbins, R. H., *The T. S. Eliot Myth*, 161.
13. Van Wyck Brooks in Unger, 114.
14. Essays on "The Function of Criticism," in Williamson, George, *A Reader's Guide to T. S. Eliot*, 54.
15. Eliot, *After Strange Gods*, 19.
16. *Ibid.*, 32.
17. *Notes towards the Definition of Culture*, 120.
18. *Ibid.*, 45.
19. 45.
20. 103–08.
21. Eliot, *Idea of a Christian Society*, 61.
22. *After Strange Gods*, 16.
23. *Ibid.*, 13.

24. *Notes towards the Definition of Culture*, 101, 103.
25. Unger, 192.
26. Eliot, *Selected Essays*, 386.
27. *Notes*, 27.
28. *Selected Essays*, 399.
29. "Catholicism and International Order," in Robbins, *The T. S. Eliot Myth*, 49.
30. *The Criterion*, July, 1932, p. 771.
31. *Christian News Letter*, Sept. 3, 1941.
32. *Selected Essays*, 390.
33. *Notes*, 122 ("Thoughts after Lambeth").
34. Cohn, Ruby, and Dukore, Bernard, *Twentieth Century Drama*, 206.
35. *Collected Poems*, 140.
36. *Ibid.*, 219.
37. *Four Quartets*, 23.
38. *Collected Poems*, 135.
39. *Time* Magazine, Feb. 21, 1969, p. 35.

CHAPTER VIII: MAUGHAM

1. Maugham, *Summing Up*, 32, 40.
2. *Ibid.*, 47.
3. 42–43.
4. *Complete Short Stories*, Preface, p. 20.
5. *Summing Up*, 124–25.
6. *Ibid.*, 7.
7. Maugham, Robin, *Somerset and All the Maughams*, 36.
8. Maugham, S., *The Moon and Sixpence*, 244.
9. *Ibid.*, 124.
10. Maugham, R., 202, 196.
11. *Moon and Sixpence*, 226.
12. *Ibid.*, 242.
13. Maugham, R., 206.
14. *Ibid.*, 110.
15. Maugham, S., *Cakes and Ale*, 4.
16. *Summing Up*, 130.
17. *Complete Short Stories*, 10, 12.
18. *Summing Up*, 36.
19. *Ibid.*, 114.
20. 118.
21. Maugham, R., 203.
22. *Ibid.*, 121.
23. *Summing Up*, 39, 44.
24. Maugham, R., 209.
25. *Ibid.*, 51.
26. *Summing Up*, 44.
27. *Ibid.*, 18.
28. Maugham, R., 209.
29. *Ibid.*, 201.
30. 123.
31. 129, 198.
32. *Summing Up*, 109.
33. *Ibid.*, 149.
34. 151.
35. *Moon and Sixpence*, 318.
36. *Summing Up*, 46.
37. *Ibid.*, 182.
38. 176.
39. *Moon and Sixpence*, 14.
40. *Summing Up*, 178.
41. Maugham, R., 196.
42. *Ibid.*, 211.
43. *Summing Up*, 134.
44. *Ibid.*, 50.
45. 22–23.

CHAPTER IX: PROUST

1. Holder, Alan, *Three Voyagers in Search of Europe*, 332–33.
2. Barker, R. H., *Marcel Proust*, 11–12.
3. *Ibid.*, 13.
4. Maurois, *Portrait of a Genius*, 37.
5. Proust, Notebooks, in Maurois, 36.
6. Proust, *Remembrance of Things Past*, Vol. III, p. 366.
7. Maurois, 152.
8. Barker, R. H., 156.
9. *Ibid.*, 93.
10. *Remembrance*, I, 246.
11. IV, 150.
12. Maurois, 116.
13. *Remembrance*, I, 237.
14. *Ibid.*, I, 18.
15. Maurois, 259.
16. Barker, 224.
17. *Ibid.*, 222.
18. Maurois, 263.
19. *Remembrance*, IX, 407.
20. *Ibid.*, I, 195.
21. IV, 293.
22. IV, 305.
23. IV, 219.
24. Maurois, 279–82.
25. *Remembrance*, V, 306.
26. *Ibid.*, IX, 312.
27. V, 40.
28. VI, 181–202; VI, 63 ff.; VIII, 21, etc.
29. VI, 164.
30. V, 44 f.
31. V, 256–391.
32. VI, 211–36.
33. VI, 264.
34. Barker, 345.
35. *Remembrance*, X, 268.
36. *Ibid.*, VII, 18.
37. VII, 48.
38. IX, 409.
39. IX, 428.
40. VIII, 138.

41. VII, 318, 321, 334; VIII, 365.
42. VII, 129.
43. E.g., Maurois, 218.
44. *Remembrance*, IX, 75–87.
45. *Ibid.*, 98.
46. 232.
47. 125.
48. 26.
49. 549.
50. 27.
51. 270.
52. XI, 13.
53. IX, 157.
54. X, 153.
55. X, 157.
56. XI, 253.
57. X, 182–86.
58. X, 245, 252, 256.
59. X, 233.
60. XI, 45.
61. 91.
62. 126 ff.
63. 188.
64. 187.
65. X, 299.
66. XI, 285.
67. 384.
68. 402.
69. VI, 102.
70. XI, 399.
71. 397.
72. 218.
73. 224.
74. IV, 96.
75. X, 266; XI, 226.
76. XI, 237.
77. In Maurois, 193.
78. *Remembrance*, III, 316–19.
79. *Ibid.*, VI, 70–77.
80. Lessing, *Laocoön, passim.*
81. *Remembrance*, VI, 46.
82. *Ibid.*, II, 238.
83. VII, 240.
84. Gide, *Journals*, II, 239.
85. *Remembrance*, VI, 125.
86. E.g., XI, 94, 296, 380.
87. E.g., VI, 148; VII, 300.
88. Ellmann, *Joyce*, 569.
89. *Remembrance*, VI, 47.
90. In Maurois, 269.
91. *Remembrance*, IV, 214.
92. *Ibid.*, 33.
93. 287–88.
94. VI, 322.
95. 321.
96. V, 125.
97. VI, 121.
98. III, 211.
99. VI, 58.

100. VII, 45.
101. Barker, 179.
102. *Remembrance*, VII, 20,
103. Gide, *Journals*, I, 304–06.
104. *Remembrance*, VIII, 237.
105. *Ibid.*, IX, 383.
106. VII, 14.
107. E.g., V, 257; VI, 138; VII, 125 f.
108. Barker, 92.
109. *Remembrance*, VI, 138.
110. *Ibid.*, IV, 176.
111. Maurois, 145.
112. *Remembrance*, IX, 250.
113. *Ibid.*, 251.
114. XI, 229.
115. Cocteau, Jean, *The Difficulty of Being*, 65.
116. Gide, *Journals*, I, 306.
117. In Maurois, 306.
118. *Remembrance*, XI, 237.
119. *Ibid.*, 241.

CHAPTER X: GIDE

1. Brée, Germaine, *Gide*, 33.
2. Gide, *Journals*, I, 15. (March, 1893).
3. Mallet, Robert, ed., *Self Portraits: the Gide/Valéry Letters*, 13.
4. Brée, 24.
5. Mann, Klaus, *André Gide and the Crisis of Modern Thought*, 161.
6. *Journals*, I, 293–94.
7. Brennan, *Three Philosophical Novelists*, 67.
8. Brée, 72.
9. Brennan, 76.
10. *Journals*, I, 335.
11. Brée, 166.
12. *Journals*, II, 53.
13. Gide, *Strait Is the Gate (La Porte étroite)*, 184.
14. Gide, *Lafcadio's Adventures (or The Caves of the Vatican)*, 171, 198.
15. *Journals*, I, 293.
16. Gide, *The Counterfeiters*, 189.
17. *Ibid.*, 158.
18. 190–94.
19. *Journal of the Counterfeiters*, Jan. 2, 1921.
20. *Journals*, II, 79.
21. *Ibid.*, 258.
22. 260.
23. Brennan, 59.
24. *Lafcadio's Adventures*, 26.
25. *Journals*, II, 198.
26. *Ibid.*, 281.
27. 292.
28. 350.
29. In Brée, 164, 202.

30. In Brennan, 101.
31. *Journals*, II, 293.
32. *Strait Is the Gate*, 207.
33. *Journals*, II, 216.
34. *Ibid.*, 123.
35. 130.
36. 175 (June, 1951).
37. In Brée, 255.
38. *Journals*, II, 123.
39. *Ibid.*, 150.
40. 137.
41. 157.
42. 175, 178 (June and May, 1933).
43. 226.
44. 227.
45. 343.
46. 234.
47. 246 (Sept. 10, 1939).
48. 247.
49. 315.
50. 249.
51. 326.
52. 360 (June 8, 1948).
53. Brée, v.

CHAPTER XI: THE PHILOSOPHERS

1. Dante, *Inferno*, i, 3.
2. I paid my tribute to Bertrand Russell in *The Story of Philosophy*. I have never dealt with his contributions to mathematics, for they are far above my head.
3. Russell, *Autobiography*, II, 66.
4. *Ibid.*, 136.
5. Wittgenstein, Ludwig, *Philosophical Investigations*, Preface, p. *x*.
6. Wittgenstein, *Tractatus Logico-Philosophicus*, Proposition 6.22.
7. *Ibid.*, 6.3.
8. 5.61, 6.13, 6.22; *Philosophical Investigations*, No. 97.
9. *Tractatus*, 6.372.
10. *Philosophical Investigations*, No. 109.
11. *Tractatus*, 5.1362.
12. *Ibid.*, 5.136.
13. *Phil. Invest.*, No. 109.
14. *Tractatus*, 4.003.
15. *Ibid.*, 4.0031.
16. 4.112.
17. 6.522, 4.1212, 6.521.
18. 6.54.
19. Russell, *Autobiography*, II, 297.
20. *Ibid.*, 165.
21. *New Republic*, June 22, 1968, p. 29.
22. Beauvoir, Simone de, *Force of Circumstance*, 38.
23. Sartre, J.-P., *Saint Genet*, 17.
24. *Ibid.*, 60–62, 68–73; Durant, *Age of Louis XIV*, 62–64.

25. Collins, James, *The Mind of Kierkegaard*, 4.
26. Lowrie, Walter, *Kierkegaard*, 132.
27. Collins, 10.
28. *Ibid.*
29. Lowrie, 192–94.
30. Kierkegaard, *Repetition*, 114.
31. Collins, 17.
32. *Concluding Scientific Postscript*, in Greene, Norman, *Jean-Paul Sartre: The Existentialist Ethic*, 5; Natanson, *A Critique of Jean-Paul Sartre's Ontology*, 5.
33. Bretall, Robert, ed., *A Kierkegaard Anthology*, 19.
34. *Ibid.*, 153.
35. 108.
36. 215.
37. Kierkegaard, *Fear and Trembling*, passim.
38. Bretall, 73.
39. *Ibid.*, 79.
40. 122.
41. 431.
42. Lowrie, *Kierkegaard*, 586.
43. Bretall, 435.
44. Husserl's *Vorlesungen zur Phänomenologie des inner Zeitbewüsstseins* (*Lectures on the Phenomenology of the Internal Consciousness*), as compiled by Heidegger, appeared in Berlin in 1928; English translation, 1964.
45. Richardson, W. J., *Heidegger*, x.
46. Heidegger, *Sein und Zeit*, 38, in Richardson, 149. Further references to *Sein und Zeit* will be to the English translation, London, 1962.
47. Heidegger, *Being and Time*, 6.
48. Heidegger, *Introduction to Metaphysics*, 74.
49. *Being and Time*, 202.
50. *Ibid.*, 42, 287.
51. Heidegger, *German Existentialism*, 9; Löwith, Karl, *Nature, History, and Existentialism*, 55; *Encyc. Brit.* (1966), XI, 305.
52. Heidegger, *German Existentialism*, 19.
53. *Ibid.*, 11.
54. Löwith, 30.
55. Marcel, Gabriel, *Being and Having*, 167.

CHAPTER XII: SARTRE AND BEAUVOIR

1. Sartre, *The Words*, 30.
2. *Ibid.*, 99.
3. 251, 102.

4. Beauvoir, Simone de, *Memoirs of a Dutiful Daughter*, 7.
5. *Ibid.*, 13.
6. 114.
7. 33.
8. 61.
9. 144.
10. *Ibid.*
11. 345.
12. 365.
13. 357.
14. 359.
15. 360.
16. 361.
17. Sartre, *The Words*, 19.
18. Beauvoir, *The Prime of Life*, 66–67.
19. Beauvoir, *Memoirs*, 345.
20. *Ibid.*, 361.
21. *Prime of Life*, 234.
22. *Ibid.*, 23.
23. 62, 25.
24. 209–10.
25. 35.
26. 39, 107.
27. Sartre, *Search for a Method*, 38.
28. Beauvoir, *Prime of Life*, 170.
29. *Ibid.*, 223.
30. *Ibid.*
31. Sartre, *Nausea*, 138.
32. *Ibid.*, 82.
33. 151, 181.
34. 179.
35. 180–81.
36. 232.
37. Cruikshank, John, *Albert Camus and the Literature of Revolt*, 15.
38. Sartre, *Nausea*, 122.
39. *Prime of Life*, 282; but *cf.* Sartre, *Search for a Method*, 38.
40. *Prime of Life*, 347.
41. Beauvoir, *Force of Circumstance*, 5.
42. *Ibid.*, 385.
43. Stern, Alfred, *Sartre*, 13.
44. Grene, Marjorie, *Dreadful Freedom: a Critique of Existentialism*, 96.
45. Beauvoir, *Force of Circumstance*, 398.
46. *Prime of Life*, 439.
47. Sartre, *Being and Nothingness*, 218.
48. *Saint Genet*, 535.
49. Sartre, *Existentialism Is a Humanism*, in Novack, Geo., *Existentialism vs. Marxism*, 84.
50. *Being and Nothingness*, 74.
51. *Ibid.*, 137.
52. 309.
53. 22, 171.
54. 617.
55. 216; Salvan, Jacques, *The Scandalous Ghost*, 22.
56. Sartre, *Situations*, III, 135 ff., in Jolivet, R., *Sartre*, 51, 53.
57. *Being and Nothingness*, 369.
58. *Ibid.*, 102.
59. In Desan, Wilfrid, *The Tragic Finale*, 66n.
60. *Being and Nothingness*, 429.
61. *Ibid.*, 47–49.
62. 439.
63. 444.
64. *Nausea*, 181.
65. *Existentialism Is a Humanism*, in Cranston, M., *Sartre*, 80.
66. Sartre, *The Flies*, Act. III, in *No Exit and Three Other Plays*, 120–23.
67. *No Exit* . . . , 16.
68. *Ibid.*, 46.
69. Beauvoir, *Prime of Life*, 471.
70. *Ibid.*, 52.
71. Sartre, *What Is Literature?*, 22.
72. *Ibid.*, 91.
73. 113.
74. 270–71.
75. 247.
76. 250, 258.
77. 277.
78. 289.
79. Sartre, *The Age of Reason*, 31.
80. *Ibid.*, 187.
81. 8.
82. 13–14.
83. 107.
84. 218.
85. 249.
86. 67–68.
87. 46.
88. Sartre, *The Reprieve*, 74.
89. Sartre, *Troubled Sleep*, 305.
90. *Ibid.*, 69.
91. Burnier, Michel-Antoine, *Choice of Action*, 42, 52.
92. Cranston, 79.
93. *The Reprieve*, 414.
94. *Ibid.*, 237.
95. 204.
96. 209.
97. See *Troubled Sleep*, 41–43.
98. Sartre, *No Exit* . . . , 262.
99. *Ibid.*, 223.
100. Sartre, *Search for a Method*, 210.
101. Beauvoir, *Force of Circumstance*, 151.
102. Sartre, *The Devil and the Good Lord*, 63.
103. *Ibid.*, 133.
104. 145.
105. Cranston, 110.
106. *Force of Circumstance*, 474.
107. Cruikshank, *Camus*, 191; *cf.* Sartre *What Is Literature?*, 287.

108. Sartre, *Forgers of Myths* (1946) in Corrigan, R. W., *The Modern Drama*, 784.
109. *Force of Circumstance*, 67.
110. Beauvoir, *The Ethics of Ambiguity*, 7.
111. *Ibid.*, 156.
112. 35.
113. 67.
114. 159.
115. 103.
116. 48.
117. 106–12.
118. *Force of Circumstance*, 162.
119. Novack, George, ed., *Existentialism vs. Marxism*, 70.
120. *Ibid.*
121. *Force of Circumstance*, 150.
122. Sartre, *Existentialism Is a Humanism*, in Novack, 75.
123. *Force of Circumstance*, 43, 45.
124. *Ibid.*, 143.
125. 230.
126. Burnier, *Choice of Action*, 23.
127. *Ibid.*, 35; Novack, 207.
128. Novack, 30.
129. Burnier, 58.
130. *Ibid.*, 61.
131. *Force of Circumstance*, 203.
132. *Ibid.*, 200; Burnier, 50, 73.
133. Burnier, 87.
134. Sartre, *Saint Genet*, 121, 124, 420, 447.
135. *Ibid.*, 536.
136. Novack, 31; *Force of Circumstance*, 360.
137. *Ibid.*, 591.
138. 545.
139. 385.
140. Sartre, *Search for a Method*, 130, 32, 43.
141. *Ibid.*, 103, 28.
142. *Ibid.*, 34, quoting Marx, *Das Kapital*, III, 873.
143. Sartre, *Search*, 34.
144. I know these remaining pages only through Burnier.
145. Stern, Alfred, *Sartre*, 252.
146. *Force of Circumstance*, 68.
147. *Ibid.*, 93.
148. 154.
149. 158.
150. 184.
151. Beauvoir, *The Second Sex*, 182.
152. *Ibid.*, 624.
153. 390.
154. 727.
155. 187–88.
156. *Ibid.*, Preface, *xxx*.
157. *The Second Sex*, 21.

158. *Ibid.*, 499.
159. 478.
160. 552–53.
161. 719.
162. *Force of Circumstance*, 187.
163. *Ibid.*, 225.
164. 229.
165. 254.
166. 255.
167. 464.
168. 35.
169. 212.
170. Beauvoir, *The Ethics of Ambiguity*, 135.
171. *Prime of Life*, 457; *Force of Circumstance*, 585, 587, 656–57.
172. Stern, *Sartre*, 17.
173. Burnier, 98.
174. Sartre, *et al.*, *Les Temps modernes*, August, 1966.
175. Robert Kirsch in Los Angeles *Times*, Oct. 9, 1968.
176. *Ibid.*, June 23, 1968, Sect. VI, p. 2.
177. *Time* magazine, Sept. 20, 1968, p. 32.
178. Cranston, *Sartre*, 5.
179. Sartre, *The Age of Reason*, 125.
180. Sartre, *The Condemned of Altona*, p. 55.
181. *Force of Circumstance*, 120.
182. *Ibid.*, 44.
183. 321, 142, 235.
184. 140; *Prime of Life*, 454.
185. *Ibid.*, 38, 118.
186. *Ibid.*, 206–07.
187. *Condemned of Altona*, p. 65.
188. *The Words*, 172; Burnier, 164.

CHAPTER XIII: CAMUS

1. Camus, Albert, *Lyrical and Critical Essays*, 7.
2. *Ibid.*, 347.
3. 191.
4. 148.
5. 242n., quoting Philip Thorly.
6. Camus, *Caligula*, III, ii; IV, xii.
7. Camus, *The Wrong Side and the Right Side*, in *Lyrical and Critical Essays*, 36.
8. *Ibid.*, 248, 351.
9. Camus, *Nuptials*, in same, 91.
10. *Ibid.*, 200.
11. Camus, *The Fall*, 11.
12. *Lyrical . . . Essays*, 306.
13. *Ibid.*, 199–201.
14. 345.
15. Camus, *The Stranger*, 84.

16. Camus, *The Plague*, 230.
17. *Ibid.*, 111, 177.
18. 166.
19. 279.
20. 154.
21. Cruikshank, *Albert Camus and the Literature of Revolt*, xix.
22. Camus, *The Plague*, 229.
23. Burnier, *Choice of Action*, 177.
24. *Ibid.*, 176–78.
25. 180.
26. 181.
27. 183.
28. 184–85.
29. 187.
30. Camus, *The Fall*, 145.

CHAPTER XIV: MANN

1. Mann, Thomas, *Essays of Three Decades*, 430. I have ventured to change the translator's "gentled" to "humane."
2. Mann, *A Sketch of My Life*, 5.
3. In Neider, Charles, *The Stature of Thomas Mann*, 90.
4. Mann, *Sketch*, 15.
5. *Ibid.*, 21.
6. 25.
7. 21.
8. Mann, *Stories of Three Decades*, 228.
9. In Neider, *Stature of Thomas Mann*, 84.
10. Thomas, R. H., *Thomas Mann: The Mediator of Art*, 33.
11. Mann, *Buddenbrooks*, I, 147.
12. *Ibid.*, I, 54; II, 93.
13. II, 85.
14. II, 81.
15. Hatfield, Henry, ed., *Thomas Mann*, 143.
16. Heller, Erich, *The Ironic German*, 68.
17. *Neue Rundschau*, XXV, 834.
18. Mann, *Sketch*, 32.
19. Mann, *Tonio Kröger*, 100.
20. *Ibid.*, 98.
21. 108.
22. 105.
23. 132.
24. *Sketch*, 46.
25. In White, Andrew, *Thomas Mann*, 85.
26. *Ibid.*, 87.
27. Hatfield, 132.
28. In Pascal, Roy, *The German Novel*, 259.
29. *Sketch*, 47.

30. Weigand, H. J., *The Magic Mountain of Thomas Mann's Novel*, 97.
31. *Ibid.*, 34.
32. Neider, *Stature of Thomas Mann*, 231.
33. Mann, *The Magic Mountain*, 587.
34. In Lukács, Georg, *Essays on Thomas Mann*, 38.
35. *Magic Mountain*, 432–34.
36. *Ibid.*, 651; Hatfield, 93.
37. Lukács, 40, 43.
38. Foreword to Mann, *Joseph and His Brothers*, iv. ed., *ix*.
39. Neider, *Stature of Thomas Mann*, 67.
40. *Ibid.*, 386.
41. 177.
42. Mann, *The Story of a Novel: The Genesis of Dr. Faustus*, 5.
43. Mann, *The Beloved Returns*, 82.
44. *Ibid.*, 101.
45. 285.
46. 292.
47. Neider, *Stature of Thomas Mann*, 188.
48. Mann, *Dr. Faustus*, 85.
49. White, Andrew, *Thomas Mann*, 49.
50. Hatfield, 4; Neider, *Stature of Thomas Mann*, 30.
51. Mann, *Confessions of Felix Krull, Confidence Man*, 104.
52. White, Andrew, *Thomas Mann*, 16.
53. Mann, *The Story of a Novel*, 113.
54. *Ibid.*, 140.
55. 116.
56. In Neider, *Stature of Thomas Mann*, 220.
57. Heller, *Ironic German*, 221.
58. In Neider, 225.
59. *Ibid.*, 224.
60. Mann, *The Tales of Jacob*, 400.
61. *Ibid.*, 3.
62. 133.
63. *Joseph in Egypt*, 178.
64. Mann, *Essays*, 422.
65. *Ibid.*
66. *Tales of Jacob*, 53.
67. *Essays*, 426.
68. In Neider, *Stature of Thomas Mann*, 227.
69. *Joseph and His Brothers*, iv. ed., 432.
70. *Ibid.*, Foreword.
71. Pp. 1282 ff.
72. Lecture at Princeton, 1939, in White, 135.
73. In Neider, *Stature*, 220.
74. *Ibid.*, 226.
75. *Joseph and His Brothers*, iv. ed., xviii.
76. In Neider, *Stature*, 226.
77. Hatfield, 123.
78. Mann, *Story of a Novel*, 38.

79. *Ibid.*, 6, 221.
80. 229.
81. Mann, *Dr. Faustus*, 90.
82. *Story of a Novel*, 29, 36.
83. White, 23.
84. In McKinney and Anderson, *Music in History*, 511.
85. Heller, *Ironic German*, 262; Durant, *Reformation*, 852.
86. Quoted in Lukács, 69; *cf. Story of a Novel*, 41.
87. *Dr. Faustus*, 175.
88. *Joseph the Provider*, 230.
89. *Ibid.*, 262.
90. In Neider, *Stature*, 29.
91. In *Rede und Antwort*, 13, in Hatfield, 49.
92. *Sketch*, 32.
93. *Story of a Novel*, 76.
94. *Buddenbrooks*, II, 286.
95. Essay, "Goethe and Tolstoi."
96. *Joseph the Provider*, 357.
97. *Neue Studien* (1948), 137.
98. *Magic Mountain*, 432.
99. In Neider, *Stature*, 229.
100. Weigand, *The Magic Mountain*, 148.
101. *Neue Studien*, 156, in Pascal, *The German Novel*, 172.
102. In Hatfield, 131.
103. Heinrich Mann in Neider, *Stature*, 86.
104. *Magic Mountain*, 42, in Hatfield, 7.
105. *Dr. Faustus*, 119.
106. Neider, *Stature*, 315.
107. Mann, *Essays*, 398.
108. White, 101.
109. In Lukács, 87.
110. *The Listener*, June 5, 1952, in White, 174.
111. *Dr. Faustus*, 505.
112. *Confessions of Felix Krull*, 197.
113. *Ibid.*
114. 59.
115. Mann, Erika, *The Last Year of Thomas Mann.*
116. Mann, Thomas, *Last Essays*, 189.
117. *Ibid.*, 203.

CHAPTER XV: KAFKA

1. Kafka, *Selected Short Stories*, 18.
2. Kafka, *Penal Colony*, 209.
3. Kafka, *Letters to Milena*, 42.
4. Kafka, *Diaries*, II, 77.
5. *Ibid.*, I, 197.
6. *Ibid.*, 15.
7. Brod, Max, *Franz Kafka*, 23.
8. *Diaries*, I, 231.
9. Brod, 78.
10. *Diaries*, I, 33.
11. *Ibid.*, 275.
12. 204.
13. 182.
14. 311.
15. Janouch, G., *Conversations with Kafka*, 29.
16. Kafka, *Letters*, 70.
17. *Diaries*, I, 27; Brod, 206.
18. Neider, Charles, *The Frozen Sea*, 59.
19. Brod, 48.
20. "Letter to My Father," in Neider, 31.
21. Janouch, 28, 43.
22. *Diaries*, I, 290 (July 21, 1913).
23. *Ibid.*, 293–94.
24. *Diaries*, II, 129 (Nov. 2, 1911).
25. Neider, 185.
26. *Diaries*, I, 19.
27. *Ibid.*, 309 (Nov. 19, 1913).
28. In Janouch, 101.
29. *Ibid.*
30. *Diaries*, I, 150.
31. Brod, 139.
32. *Ibid.*, 142.
33. 37.
34. *Diaries*, I, 296–97.
35. Brod, 143.
36. *Ibid.*, 144.
37. 146.
38. 148.
39. 76, 162.
40. *Letters*, 47, 58.
41. *Ibid.*, 77.
42. 78, 134, 101, 162, 183.
43. 98, 204.
44. Janouch, 44.
45. *Ibid.*, vi.
46. In Flores, Angel, *The Kafka Problem*, 164.
47. Kafka, *Great Wall of China*, 83.
48. Brod, 18.
49. *Diaries*, I, 23.
50. Hubben, William, *Four Prophets of Our Destiny*, 142.
51. *Diaries*, II, 22.
52. Gide, *Journals*, II, 263 (Aug. 24, 1940).
53. Neider, 24.
54. Kafka, *The Castle*, 284.
55. Janouch, 93.
56. *Diaries*, I, 207.
57. Janouch, 79.
58. *Ibid.*, 71.
59. *Diaries*, II, 114.
60. *Ibid.*, 161.
61. Janouch, 60.
62. *Diaries*, II, 20 (Feb. 14, 1914).
63. *Letters*, 66.
64. Flores, x.

CHAPTER XVI: KAZANTZAKIS

1. Kazantzakis, *Toda Raba*, 15.
2. *Id., Freedom or Death*, 374, 381.
3. *Ibid.*, 58.
4. 391.
5. 52–53.
6. 181.
7. Prevelakis, *Nikos Kazantzakis and his Odyssey*, 171; Kazantzakis, Helen, *Nikos Kazantzakis*, 33–34.
8. Kazantzakis, N., *Report to Greco*, 115.
9. *Ibid.*, 135.
10. 166.
11. 336.
12. 335.
13. Prevelakis, 174.
14. *Report to Greco*, 338.
15. *Ibid.*, 323.
16. 338.
17. 341.
18. 349.
19. Kazantzakis, N., *The Rock Garden*, 89.
20. *Id., Japan/China*, 376; Prevelakis, 185.
21. Kazantzakis, H., in *Toda Raba*, 204.
22. In Kazantzakis, H., *Nikos Kazantzakis*, 86–88.
23. *Ibid.*, 96.
24. 120.
25. In Prevelakis, 49.
26. *Ibid.*, 19.
27. Kazantzakis, H., *Nikos Kazantzakis*, 565–70.
28. Prevelakis, 19.
29. Prevelakis, 173.
30. Kazantzakis, H., 130.
31. *Ibid.*, 132.
32. 147.
33. 150.
34. 153–55.
35. Kazantzakis, *Toda Raba*, 212.
36. *Ibid.*, 39.
37. 98.
38. 159.
39. *Freedom or Death*, 27.
40. Kazantzakis, N., *The Odyssey: A Modern Sequel*, III, line 725.
41. *Freedom or Death*, p. 27.
42. *Ibid.*, 371.
43. *Report to Greco*, 180.
44. *Rock Garden*, 31.
45. *Zorba the Greek*, 142.
46. *Report to Greco*, 445.
47. *Zorba*, 71.
48. *Ibid.*, 254.
49. 158.
50. 160.
51. 254.

52. 244.
53. 115.
54. 116.
55. 118, 116.
56. 108.
57. 335.
58. 85.
59. *Report to Greco*, 447.
60. *Ibid.*, 457.
61. *Rock Garden*, 48.
62. *Ibid.*, 62.
63. 65.
64. 51.
65. 44.
66. *Japan/China*, 56.
67. *Report to Greco*, 487.
68. Kazantzakis, H., 121.
69. *Ibid.*, 116.
70. Kazantzakis, N., *Odyssey*, I, lines 378–379.
71. *Ibid.*, 556–557.
72. 1060.
73. II, 1409.
74. IV, 130–131.
75. IV, 940.
76. IV, 1263.
77. V, 852–854.
78. VIII, 552–569.
79. XII, 1264–1267.
80. XIV, 125.
81. XVI, 1098–1107.
82. XVI, 1309–1321.
83. E.g., II, 727.
84. E.g., XVI, 534.
85. II, 1018–1019.
86. *Report to Greco*, 494.
87. *Ibid.*, 250.
88. 341.
89. 234.
90. 143.
91. Kazantzakis, H., 325.
92. *Ibid.*, 63.
93. 485.
94. Prevelakis, 168.
95. Kazantzakis, N., *The Greek Passion*, 73.
96. Kazantzakis, H., 76.
97. *Ibid.*, 491.
98. Kazantzakis, N., *The Last Temptation of Christ*, 28.
99. *Ibid.*, 347.
100. 215.
101. 189.
102. 350.
103. 367.
104. 411.
105. 450.
106. 459.
107. 461.

108. *The Poor Man of God*, Prologue.
109. *Rock Garden*, 36.
110. *Report to Greco*, 334.
111. *Japan/China*, 58.
112. *Ibid.*, 47.
113. Geranos in *Toda Raba*, 114.
114. *Report to Greco*, 331.
115. *Zorba*, 22.
116. *Odyssey*, V, lines 300 ff.
117. *Japan/China*, 74.
118. *Ibid.*, 102.
119. *Toda Raba*, 186, 94.
120. *Ibid.*, 94.
121. *The Fratricides*, 56.
122. *Last Temptation of Christ*, Prologue.
123. *Rock Garden*, 36.
124. *Ibid.*, 63.
125. *Toda Raba*, 204.
126. *Report to Greco*, 493.
127. *Freedom or Death*, 41.
128. *The Greek Passion*, 108.
129. *Last Temptation of Christ*, 401.
130. *Rock Garden*, 69.
131. Kazantzakis, H., 489.
132. *Report to Greco*, 15.
133. *Ibid.*, 249.
134. 332.
135. 303.
136. 302.
137. *Japan/China*, 346.
138. Katzantzakis, H., 531.
139. Prevelakis, 180.

CHAPTER XVII: LITERATURE
UNDER THE SOVIETS

1. Slonim, Marc, *Soviet Russia in Literature*, 184.
2. Sholokhov, M., *Quiet Flows the Don*, 301.
3. *Ibid.*, 302.
4. 312.
5. 369.
6. 253–54.
7. 284.
8. 423.
9. 424.
10. Sholokhov, *The Don Flows Home to the Sea*, 245.
11. *Ibid.*, 240–51.
12. 584.
13. 6, 367.
14. 367.
15. 217.
16. 556.
17. 776.
18. 502.

19. Alexandrova, Vera, *A History of Soviet Literature*, 225.
20. *Ibid.*, 229.
21. Slonim, 187.
22. Alexandrova, 223.
23. *New York Times Book Review*, Aug. 20, 1967, p. 29.
24. Alexandrova, 231.
25. Pasternak, Boris, *Safe Conduct*, in *Collected Prose Works*, 54.
26. Payne, Robert, *The Three Worlds of Boris Pasternak*, 18.
27. Pasternak, *Collected Prose Works*, facing p. 96.
28. *Id., The Last Summer*, Introd., 11.
29. *Safe Conduct*, 48.
30. *Ibid.*, 49.
31. 62.
32. 91.
33. 95.
34. Dante, *Inferno*, V, 121.
35. Pasternak, *The Last Summer*, 138.
36. *Ibid.*, 33.
37. Pasternak, *Adolescence of Zhenya Luvers*, 16.
38. Payne, *The Three Worlds of Boris Pasternak*, 185.
39. Pasternak, *Safe Conduct*, 116.
40. In Payne, 136.
41. Slonim, 224; Payne, 79; Pasternak, *My Sister, Life*, 7.
42. Payne, 69.
43. Yevtushenko, *Precocious Autobiography*, 66.
44. Pasternak, *Poems*, 81, 17.
45. *Ibid.*, 83, 103.
46. *Safe Conduct*, 81.
47. *Ibid.*, 42.
48. Payne, Robert, in Pasternak, *My Sister, Life*, xxiv.
49. Payne, *The Three Worlds of Boris Pasternak*, 152.
50. *Ibid.*, 166–67.
51. Pasternak, *Dr. Zhivago*, 282.
52. Payne, 196 f.
53. *Ibid.*, 197.
54. 200.
55. 201.
56. E.g., Rowland, M. and P. *Pasternak's Dr. Zhivago*, 10.
57. Pasternak, *Dr. Zhivago*, 10.
58. *Ibid.*, 151.
59. 550.
60. 182.
61. 378.
62. 396.
63. 507.
64. 402–3.
65. 261.

66. 391.
67. 500–01.
68. 503.
69. In Rowland, 58.
70. Pasternak, *Dr. Zhivago*, 530.
71. Matt., v, 28.
72. *Dr. Zhivago*, 536.
73. *Ibid.*, 501.
74. 338.
75. Rowland, 161.
76. *Dr. Zhivago*, 535.
77. *Ibid.*, 523, 526.
78. 559.
79. Rowland, 186.
80. Payne, 200.
81. *Ibid.*, 210 ff.
82. Pasternak, *My Sister, Life*, xi.
83. Payne, 202.
84. Solzhenitsyn, A., *One Day in the Life of Ivan Denisovich*, Introd., *xxi*.
85. Yevtushenko, *Autobiography*, 122; Slonim, 334.
86. Solzhenitsyn, *One Day in the Life of Ivan Denisovich*, 32, 131, 140–41.
87. *Ibid.*, 27.
88. 202.
89. Alexandrova, 353.
90. *One Day*, Introd., *xxiii*.
91. Solzhenitsyn, *First Circle*, 142.
92. *Ibid.*, 259.
93. 200–01.
94. 203.
95. 553.
96. 232–33.
97. 233.
98. 289.
99. 203.
100. *Ibid.*
101. 493.
102. 523–53.
103. Solzhenitsyn, *Cancer Ward*, 18.
104. *Ibid.*, 210.
105. 218–19, 246 ff.
106. 89.
107. 444.
108. 457.
109. 400.
110. 209.

111. 294.
112. 182.
113. 153.
114. 243.
115. 501.
116. 82.
117. 366.
118. 503–07.
119. 509.
120. 510.
121. 511.
122. 513.
123. *First Circle*, 129.
124. *Cancer Ward*, 269.
125. *Ibid.*, 519.
126. 496.
127. 89, 330.
128. *First Circle*, 581.
129. Los Angeles *Times, Calendar*, March 30, 1969, p. 1.
130. *Ibid.*
131. Durant, *Mansions of Philosophy*, 475.
132. Slonim, 11; Alexandrova, 71.
133. Alexandrova, 74.
134. Slonim, 21.
135. Pasternak, *My Sister, Life*, Introd., *xii*.
136. Alexandrova, 63.
137. *Ibid.*, 68.
138. Yevtushenko, *Autobiography*, 62.
139. *Ibid.*, 70.
140. 101, 107.
141. 82.
142. 38.
143. 81.
144. *Yevtushenko Poems*, tr. Herbert Marshall, p. 111.
145. *Ibid.*, 105–09.
146. *Autobiography*, 122.
147. *Poems*, 105n.
148. *Ibid.*, 17.
149. E.g., *Poems*, 71.
150. *Autobiography*, 56.
151. *Poems*, 149.
152. *Autobiography*, 40.
153. *Poems*, 139.
154. *Ibid.*, 167–69.
155. *Autobiography*, 39.
156. *Ibid.*, 124.

Index